DILEMMAS OF DIFFERENCE

SARAH A. RADCLIFFE

DILEMMAS OF DIFFERENCE

Indigenous Women and
the Limits of Postcolonial
Development Policy

DUKE UNIVERSITY PRESS   DURHAM AND LONDON   2015

Printed in the United States of America on acid-free paper ∞
Typeset in Quadraat Pro by Westchester Publishing Services

Library of Congress Cataloging-in-Publication Data
Radcliffe, Sarah A., author.
Dilemmas of difference : indigenous women and the limits of
postcolonial development policy / Sarah A. Radcliffe.
pages cm
Includes bibliographical references and index.
ISBN 978-0-8223-5978-4 (hardcover : alk. paper)
ISBN 978-0-8223-6010-0 (pbk. : alk. paper)
ISBN 978-0-8223-7502-9 (e-book)
1. Women in development—Political aspects—Ecuador.
2. Indigenous women—Ecuador—Economic conditions.
3. Indigenous women—Ecuador—Social conditions. I. Title.
HQ1240.5.E2R34 2015
305.4209866—dc23   2015020932

Cover art: Top photo: A Kichwa woman signs her name
on an official document; photograph by the author.
Bottom texture: Robert Hamm/Alamy

For *warmikuna* and *sonala* in Ecuador
and their allies across the world

CONTENTS

ix   Acknowledgments

1   INTRODUCTION   Development and Social Heterogeneity

37   CHAPTER 1   Postcolonial Intersectionality and the Colonial Present

75   CHAPTER 2   The Daily Grind: Ethnic Topographies of Labor, Racism, and Abandonment

121   INTERLUDE I

125   CHAPTER 3   Crumbs from the Table: Participation, Organization, and Indigenous Women

157   CHAPTER 4   Politics, Statistics, and Affect: "Indigenous Women in Development" Policy

189   INTERLUDE II

193   CHAPTER 5   Women, Biopolitics, and Interculturalism: Ethnic Politics and Gendered Contradictions

225   CHAPTER 6   From Development to Citizenship: Rights, Voice, and Citizenship Practices

257   CHAPTER 7   Postcolonial Heterogeneity: Sumak Kawsay and Decolonizing Social Difference

291   Notes

325   Glossary

329   Bibliography

359   Index

ACKNOWLEDGMENTS

This book emerges out of a previous project on how indigenous transnational activism sought to leverage changes in development policy and decision-making. During that project, I carried out interviews with indigenous women, ethnodevelopment staff members, and policy-makers and found their viewpoints were often at odds and inspired by distinctive agendas. The distinctiveness and complexity of indigenous women's positioning regarding gender and development policy, and ethnodevelopment policy were forcefully brought home to me when I visited a village women's group, gathered under the iconic peak of Chimborazo volcano. I had returned to visit the central Andes and began talking with a group of kichwa-speaking women in Nitiluisa community about how they had organized a women's group. Despite the fund-raising difficulties, the logistical challenges, and the uphill task of persuading other villagers of the rightness of their endeavor, they had, by the time I dropped in, become the proud residents and active users of a single-story, light-filled room with tables and chairs for craft activities and regular meetings. These Kichwa women carried out an incremental but powerful transformation in their lives, drawing on understandings and priorities forged in adversity. Inspired by the Nitiluisa group, I started to search out and talk to elected women's representatives from diverse strands of Ecuador's indigenous movements, conducting interviews with women recently elected to a leadership role as well as historic leaders. They each spoke vividly of how low-income women in diverse ethnic groups across the country's varied geographies consistently found themselves left out of projects aimed at farmers, women, or indigenous people and the impoverishing effects of such marginalization. Women's representatives also spoke movingly of their grassroots initiatives and alternative thinking—about dignity, livelihoods, and interactions with rural spaces—that were not lifted from development plans but emerged from women's articulation of what they considered their rights, their agendas, and their politics, regardless of what others might say. Gaining momentum, these conversations led me to renew an acquaintance with Maria Andrade, one of CONAIE's first women's representatives, now a sought-after thinker and doer across a number of policy fields. Systematizing insights from preliminary interviews, I drew up a research proposal that went back and forth to Maria, as well as Ana Maria Pilamunga, Yadira Calazacón, Norma Mayo, and Alicia Garcés for inputs and changes. They bear no responsibility for what came out of this exchange, but I hope that it offers them some tools for their projects. For their steady engagement and encouragement, I wish to thank them all, mil gracias.

Once the project was under way, I worked with a wonderful range of people whose inputs contributed to the research process that has resulted in this book. Among these was my ever-engaged and engaging research assistant Andrea Pequeño, who worked tirelessly in the Tsáchila communities while I was back in the UK, and whose dedication and intrinsic interest in the project offered so much to the interpretations offered here. I am delighted to see that she is now pursuing her own research. Delia Caguana, the dynamic women's elected representative for the Chimborazo indigenous federation COMICH, was absolutely central to the process that takes material form here. Her singleness of purpose and her exemplary capacity to enthuse and inform are as evident in a village workshop as in my thinking about how Kichwa women engage and rework development. Delia not only welcomed me as a colleague and facilitated interviews and focus groups; she reflected on my interviews and then, on a bus journey or coming out of a roadside shrine, she shared her thoughts in ways that allowed me to listen and learn.

Over numerous visits to Ecuador to carry out fieldwork, I was lucky enough to catch a coffee or a meeting with a number of people whose knowledge and expertise in relation to development, and the complex situation of diverse indigenous, rural, and racialized women, has always exceeded—and will continue to exceed—my own. For her continued friendship, generosity, and interest, I owe a huge debt of gratitude to Mercedes Prieto, who not only read draft chapters but also gently encouraged me to be more circumspect about my history. Also at FLACSO Ecuador, Gioconda Herrera, Fernando Garcia, and Alicia Torres, along with various students, visitors, and colleagues, were welcoming and interested. Pilar Larreamendy and, before he passed away, Xavier Moscoso offered constant encouragement. Nely Shiguango and Luis Alberto Tuaza provided translations from kichwa transcriptions, while the Pikitsa project, together with Alejandro Aguavil and Connie Dickinson, provided a means to engage with tsafiki language material.

Nearer to home, a large number of colleagues, graduates, and postdoctoral scholars additionally provided me with intellectual stimulation and sounding boards for ideas. Denise Arnold talked over initial frameworks and provided bibliographic material, as did Laura Rival, whose knowledge of indigenous issues on the Ecuadorian *costa* is boundless. At various moments Peter Wade, Valentina Napolitano, Humeira Iqtidar, Aída Hernández, Andrew Canessa, and Liz Watson generously read draft chapters and provided feedback. Members of the Multicultural Governance in Latin America Reading Group at the Department of Geography, namely Megan Rivers-Moore, Sofia Zaragocín, Penelope Anthias, Laura Loyola Hernández, Tara Cookson, Freddy Alvarez, Sian Lazar, Istvan Praet, Sallie Westwood, David Lehmann, Jorge Resina, Sandra Brunnegger, and Andrew Webb, read parts of what became this book, and helped sharpen the argument. Carla Araujo, Conor Farrington, Dolores Figueroa, Charles Hale, Tania Murray Li, Amy Lind, Breno Marquéz Bringel, Emma Mawdsley, Cheryl McEwan, Anahi Morales, David Nally, Patricia Oliart, Jane Pollard, Stéphanie Rousseau, Lynn Stephen, Alissa Trotz, Fernando Urrea-Giraldo, Gina Vargas, and Montserrat Ventura Oller, through their writing and in person, set me thinking; thank you.

Parts of this book have been presented as seminars at the Ecole des Hautes Etudes de Sciences Sociales and the Institut des Hautes Etudes de Amérique Latine (IHEAL) in Paris, the University of Toronto Intersections seminar series, the University of Wageningen in the Netherlands, the Universidad de la Frontera, Chile, the Pro-Doc Workshop at St Gallen, the Institute for the Study of the Americas, London, and the Universities of Edinburgh, London, Manchester, Essex, Liverpool, and Bath. Thanks are hence due, in no particular order, to Guillaume Boccara, Capucine Boidin, Pamela Calla, Rachel Silvey, Betsy Olson, Katie Willis, Henry Stobart, Steve Rubenstein (now sadly no longer with us), Kees Jansen, Alejandro Herrera, Peter Wade, Maxine Molyneux, Lynn Staeheli, and Yanina Welp for invitations followed by conversations. I also gained immeasurably from conversations with Aída Hernández, who came to Cambridge in 2013–2014.

Duke University Press has supported this project from the start with enthusiasm and flexibility, first with Valerie Millholland as the commissioning editor and then Gisela Fosada, who seamlessly took over the final stages; many, many thanks to them and the team. At the Department of Geography, Cambridge, Phil Stickler and the cartographic office drew the maps and prepared the figures. I gratefully acknowledge the Economic and Social Research Council funding that permitted extended fieldwork in Ecuador, and attendance at conferences. I am also grateful to the Centre for Research in

Arts, Social Science and Humanities (CRASSH) at the University of Cambridge for funding a workshop, "The Politics of Presence in Latin America," in 2009. The research on which this book is based would not have been possible without funding from the Economic and Social Research Council (ESRC RES-062-23-0517).

And finally, my warmest thanks and *cariño* go to Guy, Jessie, Dylan, and Ben, whose flexibility, generosity, and down-to-earth support really made this whole venture possible.

Introduction

Development and Social Heterogeneity

"I just want people to respect me," says Rosario as she sits on the curb under the bright mountain sun with other women who have come into the district capital, a ragged town of two-story buildings in the central Ecuadorian Andes, for a meeting of women in similar situations.[1] Now twenty-eight years old, Rosario is a Kichwa-speaking woman from one of the fourteen indigenous peoples in Ecuador.[2] She has good reason to ask for respect; her life has offered few instances of opportunity, dignity, or security, based in an impoverished peasant economy characterized by patchy access to education, health care, and work, and hard, unpaid labor on small family-owned plots of land. Moreover, Rosario is deaf, a fact that layers into the multiple factors of deprivation affecting her and her family. Finding it difficult to understand what people say, she is swindled at urban markets, and at a young age she was raped and left with a young daughter. Walking from her village to the market where we now sit, next to street stalls selling polyester clothing and pirated music CDs, is a major undertaking, as she leaves elderly parents at home and attempts to sell potatoes and a few onions at a price sufficient to buy necessities such as cooking oil, bread, sugar, and school clothes. Speaking Kichwa but no Spanish (the language of elites, cities, and government) exposes Rosario to racist comments and disdainful behavior from urban stallholders and customers. Compounding these difficulties, Rosario was expelled from her village, similar to others in Chimborazo province (see fig. I.1), as she could not fulfill the labor and attendance requirements for membership, meaning she lacks the formal status to be involved in local

Fig. I.1. Chimborazo province, Ecuador. Photograph by the author.

decision-making. As Rosario speaks, the women around her—including Aurora and Margarita—listen intently and elicit responses to my questions, contextualize Rosario's life, and express outrage at what has happened. Although they don't share Rosario's deafness, Aurora and Margarita live a life with similar contours and struggles, as I found out talking to them later. None of these women has benefited in a sustained and equal way from the broad as well as targeted measures to improve living standards and opportunities that we call development, and hence they find themselves overlooked or not fully taken into account in programs that proclaim themselves to be acting on behalf of poor rural populations, women, or indigenous groups. At a broad level, this exclusion results from Latin America's "lop-sided development," the skewed distribution of middle-income country growth toward the urban, the male, the rich, the lighter-skinned, the able-bodied, and those unencumbered by caring responsibilities (Hoffman and Centeno 2003).

※

What does social diversity entail for development? In what ways do lines of social difference—including gender, race-ethnicity, sexuality, (dis)ability, location, and class—come to be conceptualized and then acted on in development?[3] Persistent inequalities between social groups often provide the impetus and rationale for development interventions, with projects assisting women who are poorer than men, or intervening in rural areas lacking the infrastructure common in urban districts. Lacking endless resources and personnel, development is impelled to take social difference into account in order to decide where and with whom to work. In response, single dimensions of social difference—commonly gender, income, and, recently, action on behalf of racially discriminated groups—have received attention from scholars and development professionals, leading to measures by governments and NGOs. The Millennium Developmental Goals encouraged states and multilateral agencies to address both poverty and gulfs between female and male opportunities. Yet social difference is multifaceted, generating entangled and multilayered consequences for poor populations, as gender, race-ethnicity, location, and income security each multiplies the disadvantages experienced by individuals and groups. Social heterogeneity produces highly unequal distribution of secure livelihoods in terms of life chances, dignity, and decision-making. Being a woman and rural is qualitatively distinctive from being an urban man, even if incomes are held steady. Such patterns of intersectionality—the interlocking of gender (dis)advantage, with income differentials, location, and racial group—are integral dimensions of sociospatial heterogeneity in the global South. Yet the ways this social heterogeneity shapes the outcomes of development and the ways it is taken on board in development thinking and policy proposals are rarely considered and are often dismissed as being too complex. Hence, although "slices through" social heterogeneity to take gender and race-ethnicity into account are now well established and widely accepted, the wider dilemma lies in the questions of how difference matters and how policy might take it into account without compounding existing intersectional disadvantages. If the existing policy approaches to social heterogeneity are recognized as contingent and inevitably compromised by their histories and applications, an exploration of how social heterogeneity impacts the institutionalization, operation, beneficiary experience, and the very meanings of development at play in a society opens out a wider set of questions of why and how social heterogeneity has been 'fixed' in particular ways and not others. Social heterogeneity—the continuously reproduced and ubiquitous existence of complex lines of social hierarchy and meaningful difference—remains understudied.[4] This book begins to explore these conceptual and practical challenges, offering a means by which to think about social heterogeneity, examining development's genealogy[5] of thinking about and modeling social difference, the postcolonial context in which these models are interpreted and put into operation, and the resulting interactions between on the one hand lived experiences of social difference and hierarchy and on the other development actors and institutions.

Social heterogeneity is everywhere in development. In the postcolonial societies where development is largely active, social differences frequently have huge impacts on opportunities and lives, a finding that becomes starkly evident in intersectional hierarchies (the ways groups ranked in terms of power and privilege interact to create differentiated subgroups whose relative position becomes more subtly differentiated). Latin America illustrates this issue—levels of formal education, rates of illiteracy, poverty, and insecure work are progressively worse for white men, white women, mixed-race men, mixed-race women, Afro-Latin men, Afro-Latin women, indigenous men, and indigenous women (Peredo Beltrán 2004; Calla 2006; CEPAL 2013). Likewise, development outcomes are relatively worse for rural people in each of these groups, than the corresponding urban population. In other words, social difference is key to the terrain in which development seeks to improve conditions, and cannot be considered as a residue of political economic forces.[6] This book makes the case for analyzing heterogeneous social differences as constituted through postcolonial hierarchy, that is hierarchies of difference arising in the aftermath of colonialism when dominant understandings of race, masculinities and femininities, and imaginative geographies of rural and urban areas, were established under power relations that favored the whiter, the urban, the masculine, and the wealthier over others. Rethinking domination in multiplicity means also considering the intellectual and material conditions for thinking about such heterogeneity (Dorlin 2005).

Analyzing hierarchies in relation to power repoliticizes intersectionality frameworks, while simultaneously centering materialities and embodiments in postcolonial theory. In the global South, dynamic interactions between sociocultural meanings and power-inflected relations of interlocking social differences (primarily race-ethnicity, class, gender, and geographical location) together make the basis for living conditions, authority, and voice. Combined with the uneven landscapes of global political economies and the selective provisioning of national territories by nation-states, these embodiments and associated material outcomes cannot be read directly off labor relations and capital, nor merely from discourse, as the very "matter" of (productive, reproductive, intellectual, political) labor is constituted and lived through embodiments that are always-already made through power and meaning.[7] Given this postcolonial ground, multiple lines of social difference interact within, across, and beyond development thinking, to influence policy and on-the-ground outcomes. By means of a grounded qualitative study of interlocking lines of social difference becoming coconstituted with development, the book examines the dynamic interface between development and social heterogeneity in which colonial ways of knowing social categories and their mutual interactions continue to wield enduring influence, even while development seemingly speaks to ever more refined characterizations of target populations and social difference. As this book also shows, colonial knowledges of social heterogeneity are not uncontested, being subject to reworking and resignification by social groups who do not find themselves mirrored in development categories—nor indeed in existing politicized groups—and whose critical knowledges from the margins of postcolonial development generate creative rethinking and practical knowledges about social heterogeneity in relation to development.

※

Speaking to Andean Kichwa women, including Aurora, Margarita, and Rosario, as well as women from the Tsáchila indigenous nationality on Ecuador's subtropical coastal plain, indicates that processual, granular, embodied, and governmental dimensions of interactions between those who consistently lose out from development on the one hand and those who decide what development is and who it goes to on the other require an ethnographic exploration of precisely how social difference and power are made real and enduring, and what role development interventions—from governments, overseas agencies, national NGOs, and others—play in these outcomes.[8] Development derives from and returns to two foundational features in its field of action—social heterogeneity and coloniality, which, I argue here, cannot be considered separately but only in terms of their coconstitution. Development consists of a "will to improve," an impulse to governmentality and pastoral interventions that seek to ameliorate the living conditions or social attributes of a population.[9] As such, development represents simultaneously and inextricably a form of knowing and a presumption of embodied, epistemological, and categorical social difference, through which governmentality operates. Whether at the global scale between minority and majority worlds, or in Andean NGO workers' confidence that indigenous women have primarily domestic concerns, the will to improve becomes a means by which to understand social difference—and the social heterogeneity on which it rests—as well as an impulse to power in relations across difference.[10]

In this sense, powerful myths about the composition of society guide and motivate action, making sense of complexity in ways that have enduring effects as they come to construct the social relations and categories through which development is conceived, delivered, and implemented (Cornwall et al. 2007). The will to improve these social sectors that live across a line of social difference of course occurs too within the nationalist imagined community, the dream of a common effort to overcome colonialism through achieving development, floundering against the very social heterogeneity on which postcolonial nation-states were established and built through exclusion (Gupta 1998; Chatterjee 2004). Scholars of humanitarianism and modernity-coloniality, despite profound differences in approach and sites of critical intervention, have begun to unpack the ways social categorization and their instrumentalization in moments of grave crisis—war and displacement, economic abjection that prevents dignity;[11]—serve to distinguish which subpopulations are worthy of which kind of assistance and under which conditions (Groenmeyer 1992; Agamben 1998; Butler 2003; Sylvester 2006; McIntyre and Nast 2011; Tyner 2013). What such scholarship also demonstrates clearly is that the constitution of bodies, institutions, political economies, sovereignties, policies, interpersonal interactions, and discourses layer in one on the other, expanding and naturalizing the field of social heterogeneity as well as the means by which it can be "improved."[12]

Social Difference, Development, and Intersectionality

The power-inflected outcomes of social heterogeneity have often been discussed in terms of *intersectionality*, a term referring to the need to recognize diversity in analytical (and political) categories such as "women." Intersectionality originated from the trenchant critiques by black and minority racialized women of how the single policy and political category of "women" overlooked—and in cases, actively denied—the ways overlapping forms of power resulted in violence against women of color. Since then, in the hands of women of color and postcolonial feminists, intersectionality has permitted an analysis of how active processes of racing, gendering, spatial containment, and sexualization produce, condone, and explain away violence, poorer education and employment outcomes, and other forms of discrimination and nonrecognition (Crenshaw 1991; Brah and Phoenix 2004: 78; Lugones 2007). The intersectional power of racialization, gendering, emplacement, and impoverishment operate across scales from the body through to macroeconomic patterns. In this sense, "social divisions have organizational, intersubjective, experiential and representational forms . . . and are expressed in specific institutions and organizations, such as state laws and state agencies, trade unions, voluntary organizations and the family. In addition, they involve specific power and affective relationships between actual people" (Yuval-Davis 2006: 198).[13] Racism, gendering, and so on are inscribed directly and apprehended through individual bodies. Intersectional critiques focus on the ways such power relations become naturalized and institutionalized at wider scales. In this macro-analysis, a key intersectional insight is the ontological distinctiveness of different social differences; male-female difference is not equivalent, or reducible, to race, or to class. Each has its own clusters of meanings, metaphors, and consequences, while each of these ontological distinctions compounds the extent and content of hierarchical social differentiation.

Historically and geographically contingent, categories of social difference are not fixed across time and space, as they result from articulation between interests, self-positionings, and experiences of exclusion in multiscaled configurations (Hall 1990). In any one place and time, these social differences are not singular in their effects, as they acquire meanings and practices that work to differentiate actively between an unmarked subject (men, whites, urbanites, high-income groups) and marked others (women, blacks, and minorities, rural dwellers, the poor) in ways that qualitatively inflect each other (De Lauretis 1987; Yuval-Davis and Anthias 1989; Moore 1994). In other words, any one axis of difference is relational—meanings attributed to "man" are qualities distinguishable from but related to meanings associated with "woman." Moreover, the intersection of qualities associated with an unmarked subject (such as "whiteness") reposition certain "women" closer to qualities of "man" than the social features associated with "black, minority and third world woman" (Crenshaw 1991; Carby 1982).[14] Bringing together intersectionality with a postcolonial framework (see below) seeks to more rigorously theorize intersectional hierarchies in relation to the dynamics of power associated with colonialism and postcolonial statehood and development. Drawing on postcolonial critiques of power and difference, my account of postcolonial intersectionality draws out the nuanced, relational, and multiscalar dynamics that actively work to differentiate diverse subjects, and to reinsert an account of individual and group agency in postcolonial societies. "A population affected in one moment by a process of social classification does not take on the features of a real group, a community or a social subject. Rather these features are only constituted as part of and result of a history of conflicts . . . and the decision to plait together the particular heterogeneous and discontinuous experiences in the articulation of a collective subject" (Quijano 2007: 116). Focusing on the postcolonial intersectional hierarchies found in one Latin American country, the book examines how development—an endeavor steeped in global and national postcolonial relations—brings into being social categories out of colonially inflected understandings of society that in turn impact poor rural indigenous women. It seeks to demonstrate how the meanings invested in policy categories obscure social heterogeneity by implicitly endorsing colonial imaginaries of social relations, which generate mixed, often negative, consequences for indigenous women. Development continually works amid social heterogeneity, yet it turns again and again to standard categories of subpopulations, which articulate with existing social groups in power-laden and, in the case of indigenous women inappropriate, ways. Drawing on poststructuralist accounts of subjectivities, the book develops a framework of postcolonial intersectionality to explore the conditions under which development devises and applies its social model in dynamics of material and discursive power, performativity, and embodiment, dispossession through racialization, and the production of space in terms of uneven development (Fanon 1986 [1952]; Butler 2003, 2011; Legg 2007; Foucault 2008; Smith 2008).[15]

As others have documented, social categories come to play a powerful role in development because they serve as a globalized language through which hierarchies and difference across diverse places and times can be identified quickly and smoothly enough to facilitate project interventions (Pigg 1992). While development's standard categories—peasant, village, woman—speak to international goals, they inevitably become tied to place and thereby acquire powerful national and regional associations which make them meaningful and seemingly better reflections of existing social realities. Significantly too, social categories are not merely about the external features of project beneficiaries. In the minds of policy makers and project workers, generic categories also become invested with expectations about subjects' affective properties, their psychic dispositions, and "consciousness" (Pigg 1992; Scott 1995; Klenk 2004). Later chapters document how these development expectations owe their power and endurance as much to embedded cultural tropes as to attempts by modernization and then neoliberal governmentality to forge new types of development subjects. Combining social categories, relational expectations and affective stereotypes then, development constructs its models of subjectivities and social inter-relations in ways that seep into economic, political, social and cultural projects and agendas, because they code for key social reference points—anchors for action—that seemingly predict the forms of work, attitudes and practices through which progress is to occur, and by which modern developed subjects are to be brought into being (Shrestha 1995; Hodgson 2001; Perreault 2003; Klenk 2004; Yeh 2007). Applied to public and intimate spaces, social categories associated with nature are often those that are most resilient and enduring, attaching rigid norms about social qualities to diverse forms of bodies. Race, gender, and sexuality are social features that are strongly associated with naturalized attributes, binding them to stereotypes about why indigenous women, black men, or poor farmers act in specific ways. Hence development consists of a broad political economic transformation augmented through interventions and programs and in order to achieve its ends targets subgroups of raced-gendered-located-classed subjects.

The global parameters of neoliberal development's thinking about social difference are by now relatively well documented. In the era of the so-called Washington Consensus, the need to address the social and human costs of restructuring and structural adjustment informed attempts to rejuvenate social policy. Reorganized around participation, decentralization, and antipoverty agendas, development aimed to match safety nets with particular subpopulations (Molyneux 2008). Moreover, neoliberalism's cultural politics of coresponsibility, empowerment, and active citizenship underpinned policy design and support for technologies of the self and entrepreneurialism (Lemke 2001), thereby recasting the presumptions about individuals' social core. In Latin America, social neoliberalism comprised a broad policy field in which social difference, especially along lines of gender, indigeneity, poverty and participation, come to the fore, a "rediscovery of society as a site of development needs and . . . potential," a new policy agenda (Molyneux 2006; Andolina et al. 2009: 11). Forged at the unstable hybrid meeting points of civil movements of women, indigenous groups and the urban poor with diverse institutional actors (Andolina et al. 2009; Ewig 2010), social neoliberalism relied heavily on concepts of social capital to read cultural and social difference in ways that often drew on conservative understandings of social difference just as they masked enduring power and material inequalities (Molyneux 2002; Moser 2004; Andolina et al. 2009).

The book shows how social neoliberalism's operationalization and understanding of heterogeneity carried forward and retooled existing models of social difference, both in terms of key relations between social categories (farmers and development technicians; husbands and wives; indigenous people and the state) and expectations about the affective and relational dispositions and interrelations they would have (naturalized assumptions about where different subjects' loyalties and interests would lie, how certain beneficiaries would respond to market or empowerment interventions). Tracing Ecuador's development genealogy in relation to postcolonial hierarchies of difference adds another layer of insight into social neoliberalism, namely how policy presumptions—even before neoliberalism—drew on coloniality-modernity's meanings of indigeneity, femininity, rurality, and poverty, as well as racialized meanings of family, duty, and progress. Although ostensibly post–Washington Consensus or postneoliberal, social heterogeneity in Ecuador is couched in terms that are profoundly postcolonial. Uncovering coloniality-modernity's importance in providing the contours and content of development interventions not only raises critical questions about the consequences of these framings of social heterogeneity for different beneficiary groups, but additionally prompts urgent enquiries into what alternatives might emerge to reconceptualize social heterogeneity, enquiries Ecuadorian indigenous women are actively involved in.

As noted, the category of "women" has considerable influence in development thinking. Among the first to ensure that social heterogeneity was recognized were scholars and activists who highlighted the differences between female and male positionalities in development and male bias in development thinking. Over time, women in postcolonial societies showed that focusing exclusively on female-male difference often obscured the diversified situations of racialized men and women in the global South (Sen and Grown 1987; Herrera 2003). Postdevelopment writers drew attention to how mainstream development works to represent populations in the South as particularly needy yet identified these groups by means of a shifting visibility of different social categories liable to project interventions (Escobar 1995). Moreover, these writers expanded the analysis to include the very professionals and institutions through which development occurs, highlighting the gaps between staffers and beneficiaries in professional profiles, education, authority, and mindset. Critical poststructural and postcolonial studies highlight the relational and power-drenched dynamics of social and institutional position. Postcolonial scholars additionally demonstrated the powerful ways colonial difference[16] constructed hierarchies between cultures through which social heterogeneity in the global South was apprehended and reworked through development. Whether development is considered an imminent process occurring alongside major transformations in political economy, state structures, and welfare measures or a goal-driven set of interventions structured through international organizations, nongovernmental agencies, and nation-states, social difference is foundational.

Postcolonial intersectionality matters in Latin America, as the benefits of development are so unevenly distributed across social groups. The region is characterized by the world's worst income maldistributions, with the richest 5 percent of Latin Americans receiving twice the comparable share of their OECD counterparts, while the poorest receive half. "Not only do the poor, the darker, and the female receive smaller slices, but the social pie is not large to begin with" (Hoffman and Centeno 2003: 365). Inequality leads to poorer groups working longer hours in less secure work, while economic and social policies consistently fail to address uneven development. Gulfs between rural and urban living standards and welfare support remain central to income gulfs, in part resting on highly skewed land distributions. Racialized and gendered segregation of labor markets results in darker, and female, workers concentrated in the lowest paid sectors, a wage gap that is worse in rural areas. Being female accounts for worse education, worse economic security, and less political opportunity than being male, when education and other factors are held constant. Racialization processes result in groups identified as indigenous or black being subject to discrimination and subordination across social life. Development interventions often serve to exacerbate stratification along intersecting lines of gender, race, and location. After Peru's health sector reforms, for instance, quality private services were only available to rich employees, while women—concentrated in the lower-paid, informal sector—could not participate, and racialized, largely rural, sectors were not covered (Ewig 2010). Neoliberal policy and globalized images of indigenous people with folkloric culture and arcane environmental knowledge increasingly focus on indigenous women as potential entrepreneurs, a dramatic change from previous representations (De Hart 2010; Babb 2012). Yet as later chapters discuss, such representations have ambivalent and contested effects, as they reconfigure the relations between indigenous women and men, just as they fail to address indígenas' demands for moves away from neoliberal political economies.

SOCIAL HETEROGENEITY IN DEVELOPMENT THINKING

An intersectional theoretical approach provides incisive analytical tools with which to examine the ways development policy and practice is not socially neutral. In practice, programs consistently overlook one or more dimensions of social difference. Racial difference has proven to be one of the most hidden and unexamined dimensions of social heterogeneity in postcolonial development; "the silence on race is a determining silence that both masks and marks its centrality to the development project" (White 2002: 408). Racialization underpins the social heterogeneity of postcolonial societies, yet discussion of culture, ethnicity, or location often obscures its importance. Development continues to have unexamined expectations about differently racialized subjects and the geographies they inhabit. In Ecuador, as later chapters document, colonial racialized assumptions permeate development thinking and practice and in turn ensure the hegemonic position of mestizo-white social norms at the cost of other configurations of gender, generation, economy, and meaning. By tracking the dynamics between policy framework and rural reality, the chapters demonstrate how policies fail to acknowledge colonial constructions of social difference yet continue to rely on colonial constructions of knowledge.

For these reasons, although global policy and activist networks increasingly advocate the use of intersectional policy approaches, the latter's influence remains highly conditioned by existing configurations of power. The UN Beijing conference on women of 1995 called for governments to address "multiple barriers to [women's and girls'] empowerment and advancement because of . . . their race, age, language, ethnicity, culture, religion or disability or because they are indigenous people" (Quoted in Yuval-Davis 2006: 196). Likewise the UN Durban conference against racism of 2001 validated a gender perspective in antiracism and antidiscrimination measures, diversity in plurality, and analysis of power and rights. Despite these goals, addressing intersectionality in practice remains a challenge, since "a project focusing on challenging gender inequality does not simultaneously work on challenging inequality between women from an ethnic minority" (der Hoogte and Kingma 2004: 47). One stumbling block has been the core fact of social categories' irreducible ontological difference (Yuval-Davis 2006), namely that the problems of one social group, women, may be compared with another, race-ethnic minorities, without recognizing the *qualitative* differences intersectionality makes. Moreover, development's institutional arrangements contribute to fixing boundaries between different policy approaches and working styles, and frequently hold mutually incompatible understandings of rights, the state, and professional expertise (Luykx 2000; Paulson and Calla 2000).[17] Later chapters show that these institutional and philosophical gulfs are constructed around social categories that presume particular characteristics, characteristics considered normal in the dominant population and influential in projects, despite the fact they do not correlate with heterogeneous social groups on the ground.

Development institutions and project workers are at the core of processes by which routine development intervenes in the dynamics of postcolonial social heterogeneity. As a broad-ranging and richly ethnographic set of studies reveals (Baaz 2005; Barrig 2006; Heron 2007; Cook 2008), the institutionality and personnel of development are intrinsically part of the negotiations over meaning, value, and difference that underpin expectations of modernity and development's purpose with target populations. Echoing this, the Ecuadorian case vividly illustrates how the global policy field of gender and development (GAD) draws on western liberal interpretations of gender, group rights, and development, which influence multilateral agencies, international NGOs, and national institutions.[18] In development, "those with power appear to have no culture [race, gender, location], those without power are culturally endowed" as well as gendered, raced, and so on (Volpp 2001: 1192). Target populations moreover are associated strongly with specific embodied attributes that gain traction in development thinking, such as dexterity, docility, or physical strength. In light of these blocks to applying intersectional policy, policy legacies are not "neutral political factors, but . . . carry with them clear implications for gender, race and class inequality" because they "entrench the class, gender and race inequalities on which they arise" (Ewig 2010: 200; see Boesten 2010). Policy legacies are powerful because development institutions and personnel continue to embrace deeply held understandings about core human attributes of project beneficiaries, concerning issues related to (lack of) agency and (lack of) relevant knowledge. In these relational understandings, development actors often associate themselves with a normalized modernity, in contrast to a pathologized, unchanging society, a viewpoint that permeates policy approaches to all social categories and intersectionality (Schech and Haggis 2000). Moreover, "intersectionality" as a policy approach often remains associated with already-problematic subpopulations and vulnerable subaltern groups rather than with the full range of social categories formed at the intersection of race, class, gender, and location (Paulson and Calla 2000: 119).[19] As later chapters show, GAD's coloniality not only impacts how indigenous women's gender positionality is viewed but also informs how development debates around intersectionality play out in specific policy initiatives, such as ethnodevelopment (proindigenous and pro-Afro-Latin development). In Latin America, these postcolonial dynamics come to the surface in debates between development workers and "beneficiaries" over the relative value of individual and collective rights (der Hoogte and Kingma 2004: 50). Friction between policy notions of femininity, womanhood, and racialization, and indigenous women generate in turn innovative responses by indigenous women to their positionality and standpoint.

In this sense, social heterogeneity cannot be apprehended merely by examining the genealogies and forms of governmentality inaugurated by development, crucial though this is in providing critical comparative analysis of policy (dis)continuities. The Ecuadorian case illustrates how successive waves of policy approached social heterogeneity and entrenched social hierarchies. Bringing into focus both colonial and policy legacies illustrates precisely why development struggles to adopt approaches that are flexible, nuanced and sensitive enough to address social heterogeneity. In the words of Andrea Cornwall, the challenge remains to identify "an approach and interactions that are part of everyday life, rather than imposing categories and concepts from conventional . . . approaches. To do so calls for strategies that are sensitive to local dynamics of difference" (Cornwall 2003: 1338). While aid organizations are increasingly taking complexity, volatility and the unexpected into account (Ramalingam 2013), much remains to be done in discerning what is required in relation to social development and differentiation. A critical genealogy of successive development frameworks for dealing with social heterogeneity and social categories they call into being demonstrates the ways policy recurs again and again to malleable and powerful colonial templates and stereotypes. Close attention to the content and meaning of categories over time identifies which meanings and lines of difference are mobilized and which are left unspoken and unacknowledged.

Coloniality, Postcolonial Intersectionality, and Development

> We women usually have our [ethnically distinctive] clothes, but men hardly
> put their poncho on. Always when we arrive at the hospital, they treat us like
> "Marías." They don't attend to us properly.
> TERESA, KICHWA WOMAN, SPEAKING IN RIOBAMBA (2009)

Colonial legacies continue to shape countries in the global South as they establish the parameters for treatment of different social groups, and the moral and political grounds on which certain dimensions of social heterogeneity are ignored and dismissed. Colonial constructions of social difference thus become marked on a daily and generational level through representations, dispossession of populations, colonial administration, and description of spaces, regional political economy, and hybrid dynamics of encounters between colonizers and the colonized (Stoler 1995; Sylvester 1999; Loomba 2005). Everyday understandings of social heterogeneity hence owe their veneer of commonsense to routine and normalized colonial vocabularies and procedures. Teresa, from the central Ecuadorian Andes, quoted in the epigraph to this section, is treated by public services as a generic, interchangeable racialized woman who is less deserving of quality attention, in comparison with men and nonindigenous users.

Varying with colonial power, history, and geography, western representations and government produced social heterogeneity through colonialism's procedures of demarcation and violence, by reifying social (especially racial-ethnic) categories and inscribing meanings on diverse bodies and by generalizing and denying colonized social difference (Said 1993; Escobar 1995; Ferguson 1999). Chandra Mohanty (1988) termed this "discursive colonialism," a power exerted by demarcating a fundamental difference between the West and the rest, denying relational meanings and social exchange. Accordingly, coloniality refers to the ways colonialism has shaped "longstanding patterns of power that . . . define culture, labor, inter-subjective relations and knowledge production" into the colonial present (Mignolo 2000; Quijano 2000; Gregory 2004; Legg 2007). Coloniality's social classifications in Latin America distinguished between groups according to the type of labor power required, thereby locking into place crosscutting racialized and gendered subcategories, even if in reality these laborers were always heterogeneous, discontinuous, and conflictive (Quijano 2007). Latin American colonialism established institutional dispositions, structural inequalities, displacement of populations (indigenous populations from historic territories, black slaves from Africa), and naturalized divisions of labor between men and women, elites and laborers, colonizers and colonized, which were in turn solidified in law, routines, and inscriptions on bodies. Although Spanish colonialism ended in the early nineteenth century, coloniality continues to shape development outcomes today, producing the region's lopsided development, with markedly different outcomes for social groups (Galeano 1973; Mignolo 2005; Mahoney 2010).

In Latin America, state-building was widely established over indigenous territories and populations by means of the creation of internal colonies, which facilitated national "development" while racializing and containing these places and people as sinks for low-value labor power (Gonzalez Casanova 1965). Internal colonies were and often continue to be tied firmly into exploitative macro-economies through trade, political, and employment relations. "Internal colonialism is not only or principally a state policy as under foreign occupation; it is rather a widespread social grammar which traverses social relations, public and private space, culture, thinking and subjectivities" (De Sousa Santos 2011: 27), becoming an intrinsic part of wider social, spatial, and governmental processes of state formation in which "scaled contempt" (Rivera Cusicanqui 2010: 47) simultaneously integrates and differentiates. In the words of Mahoney (2010: 19), "institutions that produce hierarchical forms of domination are . . . of great importance. Thus attention must turn to colonial rules for securing indigenous labor, for securing indigenous land rights, and for designating local political power holders. Such institutions often connect ethnoracial categories to patterns of resource allocation . . . and ethnic identities into highly enduring axes of contention."

However much indigenous Americans are treated as traditional, ancestral, and unchanging, the reality has been that they have experienced the most direct effects of the entangled dynamics of coloniality and modernity. Ecuadorian internal colonies today consist of spaces for the low-cost subsistence of low-wage labor underpinned by urban migration, informal social welfare measures, and poor public infrastructure, the racialized form of development's contemporary will toward enclosure and enclavization (Sidaway 2012). Internal colonies have not lost relevance to development governmentality and postcolonial state formation, as they are retooled for present concerns.[20] While primarily serving to locate and fix indigeneity, internal colonies coconstitute class and gender differences and sexuality. "The conquest, colonization and appearance of the hacienda system constituted a space through which [female-male] differences were deepened" (Palacios 2005: 327), impacting social differences in work, resources, and status. Gatherings of bodies that do not matter to elites, internal colonies are granted low priority in public investment, compounding state neglect and minimal living standards and becoming a form of "disenfranchisement due to racism and the legacies of colonialism" (Volpp 2001: 1217; also Rivera Cusicanqui 2012).

Under the colonial gaze, stereotypes about the clumsiness, inarticulacy, and lack of agency of an indigenous woman confirm social difference while leaving in place underlying ambivalence about distinctions, even as it imposes impossible demands on subalterns. Accordingly, "it is the force of ambivalence that gives the colonial stereotype its currency; ensures its repeatability in changing historical and discursive conjunctures; informs its strategies of individuation and marginalization; produces the effect of probabilistic truths and predictability which, for the stereotype, must always be in *excess* of what can be empirically proved or logically construed" (Bhabha 1996: 87–88, original emphasis). In postcolonial intersectionality, indigeneity[21] is performed and embodied—through clothing, speech, bodily expression, and inscriptions on the body—in daily interactions, under the racializing gaze of dominant groups. Latin American politics of indigeneity are entangled with tensions between elite-state labeling and postcolonial processes of self-identification. In this book, the term *indigenous* is used to signal state labels as well as broad self-identification, while the terms *nationality* and *pueblo* refer to larger and smaller ethnocultural-linguistic groups, respectively. As later chapters demonstrate, colonial stereotyping is found through development policy—from modernization to multiculturalism— although it originates in a broader biopolitics that marks a sharp distinction between bodies that are worth valuing and subalterns who are not, a modern nonethics arguably originating in sixteenth-century debates over whether Indians had souls (Maldonado-Torres 2007). Latin American nation-states' colonial discourses disavow indigenous claims over material plenitude and epistemic equality, frequently placing them outside the imaginative, legal, and material category of sufficient humanity (Agamben 1998; Anderson 2007). Colonial criteria set the stage for development governmentality just as it rendered subaltern claims fragile. Although nominally covered by development's remit of poverty alleviation, indigenous and other racialized groups in Latin American countries are construed in the colonial present as dispensable (Fanon 1986 [1952]; Wright 2001; Maldonado-Torres 2007; Butler 2011). In this sense, indigenous experiences of development in Latin America link to analyses of how abject and surplus populations are produced as disposable through sociospatial relations (Wright 2001; McIntyre and Nast 2011; Tyner 2013). The "epidermalization" (Fanon 1986 [1952]) of marginalization is experienced physically and psychically in the forms of quotidian epistemic and physical violence, against individuals and groups viewed as raced—conquered, gendered, and sexualized.

In Latin American postcolonial societies, indigeneity is intersectional (de la Cadena 2008: 344; Valdivia 2009), an inherently multiple and context-dependent social position and subjectivity constituted through interrelating sociospatial relations and incomprehensible outside of them, as indeed are race and gender.[22] Indigeneity, being identified with prior claims to territory and sociocultural difference, is associated in Latin America with impoverishment, an insecure segment of labor markets, and a low socioeconomic class status. Indigeneity is also largely a social position associated with rural places and social abandonment.[23] Populations claiming originary ties to the American continent are highly diverse, yet they strategically identify common demands arising from their position after conquest, as the UN'S definition of indigenous peoples makes clear:

> Indigenous communities, peoples and nations are those which, having a historical continuity with pre-invasion and pre-colonial societies that developed on their territories, consider themselves distinct from other sectors of the societies now prevailing on those territories, or parts of them. They form at present non-dominant sectors of society and are determined to preserve, develop and transmit to future generations their ancestral territories, and their ethnic identity, as the basis of their continued existence as peoples, in accordance with their own cultural patterns, social institutions and legal systems.[24]

As a colonial legacy, land distribution is most skewed and uneven in Latin American countries with large indigenous populations. Moreover, countries with large indigenous populations have tended to be those where the liberal politics of oligarchic elites have been more strictly exclusionary and harshly authoritarian. "Indigenous" identity, whether adopted or ascribed, thus reflects a political positioning in global, national and local power structures. While indigeneity is at times defined through resistance to dam construction or large-scale mineral extraction (for example, Chile's Bio-Bio dam, Peruvian antimining activism, and Panama's Ngobe-Buglé), elsewhere it is constituted through lives of quiet desperation and everyday resilience.

"Coloniality does not just refer to racial classification. It is an encompassing phenomenon . . . and as such it permeates all control of sexual access, collective authority, labor, subjectivity, intersubjectivity and the production of knowledge" (Lugones 2007: 191). In coloniality, the intractable production of difference occurs where interlocking relations of gender, sexuality, race, class, and location constitute colonial power and the nature of resistance to it (Anthias and Yuval-Davis 1992; McClintock 1995; Stoler 1995). Male-female difference remains intrinsic to postcolonial indigenous experience, as labor markets, technical assistance, expectations about productive and reproductive inputs, and authority continue to be strongly biased against female agency and toward nonindigenous norms, with women's position often viewed as "more Indian" than men's (de la Cadena 1995). Central to Latin American coloniality in this regard has been white(r) men's sexual access to, and rape of, low-income, largely rural, indigenous women, a process that has contributed to the emergence of a mixed-race (*mestizo* in

Spanish) and increasingly middle-income, urban class group. In coloniality's field of social differentiation, the "rapeability" of indigenous women informed elites' feminization of indigenous men, and indigenous femininity's association with lack of worth (Curiel 2007; Maldonado-Torres 2007; Wade 2009; Galindo 2013). Although indigenous women bore mestizo children, they remained at the bottom of postcolonial hierarchies, whereas indigenous men were permitted highly conditional entry into law, paid work, and literacy (Rivera Cusicanqui 2012; Galindo 2013).[25] The colonial category of "indigenous women" hence established a specific context in which development projects came to operate. As postcolonial critic Gayatri Spivak argues, the archetypal woman of the global South is placed in a highly unstable and ambivalent position, as she represents the subject who is the not-yet-modern yet the archetypal remains-to-be-modernized. Hence "the displaced figuration of the 'third world woman' [is] caught between tradition and modernization" (Spivak 1993 [1988]: 102; also Minh-ha 1989; Mohanty 1999). In development programs, the "thirdworldwoman" becomes a boundary-marker for cultural difference, as policy views her in ways that bear no relation to ordinary women's lives. As later chapters document, Ecuadorian indigenous women respond to their positionality in coloniality-modernity by critically reworking the colonial framework and presumptions about difference and subjectivity in ways that contribute to alternative modernities. To signal the multiple and fluid nature of postcolonial intersectionality as an experience and a political category, this book uses the term indígena to refer to subjects self-identifying with indigeneity and femininity, a context-specific concatenation of claims.[26]

Rather than listen to policy-makers and development professionals talk about intersectional goals, the book centers the perspectives of indigenous women talking about connections between existing policy, entrenched inequalities, and the costs of postcolonial intersectionality (see Hodgson 2001; Escobar 2008; Asher 2009). Racialized female beneficiaries' words about postcolonial development reveal how they learn from bitter experience how interventions consolidate inequalities rather than tackle them, and hence provide key insights into the underbelly of development's selective and colonial engagement with social heterogeneity. The deeply contextualized case study analysis provides a window onto the shifting developmental visibilities of different social categories and their consequences for variously situated groups at diverse intersections of postcolonial hierarchies.[27] The critical institutional and community ethnographic focus on low-income indigenous women demonstrates how the nonrecognition of diversity within diversity results in indigenous women's limited gains, and their dissatisfaction with development's reading of social heterogeneity. Their experiences provide key insights into the power relations that result in developmental approaches to social heterogeneity at multiple interlocking scales from household to village and to region, indigenous ethnic group, nation, and the global scale. Indigenous women are treated differently in development from indigenous men, nonindigenous women, and nonindigenous men, as interlocking inequalities of power variously deprive them of resources, make their specific positionality and needs invisible, prejudge their social disposition, and/or override their demands in the name of a greater community. Pinpointing the proximate power-holders in these dynamics suggests that the nation-state, development agencies (global, national, and nongovernmental organizations), women and men in dominant class-race-locational positions, and indigenous men are significant, if not equally influential, in every context or moment in history.[28]

The Politics of Postcolonial Intersectionality, Development, and Citizenship

Critical accounts of development highlight the need to distinguish between citizenship as a set of practices ensuring voice, authority, and resources, from development and welfare interventions that work to contain and channel claims to resources and decision-making power (Lemke 2001). According to Partha Chatterjee (2004), republican citizenship ideals were "overtaken" by the developmental state and were reoriented toward fulfilling dreams of prosperity and modernity. In this way, postcolonial governmentality and biopolitics became bound up in distinguishing between groups in need of intervention and other groups who became bearers of full substantive citizenship.[29] This divergence in goals and interventions, however, also becomes bound up with pinpointing particular social groups for improvement: "The protection of woman (today the "third world woman") becomes a signifier of the establishment of a *good* society" (Spivak 1993 [1988]: 94, original emphasis). Security and welfare agendas gave rise, in this context, to a different kind of citizenship. By drawing attention to the irreducibility of development to citizenship, Chatterjee's incisive analytics forces us to query how social heterogeneity becomes bound up with differentiated claims, rights, acts, and protections across a highly fractured political terrain.

According to Chatterjee, development governmentality has as its end the reduction of poverty within designated subpopulations, prompting the developmental state to invest in acquiring knowledge about subpopulations, a process whereby "older ethnographic concepts [became] convenient descriptive categories for classifying groups of people into suitable targets for administrative, legal, economic or electoral policy. In many cases, classificatory criteria used by colonial governmental regimes continued into the postcolonial era, shaping the forms of both political demands and developmental policy" (Chatterjee 2004: 37). Under the developmental state, policy thinking and interventions viewed social difference through a postcolonial lens that attempted to distinguish unmodern and modern characteristics (Schech and Haggis 2000). Liberalism's field of differentiated subjects and substantive citizenships infuses interventions' framing of social heterogeneity and the suitability and content of what development "should do." The existence of social categories through which development is governed and directed reflects not a fixed grid of subpopulations but the constitution of relational, context-dependent categories that come into being informed by mainstream understandings of social difference, as well as challenges to the boundary between citizenship and development. Citizenship's negotiable substantive content remains in tension with colonial distinctions between categories of human, as exemplified in recent Ecuadorian nonwestern policy of *buen vivir* development.

Although colonial rule created endless fissures and social heterogeneity, there remain subterranean points of political articulation, leading to interruptions to governance and development (Bhabha 1994; Li 2007; Quijano 2007). Mobilized around grievances at being marginalized or discriminated against, contingent groups galvanize to press for reformulations of development's reading of the postcolonial terrain (Chatterjee 2004), resulting in some cases in the incorporation of single lines of social difference into development (e.g., global women's movement's gender mainstreaming). Such struggles often straddle the boundary between development and citizenship, between redistribution and recognition, and arise out of coloniality's exclusions and subaltern disadvantage (Young 1990; Fraser 1997; Isin and Nielsen 2008). Political mobilizations outside the frame of development, as well as at times the unintended consequences of participatory development, generate disruptions to the contingent and fragile boundary between citizenship and programs to alleviate disadvantage (Alvarez et al. 2003; Chatterjee 2004; Hickey and Mohan 2004; Holston 2009). Such politics—if it is to occur at all—has to be forged through new forms of communication and practice (Spivak 1993 [1988]; Chua et al. 2000; McEwan 2009). Through colonial and republican history, Latin American indigenous women and men periodically contested the colonial terms of recognition (how to be indigenous) and redistribution (colonial allocations of land, postcolonial distributions of education, investment, dignity).

In this regard, multicultural recognition of plural cultures and ethnicities seemingly reformulates political and developmental responses to social heterogeneity on more equitable grounds (for an overview on Latin American citizenship, see Dagnino 2003). Latin America's multicultural reforms reconfigured the dynamics between racialization, development and citizenship from the 1990s, while indigenous movements in some countries seized the moment to pursue deeper redistribution and recognition goals (Postero 2006; Gershon 2011). In the region, multiculturalism worked its way quickly into constitutions, political rhetoric, and state institutionalization, although racialized, poor, rural, and female subjects saw uneven gains in economic, social, and political rights (Hale 2002; Yashar 2005; Walsh et al. 2009). Informing social neoliberalism, policy recognition of indigenous difference through the lens of culture resulted in specific development interventions that entailed mixed outcomes for racialized groups. Although Ecuador adapted the millennium development goals for indigenous needs (Ecuador Indígenas 2009), multicultural reforms in development and health had only partial impacts on indigenous women, as long-standing social assumptions remained largely in place. Fundamentally, multiculturalism did little to challenge, let alone overturn, entrenched colonial hierarchies, as it tended to regulate expressions of difference while retaining forms of privilege and stigmatization (Bhabha 1994; Hale 2002; Melamed 2006), generating paradoxical effects in development programs. If gender policy did little to acknowledge postcolonial power differentials between women, neoliberal multicultural policy worked from reified, culturally focused definitions of indigeneity, thereby closing down consideration of material inequalities and male-female difference.

Yet to the degree that multicultural development arises from rights to cultural recognition, it resembles the rights-based agenda in development, which seeks to use a rights framework in order to ensure more equitable well-being and security (Cornwall and Nyuma-Musembi 2004). Rights-based development influences Latin American measures to tackle female-male inequality, and racial-ethnic disadvantages, and recently in Ecuador's "postneoliberal" buen vivir development (see chapter 7). Scholarship demonstrates the challenge of moving from abstract rights in law toward the realization of rights in the context of development interventions. Later chapters add another dimension to this, exploring how postcolonial intersectionality means that even if rights are specified for one group, the heterogeneity and crosscutting power relations within that group results in uneven access to rights. The result can be the homogenization of rights-bearers, rather than a heterogeneous politics of presence (Phillips 1995). Hence, although the human rights framework is widely vernacularized among Ecuadorian indigenous women, as well as celebrated in development agencies, it remains a profound challenge to ensure that rights come to be practiced in a socially sensitive manner.

Reflecting postcolonial intersectionality, indigenous women's rights and citizenship are structured differently from indigenous men's and nonindigenous women's, whether under political liberalism or neoliberal multiculturalism (Rivera Cusicanqui 2010).[30] In later chapters, indígenas' postcolonial positionality in citizenship becomes evident. Feminism's liberal politics assumes that thirdworldwomen will be empowered by individual rights instead of by ethnic communities, and that subalterns will become individual subjects, combining social detachment and self-authorization (Povinelli 2005).[31] Aurora's and Margarita's solidarity with Rosario, described earlier, speaks to indigenous women's struggles to work together to change development in ways that upset coloniality's liberal expectations. Shortly before our conversation under the midday Andean sun, we had all attended a workshop about sexual and reproductive health in a simple community hall, an event organized by the women's representative for the provincial indigenous federation, the redoubtable and cheerful Delia. Over one hundred women—some carrying babies in bright carrying cloths on their backs—and a few men listened to Delia's talk, which was given in a mix of Spanish and Kichwa. On the bus later that day, Delia expressed outrage on hearing Rosario's story and vowed to talk to her ethnic organization. Her response was characteristic of Ecuadorian indigenous women's affiliations. Rather than pinpoint gender as the major axis of Rosario's disadvantage or view the state as an effective arbiter, Delia turned to civil organizations of indigenous women and men, whose widespread legitimacy and authority might get Rosario readmittance to her community. Meetings, acts of solidarity, and confederation spaces echo with indigenous women's agency and strategies for sociocultural change. Not that Delia believes women are always best served by ethnic politics tout court. She is also a vocal advocate for action by and on behalf of indigenous women to gain autonomy, education, and decision-making, and so she contributes to templates that copy neither development nor ethnic agendas. Although struggling to leverage resources and power, indigenous women forge unique agendas for development and citizenship that selectively borrow from development, feminism, and intersectional indigeneity to create an alternative formulation of rights and dignity.[32]

Ecuadorian women from many indigenous nationalities are active participants in ethnic rights groups, alongside men, and jointly pursue anti-racism, recognition and redistributive goals, with a number gaining leadership positions (Cervone 1998, 2002).[33] Women's activism in ethnocultural movements reflects indigeneity's postcolonial intersectionality, the existence of diversity within diversity, where demands for antiracism exist in tension with colonial representations of women's tradition (Safa 2005). Indigenous women experience worse racism than male counterparts in markets, schools, public offices, and streets, prompting active engagement with antiracist and group rights demands (Palacios 2005: 325; Encalada 2012; see chapters 1, 2). However, indigenous women in Ecuador are increasingly unwilling to condone representations of female quiescent culture-bearers. In everyday contexts, Kichwa and Tsáchila women's granular, recombined practices contribute to a reimagining of political subjectivity and agendas, at the intersection of racialization and gendering. As the Ecuadorian case demonstrates, indigenous women appropriate multicultural spaces with a distinctive raced-gendered politics that creates innovative and creative political subjectivities and agendas. To these ends, indigenous women form practical and strategic alliances across national borders, across and between social differences. Indigenous women across Latin America struggle against coloniality's understandings of subalterns to dissociate themselves from social labeling that reinforces gendered racialized power, adopting a multiplicity of tactics and methods (del Campo 2012).

Although it promised substantive citizenship via development, Ecuador in practice has delivered irregular, highly conditional development, in which a small coterie of elite families have dominated political economic activities in export agriculture, resource extraction, politics, and statecraft, against which a small, tenuous middle class and large numbers of diverse low-income subjects struggle to maintain dignity and livelihood. With weak state institutionalization, Ecuador's postcolonial state has one of the world's worst income distributions, alongside the United States and South Africa, with a Gini coefficient of 49.3 in 2010, and inequalities that remain entrenched, as an underclass is granted minimal social protection (Ramírez Gallegos 2008; Mahoney 2010). Racialized inequality is marked: unlike nonindigenous Ecuadorians, self-identified indigenous peoples living on less than $2 a day rose from 45.8 to

69.4 percent, while indigenous people with unmet basic needs (another measure of poverty) remained above 80 percent.[34] Formally democratic, Ecuador is a middle-ranking country in global terms,[35] yet the richest 10 percent control 35.2 times the income of the poorest tenth.[36]

Producing Knowledge on Postcolonial Development

O my body makes of me always a man who questions.

FRANTZ FANON, BLACK SKIN, WHITE MASKS (1952)

Development's reliance on and instrumental deployment of social difference speaks to processes of knowledge production. Knowledge about beneficiaries' social characteristics constitutes development procedures as manageable and grounded. Existing accounts of indigenous women's development experiences are framed through colonially inflected forms of knowledge, statistically shown to be disadvantaged in education, income, landholdings, credit, political office, and health, in comparison with women in dominant racial-ethnic categories, and indigenous men (Vinding 1998; Cardenas et al. 2011; CEPAL 2013). In Ecuador, too, government data suggests that indigenous women are worse off as a group at the start of the twenty-first century than a decade previously.[37]

Analyzing the operations of postcolonial intersectional development hence requires discussion of knowledge production, methods, and positionality in institutional and community contexts. As noted by women of color, power relations generate differently positioned forms of knowledge, while being at the margins generates a double sight that draws on dominant and marginalized experiences alike (Anzaldúa 1987; Rappaport 2005). Building on these insights, this study gathered information through a process informed by a decolonial attitude, seeking "responsibility and the willingness to take many perspectives, particularly the . . . points of view whose very existence is questioned and produced as insignificant . . . [and] recognize their intellectual production as thinking—not only as culture or ideology" (Maldonado-Torres 2007: 262; Tuhiwai Smith 2012). Consistent with explorations of the epistemologies under modernity/coloniality (Mignolo 2000; Walsh et al. 2009; Jazeel and McFarlane 2010), a critical examination of social heterogeneity in postcolonial development entails careful theorization of development "from the perspective of postcolonial people and their daily dilemmas" (Sylvester 2011: 189).[38] For these reasons, this account of indigenous women's experiences of development arises out of a collaborative and ethical process in which I take responsibility for the organization, selection, and theorization of findings generated through participatory methods (also Jazeel and McFarlane 2010; Noxolo et al. 2012; Hale and Stephen 2013).

The *experience* of development for marginalized groups refers to social processes, emplaced meanings, and expectations of carefully calibrated differences that are best captured through ethnographic and qualitative approaches (Hart 2004). Indigenous women's encounters with development are experienced as raced-gendered-sexualized as well as fractured, disparate, uneven, episodic, inappropriate, dismissive of their knowledge, and insufficient. Women gain knowledge of being ignored in project planning and racist abuse from state officials. Yet indígenas' insights inform us not merely of the limited reach of development—an empirical description coming from the global South. Rather, indigenous women become observers and embodied knowledge-holders about the types of intervention they encounter, illustrating "the ways in which theory and practice interact. . . . The real life solutions that women craft often navigate them between theory and practice, the local and the global" (Perry and Schenck 2001: 2). Latin American indígena organizations incisively critique the ways global development frameworks describe their social situation and prescribe policy.[39] As in Africa, "the planners may have historical amnesia but those who are the target of repeated development efforts remember the struggles, successes and failures all too well" (Hodgson 2001: 11). Taking this knowledge as its starting point, this book documents indigenous women's process of learning about development's socially uneven and exclusionary effects, which constitute them in relation to a wider political and moral project. Indigenous women's embodied and grounded experiences of interventions—often short-term, uninformed, and deaf to women's situation—give rise to uniquely positioned forms of critical border knowledges, providing extensive evidence on development's blind spots and egregious failures, their bodies making of them a questioning, troubled subject, to adapt Fanon. Although unacknowledged in much development policy and analysis, indigenous women are actively involved in rethinking development knowledge and practices, informed by their unique positionality at the crossover of ways of life with development governmentality (Hernández 2008; Lugones 2008; Paredes 2010; Galindo 2013). In doing so, they rethink dominant epistemologies on how to achieve well-being and dignity as they become knowledgeable critics of lopsided systems of distribution and welfare, citizenship, and the postcolonial state.

Across the world, subalterns are denied a voice through the deployment of epistemic violence that misrecognizes their knowledge and denies epistemological equivalence and validity (Spivak 1993 [1988]; Mignolo 2000; Maldonado-Torres 2007).[40] Postcolonial writer Gayatri Spivak (1993 [1988]) famously argued that knowledge and difference are particularly fraught for subaltern women as the powerful—northern nations, capitalist political economies, states, masculine power, and western feminism—claim to always already know them. In Ecuador, feminist development experts, indigenous social movements, and the nation-state each claim to speak on Andean indigenous women's behalf and represent them as muted, and unable to express themselves independently. By contrast, critical scholarship documents the numerous and wide-ranging registers through which female subalterns articulate, systematize, and make effective their agency and provides extensive evidence of women's diverse voices, forms of authority, creativity, and knowledge (Arnold 1997; Burman 2011).[41] Decolonizing knowledge production regarding Latin American indigenous women hence involves recognizing their diverse and distinctive standpoints, off-center perspectives, and varied tactics. Critical ethnographic work documents the diversity of Ecuador's indigenous women and the increasingly urban-based, market-influenced, and hybrid cultural contexts of their lives (for example Crain 1996; Weismantel 2001; Prieto et al. 2005; Garcés Dávila 2006; O'Connor 2007; Swanson 2007, Prieto 2008, Pequeño 2009).

Ecuadorian indigenous women vividly exemplify "a confrontation with the racial, gender and sexual hierarchies that were put in place or strengthened by European modernity . . . [generating] oppositions to the coloniality of power, knowledge and being" (Maldonado-Torres 2007: 245). This decolonization process arose from ordinary indigenous women rethinking development in ways that challenge modernity-coloniality's material and epistemological exclusions and that produce alternatives in political and policy debates.[42] If Mohanty offered us the concept of "colonial difference" to signal how metropolitan knowledge "knew" about the majority world, decolonization urges engagement with what might be called the "postcolonial difference," that is, how diversely positioned groups across the global South come to know and systematize knowledge about modernity-coloniality. "Postcolonial difference" indexes the richly practical, embodied, and intellectual knowledges held by majority-world subjects about development and the colonial present. Nevertheless, as Kichwa and Tsáchila women show, the postcolonial difference offers no secure or stable platform on which to

Fig. I.2. Tsáchila women sit outside their house. Photograph by the author.

construct a "solution" to development's lacunae, no rallying articulation of identity and culture through which to overturn the status quo in a neat political reversal. Accordingly, examining social heterogeneity in postcolonial development offers no easy policy-relevant answers or neat authorial positions.[43]

This book arises from and reflects on over seven years of collaborative and qualitative research with national-regional indigenous women's representatives, as well as sustained interaction with village women in two indigenous groups.[44] Prior to village-based fieldwork, I spent many months working and talking with a politically, ethnically, educationally, and institutionally diverse set of women, who held positions as ethnic movement leaders, elected women's representatives, NGO workers, and civil servants (some of them indigenous women). Conversations focused on the key themes indigenous women were interested in, to which further exploration and research could contribute. Discussions also provided initial research questions, refined via email. In this sense, I was attempting to engage in a decolonial approach, which reaches for "making visible the invisible and . . . analyzing the mechanisms that produce such invisibility or distorted visibility . . . [including] the critical reflections of the 'invisible' people themselves. Indeed, one must recognize their intellectual production as thinking—not only as culture or ideology" (Maldonado-Torres 2007: 262; Tuhiwai Smith 2012; compare Chibber 2013). On return to Ecuador for fieldwork, these conversations continued informally, as I traveled around the country on buses, walking up hills and through banana groves, and were pursued over lunch and in snatched moments with leaders, workshop participants, and diverse development workers.[45] Questions about access and mutually agreed qualitative methods with Kichwa women in Chimborazo province and Tsáchila women in Santo Domingo province (see fig. I.2) were negotiated through sustained interactions with provincial federation and indigenous group leaders, particularly with the Chimborazo women's representative.[46]

Argument and Structure of the Book

Analyzing the genealogy of development's treatment of social heterogeneity from modernization, integrated rural development through to GAD, neoliberalism, and beyond reveals how technical simplifications of social diversity combine with colonial designations of social and psychic dispositions to shape development thinking and policy. Rendering an issue technical in development, according to Tania Murray Li, encompasses an array of processes, from representing a domain for intervention, to assembling information and devising techniques, to confirming the boundary between development expert and non-experts (Li 2007: 7–112). This book shows how policy's social categories carry with them malleable yet stubborn colonial associations, meanings, and expectations that shape how social difference is encountered, problematized, depoliticized, and instrumentalized. Although development thinking does not directly address social heterogeneity in all its intersectional dimensions, policy from the 1970s began to identify single axes of difference (location, gender, race-ethnicity). In the postcolonial context of Ecuador's lopsided society, these policy frameworks were implemented in ways that drew on global policy design, which was interpreted through postcolonial intersectional hierarchies. Most recently neoliberal development thinking has paid attention to social difference and risk, through policy interventions that have relied on prior readings of social diversity. Juxtaposing these insights and indigenous women's critiques of how development consistently lets them down suggests that development relies on models of social heterogeneity that misrepresent the interests and positionality of individuals and groups at the margins of postcolonial hierarchies. The book shows that subalterns (in this case, racialized rural low-income women) experience development in relation to its continually repackaged yet stubbornly colonial understandings of social difference and, in certain circumstances,

build alternative epistemologies as the basis for change. Beyond documenting the development situation for indigenous women, the book analyzes
the dynamics that shape diverse racialized female subalterns' positionality
in development in order to throw light on how interventions—global, national, modernizing, neoliberal, and postneoliberal—address postcolonial
social heterogeneity. While there are many other possible starting points
for such an analysis (see Hodgson 2001; Asher 2009; Ewig 2010), a critical
examination of the conditions, mechanisms, and social meanings bound
up in development efforts to address social heterogeneity merits careful
discussion.

Departing from indigenous women's everyday resistance and practices,
this book brings into focus the gendered consequences of development's
explicit models of and implicit expectations about social heterogeneity. In
order to examine the politics and consequences of humanitarian policy and
social heterogeneity, the book combines qualitative analysis of subaltern
experiences with a genealogy of policy formulation. The relational poststructural account of two groups of indigenous women avoids reifying a
category and development as a fixed form of governmentality, while it
reveals how material and discursive fields are coconstituted as meaningful.
In this way, the book presents the first systematic discussion of how indigenous women have been categorized and treated in development, indígenas'
diverse responses, and their reworking of development's knowledge about
social heterogeneity. Comparing two indigenous groups provides insights
into grounded forms of coloniality and development that construct and respond to existing social difference, rather than merely highlighting ethnic
cultural difference. Although the nature of social categories, their meanings, and their internal relations transform steadily over time, development
remains deeply embedded in understandings of social difference that draw
for their power on colonial understandings, the hegemonic frames emerging out of postcolonial nation-building and naturalized intersectionality,
in ways that put rural impoverished indigenous women at a consistent disadvantage. Yet from these margins, indigenous women resist, rework, and
selectively accommodate to development's governmental categories and social dispositions, creating an alternative vision of postcolonial social difference informed by priorities that meld but transcend global technologies of
conduct and anticolonial resistance.

The book is structured as follows. Chapters 1 and 2 establish Ecuador's
development trajectory in relation to postcolonial political economies and
social fault lines of power to identify (dis)continuities between colonial

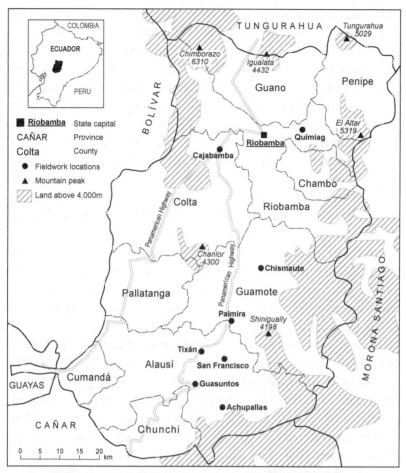

Map I.1. Chimborazo province showing districts (cantons) and key field sites. Map by the Cartographic Unit, Department of Geography, University of Cambridge.

rule and contemporary development and contextualize the forms of power through which rural low-income indigenous female subjects are constituted. This background also introduces the two case study indigenous groups at the heart of the book, namely Kichwa and Tsáchila women who occupy postcolonial intersectionality in both similar and different ways. Living in the central Andes (see map I.1), Kichwa women experienced colonial settlement and displacement through the hacienda system and have mobilized extensively and articulately in mixed-gender indigenous rights movements to contest marginalization and lack of development.[47] In the Kichwa language, used by Andean *runa* (people), woman is *warmi* and women are *warmikuna*, terms used through the book to signal the qualitatively distinct positionality of Andean rural indigenous women (and their difference from Tsáchilas). The Kichwa Puruhá pueblo in Chimborazo province has been the subject of frequent development interventions yet remains one of the poorest in the country. By contrast the Tsáchila, a group of around 2,500 people in the Pacific tropical lowlands, were impacted from the mid-twentieth century by settler colonization and rapid expansion of agro-export plantations. In the Tsafiki language, used by the Tsáchila, the term *sona* means woman, *sonala* women. Using these terms signals that the women at the heart of the book are not equivalent to "women" in mainstream development and profound differences exist across the two groups. The terms *indigenous women/indígenas* are used by contrast to indicate heterogeneous women from numerous nationalities and pueblos. Less politically visible than Kichwa Andeans, Tsáchila villages have experienced many fewer interventions than Chimborazo, and female-male relations in these villages are distinctive (see map I.2). Kichwa and Tsáchila women's criticisms of development offer insights, as partial and compromised as any other, into how distribution, fairness, and justice become bound up with postcolonial meanings of social difference that lie—however unacknowledged—behind the will to develop.

Chapters 3 and 4 examine in depth how a range of development interventions have addressed Ecuadorian social heterogeneity, and how specifications of social difference have shown persistent elements even as they have been amended with shifting policy priorities. From modernization through to social neoliberalism, the chapters document the experiences and responses these interventions have generated for Kichwa and Tsáchila women, who have drawn on interactions with projects to critically evaluate and rework the terms of engagement and resignify their differences. Chapters 5 and 6 bring to the fore the political context in which indigenous women contest, subvert, and rework development's framing of social heterogeneity, including their unique perspectives on ethnic movement demands for alternatives to western development. Indígenas' granular everyday acts demonstrate mobilization to articulate a creative reframing of citizenship, development, and social heterogeneity. Situated in contexts of profound inequalities, the chapters evidence the emergence of decolonial ways of thinking around development, dignity, and well-being, explored in chapter 7, which is about *buen vivir* (living well).

In addition to its thematic-chronological logic, the book can be read contrapuntally. Rural low-income Kichwa and Tsáchila women's daily experiences are documented in chapters 2 through 6. The dynamic between women and indigenous politics is foregrounded in chapters 5 and 6; the dynamics of

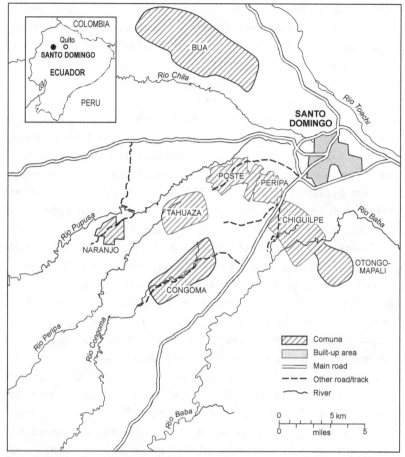

Map I.2. Sketch map showing Santo Domingo city and Tsáchila villages. Map by the Cartographic Unit, Department of Geography, University of Cambridge.

postcolonial development (chapter 1) and decolonization and development (chapter 7) book-end the discussion. Close attention is paid to policy in chapters 1, 3, and 4, which together provide a genealogy of successive development approaches to social heterogeneity.

Chapter 1 describes the ways indigenous populations, including women, have been incorporated into key transformations in postcolonial development. Colonial and then development governmentality brought about the routinization of control, boundary maintenance, and uneven political economic development, which dispossessed indigenous women and men in material, embodied, and discursive ways. Since the mid-twentieth century, Ecuadorian postcolonial narratives of modernity have been bound closely with expectations about development improvement (Ferguson 1999), promising the country's middle-income ranking and modernity. Yet, simultaneously, republican "civilizing" projects and modernization subjected indigenous populations to sociospatial force that "nearly irrevocably set broader levels of socioeconomic inequality" because "colonial institutions exerted their effects by allocating resources in systematically uneven ways" (Mahoney 2010: 263, 266). Deepening an account of the underbelly of national development (Mbembe 2003; Gregory 2004), the chapter also sketches a counternarrative, a subaltern history of ongoing exclusions that maintain the social distinctions against which "progress" is measured (Pigg 1992). The chapter ends with a critical analysis of current Ecuadorian development institutionality, organized around single lines of social difference, namely gender and ethnicity. Ethnodevelopment becomes associated with protection of "tradition," while GAD promotes western, "modern" goals of female-male relations. As the chapter demonstrates, these policy framings of social heterogeneity are not as separate as first appears, and exploring hidden connections reveals important points about postcolonial intersectionality and its interface with policy worlds. Chapter 2 employs a counter-topographical (Katz 2001a) analysis of Kichwa warmikuna's and Tsáchila sonala's situation in relational comparison with nonindigenous women and indigenous men, thereby mapping out the extent and nature of social differentiation behind the statistics that place these groups among the poorest and most disadvantaged.[48] The chapter also introduces indígena women's critical description of the shortcomings of development interventions, documenting sporadic, uneven, and short-term interactions with neoliberal, rural, gender, and ethnodevelopment projects and begins to contextualize indígenas' acquisition of critical knowledge about development and social heterogeneity.

Chapter 3 extends these themes by examining how participatory development has been applied in Chimborazo province among rural Kichwa runa. Comparing three participatory development projects, the chapter describes women's experiences and active responses to participatory development's construction of a "social consensus" as the means to achieve its goals. Kichwa warmikuna draw selectively and creatively on the spaces opened for social organization while refining critiques of the social communities that development instrumentalizes. Chapter 4 deepens understanding of the interplay between policy, subaltern positionality, and resistance by examining in depth a neoliberal policy for "indigenous women" and indígenas' critical responses to it. Organized around programs for female leadership, and disaggregated statistical information regarding social disadvantage, the "indigenous women" policy embodies a liberal gender program that recapitulates the colonial difference, against which indigenous women clarify their political agendas and knowledge formation. Discussing the politics of vulnerability and social heterogeneity, the chapter contrasts policy fixations on abject racialized women with the agency and creativity of networked indigenous women.

Chapter 5 analyzes in depth the positionality of indigenous women in a policy field that has permitted a hybrid of "mainstream" (postcolonial national) and "alternative" (ethnic) agendas, namely intercultural policy in sexual-reproductive health. Indigenous women support ethnic intercultural programs to strengthen collective rights yet combine that with vernacularized decolonial constructions of women's rights. Remaining with Kichwa and Tsáchila women's everyday lives and problems, chapter 6 explores the practices indigenous women use in various spaces and scales to bring into being a substantive form of citizenship that speaks to their position in postcolonial intersectionality. In communities, social movements, development projects, and local elected positions, indigenous women vernacularize the notions of rights and citizenship and at the same time infuse them with innovative content, thereby forging a globalized yet socially sensitive, modern culture of politics (Merry 2006; also Bhavnani et al. 2003). Indigenous women's rethinking of development has generated frameworks that have been important in bringing about the incorporation of the alternative conception known as buen vivir into the 2008 Constitution and subsequent public policy. Given its subaltern genealogy, indigenous women feel a strong sense of propriety and depth of knowledge about buen vivir that informs their responses to Ecuadorian development's latest turn. Chapter 7 examines the extent to which an unprecedented and partially indigenous development model, known as buen vivir, challenges postcolonial readings of difference and how buen vivir policy addresses social heterogeneity. The chapter also documents indigenous women's concerns, before moving on to analyze what decolonizing development might look like from indigenous women's perspectives.

Tracing development's genealogy of engaging with social difference moreover highlights the ways coloniality-modernity continues to inform the categories and content of development interventions. Yet Ecuadorian racialized-feminized rural subalterns—indigenous women—then theorize and produce alternatives to social exclusion, highlighting a contingent and delicate process of decolonizing development. Interrogating complacent metropolitan universality and the rifts that extend through postcolonial nationalism entails a careful critique of development's unexamined treatment of social heterogeneity and a reorientation of how knowledge of development is constructed. Paying close attention to the power relations that produce postcolonial intersectional hierarchies while analyzing the genealogy of development's shifting approaches to social difference offers the possibility of discerning motley alternatives that can provide dignity and well-being to people and socionatures.

ONE

Postcolonial Intersectionality and the Colonial Present

Ecuadorian policy arises in relation to postcolonial difference and inequality, inextricably entangled with the process of grappling with social heterogeneity while all the time aspiring to international models of how society works. In this context, global policy approaches are merged with deeply established national ways of discerning colonially inflected social difference, and international policy's global postcolonial context. Grappling with the existence of marked social inequalities, development's dilemma became finding frameworks through which persistent axes of inequality could be organized. Over recent decades, multilateral and bilateral agency thinking began to pay attention to social difference in order to ensure that benefits target populations more effectively, and in doing so made marginal groups visible. Policy and thinking around female-male difference, known as GAD, challenges development to confront its male biases and advocates close attention to gendered differences in resource control (Rathgeber 1990; Kabeer 1994). Similarly, approaches to ethnoracial difference aim to include impoverished indigenous and black populations (Stavenhagen 1986; Assies et al. 2001). As in other Latin American countries, Ecuador has organized this growing attention to social difference around separate institutions for gender in one case and for race-ethnicity in another institution. Norma, the elected women's representative for CONAIE, and the women she represents know through bitter experience that their multifaceted needs and aspirations cannot be separated out so simply. Tracing the genealogy of Ecuador's social development, this chapter argues that development thinking views female-male difference and ethnoracial difference through malleable yet persistent stereotypes that owe their content to dominant colonial understandings of how society works.

Indigenous women's disadvantage has often been described as resulting from overlapping forms of oppression. Peruvian anthropologist Marfil Franke identifies a "plait" of interwoven oppressions of indigenous women; Audrey Bronstein describes Andean women's "triple struggle" against the disadvantages of being female, peasant, and from the global South; even policy refers to the "triple discrimination suffered by indigenous and Afro-Ecuadorian women in politics and work because of their gender, race and social class."[1] Such frameworks treat race, class, and gender as if they were discrete and cumulative forms of power, whereby gender inequality is layered on top of preexisting racial hierarchies and onto prior class hierarchies (Quijano 2000; Lugones 2008). This chapter argues that although policy may nod to additive understandings of social heterogeneity, in practice social difference and developmental thinking are better understood as outcomes of coloniality's relational and qualitative constitutions of race, gender, and class.[2] Moreover, the chapter argues that social heterogeneity is coproduced within and through spatial heterogeneity, resulting in uneven landscapes of wealth and poverty, as "geographies are part of the process by which certain individuals and groups are reduced to bare life" (Pratt 2005: 1055).[3] Examining how and where associations between femininity, indigeneity, rurality, and poverty are forged and made material, the chapter covers how these intersectional associations were slowly institutionalized and tied to development from the colonial period to the neoliberal present. The chapter traces how powerful colonial discourses and material processes constitute indigenous women as relationally distinctive to indigenous men, and to nonindigenous women and men.

Colonial Histories: Power and Dispossession

Ecuador's colonization by the Spanish inaugurated a pattern of sociomaterial relations that continue to resonate today through what geographer Derek Gregory terms a series of "intrinsically spatial strategies" that connected "colonial projects, the production of space and various modalities of power-knowledge" (Gregory 1994: 168; Banivanua and Edmonds 2010; McIntyre and Nast 2011). Having recently been conquered by the Inka empire to the south, women and men from diverse ethnic nationalities shared the experience of Spanish colonial power and continue to feel its force, concentrated in marginal resource-poor areas with high levels of social deprivation. Indigenous populations in Ecuador experience development as subalterns, subjects of colonial-modern power in ways that systematically deny them authority, legitimacy, and equality. The region later known as Ecuador resource-poor, yet its ready supply of indigenous labor in the highland S underpinned Spanish settlers' wealth extraction, especially through te production, giving rise to mercantilist elites (Mahoney 2010). Diverse Andean indigenous populations were required to engage market-based economies by tribute obligations (generating one-third of state revenues) that endured into the republican era (De la Torre 2007: 153). The Spaniards established their first city, Riobamba, in what became Ecuador, in the central Andes in 1534, two hundred kilometers south of Quito, the present capital. Outside the textile economy, indigenous people were displaced from productive land and recruited as unpaid (or minimally remunerated) labor into large agricultural estates resulting from land grants awarded to Spanish colonizers and a small, locally born white elite.

Consequently, the "early association of the new racial identities of the colonized with the forms of control of unpaid, unwaged labor developed among the Europeans the singular perception that paid [professional] work was the whites' privilege" (Quijano 2000: 539). Treating indigenous groups as an undifferentiated mass of raw embodied energy, colonial structures created legacies of fracture with continuing force today (Mbembe 2003; McIntyre and Nast 2011). Indigeneity began to accrue meanings of racialized difference, associations with marginal rural districts, and with unskilled labor, a biopolitics that would come to inform calculations of indigenous "surplus" to national priorities. Indigenous women's labor and resources were as much affected by conquest and colonialism as men's, producing forms of bare life that combined racial and gendered differentiation.[4] Women worked in textile production for less than the minimal payments for menfolk, while independent inheritance claims to land were disallowed under Spanish law. Through the steady processes of dispossession and displacement of indigenous populations—largely in the Andes—women were deprived of animals and land and excluded from decision-making through the reservation of authority posts for men.

After formal independence in 1830, Ecuador's political economy perpetuated a racialized socio-spatial distribution through which consistent routines of exclusion, discrimination, and privileges made indigenous embodiments "surplus" to core activities and statuses, yet whose spaces of abandonment were tied into unequal power relations. By 1900, Ecuador's economic position lagged behind other South American countries, a situation that twentieth-century modernization would do nothing to shift. Its GDP per capita remained sluggishly around half the Spanish American average, masking massive income gulfs (Mahoney 2010: 219). Colonialism had also inaugurated a cultural politics of representation whereby diverse native ethnocultural populations were labeled primitive "Indians," the binary opposite of civilized European descent and cultural identity. Increasing numbers of mixed-race mestizo populations began to blur the lines between colonizer and colonized while keeping hierarchies firmly in place, as mestizos were frequently the offspring of indigenous mothers and white fathers. Indigenous subalterns were subjects whose claims on resources, attention, and rights were occluded, although in practice mestizo and indigenous were relational categories shaped by power-laden performance, location, and relational social interactions (Said 1993; Muratorio 1994). Coloniality denied racialized subalterns the status of fully recognized subjects in what Gayatri Spivak terms "the heterogeneous project to constitute the [colonized] subject as Other" (Spivak 1993 [1988]: 76). By means of racial discourses highlighting a lack of modernity, indigeneity was constituted as subjects whose rural locations, culture, and sheer difference from mestizo norms placed them beyond the limit of inclusion as full citizens (Agamben 1998; Chatterjee 2004). Such disavowal of connection informed biopolitical programs—development—that worked to further dehumanize racialized groups. In Ecuador this resulted in an exclusionary liberalism and politico-spatial containment, as well as the creation of intermediaries who ventriloquized for subalterns (Guerrero 1997; Prieto 2004). In this context, subaltern voice, authority, and autonomy were removed through the force of the colonial gaze, creating a "series of (stereotyped) parts" (Bhabha 1986: xi, drawing on Fanon 1986 [1952]) of indigeneity and the places where they resided.

Through the nineteenth century, the material basis for postcolonial hierarchies was further consolidated by elite land grabs of indigenous communal areas, resulting in highly skewed land distributions and associated sociocultural power. Into the twentieth century in Andean haciendas, as well as on burgeoning export-crop plantations on the coastal plains, and in incipient Amazonian extractive economies, indigenous and Afro-Ecuadorian groups provided the labor power for national economic expansion. In capitalist economies of trade and market-oriented food production, subaltern indigenous workers in Andean estates were subject to postcolonial forms of control and valuation. Large Andean landholding estates, haciendas, relied heavily on the rural, often Indian, communities who were tied into unequal feudal-type relations in which unpaid labor was on call for landowners in return for usufruct of tiny plots of land and rights to firewood and grazing, in a system known as huasipungo (tenants were known as huasipungueros). Indian tenants worked up to fourteen hours daily four or five days a week, leaving little time to cultivate subsistence crops on small, generally low-quality parcels of land to which they had no formal title. Rural indigenous women in huasipungo tenant families additionally had considerable social reproductive responsibilities. In one hacienda in Guamote canton, Chimborazo, tenant households contained an average of eleven people, a situation that engaged women in endless food preparation, washing, and collecting of firewood and water. Households reflected "a family structure growing in members over time and in charge of reproducing the huasipungo workforce" (Ferrín 1982: 162). Indigenous groups made up 39–60 percent of the national population, the vast majority in the Andes (Prieto 2004). Extra hacienda labor was recruited through the allegados/arrimados system, whereby villages around haciendas provided labor in return for limited access to firewood, pasture, and water. Estates reinforced racial difference by keeping laborers in distinctive clothing, preventing their education and maintaining crippling levels of indebtedness. Coloniality's spaces of exception produced uneven extensions of liberal rights over the national territory, and feudal peonage relations persisted well into the twentieth century, perpetuating women's daily grind of backbreaking work (chapter 3).

Cultural political economies became racialized territories where white-mestizo cities (and rural elite enclaves) were construed as modern in relation to rural internal colonies with nonmodern indigenous populations, exacerbating and racializing uneven development.[5] Development thereby reproduced and exacerbated a spatial governmentality in which concentrations of low-cost labor provided resources for other economic sectors and spaces. Although not formalized as such, these internal colonies[6] functioned primarily as reserves of cheap labor and products while forcing performances of abject indigeneity. Internal colonies made material the racial, class, and locational hierarchies of postcolonial society by binding together bare life and remote places (Pratt 2005: 1068). Internal colonies were not so much coordinated by the state as devolved to governance by landowners, estate managers, and local strongmen, and their variable pastoral and coercive power (Guerrero 1997; Prieto 2004),[7] reinforcing the point that "land and the organized spaces on it . . . narrate the stories of colonization" (Banivanua and Edmonds 2010: 52). In Ecuador, indigenous work sustained urban and rural elite families' living standards and status, whose claims to socioeconomic development prevailed unquestionably, embodying the epistemic and psychic violence of colonial hierarchies.[8] At the time Frantz Fanon and Alberti Memmi were critiquing colonial subjection in North Africa, indigenous Andeans faced normalized humiliations and structural disadvantage on a daily basis.[9] White-mestizo elites feared the Indian masses and responded to this dilemma of their own making with a mix of containment and boundary-marking, whereby discourses of indigenous primitivism legitimized hygienic measures and naturalized legal abandonment (Prieto 2004; see Spivak 1993 [1988]: 86). The category of "Indians" became associated with dirt, depreciation, and disease, establishing discursive, material, and embodied freight that resonated through later development.

Women and men in huasipungo households were equally but differentially subjected to racialized dynamics and postcolonial discipline. Female huasipunguero family members were obliged to contribute to cooking, cleaning, and generally maintaining the landowner's house under tribute relations called huasicama. These relations continued well into the mid-twentieth century. According to oral testimony from Guamote district, Chimborazo province, "They treated us poorly as huasicama and during the shepherding. And if something broke in the hacienda, they charged us— they didn't give us anything. . . . We were slaves" (quoted in Rosero Garcés and Reyes Ávila 1997: 17). The gendering of social reproduction constituted the harsh exigencies of subaltern embodiment and contributed to female-male distinctions in indigenous settlements, as indígenas' testimonies recall. Lucinda, a Kichwa woman, who never attended school and is now married with eight children, remembers: "My father worked for the hacienda, they called him in the mornings. With my mother, we went to work for ourselves in the lands they loaned us, until six at night."[10] As women were called periodically from the fields into the landowner's house, women's claims over agricultural land were repeatedly eroded. Female hacienda work has for this reason been described as "the starting point to understand the contemporary situation of women in communities and the undervaluation of their labor power, and representation in the family, the community and in development."[11] Despite geographical and ethnic diversity, the hacienda-based divisions of labor forged a degree of similarity for Andean rural racialized women, while also differentiating them from men-folk.[12] As a result, indigenous women "are the last link in a chain of exploitation . . . [and given the] hardest and least dignified tasks. They were considered absolutely as objects in a series of useful items in the hacienda system" (Palacios 2005: 19). Nevertheless, women's lack of economic-political leverage over land became a socio-symbolic tool in protests against hacienda power. As men were the household's official representatives in estates and women had no land rights, rural protests often granted women a prominent role in public opposition to haciendas, as they could not be penalized by the removal of land rights. Their very marginality in land-territory made them harder to discipline yet symbolically key to emergent ethnic movements (Crespi 1976; Centro Maria Quilla 1992).[13] According to an indigenous Salasaca woman speaking to an ethnographer, "All our lives we have been runas [Kichwa, people], with no more rights than a dog" (quoted in Poeschel-Renz 2003).

Through the first half of the twentieth century, a stronger central state supplanted devolved pastoral power and embarked on a governmental role in relation to indigenous populations. From the late 1950s, precarious and feudal labor practices became the subject of liberal debate among intellectual and government elites, leading to social welfare institutions, especially, after 1925, through the Ministry of Social Provision and Labor (Guerrero 1997; Prieto 2004; Ramón and Torres 2004). Informed by productivist logics, national legislation consolidated agricultural units from scattered household plots (in "independent" communities) and established more direct forms of political control. The creation of comunas (communities) under 1937 legislation was designed to contain the "dangerously" mobile indigenous class while establishing oversight by government-appointed officials. In return for registration, villages gained limited collective rights to land and autonomy, exemplifying counter-movements' management of indigenous dispossession (Li 2010).[14] By law women and men were equally able to claim comunero membership status in these new landholding and political units. Overall, however, indigenous populations were "prevented from partaking in whatever benefits and possibilities economic growth might have created" (Mahoney 2010: 263). Homi Bhabha (1994: 43) notes how the epistemic violence required to perpetuate a postcolonial system can never be acknowledged as the "determinate conditions of civil authority." In Ecuador, although subaltern exclusion pervaded the very matter of development at scales from the individual body through to the nation-state, the privilege of some at the cost of many could never be admitted.

Modernization, Mestizos, and Development: Ecuador in the Mid-Twentieth Century

From midcentury, the forms of governmentality regarding social difference increasingly came under the sign of development, as which, according to the logics of modernity, could not not be desired (Gupta 1998; Wainwright 2008). The will to improve meshed with a growing awareness of populations who would never reach the status of full citizen but whose needs could be addressed (Gupta 1998; Ferguson 1999; Chatterjee 2004; Li 2007). As indigenous woman leader Carmen Tene noted when writing of these issues, "although indigenous women and men no longer live as slaves on the haciendas, we have converted ourselves into very poor salaried workers. Even now, we don't get paid fairly just because we are indigenous. Then as women, as an additional problem, we receive unequal treatment. . . . They pay us a daily wage lower than what any man earns, a payment that isn't even always in money—it can be payment in products, or given to our husband [instead of directly to us]" (2000: 204–5). As noted in Carmen's statement, development transformations came to change women's lives in ways that continued to compound intersectional disadvantage. In interventions to promote agricultural productivity and market efficiency, racially unmarked actors such as government officials, landowners, and foreign capitalists drove forward economic development that was defined in ways that ignored indigenous aspirations and imposed a postcolonial project of development. In Ecuador, the will to improve was cast as a task of providing indigenous subalterns with the means—education, social work, local organization—through which to become modern, developed, mestizo subjects shorn of cultural difference.[15] Mestizo developmentalism kept intact colonial material and discursive hierarchies of difference (largely because spaces of exception and forms of dispossession could not be acknowledged), just as it reworked understandings of the malleability of social difference, offering mestizo modernity as a route out of disadvantage.[16]

Key drivers of modernist developmentalism were to be industry and processing, although large companies were owned by a small, closely knit group of dominant white-mestizo families. Governments propounded the mantra that increased production would occur in the newly emergent "racial democracy" if only a few "racial barriers" were removed, to be replaced with "intercultural relations [thereby] creating new possibilities of access for marginal social groups" (Junta Nacional de Planificación 1970: 8; see also Ecuador Bienestar Social 1984). Although the nation-state's plans about development were expansive, the presence of the developmentalist state was weak, especially in rural areas, despite state centralization from the 1950s. Successive governments dismissed the detailed development plans prepared by planning boards, leaving swathes of territory under the devolved authority of regional power-holders such as hacienda owners and managers. Indigenous areas continued to receive a disproportionately low level of state investment, resulting in an "aggravated lack of essential services (schools, hospitals, water, and electricity)," thereby perpetuating the postcolonial associations between place, race, and poverty (Gonzalez Casanova 1965: 35).[17] Andean and tropical lowland areas inhabited by diverse indigenous groups were overwhelmingly characterized by exclusion from programs for credit, commercial outlets, health care, schools, and technical training in agriculture. In the early 1960s, national illiteracy rates stood at 31.9 percent while Indian-majority areas like Chimborazo and Morona Santiago reached 53 percent and 41.4 percent, respectively (Junta Nacional de Desarrollo 1964).

Despite liberal efforts to improve the conditions of rural impoverished racialized populations, the third quarter of the twentieth century witnessed the continued valance of colonial legacies, which were particularly marked in relation to land distribution. Andean indigenous and mestizo communities were and are concentrated in poor-quality, marginal, and small-sized plots, reliant on precarious peasant livelihoods in diverse socionatures. In the 1970s, nine-tenths of all Ecuadorian agricultural units were so small that "they could not provide full-time employment for and satisfy the basic needs" of the family (Lindqvist 1979). Families often relied on a combination of subsistence, small-scale commercialization of products, and outmigration. Development programs encouraged entrepreneurialism and civil infrastructures while avoiding a commitment to universal welfare. President Galo Plaza (1948–1952) and the "Andean Mission" (Misión Andina) committed to modernization through expanding ethnic craft production with the dual objective of boosting national exports and relieving rural—largely indigenous—poverty.[18] The Andean Mission reprieved the geographies of internal colonialism by intervening in highland areas above the altitude of fifteen hundred meters (see fig. 1.1). Beginning with weavers' cooperatives in the Otavalo region, the Mission recommended centralized community councils, agricultural cooperatives, and sports clubs. In 1956 the mission expanded into Chimborazo province in the central Andes (another indigenous-majority area) with education, health, civil engineering, training, and housing projects. It supported specialist craftspeople, to "accelerate the transformation of the productive structure, organize and help peasants, and promote commercialization and public services, as well as favor intercultural relations and create new possibilities of access for marginal social groups," without creating any sustained change in indigenous political economies (Junta Nacional de Planificación 1970: 8).

At the same time, female-male difference was resignified in ways that were to extend mestizo norms of femininity and mestizo-type domestic spaces into rural communities. The Andean Mission encouraged rural racialized women to embark on domestic transformations that would bring Indian communities closer to urban norms. Normalizing (post)colonial discipline to distinguish clean modern citizens from Others (McClintock

Fig. 1.1. Andean women speak to Andean Mission panel, date unknown. Espín 1966.

1995), the Andean Mission trained "mejoradoras del hogar"—literally "female household improvers"—to install modern hygienic and nutritional standards and to become midwives and nurses.[19] Distinctions between developed and undeveloped groups were made on criteria of respectability and cleanliness. From 1955, the Ministry of Agriculture's Department of Household Improvement continued to train rural women in household maintenance, domestic tasks, and feminine manual craftwork. Such programs refined and massified developmental understandings of modernity, via project attempts to discipline—and hence bring into performative existence—a mestiza subject, a nationally endorsed form of whitening, modernizing femininity. In this context, the figure of "indigenous women" came to symbolize the country's development challenge.[20] Pitting the achievements of urban mestizos against the failings of female subalterns delineated the extent and challenges of modernization, legitimizing action to unite society (Yuval-Davis and Anthias 1989; Goetschel et al. 2007; Wade 2009).[21] This was the first of many efforts to treat indigenous women as "mestizas in the making," protomoderns on coloniality's terms, as later chapters document. Such measures could only operate across the field of social heterogeneity through disavowing postcolonial power differentials through the twentieth and into the twenty-first century. Programs also made meaningful in discursive and material terms a female-male difference within rural racialized communities, as subalterns were allocated gendered positions that reflected mestizo urban expectations and gendered subjectivities more than rural realities.

As noted, Ecuador has had one of Latin America's most concentrated patterns of landownership, entrenching associations between poverty, rurality, and racialization. Smallholder farms accounted in 1960 for half the agricultural labor force, around four-fifths of whom were unpaid family members consisting of the wives, sisters, mothers, and daughters of the developmental category of "smallholder farmer." In Chimborazo from the early 1960s, profound restructuring of local labor markets occurred as former workers were "freed" from obligations to haciendas that had captured over two-fifths of huasipungo labor and around one-third of "independent" community labor (Gangotena et al. 1980: 18).[22] Households often sent out labor in order to subsidize agriculture, yet to do so was to enter regional employment markets suddenly filled by others desperate to earn money. Immediately after the breakup of haciendas in Guamote district, Chimborazo, daily wages fell to one-seventh the rate in Quito or Guayaquil (Gangotena et al. 1980: 62, 63–64). In Quimiag parish, Chimborazo, large farms continued, despite the land reform, tying indigenous laborers to local labor markets. Increasingly the outmigration of younger family members became a survival strategy, reducing the burden of subsistence food production and generating income. Yet many households retained only an insecure foothold in cities, forcing short-term employment in lower-end jobs (laboring, construction, domestic service) with seasonal maintenance of semisubsistence plots. In Chimborazo province, 85 percent of households lost at least one member to migration during these decades (Rosero Garcés and Reyes Ávila 1997: 12). Racialized labor commanded the lowest wages in both rural and urban economies, so households made careful calculations about how to balance rural labor requirements and potential wages without threatening land tenure. Men earned more than women; consequently many Andean areas saw women assume increasing responsibilities and long hours of work in hand-to-mouth agriculture.

In the early 1960s, uncontainable challenges punctured elite complacencies around land, development, and progress.[23] In December 1961, twelve thousand Andean huasipungo workers and comuneros marched on Quito protesting hacienda labor conditions. In the immediate aftermath of the Cuban revolution, such protests were geopolitically significant and pushed the government to remove feudal agrarian relations.[24] Indigenous women mobilized as rural workers and hacienda tenants, expressing interests regarding interlocking postcolonial exclusion that were time- and place-specific. "In Ecuador the agrarian reform left one third of the agricultural land in the hands of large landowners and one third in the hands of medium-sized private entrepreneurs. Indigenous subsistence farmers split the remaining third with mestizo market-oriented smallholders, an outcome that delayed peasant rebellion only temporarily" (Stocks 2005: 89). The 1964 Agrarian Reform granted property rights to huasipunguero tenants who could demonstrate ten years residence and work on a plot of land, and abolished feudal working relations. Between 1964 and 1972, around 17,500 households acquired land in this way, a total of sixty thousand hectares, and by 1970, nine-tenths of farms were smallholdings (minifundios) that covered less than 20 percent of the land (Lindqvist 1979: 102). However, the amount of land distributed did not address land hunger and was often of poor quality, and precarious and exploitative work persisted (Junta Nacional de Planificación 1970: A3: 17).[25] The model of the "family farm" (finca familiar) underpinned reform objectives, yet plots could often not support families, generating temporary and permanent moves to cities and tropical lowlands. Modernizing land reforms furthermore restructured indígenas' position, reworking access to socio-environmental resources and legitimacy in enduring ways. As Carmen Tene's statement makes clear, the gendered divisions of hacienda labor constructed hierarchies of value that mutated into rural women's long-term disadvantage under agrarian reform. Although women had been laborers, their work in fields and in domestic spaces was invisible to indigenous men and state officials. Western-inflected values about public versus "private" labor became the lens through which indigenous women's claims were settled.

From the 1960s, Ecuadorian development took a number of important turns, resulting from the combined impacts of state encouragement of colonization in lowland tropical areas, the discovery of petroleum deposits, and the growth of export agriculture on the coast. Class structures and income-power differentials remained in place, although on a transformed basis. Oil wealth did not change Ecuador's regional ranking in terms of GDP per capita, yet it did permit expenditure on social development to a level unexpected for the country's economic size.[26] State expenditure trebled between 1971 and 1975 on the back of oil price rises and funded the extension of school-building and core social investments (health centers, teachers' salaries, road-building) in more rural areas than previously. However, postcolonial stratification reproduced highly uneven socionatural landscapes. The majority of indigenous groups failed to benefit proportionately from state spending derived from oil revenues, while Amazon indigenous groups increasingly paid the environmental, livelihood, and human costs of the new resources. Even where governments invested in rural schools and clinics, coloniality continued to be expressed through quotidian and normalized racism. Oil-fueled development deepened class and regional income disparities, shifting attention to transport infrastructure and away from sectors of agriculture, social services, and housing and hence indirectly benefiting a rising urban middle class and recent migrants who had become mestizos. Combined with the racial segregation of urban labor markets and the normalization of postcolonial racial hierarchies, migrants came under intense pressure to cease making claims as indigenous subjects, as urban opportunities were associated with mestizo cultural politics and performance. As Gonzalez Casanova has noted, postcolonial relations perpetuate the spatial outcomes of colonial difference, reinforcing income and development "gaps" between core areas inhabited by dominant groups and the peripheries inhabited by racialized subalterns (Gregory 2004; on Ecuador, Bromley 1977: 83, 85). In 1950, although only one-quarter of citizens were urban, the next three decades saw urban investment outstrip rural spending three to one, establishing rural-urban disparities in well-being and security. In this way, the glib narrative of mestizo development naturalized sociocultural transformations while it veiled postcolonial hierarchies and the dire conditions of racialized subalterns especially in rural areas.[27]

In rural areas with indigenous majorities, rural development programs strived to raise living standards while contributing to national economic growth. Initiatives continued halfheartedly to promote craft production, small-scale production, and job creation in the Sierra, although health care services were reduced.[28] In rural development programs, indigenous poverty was cast as a question of economics. According to the Ministry of Social Welfare, "the Indian is the rural inhabitant who carries out generally unskilled jobs, in the most part physical labor, and as such is low paid. In the agrarian system, this means a series of roles characterized by access to insufficient land resources (smallholders and community members), or servile forms of agricultural labor (huasipunguero and related forms, 'free' peons, etc.)" (Ecuador Bienestar Social 1984: 167). When ethnic difference was acknowledged, for example in the SEDRI program in the 1980s (which attempted to reorganize relations between land, indigenous labor, and productivity), it kept coloniality's assumptions and exclusions firmly in place, disavowing subaltern knowledges and leaving intersectional hierarchies unchallenged (Yashar 2005; De la Torre 2007). Development treated the female, racialized, and rural person as the most anachronistic in the modern nation, the sign of the development/no development boundary (Muratorio 1994; McClintock 1995).

Despite modernization, internal colonialism continued to have great resonance during the mid- to late twentieth century, although the location of internal colonies shifted from the Andes to the tropical lowlands east and west of the Andes. Under government auspices, smallholders and larger agrarian corporations colonized the tropical lowlands on either side of the Andean Sierra. In colonial-modern discourses, Amazonian Indians (around 10.7 percent of indigenous populations) and coastal populations (around 9.3 percent of indigenous populations) were perceived as particularly unmodern, which in turn justified development interventions. State encouragement of tropical lowland colonization was rationalized as the expansion of agricultural frontiers, based on myths of unoccupied fertile areas and dreams of medium-scale intensive agrarian entrepreneurship. Low-income or landless mestizo families were encouraged to settle on "empty lands"—"tierras baldías"—denying indigenous presence (eight groups in the Amazon alone). Agrarian frontier programs thereby reinscribed colonizing territorial expansionism and racialized understandings of modernity, erasing native habitation and furthering the unconditional sacking of indigenous resources. Ecuador's Amazon basin became an oil-era internal colony during this period, generating 45–53 percent of state budgets and receiving 2.34 percent of state expenditure in return (Espinosa 1997; Sawyer 2004; Valdivia 2009).[29] An extractive economy established a male-biased labor market of state employment and state-sponsored colonization. In parallel, the expansion of banana production on Ecuador's coastal plains through the 1950s to the 1970s drew in indigenous and peasant migrant laborers, displacing Tsáchila, Chachi, and other coastal indigenous populations from their historic territories. Tsáchila became confined in ever-smaller areas, while livelihoods switched from hunting-gathering and subsistence to cash crop production (see chapter 2). Indigenous populations became entangled in oil- and settlement-driven socionatural and spatial transformations, which filled government coffers but failed to reverse three decades of colonization and oil extraction. Mestizo developmentalism hence entailed what we can term "dispossession squared," that is, displacement from land-territory × ever-more exiguous social and economic resources = hollowed-out means of social reproduction and reduced capability to mount robust defenses of Other lifeways (also Katz 2001b; Glassman 2006).

Despite its rhetoric of inclusion, in practice mestizo developmentalism recast internal colonies less as sites for cheap products than as spaces of social abandonment, where residents increasingly lived in shadow economies of semisubsistence, outmigration circuits, and low-paid local rural labor for commercial agrarian enterprises. Efforts to modernize agriculture entailed the entrenchment of land distribution inequalities while creating few dignified jobs. Female difference in this backdrop of social heterogeneity was perpetuated through legislation around land title, development interventions in capacity-building and credit extension, and gender-segregated labor markets. Mestizo norms of a male household head and a female homemaker infused development projects, embedding modernization in unexamined colonial visions of social heterogeneity. Subjects who were female, rural, poor, and racialized continued to be associated with a problematic nondevelopment, a reified subject firmly located in the public eye as the face of traditional peasant communities.[30] Mestizo cultural politics compounded these female-male differentials as migrants discarded markers of indigenous identity in response to urban racism, and rural residents became associated with "purer" ethnic difference.[31] In reality rural subalterns were located at the front line of uneven processes of commercialization and urbanization, as later chapters document, yet these cultural politics entailed enduring consequences in policy's approach to social heterogeneity in rural indigenous areas. The Ecuadorian nation-state repositioned indigeneity in a cultural slot, with the Office of Indian Affairs and the Ministry of Social Welfare issuing urgent calls to "strengthen culture" with "respect for, and encouragement of, the cultural expressions of distinct communities,"[32] a politics that echoed President Galo Plaza's work with Tsáchila in previous decades (see fig. 1.2). Strengthening "culture" also meant protecting racialized beneficiaries from the worst excesses of the market, as they had inadequate work, poor socionatural conditions for livelihood (limited irrigation, soil degradation, deforestation), poor mobility, and low social security coverage (Li 2010; see also Ecuador Bienestar Social 1984: 167; Consejo Nacional de Desarrollo 1991: 24; compare Carlos de la Torre 2007). It all added up to what the National Development Council in 1996 called "insufficient development of indigenous and black populations." Such formulations of indigenous "lack" continued in step with racialization practices that marked ethnocultural difference through daily reinscription on bodies and spaces, maintaining Spanish as the hegemonic language, and everyday racism. In the Andes and Amazon, racialized groups report verbal abuse, discourtesy,

Fig. 1.2. President Galo Plaza and Tsáchila women, 1950. C. de la Torre and M. Salgado (eds.), *Galo Plaza y su época* (Quito: FLACSO-Fundación Galo Plaza Lasso, 2008).

lack of attendance from state officials, and requests for bribes, a situation that worsens during economic crisis (Cervone and Rivera 1999; De la Torre 1999; Encalada 2012).

At the end of mestizo developmentalism, Ecuador's reputation was in tatters. While superficially characterized by oil-led growth and national inclusion, development planning in reality was a "masquerade to impress Ecuadorian and foreign interests," according to a British development expert at the time.[33] The mid- to late twentieth century was haunted by ongoing exclusion and maldevelopment for indigenous—and Afro-Ecuadorian—groups. Although some indicators showed progress, the overall trajectory of development stalled, not least during the "lost decade" of the 1980s. Although development practice was increasingly devolved to NGOs in order to tighten connections with civil society, it remained highly uneven in scope and impact (Bebbington 2004). Mestizo developmentalism, from the perspective of racialized subalterns, represented "a re-articulation of the coloniality of power over new institutional bases," according to postcolonial critic Anibál Quijano (Quijano 2000: 567). Indigenous organizations' growing mobilization brought about vociferous critiques of postcolonial development as regional federations and the national confederation CONAIE defended landscapes and livelihoods.[34] Demanding rights and justice, ethnic agendas were located "at the crossfire of power and history, political economy and grounded struggle pervading cultural practices situated in any landscape of resistance" (Moore 1997: 103). Women actively participated in ethnic protests. Yet successive governments treated ethnic demands for recognition and redistribution as excessive and unrealistic; only in 2008 would indigenous rights to prior informed consent and decision-making over development be recognized constitutionally. In the meantime, mestizo developmentalism treated indigenous populations as "too immature" to exercise citizenship rights.[35] Although mestizaje (literally mixing; mestizaje refers to mixed European and indigenous populations, and highlights the desirability of European social characteristics) pedaled a myth of the irrelevance of race-ethnicity while privileging whiteness, intersecting hierarchies of male-female and rural-urban difference acquired new meanings that would resonate through later development thinking and practice.

Single Issue Development: Gender, Ethnicity, and Postcolonial Intersectionality

By the end of the twentieth century, development thinking began to grapple with social heterogeneity in ways that differed from previous decades. Just as development was increasingly becoming a globalized model for social intervention, a characteristic that reflected and grew out of the neoliberal "Washington Consensus," development increasingly grappled with the issue of how to target populations who were particularly impacted by market-led political economies. In other words, new responsibilities for populations came to define how and in what ways beneficiaries would be identified and engaged. Social neoliberal policy dealt with social difference not as politically contested categories and outcomes of power but as metrics of technocratic and efficient decision-making in what I term "single issue development." Accordingly, axes of social difference—gender, race-ethnicity, age—became technical categories through which subpopulations could be targeted in neoliberal measures of poverty alleviation (Schild 1998; Andolina et al. 2009; Boesten 2010; Ewig 2010).

It was in this context that measures to develop indigenous populations—ethnodevelopment—emerged and gender programs were extended. Gender and ethnic-racial difference were imagined, institutionalized, and operationalized in programs in Ecuador from the 1990s. A critical postcolonial analysis of gender and ethnodevelopment reveals the beguiling simplifications and the epistemological and organizational reasons behind persistent colonial thinking. The enduring power of colonial understandings of social difference suggests that not only do dominant power relations operate in agencies to exclude nondominant groups' interests, but that policy relies on implicit social models about social heterogeneity that, as in Ecuador, are infused with colonial-postcolonial expectations about the developmental qualities of diverse subjects. These postcolonial templates for action have profound influences on how policy addresses heterogeneity in ways that work against decolonization. Ecuadorian development has long been institutionalized around the separation of gender programs from ethnic development.[36] From the 1990s, gender policy's institutional separation from policy on racial-ethnic groups was encapsulated in the difference between the National Women's Council (CONAMU), which promoted gender mainstreaming, and the indigenous development council (CODENPE), which devised and implemented "development with identity."[37] Each institution operated largely independently of the other, despite low-level efforts to coordinate activities and create dialogue. In addition to distinct institutions and personnel, many policy-makers, agency staff, and state employees viewed GAD and multiculturalism as incompatible and at odds. The institutional arrangements and their influence on specific programs, among Kichwa, Tsáchila and other indigenous women is summarized in Table 1.1.

SINGLE ISSUE DEVELOPMENT 1: GAD AND THE HIDDEN HISTORIES OF POSTCOLONIAL INTERSECTIONALITY

Development's modernization agenda incorporated a concern for male-female difference and women's disadvantage from the mid-1970s (Consejo Nacional de Desarrollo 1991: 102), although women-oriented programs had been part of Ecuadorian development thinking from the 1950s. Standard commitments to empowerment and equality principles were consolidated in key institutions where gender policy was formulated, supported, and resourced (Lind 2005). As with rural development policy, gender policy addressed one dimension of social heterogeneity, setting in train processes that reestablished or reconfigured postcolonial intersectional hierarchies while attempting to empower women (compare Richards 2004 on Chile). Gender policy's entanglement with coloniality had numerous ramifications for Kichwa and Tsáchila women, as subsequent chapters discuss. Moreover, toward the end of the twentieth century, gender was increasingly enrolled into governmentality around ethnodevelopment, reflecting gender policy's postcolonial genealogy and the position of indigenous subalterns in development debates.

Due to strong feminist and women's movements, Ecuador became internationally recognized for its gender rights administration, adapting and legitimating gender development policies.[38] The National Women's Council gained oversight of gender policy, constituting an arena for feminists willing to work with/inside the state.[39] Founded in 1997, CONAMU worked to extend women's empowerment across an array of government policies, an agenda known as gender mainstreaming. Ecuador's relatively strong institutional base for GAD owes much to women's social movements globally, regionally, and nationally, in turn molding its engagement with social heterogeneity.[40] One strand of the country's women's movement, the influential CPME Ecuadorian Women's Political Network, strongly supported engagement with the state and mainstreaming policies.[41] Hence CONAMU was linked to a strand of urban middle-class feminism that "normalize[d] a certain set of ideas about women's roles in development, while rendering others invisible or less important" (Lind 2005: 120), which had profound implications for CONAMU's interaction with indigenous women's development agendas. Whereas gender experts often employed indigenous women as domestic help at home, an awareness of their lives was not generally brought into mainstreaming institutions, reflecting intersecting postcolonial hierarchies of race, class, and gender (Barrig 2004, 2006).[42] The global tendency for GAD institutions to be associated with racially unmarked, often affluent femocrats was replicated in Ecuador. Although the council established several initiatives on gender and ethnicity, it lacked "a coherent national leadership geared to achieve these goals" (Oliart 2008: 9–10), reflecting the normalization of particular gender agendas despite heterogeneous civil society.[43] Where programs included a component for (ethnic) women, these were often "add-ons" to mainstream projects. For example, a 1970s credit program aimed to recognize "women's indispensable role in subsistence" yet offered them only a marginal subproject (Ecuador Bienestar Social 1984). Mestiza femininity remained the implicit norm, as in the National Development Plan for 1980–1984. Founded on unexamined assumptions about households,

TABLE 1.1 Single issue development and indigenous women in Ecuador, c. 1970–2010

Project name/description	"General" beneficiary	Indigenous men or indigenous as group	Women	Kichwa and Tsáchila women	Chapters of book that discuss exemplary projects
			BENEFICIARY GROUP		
Agricultural modernization					
IRD general, 1970s and 1980s	√	(√)	√	(√)	1, 2
State colonization	√				1, 2
Rural income generation	√				3
UNDP and UNIFEM: Rural Development Secretariat, 1974–1983			Projects for peasant women, small animal care, etc.	(√)	2
Neoliberal					
PRONADER land titling (1991–)	√		(√)		3
Rural women's participation					
EU Chimborazo (1994–1998)			√ Rural women in Chimborazo	(√) Kichwa women only	3
Spanish Cooperation			√	√	
IBIS leadership program		(√)		√ Tsáchila women only	4

Ethnodevelopment			
PRODEPINE (1998–2002)	√	√ Kichwa (and Tsáchila)	3
FODEPI credit program		√ Kichwa and Tsáchila	1
Other social programs			
Education and EBI		√	
	√	√	
Free maternity care (2006–)		√	3
		(√)	
Conditional cash transfer ("bono")		√	7
		(√)	

Key: √ Target beneficiary group

(√) Beneficiary category by default included this group

projects retrenched indigenous women's disadvantage even under programs that tried to raise living standards. As rural dwellers, indígenas were offered assistance through small-scale animal sale projects, such as FODERUMA in the mid-1990s, which assumed that indígenas had the same relationship with urban markets, consumers, and workloads as mestiza women.

In this postcolonial context (mestiza) women's empowerment became a normative part of national development such that "among certain public functionaries, a gender perspective is converted into a neutral element of modernization and development, into a civilizing discourse,"[44] smuggling dominant norms into the colonial present. In this sense, "ladies' spaces were not enough to transform gender relations and other structural inequalities that resulted from Ecuador's colonial legacy" (Lind 2005: 44, 51). The acceptability of gender policy arose from the legitimacy of mestizo urban values expressed via this modernizing and civilizing agenda (Fellows and Razack 1998; Martínez Flores 2000; Herrera 2003: 23). Discussing indigenous women's exclusion from gender policy, an indígena regional leader voiced the opinion that "the National Women's Council in my province of Tungurahua was only for mestiza women. They never gave us even a part; they only ever used us."[45] Under the colonial association of indigenous populations with a lack of civilization, gender thinking in development became firmly embedded in the mestizo racial project, articulated around "modern, technical" solutions. By the early twenty-first century, the National Women's Council was becoming subject to critiques for its "deficiencies in its treatment of ethnic themes" (Larrea 2002: 11), while racialized subaltern women were increasingly speaking out against what they perceived as a middle-class, white, and urban enclave. Just when indigenous women were becoming more vocal in putting forward development agendas, neoliberal strictures and governmentality forced greater dissociation between gender professionals and grassroots populations, exacerbating class and racial cleavages, as later chapters discuss (Schild 1998; Lind 2005; Molyneux 2008; see also chapters 3 and 4). Consequently, gender policy was subject to significant reworking of its objectives and meanings during neoliberal restructuring in the 1990s in Ecuador, as elsewhere in the global South, where budget cutbacks and free-market ideologies undercut feminist demands for welfare, rights, and justice (see Molyneux and Razavi 2003; Rai 2003; Assies et al. 2005). Neoliberal gender policy was entrained into a vision defined in relation to global whiteness and formal political economic gains, further delinking gender development thinking from the informality, insecurity, and racialized experiences of indígenas and other subalterns.

Moreover, in Andean postcolonial societies local development workers were reluctant to intervene in "ethnic" cultures and so left indigenous gender relations unexamined and unknown, a point discussed later (Junta Nacional de Planificación 1970). Andean nation-building narratives stress the closed and traditional nature of Andean communities of indigenous peoples, with the consequences that indígenas are associated primarily with ethnic communities and seen as subordinate to ethnic cultures and power relations. Ecuador's development thinking owes much to coloniality's framing of Andean male-female relations in terms of what is termed "complementarity" (*complementariedad*), a colonial interpretation of indigenous relations as culturally driven, nonmodern, and incompatible with modern feminism.[46] Global development thinking then reproduces these views, with multilateral staffers in Latin America arguing that policies for indigenous populations are incompatible with gender. According to a male ethnodevelopment expert, "it's not easy to incorporate gender into indigenous organizations as it's outside their area of concern; it's more important in the western world."[47] Consequently development workers hold preconceptions about Andean indigenous male-female relations that shape expectations and behaviors while reinforcing hierarchies of difference. As later chapters show, this policy configuration produced interventions experienced by subaltern female subjects through the prisms of male-biased policies for racialized populations (Cornwall et al. 2007; Heron 2007).

> The ideology of gender solidarity [means that] differences between
> rich and poor women disappear, between citizens and peasant women,
> between white-mestiza women and indigenous women, all for women's
> unity. (Vicenta Chuma, indigenous female leader, presentation at 2004
> Indigenous Summit, Quito)

With gender policy's primarily economic focus on female work, the qualitatively distinctive aspects of indígenas' labor experience were moreover excluded from consideration (Ong 1988). The 1993–1996 National Development Plan included a brief mention of indigenous women, who were to be offered "productive employment," although the market-led Plan failed to identify in which labor markets women were to earn a living wage (Consejo Nacional de Desarrollo 1996: 27). In practice, small numbers of indigenous women were recruited into booming export flower farms concentrated in the north-central Andes.[48] A handful found work in urban and rural tourism, often performing and embodying the "united colors of capitalism" for rich customers (Mitchell 1993; Crain 1996). As chapter 2 shows, indigenous women outside these sectors struggled to find off-farm work opportunities. Many more indígenas became subject to policy initiatives to convert low-income women into entrepreneurs through provision of microcredit (see discussion later). Problematic and insufficient as they were, neoliberal microcredit programs "linked women to development processes and modernization and the possibility of getting away from images of backwardness and poverty" (Cervone 1998: 231, 235). Unfortunately, however, indigenous women moved from being "invisible to excessively visible" (Maldonado-Torres 2007: 257) without a sustained change in their relative positioning in postcolonial hierarchies (see chapter 4).

SINGLE ISSUE DEVELOPMENT 2: ETHNODEVELOPMENT AND POSTCOLONIAL INTERSECTIONALITY

In the early 1990s only 1 percent of state social and economic projects were for indigenous populations in Ecuador, although they composed approximately one in four of the country's citizens, a figure that brings into sharp relief the systematic sidelining of racialized populations during mestizo developmentalism. Yet from the early 1990s a form of development thinking arose that was to have significant impacts on how development grappled with race-ethnicity (Stavenhagen 1986). As existing scholarship shows, ethnodevelopment was a policy hybrid, emerging in part from indigenous activism to counter systematic exclusion from development decision-making and lack of enforceable rights to territory, water, and resources and in part from neoliberal measures to boost indigenous and Afro-descent populations' human capital and tackle poverty (Andolina et al. 2009).[49] "Although the most egregious systems of labor exploitation have mostly ended, the available evidence consistently demonstrates that [blacks and Indians] continue to be more likely to live in poverty, be illiterate, die at a younger age, reside in substandard housing and bear the greatest burden of police abuse" (Telles 2007: 189). Reflecting sustained social movement mobilization, widespread civic unrest, and indigenous and black engagement in new forms of state- and nation-building, various forms of multiculturalism were introduced across the region after the 1980s. Indigenous demands to extend political, economic, cultural, and social rights galvanized transnational networks of donors and cultural interpretations of indigenous development potential, resulting in ethnodevelopment planning, also known as "development with identity" policy.[50] In the resulting uneasy compromise, racial-ethnic difference was to be managed through selective development programs for low-income racialized populations.

In Ecuador, multicultural reform and sustained indigenous pressure resulted in the foundation of the indigenous development council, CODENPE, which quickly established a budget in excess of the National Women's Council's; CODENPE oversaw various programs, for example an Amazon ecodevelopment institute, an indigenous credit fund, bilingual intercultural education and health, and PRODEPINE, an indigenous and black development project (Laurie et al. 2005; Bretón 2005; Quintero López 2008; Andolina et al. 2009).[51] As documented across Latin America, ethnodevelopment initiatives and institutions reworked—but could not shift—forms of racialized governmentality, mired as they were in neoliberal forms of conduct and postcolonial criteria of worth and difference (Hale 2002; Andolina et al. 2009; De Hart 2010).[52] Neoliberal multiculturalism's focus on cultural difference gained "strategic force, not from the fixity of [its] essentialisms, but from the internal malleability assigned to the changing features of racial essence" (Stoler 2002: 144). In this sense, multicultural development represented a top-down cultural politics of recognition founded on postcolonially inflected concepts of social capital (Radcliffe 2007b; Andolina et al. 2009).

From the late 1990s, Ecuador retreated from lopsided stratified welfare and moved toward focused social neoliberal programs that targeted the groups most affected by economic restructuring, while it delegated operations to NGOs and local governments. The country's social expenditure halved, prompting the introduction of programs for "vulnerable" populations using criteria that owed (once again) their content and meanings to colonial framings of social difference.[53] Policy discourse prejudged indigenous groups according to stereotypes about rural locations, agrarian livelihoods, traditional authority structures, and cultural authenticity, establishing a highly disciplining governmentality. Ethnodevelopment projects operated in local areas with unpaid community labor, under predominantly male leaderships, and with free-market optimism about culturally distinctive products and services (Yúdice 2004; Radcliffe and Laurie 2006). In single issue development, ethnodevelopment was largely separate from gender policy, although occasionally subject to interventions (see chapter 3 for a detailed discussion of how these interventions impacted an ethnodevelopment project in Chimborazo).

While ethnodevelopment justified and funded small-scale projects, racialized populations continued to face segregated labor markets, resource grabs, and privatization in the broader economy. Neoliberal macroeconomics continued to put downward pressure on wages and welfare budgets,

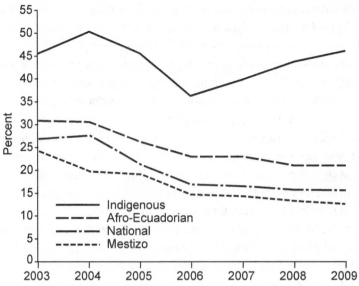

Fig. 1.3. Poverty rates by racial-ethnic group, Ecuador, 2003–2009.

ensuring that racialized populations bore a disproportionate cost of restructuring (Hall and Patrinos 2005; Telles 2007) (see fig. 1.3 for poverty differentials across racial groups). Neoliberal restructuring was associated with
worsening income distributions, greater inequalities, and a rise in impoverishment among racialized subalterns in Latin America, including indigenous
and Afro-Latin populations, despite multicultural reforms and development.
Moreover, discrimination rose in Ecuador, with nearly half of indigenous-
nonindigenous wage differentials due to discrimination, making it Latin
America's most discriminatory country.[54] In addition, the lopsided political economy remained firmly in place: by the late 1990s, 92 percent
of indigenous families worked in agriculture (89 percent owned small parcels of land), with one-fifth of income from subsistence production.[55] Informed by agendas to decolonize the state, development, and knowledge,
indigenous organizations voiced devastating critiques of national development, especially neoliberal attempts to undercut popular control over water
and land. Nationwide popular uprisings called Levantamientos Indígenas
erupted regularly between 1990 and 2012. Serving as what anthropologist
Nancy Postero calls "a site of articulation and contestation with unexpected
results," this political interruption severely challenged dominant interpretations of development needs and citizenship and gave rise to a widening

politics of postmulticulturalism and postneoliberalism (Postero 2006; see chapter 7).

❋

As this genealogy of Ecuadorian development sketches out, policy's apprehension of social heterogeneity has been strongly influenced by colonial categories of difference and its characterization of femininity, indigeneity, and rurality as problematic, stereotyped, and "in excess of what can be empirically proved or logically construed" (Bhabha 1996: 88). In this context, it is unsurprising that single issue development (GAD, ethnodevelopment) perpetuates such thinking even as it seemingly addresses major fault lines in the distribution and reach of development. Although social heterogeneity exists relationally, policy frameworks arising out of colonialism demarcate specific axes of social difference around which to organize development.[56]

Coloniality, Social Neoliberalism, and the Persistence of Single-Issue Thinking

In Ecuadorian policy history, two dimensions of social heterogeneity have been institutionalized in ways that prevent a broader understanding of social difference, and how interlocking hierarchies of gender, rurality, and race-ethnicity are maintained. While in theory multicultural legislation and practice should be able to recognize and work from women's rights at the global scale, in practice the means to mesh women-sensitive development with development with identity are not straightforward.[57] Feminism and multiculturalism are often represented as opposing interpretive frameworks for dealing with rights, citizenship, and representation, despite a shared philosophical commitment to challenging power inequalities. The capacity of (neo)liberal multiculturalism to fully acknowledge and provide effective voice to racialized minorities in multiethnic, frequently settler, societies has been extended by interrogations of multiculturalism's capacity to address women's rights.[58] Feminist arguments point to multiculturalism's tendency to reinforce communal patriarchal structures and authority within ethnic minorities, in many cases blaming minority men for discrimination. Two dimensions often become conflated: "The recognition that multiculturalism may entail risks for minority women can then easily become squared with a belief that multiculturalism is (intrinsically) bad for women" (Phillips and Saharso 2008: 295). Postcolonial critics by contrast highlight the multiple factors influencing ethnic women's disadvantage, for example political economies, citizenship status, religion, legal jurisdictions, and so on, while geographers point to the multiscalar and overlapping nature of exclusion, self-positioning, and resistance (Sen and Grown 1987; Grewal and Kaplan 1994; Fisher 2004).[59]

Accordingly, gender and ethnicity appear as if they were "polarized, mutually exclusive concerns . . . at the level of political practice" (quote from Luykx 2000: 150; also Paulson and Calla 2000).[60] Yet "pitting feminism against multiculturalism has certain consequences: it obscures the influences that in fact shape cultural practices, hides the forces apart from culture that affect women's lives, [and] elides the way women exercise agency within patriarchy" (Volpp 2001). To pursue a critical analysis of apparently polarized concerns, this section uses Diane Fuss's (1989) deconstruction of essentialisms to examine the two policy fields not as fundamentally opposed but as both reliant on coloniality's understandings of how society works. Juxtaposing policy frameworks rather than treating them separately reveals how each policy field relies on the other to shore up dominant postcolonial norms about gender, race, location, and class while bolstering imaginaries of always-already gendered-raced development subjects. Although GAD and ethnodevelopment are "single issue development" approaches, they are connected, through their constant reliance on a colonial present, which is normalized through claims to modern, technically discrete, and politically effective axes of policy.

Ecuadorian gender policy consistently treats Andean communities as bastions of "traditional" male-female dynamics that require the unilateral introduction of modernized gender relations, as articulated in feminism and GAD policy. Feminist policy-makers see multicultural development as inadequate in guaranteeing women's rights, critiquing ethnodevelopment projects for not "doing" gender and justifying the introduction of gender equity components. In other words, gender policy treats indigenous (and peasant) communities as if they were homogeneous and not ethnoculturally diverse, as universally exemplifying unmodern female-male relations in self-referential ethnic cultures (Larrea 2002: 9). Hence, despite institutional separation from ethnodevelopment, GAD can be understood as embedded in colonial readings of intersecting gender, race, and class differences. Ecuadorian gender thinking is saturated with feminist norms consolidated and validated throughout urban mestizo developmentalism, a set of goals intrinsically defined against rural, racialized difference. Although gender policy did not ostensibly deal with "culture"—which was supposedly left in ethnodevelopment's realm— it did rely on expectations about the relative values of (racialized) cultures. These understandings of culture in gender policy in turn positioned indigenous women as invisible to gender policy, or pathologized them as discrete problems, as later chapters explore. Gender policy moreover essentialized "culturally different" women as passive, unchanging, traditional, and subordinate to ethnic patriarchies. In turn, these understandings bolstered liberal feminism's claims to privileged influence in policy solutions.[61] Neoliberal ethnodevelopment also relied on notions of community, with Ecuadorian policy placing strong emphasis on the distinctive cohesive social relations of ethnic groups, especially with reference to the internal homogeneity of rural villages and their practices of labor exchange, reciprocity, and robust local identities. Development policy interpreted these characteristics as a form of social capital, a development "good" to boost antipoverty interventions. In this way, nationalist discourses about the sociospatial distinctiveness of indigenous communities meshed with international policy frameworks to provide an apparently seamless route into policy design (Bretón 2005; Larrea, Montenegro et al. 2007; Andolina et al. 2009).

The often-cited distinction between gender and ethnic policy is blurred too by a shared failure to address interconnecting hierarchies of difference. Gender approaches tend to work with women (more rarely with men) and, in doing so, with dominant racial-ethnic women, while ethnodevelopment focuses on racially marked populations, leaving intact the privileges of whiteness. Moreover, gender policy and, to a lesser extent, ethnodevelopment tend to downplay the imbrications of race-gender-class-location within and across the spaces of development. Likewise, both approaches intervene in beneficiary social relations, not in social relations involving development workers. Mestizo-white staffers remain racially unmarked, despite development's role in reproducing racial hierarchies.[62] In Ecuador "many white-mestizos/as that work in Indian development consider themselves allies with the Indian movement, as left-oriented and critical of the state and nationalist homogenizing ideologies" (quote from Lilliott 2000: 3–4, also Martínez Flores 2000). Likewise, ethnodevelopment and gender policy struggle to think through how female-male dynamics constitute project interactions and how project staffers perpetuate racialized-gendered privilege. Multicultural development agencies such as CODENPE are staffed by largely male ethnic movement activists and professionals, a growing (but small) number of individuals with university or professional training.[63]

Moreover, another arena where gender and ethnodevelopment policy are less polarized than is often recognized is that of expectations about household structures and authority. Gender policy advocates in Ecuador lobbied for many decades to shift the stubborn official emphasis on male heads of households in rural peasant areas (Herrera 2003: 20, Cuvi Sánchez 2000:

20). Yet what rural development staffers and their gender critics overlooked consistently was the fact that development interventions were targeted at a male and mestizo agricultural producer, a racially unmarked subject privileged by association with modernity (Carrión and Herrera 2012). In a parallel move, World Bank feminists advocate an intrahousehold negotiation model, which perpetuates "a universalizing portrayal of the household economy and family life as mired in patriarchal tradition" (Bergeron 2011: 151). In Ecuador, for instance, World Bank lending to ethnodevelopment projects normalized what Kate Bedford has termed "ideals of sharing monogamous partnership" (Bedford 2005). Although ethnodevelopment and gender policy hence claim different spheres of interaction, they share uninterrogated understandings of household structure with strongly racialized and gendered meanings, despite the fact that in Ecuador, household structures and authority vary across ethnic groups and regions. In the central Sierra, locals say they have "two-headed households."[64] Female-headed households, women separated for long periods from migrant husbands, and other complex multigenerational forms give rise to variegated forms of decision-making, leadership, and resource use, a variability that is poorly captured in policy categories. Indigenous women leaders are much more careful to differentiate these gendered-raced-cultural forms. At a meeting, a CODENPE female employee spoke specifically about "the Siona indigenous group work together, men together with women," while pointing out that "development wants to work like in Western society."[65] Ethnodevelopment and gender policy are also not so far apart in their conceptualization of indigenous women's agency and power. Ecuadorian gender policy-makers often describe indigenous women as thwarted by communal patriarchies. The recent plan of action of CONAMU associates indigenous (and black) women with vulnerability and a lack of agency (chapters 3 and 4). From a different starting point, ethnodevelopment suggests that colonialism's legacies of male power stunt indigenous women's power and capability. Each policy framework thereby elides from its account of social heterogeneity subaltern women's agency to challenge, disrupt, and question an array of "solutions" offered in the name of progress. As subsequent chapters document, however, indígenas in practice do actively rework and resist forms of development that work against their interests, whether these are ethnodevelopment, GAD, or neoliberalism.

Exploring the shared ground between GAD and multiculturalism demonstrates how despite the institutional separation of gender and ethnicity, their readings of social difference are rooted in legacies of colonialism. The separation of gender and ethnic policy is less clear-cut and oppositional than is often portrayed, and the policy approaches share core premises of postcolonial hierarchies. Nevertheless, institutional and conceptual disaggregation into single issue development does important work, making intersectional hierarchies less graspable, absolving development from responsibility for sustaining hierarchies, and leaving uninterrogated deeply held understandings of modernity and social heterogeneity. Ecuadorian development relies extensively on imaginaries of what are always already gendered and racialized, classed, geographically situated people, naturalizing dominant interpretations of race, gender, class, and location (see Table 1.2). As practiced and implemented in Ecuador, gender development and ethnodevelopment are permeated by taken-for-granted norms about divisions of labor, intra-household interactions, and sexuality, norms rooted in dominant postcolonial national understandings of what makes modern social relations.

※

Returning to the notion that indigenous women's development disadvantage arises from the "triple oppression" of being poor, indigenous, and female, Ecuador's development genealogy demonstrates how "difference" in postcolonial social heterogeneity is born of power-laden relational comparisons between minority and majority worlds, masculinities and femininities, racial-ethnic groups, and across wealth gaps.[66] Whether as mathematical steps or technical single-issue development, additive models moreover reproduce the postcolonial move of making certain subjects into the epitome of national progress, against whom other embodiments represent obstacles or limits to development intervention. As this chapter shows, these readings of postcolonial social heterogeneity are not discursive interjections but intrinsic to the materialization and power relations of development and macroeconomics. The mutually constitutive nature of social categorizations and the associations they acquire have qualitative, not additive, effects on individuals and groups (De Lauretis 1987, Fuss 1989, Moore 1994). Postcolonial intersectionality generates disadvantage greater than the sum of its parts. In Mexico, poor indigenous women in rural areas have worse health outcomes than would be expected with the single effects of class, race, and gender. Likewise in Ecuador, the combination of race, gender, and educational factors has been found to have a disproportionate impact on indigenous women's work prospects, although it is crucial to note that "there are real limitations to generalizing across the experiences of men and women,

TABLE 1.2 Social difference and development in Chimborazo and Santo Domingo provinces, in the Ecuadorian context, c. 2005–2012

	Chimborazo 458,581	Santo Domingo 368,013	Ecuador 14,483,000	ECUADOR SOCIAL DEVELOPMENT			
				Average monthly income ($)	Percent social security coverage	Years of schooling M	F
Total population	458,581	368,013	14,483,000				
Ethno-racial groups (%)							
Mestizo	57.4	81	71.9	325	21	10.3	10
Indigenous	38	1.7	7.0	196	12.7	6.5	4.7
White	3	6.8	6.1	420	24.7		11.2
Afro-Ecuadorian	1	7.7	7.2	282	20.3		
Other (& Montubio)	0.6	2.8	7.8	n.a.	n.a.		
Women's employment							
Agriculture	35.1	4.4	12.5				
Services & retail	18.2	34.6	21.2				
Elementary occupations*	18.1	21.3	14.7				

Illiteracy			
Provincial	13.5	6.3	Mestiza women 6.2; Afro-Ecuadorian women 7.9; indigenous women (natn) 26.7
Unmet basic needs			
Kichwa Puruhá	96.2 (50.9 in province)	–	Mestizo 60; white 40.5; Afro-Ecuadorian 70.3
Tsáchila	–	97.1 (49.5 in province)	

* Includes cleaning, domestic service, street vendors, peons, and others.

Source: Adapted from Telles 2007; De La Torre 2007; INEC Census 2010; CODENPE 2010b; Ecuador 2013.

and across racialized and gendered forms of abandonment, and—most importantly—that gender hierarchies support and relay the split between biological and political life, which is both cause and effect of abandonment" (Pratt 2005: 1057).[67]

Despite the hegemony of single issue development, Ecuadorian policy began at the turn of the twenty-first century to address specific subpopulations, including indigenous women, as particularly needy groups. Development's sudden interest in indigenous women emerged from the increasing micro-scaling and targeting of neoliberal development and in the context of policy on reproductive health and microcredit (on reproductive health, see chapter 5). Optimizing the facets of social difference, neoliberal policy sought "to create neither a discipline nor a normalizing society, but instead a society characterized by the fact that it cultivates and optimizes differences" (Lemke 2001: 200). In this vein, Ecuador's 1996 National Social Development Plan (Ecuador 1996: 163) mentioned racialized women twice in relation to their childbearing capacity, combining the problematic features of a high fertility rate and low education. Such policy discourses implied "that rural women have more children as they are ignorant, whereas enlightened, urban and empowered women have fewer children" (Cuvi Sanchez and Ferraro 2000: 117). Such discourses reworked colonial power relations to imply that subaltern women merely needed to become modern, national subjects.

The same logic underpinned microcredit programs, although indigenous women were expected to become entrepreneurial in a culturally distinctive way while behaving otherwise like domesticated, neoliberal female subjects.[68] The FODEPI credit program aimed to boost indigenous business capacity. Credit was disbursed via one program for indigenous groups and individuals and a second program exclusively for women individually or in groups, the "Llankari Warmi" scheme, Kichwa for "Entrepreneurial Woman."[69] This type of credit echoes neoliberal microcredit programs found across the global South, in that it targets low-income groups to release women's business potential through small cash inputs (Mayoux 2001; Rankin 2001; Lazar 2004). Yet through its structure and expectations, FODEPI's program reproduces postcolonial expectations about ethnic communities' social cohesion, the existence of traditional communal authorities, and the docile, predictable behavior of married women, who make up the majority of credit recipients. In this way, FODEPI merges neoliberal individual entrepreneurial models with colonial narratives about how indigenous subjects behave (see chapter 4). Unsurprisingly, indigenous women experience the program in contradictory and paradoxical ways, as it offers them a degree of financial autonomy while public services, socionatures, and women's knowledges continue to be slowly hollowed out. Hence indígenas begin to articulate decolonizing critiques of development and to focus their attention on development's "second generation" challenge—namely, the need to address disadvantage in relation to postcolonial intersectionality.

Conclusions

Development is intrinsically a postcolonial endeavor, a discursive and material project resting not only on the aspirations to a nationally distinct modernity but also crucially on the variable and differently valued labor of racial-ethnic populations and resources, whose incorporation into colonialism established long-standing consequences for their populations. In continuity with colonial governmentality, development is embedded within a routinization of control, boundary maintenance, and uneven political economic processes that dispossess indigenous women and men in material, embodied, and discursive ways. As this chapter demonstrates, indígenas in Ecuador are located firmly in the postcolonial dynamics of ongoing and often policy-driven transformations that reconfigure relations between resources, populations, and the goals of modernity. In the words of a historic female leader, Vicenta: "the system has gone on co-opting women and children into enslaving work, maximizing its profits and destroying even more indigenous economies and family structures" (Chuma 2004: 2). Indigenous women are subject to dispossession because of relational qualities of femininity, poverty, and cultural difference, a positionality that cannot ever be recognized as such within the terms of postcolonial development. "Liberal and neoliberal promotion of women's civil and political rights does not address the inequalities of class, ethnicity, and territory . . . leaving indigenous, afro-descent and popular women outside" (Transition Commission 2011: 22). Single issue development relies—often implicitly—on a "standard model" of social heterogeneity. As with many forms of knowledge in modernity, development's approach to social heterogeneity is deeply compromised by its genealogy and association with postcolonial privilege.

A postcolonial analysis of development brings to the fore how intersectional marginalization and impoverishment are, according to Victoria Taulí Carpuz, a Filipina indigenous activist, "a collective phenomenon, arising from historical and structural causes, and as a result [why] it cannot be dealt with simply at an individual level" (quoted in Pazmiño 2008). Intersectional hierarchies are collective not due to an essential link between indigeneity and poverty or to ethnic communities, or to women. Rather,

Tauli argues that the issues pertain to a group of subalterns because the interlocking exclusions and inequalities in settler societies reinforce the associations between lack of humanity, poverty, racialization, and gendering (also Maldonado-Torres 2007). Although symbolizing the past—that which is culturally outdated, slow, racially distinctive—indigenous women in fact find themselves throughout postcolonial history at the heart of lopsided and exclusionary growth and sociospatial restructuring. This very lack of correspondence between elite discourses of modernizing development and the embodied realities of indigenous women provides a key to their experiences discussed in later chapters.

The technical separation of gender and ethnoracial difference as the grounds for institutionalizing development responded to multiscalar mobilization and the politicization of prior simplifications of social heterogeneity in mainstream development, on behalf of women and of indigenous populations (and to a lesser extent Afro-descendants). Gender and ethnodevelopment in turn have been charged with depoliticization and technical fixes, features that can also be identified in the Ecuadorian case. Yet bringing these genealogies in conversation with postcolonial analysis extends these critiques by bringing into focus how the postcolonial condition for this recognition reinforced—or did not raise for sustained scrutiny—the more complex ground of social heterogeneity against which this technical division of labor and intervention was to occur. In this respect, single issue development deals with postcolonial social heterogeneity with an "axis" model, each line of social difference separately circulating around its own pole of interests. As discussed earlier in this chapter, in Ecuador, gender and ethnic issues were overseen by separate councils, each reporting directly to the president, each with a stand-alone budget, and each dealing with a singular target population. One metaphor that has been applied to the intersectionality of gender, race-ethnicity, and income is that of multiple "axes" of difference that together create disempowerment and marginalization for the subaltern third world woman. "Axis" is defined in the Oxford English Dictionary as a straight line around which a body rotates, thereby signaling the concept's origin in a Newtonian ordered world. An axis works in a universe with a stable rational dynamic that is established by the relative positions of subjects (bodies) moving in a predictable and finite way and that is determined by existing conditions and prevailing forces. In this way, the definition of "axis" calls to mind the teleologies of development and its technical and conceptual rendering of social heterogeneity as "gender" and "ethnodevelopment."[70] Development agendas of ethnic rights and women's rights do not simply provide a positive synergy for female racial subalterns, yet neither are they independent variables.

A second definition of axis is a geopolitical alliance where a political agenda unites a number of disparate subjects in opposition to a common enemy. This geopolitical connotation draws attention to the strategic but ultimately weak coalitions between ethnic and women's movements to challenge neoliberal restructuring and democratize the state. Ecuadorian ethnic and women's movements proved to be uneasy allies, divided by incompatible positions in postcolonial hierarchies and with few shared visions.[71] As scholars of intersectionality argue, power relations underlying racialization, gendering, and class stratification contribute to political factionalism and division, accusations of treason, and a fragile process of coalition building (Crenshaw 1991; Phillips 1995). In Ecuador, such political divisions are blamed for undercutting racialized women's gains in land titling under neoliberal multicultural reforms (Deere and León 2001a; Radcliffe 2014b). Unless racialized women's perspectives are systematically accorded space and authority in political movements to overturn postcolonial disadvantage, the complacent stereotypes that inform public policy remain unchallenged.

Moreover, a critical account of postcolonial intersectionality points up the inadequacy of single issue development in the grounded realities of colonial governmentality. Indigenous women alongside indigenous men were incorporated into postcolonial power relations and attendant forms of dispossession and representational Othering. Likewise, women and men were brought into agrarian labor as unpaid or nearly unpaid workers and displaced from historic territories. Yet the embodiment of colonial racialization was differentiated between women and men in ways that compounded gendered experiences in colonially inflected segregated labor markets. Although indigenous women and men were treated indiscriminately as disposable, low-cost labor with no rights to security or recognition, women had fewer claims than men. Likewise, with regard to land and resources indigeneity determined minimal claims, and for indígenas that minimal claim was yet more problematic. Postcolonial development hence entrains racial and gendered (as well as locational and class) difference simultaneously and relationally, generating differentiated experiences of development for indigenous women while making them frequently invisible or imagined as minor. Analyzing development as processual and power-laden highlights how racialized female subalterns are positioned differentially from indigenous men, nonindigenous women, and nonindigenous men. Their uniqueness arises from the interplay of interlocking hierarchies, not some essential qualities of being an indigenous woman. As the chapter also has demonstrated, development understandings of social heterogeneity are constituted in and through the postcolonial histories of labor, territory, and exclusion. Policy expectations around households, beneficiaries, and development modernity refer back continuously to postcolonial nationalist norms about male, female, and racialized subjects. It is not just that "women" become a reified category of GAD and depoliticized and colorful Indians the beneficiaries of ethnodevelopment. Each of these "cookie-cutter" formulations of social heterogeneity are thoroughly saturated with meanings and associations given to the category by the postcolonial dynamics in which they emerge.

Subaltern women's marginalization is embedded in the procedures, practices, and discourses of national development in the mutually influential relationships of race, class, gender, and location. Development's chains of association systematically remove from consideration indigenous women's agency as subaltern subjects. Ecuadorian indígenas are coming to know how "one's subject position is constituted through links among thoroughly unequal social forces" (Spivak, quoted in Grewal and Kaplan 1994: 352). Regardless of uneven efforts to speak on their behalf, indigenous women acquire a deep and critical knowledge of their situation and their problematic relationship with development and citizenship. The words, thoughts, and interjections of variously positioned indigenous women reflect no claims to privileged or essential insight, but a partial and situated truth. From their unique standpoint in postcolonial development, indigenous women become knowledgeable critics of how social heterogeneity is framed in the colonial present.

___

TWO

The Daily Grind

Ethnic Topographies of Labor, Racism, and Abandonment

Born in Cóngoma village, sona Rosa was raised by her mother and then married at age thirteen to a boy of the same age, entailing a move to Naranjos village. She wakes at five o'clock in the morning to prepare breakfast before working in the banana groves, her adult sons helping to harvest and sell crops. Rosa has never attended school but occasionally goes along to village meetings. Many kilometers away lives Concepción, who was removed from primary school when she was young to care for her siblings and the family's small goat herd. Living in the central Andean province of Chimborazo, Concepción was married young, only to see one of her children die, and scrabbles a precarious hand-to-mouth existence as a semisubsistence farmer. In Cajabamba, one of Chimborazo's district capitals, located on an accessible and irrigated plain, twenty-four-year-old Carmen lives at home with her parents, farming a relatively large set of plots for sales and self-sufficiency, and caring for younger siblings. Having attended the village school, she undertook long-distance learning to gain a partial secondary education. Rosa, Carmen, and Concepción are unlikely to meet, as the paths they travel do not overlap; their lives are multiply diverse and reflect an uneven landscape of power relations and socionatures. In what sense then can we speak about indigenous women's positionality? What does being a Tsáchila sona or Kichwa warmi mean today? To address these questions, I use the analytical tool of countertopography to unpack the processes shaping the lives of Rosa, Carmen, Concepción, and other Ecuadorian raced-gendered-rural subjects. With the term *counter-topography*, geographer Cindi Katz refers to "the historical examination of social process in three-dimensional space" in order to situate and describe the "uneven yet interconnected processes associated with global and developmental restructuring and its ramifications for variously situated actors" (Katz 2001a). To use their own languages, Kichwa warmikuna's and Tsáchila sonala's lives vary because of ethnocultural differences in divisions of labor, expectations about residence after marriage, and the ways racial-ethnic identity is disciplined. Yet the counter-topography also highlights how, despite these ethnocultural differences, and regional differences in political economy and development histories, Tsáchila and Kichwa women often share characteristics and positioning in development that exemplify wider power-laden articulations of place, race, class, occupation, and gender, without reifying the category of indigenous women. Encompassing the spheres of social reproduction, informal and formal economic sectors, and enduring legacies of racialized enmity, the notion of counter-topography situates global change across multiple scales, keeping sight of individuals' embodied constraints and access to resources.[1]

Counter-topography hence serves to contextualize women's lives in two ethnic groups, while signaling the importance of processes that shape their lives in ways unconnected with ethnicity. Ecuador has fourteen indigenous nationalities, differentiated culturally, materially, linguistically, and politically, each crosscut by class, generational, education, and occupational differences. Tracing lines of (dis)connection across Kichwa and Tsáchila groups unpacks the local and embodied consequences of postcolonial intersectionality on the ground, given their diverse ethnocultural dynamics, environments, and regional economies. Postcolonial critic Gayatri Spivak challenges us to understand the connections between individuals and the lumpen categorization of the subaltern by unpicking the threads of power to understand how a group of people become mired in structural poverty, marginalization, and disadvantage (Spivak 1993 [1988]). In the relational and power-drenched interpretation of terms such as "indigenous women," "nonindigenous men," categories emerge as if they were self-evident and separate. Yet to understand postcolonial social heterogeneity, it becomes important to identify the parameters and extent of social differentiation between clusters of individuals, and the relations of power across categories (see McCall 2005). In the words of postcolonial critic Maria Lugones (2007: 192), "Intersectionality reveals what is not seen when categories such as gender and race are conceptualized as separate from each other."

For this reason, this chapter moves between comparisons of indigenous women with indigenous men and nonindigenous women, and the substantive detail of indigenous women's lives, to reveal the contingent relational quality of intersectional postcolonial hierarchies and inequalities. Rather than highlight the complexity of indígenas' lives the purpose of this account is to indicate the processes and inequalities that development might tackle.

The predominantly rural province of Chimborazo, with a population of under half a million, 60 percent rural, has a population that is 40 percent Kichwa, most of them from the Puruhá pueblo. More than nine out of every ten Puruhá Kichwa have unmet basic needs, while Chimborazo province has one of Ecuador's lowest human development indices.[2] By contrast Santo Domingo province is rapidly urbanizing, and the provincial capital of the same name is the country's fourth largest urban center. A predominantly mestizo province, with its indigenous population under 2 percent, in 2010 Santo Domingo de los Tsáchilas had a population marginally smaller than Chimborazo's (around 400,000), three-fourths of it urban, and with the racial-ethnic makeup four-fifths mestizo, 7.7 percent Afro-Ecuadorian, 6.8 percent Montubio, and 1.7 percent indigenous, most of the latter being Tsáchila. The Tsáchila are experiencing 97.1 percent unmet basic needs. Although neither the Kichwa nor Tsáchila are currently impacted by large-scale mining investments or enclave industrialization, their livelihoods are constituted through dynamic and extraregional (in some cases global) labor and product markets, patterns of social reproduction, and embodied outcomes of postcolonial racialization. Whereas Tsáchila sonala live in communities that are increasingly being encroached upon by land-grabs and rapid urbanization, warmikuna inhabit a shadow space consisting of a floating surplus population and declining agrarian economies reliant on outmigration and semisubsistence agriculture. Mapping the topography of connection—and disconnection—between and across Chimborazo and Tsáchila villages in Santo Domingo reveals the hidden side of development as it is experienced: the weight of racism and social abandonment and their pervasive impacts on women's occupations, educational histories, embodiments, and security and dignity of livelihood (see table 2.1). This account hence captures the reproduction of enclaves as distinctively indigenous, even while institutional and socioeconomic dynamics within political economy and state interventions shift uneven development in and around these geographies (Bebbington 2000; compare Chibber 2013).

TABLE 2.1 Characteristics of the two field sites in the Ecuadorian context

Aspect or phase	CHARACTERISTICS		
	Chimborazo province	Santo Domingo province	Ecuador
Racialized female subalterns	Kichwa nationality, Puruhá pueblo; "woman" = *warmi* (singular), *warmikuna* (plural) in kichwa language	Tsáchila nationality; "woman" = *sona* (singular), *sonala* (plural) in tsafiki language	14 distinct indigenous nationalities (groups)
Socionatures	Andean mountain range and high valleys, altitudes range from 2,500 to 6,268 meters (Chimborazo volcano)	Subtropical area, altitude 400–500 meters	3 main regions: coastal subtropical zone; Andean cordillera with high valleys; Amazon basin region. Total land area 283,520 square kilometers (equivalent in size to Colorado, Italy, or New Zealand)
Pre-Columbian society	Northern part of Inca state from late fifteenth century	Hunter-gatherer groups, with extensive territory and trade with Andes	Diverse mix of languages, political systems, and social relations
Conquest and European settlement	Riobamba was first city founded in colonial Ecuador, 1534; displacement and marginalization in small land plots	From mid-nineteenth century, center of wild rubber trade; some missionaries	1531 Spanish arrived in Ecuador; Quito founded 1534; under Spanish Crown until 1822; independent republic 1830

Relation with colonizers/settlers	Labor obligations to haciendas; tax obligations to colonial state	Displacement by banana colonization, urban boom from mid-nineteenth century	Spanish Crown awarded encomienda (grants of tribute or labor from indigenous people) landholdings to 500 families
Twentieth-century political economy	Combined subsistence, local wage labor in agriculture and informal urban sectors; migration to coastal plantations and major cities	State planned colonization and spontaneous settlement by nonindigenous from 1940s; land awarded on condition that land cultivated; cultivation of commercial crops of banana, coffee	Petroleum (40% of exports), tropical crops (bananas, flowers, cocoa)—mainly to USA, China, Colombia
Administration	Comunas from 1937 Law, numbers increased after 1964 Agrarian Reform, subsequent land transfers and sales	Tsáchila comunas recognized as means of cultural protection in early 1970s	Republic with president and unicameral National Assembly; civil law; 24 provinces as main political-administrative divisions
Forms of local organization	Active village associations; cabildos (councils) in comunas; OSGs and OTGs; progressive Catholic church; Provincial indigenous federations; numerous NGOs	Tsáchila governor (formerly an inherited position, now elected), Tsáchila council; missionaries; a few NGOs, largely international	Active civil society with numerous religious, civic, urban and rural associations, Federations, etc.
Indigenous women's representatives	Provincial federation elects women's representative; village women's associations	Tsáchila women's representative (chosen by Council)	CONAIE-elected women's representative, CONMIE, and individual nationalities' women's representatives

Multiple Lives, Fluid Patterns, Cumulative Disadvantage

While "it is essential that indigenous women's problematic is not homogenized" (Pacari 1998b: 59), the specifics of women's lives—the kinds of animals they herd, the crops they grow, the sources of their livelihood, their children born, and their political voices—are shaped profoundly by uneven development and the spatial realities of the colonial present. As Inderpal Grewal and Caren Kaplan (1994) note, these factors work to create differentiated forms of everyday life and long-term development opportunities for women of color, although they often remain subordinate overall to the "scattered hegemonies" of institutional, state, economic, and male power. In Ecuador's case these scattered hegemonies result in nearly nine of ten indigenous households living below the poverty line and nine in ten indigenous women having unmet basic needs (Palacios and Chuma 2001). Here four forms of scattered hegemonies are discussed: work and livelihood; capabilities and education; resource control; and experiences of racialization and gendering.

"ALL IN A DAY'S WORK": INCOME, WORK, AND SECURITY

In Ecuador, as across Latin America, indigenous women work long hours in largely rural and agricultural settings for little monetary compensation (see map 2.1). As María Andrade, onetime CONAIE women's representative, noted twenty-five years ago, "the situation of indigenous populations in general and of indigenous women particularly is determined by the structural conditions of Ecuadorian agriculture. The fundamental problem of the rural sector is land tenure. Government-promoted reforms have not solved the problem, which has worsened polarizing land distribution. As participants in this reality, indigenous women have had to undertake a series of social and economic reproductive roles" (Andrade 1990: 8–9).

In Ecuador's rural areas, indigenous women are more likely to work in agriculture than nonindigenous women, although they are also highly likely to be working unpaid on family farms (Giarracca and Teubal 2008; CEPAL 2013). In the postcolonial distribution traced in the Introduction, women struggle on a daily basis additionally with the consequence of uneven state investment in road-building, infrastructure, and social welfare. The risk of being poor is more associated with being indigenous than with being female: while 87.1 percent of indigenous women are at risk of poverty, so too are 84.0 percent of indigenous men, compared with just over half of nonindigenous women.[3] Indigenous women's accounts of hard lives lived in land-

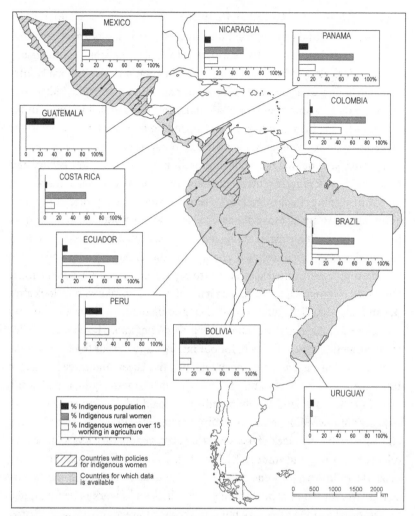

Map 2.1. Indigenous women in rural areas and working in agriculture, Latin America, c. 2010. Map by the Cartographic Unit, Department of Geography, University of Cambridge.

scapes of social abandonment, and the work that goes into battling daily for existence, also reveal how precarious livelihoods are, how vulnerable indigenous women are to major upheavals caused by illness, death, or a lost harvest.

Among Ecuadorian women over fifteen years old, 59.6 percent work in the primary sector (primarily agriculture) in comparison with 51 percent of indigenous men, and 11 percent of nonindigenous women nationally

(CEPAL 2013: 99).[4] Warmikuna confront their precarious situation of inadequate land and work by combining diverse strategies into a web of minimal income and measures to cope with risk. In a subsistence and commercially oriented agriculture, they work long hours in rural areas in a globally integrated economy as a source of cheap labor and cheap foodstuffs. Indigenous women tend to work unpaid for other household and family members, or for lower wages than male counterparts. Depending on local market conditions and resource base, women grow primarily potatoes, maize, onions, vegetables, barley, and quinoa (an Andean protein-rich grain), for subsistence and small-scale sales in nearby urban markets. Women are associated more than men with keeping small animals for resources (wool, meat, protein, eggs) and as an insurance against loss of harvests. Poor women often keep a few *cuyes* (guinea pigs, used for meat), a pig, and some sheep and chickens; resource-endowed women might own five cows, some sheep, and five pigs and ducks. In remote villages, women keep llamas to carry heavy goods down to the road. One poorer woman explained as we sat in conversation, "We women look after the animals, especially guinea pigs; they give us food. We have a guinea pig house in the village, and we sell them for $4.50 per kilo. This is what we live from. Sometimes we sell sheep, for our families and for our food." A wealthier woman, Amelia, owns ten sheep, one pig, five cuyes, and three llamas for transporting her products, and she grows potatoes, maize, quinoa, and peas.[5]

Using their own and family members' unpaid labor, women work long days seeding, weeding, and harvesting crops, with little protection against climate variability or lack of markets. However, gender divisions of labor are relatively flexible, and Andean Kichwa women have relative autonomy over tasks (Hamilton 1998; Rens 2003).[6] Despite widely voiced cultural taboos against women's use of plows, the gender division of work is being rapidly transformed as men and boys migrate for ever longer periods out of rural communities. Rather than being cowed by tradition, women question the basis for taboos and stress the urgency of undertaking heavy agricultural labor in order to guarantee food supplies and income. Disabled women and widows have less secure control over resources, while female-headed households face an uphill struggle to contract labor for agricultural production, as they cannot access male labor through kin and marriage ties. Malnutrition and the lack of nutritious cheap food are widespread, a factor mentioned by women responsible for food preparation. One-fourth of Chimborazo's households regularly find it difficult to pay for food (CEPAR Chimborazo 2004). Small amounts of potatoes, onions, and beans are sold once a week in the nearby district capitals, reflecting women's historic ties to informal sectors of petty commodity production and service work.[7] Warmikuna travel to local and regional markets to sell small quantities of foodstuffs in order to raise cash for necessities such as oil, rice, and medicines. The sale of small amounts in saturated markets means women gain little in return for their long hours in the fields yet rely on these few coins to purchase otherwise unavailable items. When rural indígenas attempt to sell produce, they face high transport costs and intermediaries who keep prices low, use false weights, and impose disadvantageous terms of sale. Women with more regularized and larger-scale marketing activities, dubbed cholas, are viewed by dominant groups with ambivalent fear and admiration yet are disproportionately subject to state intervention as "matter out of place" in urban spaces (Weismantel 2001). A thirty-nine-year-old grandmother, Caterina works on Riobamba's streets selling fruit and herbal teas. Carrying a grandson on her back, she often gets moved on by municipal officials "who treat us badly, beat us. It's not just me; one woman lost her baby when they threw us off one patch."[8] In urban markets, women experience considerable discrimination based on intersecting gender and race-ethnic hierarchies. With access to unreliable information, women also are cheated by middlemen, as Tsáchila and Kichwa indígenas told me, because daily racial and gendered discrimination affects them in produce and labor markets. One Andean leader vividly described it to me as "an exclusionary market— middlemen give us the price they want then cheat on weights."[9] In urban areas indígenas often face intimidation from urban-based sellers and are pushed into the corners of municipal markets, reducing their sales.

Warmikuna's labor input and responsibility for sales usually guarantees them an independent monetary income, although they tend to use that income immediately for household expenditure (children's schooling supplies, salt, butter, sugar, bread). Around a third of women additionally weave homespun cloth (bayeta) or fiber bags (shigra), largely for personal use and village sales. Despite predominantly foodstuff production, irrigated areas around Lake Colta are increasingly contracted by supermarkets to produce broccoli, which promises profit but exposes warmikuna to insecurity, as supermarkets have the power to reject a harvest, leaving women with no income. Although national policy promotes nontraditional export agriculture, indigenous women's limited landholdings and lack of insurance make it a risky option, and women dislike using chemical inputs, despite higher yields,[10] preferring organic agriculture as a mutually beneficial relation with the living earth, Pachamama (chapter 7). In high altitude areas, women often produce quinoa, which commands good prices. In her forties with nine children, Florinda described its importance: "The quinoa came from the [local NGO] project—they gave me seed two years in a row. So they take it and pay—it's the only help we have!" Encouraged by the progressive Catholic diocese,[11] organic quinoa production boomed after 2005 with rising fair-trade export prices, although poorer households now cannot afford to eat quinoa.

Most families in Chimborazo hold a series of small subfamily plots as a form of insurance, a resource base for social reproduction of cheap migrant labor, and for peasant agriculture. Warmikuna's households during the period of my fieldwork held around one hectare of land, although considerable differentiation occurred.[12] State gender bias of over a generation ago reverberates down to women.[13] Although all households are passing smaller and smaller numbers and sizes of plots to daughters and sons, they start with disparate quantities and qualities of land. Centuries of dispossession mean that one in five Kichwa women interviewed had no land, as parents' land had not yet been subdivided (these women were single and living at home), because they were orphans, or because parents were landless. While the majority of warmikuna inherited land from both parents, three times as many mentioned fathers as mothers regarding inheritance, while mothers' landholdings were smaller than fathers. Warmikuna inherit on average just less than half a hectare of land, whereas men contribute two to three times as much land on average to the household.[14] Warmikuna acquire land through various mechanisms: inheritance only (34 percent of interviewees), inherit and buy (18 percent).[15] Just over one-quarter of Kichwa women bought land, although these purchases were generally small; demand for land outstrips market supply. In Pucupalla village, Florinda inherited one small plot from her parents and worked as a cook for a hacienda estate to earn money for another small plot after her husband left her, in order to raise nine children. Young married women undertake productive and reproductive tasks for in-laws, in the expectation that their household will eventually receive a share. Warmikuna's common refrain is land shortage, although lack of land and the need for greater labor input into existing plots does not raise the value of women's labor, and is perceived a leading factor in male wage migration and leaves women with production and reproduction responsibilities. During a visit between Kichwa and Tsáchila women at the end of field research, one Chimborazo woman looked around the Tsáchila village where we were gathered.[16] We had all spent the morning discussing similarities and differences between highland and coastal indígena lives. As she gazed around at the dense growth of cocoa and banana trees, so different from the open patchwork fields of her village, Delia said in a surprised tone, "Up in the Sierra we have a single ditch! Here it's all hectares!" She continued, "If you have land, you have food, animals, somewhere to work—with that, I'm not a worker for anyone else!" Her comments were not purely mathematical, as she articulated a sense of Andean land-territory relations forged through colonial labor exploitation and the continued hard physical labor required on small, scattered plots. Her words also vividly illustrate the continued insecurity of landholdings for female racialized subalterns whose options in nonagricultural rural work and urban labor markets are so limited. Between the fracturing comuna, insufficient legal structures, and lack of welfare, warmikuna cling to land-territory not as a market instrument but as the basis for political mobilization and dignified survival.

As this anecdote suggests, the dynamics between indigeneity, uneven development, and postcolonial development in Tsáchila villages is distinct from Andean patterns.[17] Among Tsáchila interviewees, households had an average of 4.72 hectares (range 1–12).[18] As land pressure increases, land plots become smaller and inheritance is increasingly patrilineal, so women are granted inheritance plots that are insufficient to support a family.[19] Tsáchila women generally received just under 3 hectares in inheritance; by contrast, husbands brought around 5.69 hectares into the household.[20] As Elizabeth, a college-educated trainee teacher, explained, "Sure, I got some land from my parents but among the Tsáchila men receive more, husbands." In conversations, sonala consistently associated land-territory with fathers and, to a lesser extent, brothers, unlike Kichwa women, who spoke of mothers, fathers, and siblings (see Radcliffe 2014b). Around one-quarter of sonala had no land-territory, living solely on husbands' land; whereas their brothers received more land—between four and twenty times as much. Although Tsáchila women inherit pieces of land that Kichwa women could only dream about, these plots of land are firmly embedded in male-centered systems of control. Tsáchila women hence find it difficult to use the "customary" system to secure land, especially if they are single or widows.

Between the ages of twelve and sixteen, young indigenous women begin to work on varied and heavier tasks around the farms. Older indígenas, too, work long days, there being no retirement age or pension; widows care for the household's sheep in high mountain pastures or scrape together a living on small plots (Censo Agropecuario 2000: 126). Postcolonial hierarchies of race, place, and gender are reinforced when women return to villages as impoverished and as unable to lever living wages. As a middle-aged Kichwa woman told me, "My work is in agriculture. I get up very early and we are always the last to go to bed. I get up at 5 a.m. I work in the fields planting potatoes, beans, irrigating the land to get pastures for the cows and cuyes." The compound disadvantage of rural warmikuna is demonstrated by the greater likelihood of extreme poverty in rural households with larger numbers of women.[21] The reason is that overall women have less leverage in kin relations and cash transactions than men to enable autonomous socionatural resource control, and men generally retain greater decision-making power. For instance, men and women have different interests regarding irrigation water, as men predominate in water committees. Whereas single women may have independent water rights, these transfer to husbands after marriage, as only men's names are customarily registered in village lists. Nevertheless, women remain creative in reworking labor inputs, resource use, and income diversification: women in one community bought a plot of land jointly, while in another they used a village plot to produce foodstuffs collectively.[22]

According to recent figures, 40 percent of indigenous women work in rural family farms (and half of them are not paid wages), and 44 percent work in unskilled work (CEPAL 2005). Like their Andean counterparts, sonala also work unpaid on family farms primarily in agricultural production for subsistence and sales. However, different gender divisions of labor and regional markets for products result in distinct outcomes. Tsáchila households rely on bananas, coffee, and cocoa production for income and yucca, fruit, and malanga for subsistence. Unlike mestizo landholders in the Santo Domingo region, they do not keep cattle, although women usually keep small numbers of pigs and chickens for subsistence and village-based sales. Women work alongside men with machetes and other tools to clear tropical forest and maintain tree crops. Tsáchila communities are embedded in a dynamic regional economy based on Andean-coastal trade, resulting in Santo Domingo city's rapid expansion and an intensely monetized rural economy. The neoliberal boom in export-led production has resulted in encroachment on Tsáchila territories that historically provided for hunting and fishing in the tropical forests, a practice that has now disappeared almost completely. In commercial banana and coffee production, men transport crops to market and negotiate sales, leaving women without an independent income. Women keep a small number of chickens in the house yard; some grow cocoa near the house and dry the beans. Tsáchila women, especially older generations, learned to weave the distinctive clothing worn by men and women, although younger generations buy from traders; cloth production is now increasingly in the hands of Andean Otavaleño merchants. Tsáchila women are unevenly and precariously being drawn into craft production for a national tourist market, making jewelry from seeds and woven bags, although income is extremely erratic and minimal because tourist numbers are low.

> Collective hunting trips to the jungle have declined, which generates complaints particularly among [Tsáchila] women. The new economic situation has confined women to domestic spaces and solitude; they take charge of child care, cooking, agriculture and small domestic animals; they sometimes accompany their husbands for banana collections. . . . This new order has likewise generated an increase in the time men spend working outside the home, and the power they derive from relating with the outside world. (Ventura 2012: 57)

Labor markets reproduce and underscore male-female difference in ethnic populations. Whereas Kichwa men find paid work through the expansion of export agriculture on the coast in gender-segregated labor markets, women receive considerably lower wages in highland estates.[23] On banana plantations, Andean migrant men earn a basic salary of $300 monthly, which compares favorably with women's plantation pay of $200, yet both are favorable in comparison with Chimborazo's male average wage of $226, although migrants face racial discrimination in predominantly mestizo Guayas province (ODM Chimborazo 2007: 77). The few indigenous women who are drawn into export-oriented agriculture on Ecuador's coastal plains earn around $20 weekly and live in basic accommodation, yet Tsáchila women were not among them and did not report undertaking paid rural work, in part because coastal plantation agriculture is largely male-dominated. In Chimborazo, a small number work in paid agricultural work in local farms. Among Kichwa interlocutors, unmarried women are less likely than married women to have land so work locally for wages.[24] Taken up by poorer and unmarried younger women, seasonal jobs provide vital inputs to family budgets but are based on labor costs established under postcolonial hierarchies. Indigenous women in Chimborazo earn $6–8 daily, depending on age, for eight hours of backbreaking work, while men alongside them earn $8–10 daily.[25] For the few women who work as laborers in export flower greenhouses, wages are higher ($10–30 daily) but come with health costs, due to high pesticide use. Another source of paid work for a few women is in low-level government employment, focused in the feminized sectors of education and child care. Among the Tsáchila women interviewed, two women in their twenties were earning as part-time educators in bilingual literacy programs, having completed secondary education. In Chimborazo, Lucia, nineteen years old, worked full-time for the local INNFA program (a subsidized state preschool provision in poor areas that costs families $1 per month), having completed three years of secondary education. She lives with her parents and six sisters, contributing her earnings to the household. Across Ecuador, widespread gender segregation in labor markets results in significant rural-urban wage gaps; in rural areas women's wages average 53.6 percent of men's. Indigenous versus nonindigenous earnings gaps are partly explained by differences in years of schooling, while gender gaps in wages are mostly explained by discrimination against female workers.[26] Indigenous women hence face compound inequalities in highly segregated wage-labor markets (see Mc-Call 2005).

High rates of temporary male migration into urban labor markets characterized the situation during much of the late twentieth century, affecting the highlands and the coast and impacting Kichwa and Tsáchila women unevenly.[27] Whereas many Chimborazo households rely on migrant remittances, Tsáchila villages remain relatively untouched.[28] Off-farm employment has disproportionately incorporated rural men, resulting in the feminization of subsistence agriculture, as women are left with responsibility yet often without the political, economic, and social resources required to ensure secure and dignified livelihoods. One young woman from rural Guamote spent three years working on a clothing stall in a low-income barrio of Caracas; migrants also go to the United States and Europe. Male migration incurs payments to human traffickers of $4,000, which impoverishes families for years and locks women into disadvantageous divisions of labor. Age, generation, and gender lie at the center of household strategies, shaped by broader postcolonial hierarchies and geographies of political economy and abandonment (Cárdenas et al. 2011: 57). The introduction of a national minimum wage did little to raise provincial wage rates, meaning indigenous women and men continue to be paid extremely low wages. Sitting under the harsh sun, fifty-year-old Mercedes recounted how her two daughters are live-out domestics in Quito, one son works in the United States, and another in Cuenca city, leaving a daughter helping at home.

As part of this floating surplus labor, a few warmikuna migrate to cities on a temporary basis and find work in the poorly paid and unprotected sector of domestic service.[29] Nationally around 15 percent of employed urban indigenous women and 5 percent of rural indigenous women are found in domestic service jobs (CEPAL 2013: 102). Andean households send daughters from the age of fourteen into domestic service in the cities of Riobamba, Quito, and beyond. Domestic service remains much more common among Kichwa than Tsáchila households, reflecting historic feudal ties between urban middle classes and rural communities as well as differences between the nationalities in the control exerted over young unmarried women.[30] In postcolonial economies of value, domestic service is a paradigmatic segregated urban employment sector for female subalterns, constituting a workspace where celebrations of mestizaje and national progress work to control and discipline employees. Young girls are ruthlessly exploited; one woman recounted in horror her monthly $5 wage and being stopped from attending school. Live-out wages are higher (averaging $110 monthly) yet incur costs that women cannot cover, such as accommodation and child care. Domestic servants overwhelmingly come from poorer households that command no land or small parcels, meaning migrants are not in a position to command dignified wages. Magdalena, the third oldest child of a land-poor household from Achupallas, entered domestic service at nine years old to send remittances and worked for two years in Riobamba. From the same district and a family with one hectare of land, Lisa, the fourth of nine siblings, went to Quito as a live-in maid at the age of fourteen. She stayed for six years, first in a private house and then in a religious institution, earning $80 monthly with no social security. Despite neoliberal policy moves to "modernize" domestic employment, warmikuna are racialized by low-paid, hard manual labor, with limited opportunities for acquiring skills and cultural recognition.

Postcolonial uneven development and economic restructuring impact gender-segregated labor markets, profoundly impacting women's working lives and employment insecurity.[31] Neither in domestic service nor in agricultural labor do Ecuadorian indigenous women receive social security protection, reinforcing the association between gendered racialization, minimal protection, and content-less citizenship. Income insecurity hence characterizes many rural indigenous women's lives and perspectives.[32] Over half of all indigenous women work without pay, compared with nearly 30 percent of nonindigenous women, and around the same percentage of indigenous men. As a result, indigenous women are less likely to make a monetary contribution to household livelihood. Whereas two-fifths of indigenous men bring in monetary income, only 21 percent of indigenous women could economically support their households (less than among nonindigenous women, where totals reached 27 percent) (Prieto 2005: 275–76, 284). In the early twenty-first century, whereas Ecuadorian indigenous workers received only 64 percent of nonindigenous salaries on average, the gap for indigenous women was even greater (Telles 2007).

In contexts of economic disempowerment, there are few examples of income generation that grant women autonomy and security in rural communities. Rural indígenas often search desperately for off-farm income but are faced with discrimination, particularly when they have little or no education (García-Aracil and Winter 2006; INEC 2008). Consequently, women's ability to earn money by weaving of shigra bags from *cabuya* (agave) fiber in the village of Nizag in southern Chimborazo is exceptional. Supported by village leaders and spouses, Nizag's women began to make the woven bags for local consumers and—crucially—tourists who come along the tourist railway to the internationally famous Nariz del Diablo site. Making the bags is a time-consuming task, undertaken in snatched moments outside the many other calls on their time; a large bag takes a month to complete. In remote villages women sell shigras to each other for under $10; in Nizag, by contrast, prices are treble that or more. Although Nizag appears to illustrate policy prescriptions for women to take off-farm work as discussed in chapter 1, in reality women's confidence and organizational capacity grew as a function of sustained kin and communal support, proximity to a major tourist hub, and dynamic female leadership that supported diversification into herbal tea production. In Ecuador's uneven postcolonial landscapes, few are the rural sites that can generate such off-farm employment and globally linked livelihoods. Most rural indigenous women are distant from, and face barriers to entering, wider secure political economies, despite craft fairs, fair trade, and tie-ins with tourist establishments, as sonala demonstrate.

> Rural women, to whom falls the majority of agricultural labor that feeds the country, are those with the worst labor conditions in terms of precarity and incomes. Moreover they face a greater workload than any other social group, being responsible for production, the commercialization of agricultural products as well as reproductive work at home, care work and tasks related to community organization. (Carrión and Herrera 2012: 147)

Women's labor contributions often remain unrecognized by household members, parents-in-law, husbands, and communities. Even in increasingly market-led economies, women's labor is undervalued.[33] In the central Andes, the devaluation of women's work has been naturalized to such an extent that neither indigenous women nor men recognize its significance. Tasks of social reproduction are often gendered as female in households, and married women or older daughters pick up tasks of cleaning, child care, and so on. Given the lack of infrastructure, social reproduction is extremely time-consuming and requires juggling of time and energy. Andean indígenas rely on firewood—and when cash is available, gas—for cooking. In Tsáchila villages, water is piped to house yards, but only one-third of Chimborazo rural households have piped water. Magdalena, from an inaccessible eastern village, told me, "I don't have water or electricity at home. I cook with gas. I supplement that with firewood, but you have to go far away to look for it. I get water from the springs, walking about twenty minutes as it's far away." Women in Chimborazo spend six times more hours than men cooking, three times longer washing and on child care (ODM Chimborazo 2007: 79). The location of development resources shapes the quality and nature of indigenous women's daily workloads; racialized geographies of abandonment result in poor provision of water and sewerage systems, making rural indigenous women's domestic work more burdensome than that of urban women or rural women outside contemporary internal colonies. In settlements without running water and electricity, women spend much time collecting the resources to wash clothes, care for small domestic animals, and prepare meals.[34] The highly monetized regional economy surrounding Tsáchila villages results in greater time spent on food purchase and travel. In other words despite very different environments and ethnocultural distinctions, Tsáchila and Kichwa women spend long hours in social reproduction, causing them to cut into time for rest and sleep. Moreover, indígenas' labor in social reproduction often remains unrecognized, as the bodies and lives they nurture are disdained in postcolonial hierarchies. National surveys comparing indigenous, Afro-Ecuadorian, and mestiza women found that on average women work eighteen hours more each week than men. This workload peaks among indigenous women in midlife, when reproductive and productive responsibilities require thirty hours' more input than indigenous men's.[35] Kichwa and Tsáchila rural women regularly work fourteen to sixteen hours daily, and in addition warmikuna in Chimborazo do the most domestic work at the same time that they undertake hours of extradomestic work equal to mestiza women (CONAMU 2006: 59) and which includes four to five hours in production, an amount equivalent to male agricultural work on the coast, although the latter then had afternoons free, whereas domestic labor keeps women busy into the evening. In Chimborazo, indígenas's organizations draw attention to their long workdays and demand equity between household members. According to a leader who lives in a small village, "women certainly work longer hours than men, and have hard work—even if they don't plow. Women get up at 4 a.m. to get everything done for example, breakfast, getting kids ready for school, and milking cows. Men stay in bed, and if men get up early then they just walk around the farm. They don't help the women by doing the chores."[36]

RESTRICTED CAPABILITIES: BARRIERS TO EDUCATION AND TRAINING

Postcolonial hierarchies expressed in social and place-specific abandonment in combination with the proximate factors of poverty, long days of work, and limited resources contribute in turn to indigenous women's disproportionate exclusion from sustained and quality formal education and training opportunities. Across Ecuador indigenous women—including Tsáchila and Kichwa—receive significantly lower access to all levels of education, meaning that over their lifetimes indigenous women acquire fewer endowed capabilities than nonindigenous women and indigenous men. Indigenous leader Nina Pacari (2002: 54) views this as a "structural problem," highlighting the compounded nature of postcolonial uneven development on educational investment in rural and indigenous areas.[37]

Although the national education gap between girls and boys closed during the 1990s, it did not do so among indigenous populations (Prieto et al. 2005: 175). Over the past decade, indigenous-majority districts tend to have the starkest gender inequality in educational achievement, particularly among older generations, reflecting the lesser value placed on girls' education in mestizo and indigenous households.[38] Faced with extreme poverty, families often decide against investment in girls' education, compounding the disadvantages associated with poor-quality rural schools. Poorer Kichwa and Tsáchila households rely on girls for child care of younger siblings and herding sheep, removing them from regular schooling. Sonala told me how they only recently started to have some access to formal education. In the early 1970s, the Tsáchila governor Abraham Calazacón was vehemently against schooling, viewing it as assimilation into mestizo national society, an attitude with strongly gendered effects. Yet resistance diminished in the mid-1980s, when village-based schooling was introduced; now the majority of under thirty-five-year-old women have complete primary education.

However, the take-up of secondary education is highly gendered among sonala and warmikuna. Among interviewees, their siblings, and their children, women outnumber men 6:1 among those with no education and among Tsáchila with only primary education 16:3. By contrast, four times as many men attend or have attended secondary education as women. In comparison with Kichwa, sonala's educational histories end sharply at the end of primary school, according to Tsáchila parents, because secondary schools are in Santo Domingo town, which is costly and time-consuming to access.[39] In these uneven landscapes of provision, young women are further tied to villages by social reproduction commitments (child care, or an ill parent). Now seventeen, Rosita left school at twelve years old, with completed primary bilingual education, to care for younger siblings and help her parents, yet her brothers continued to secondary school, one younger teenage sister attends literacy classes, with one eleven-year-old brother at primary school. The gendered power of ethnic nationalist discourse also contributes to women's disadvantage: Tsáchila public discourse represents the city as a sexually dangerous place for women, a site of seduction and sexual violence, representations that influence attitudes to city-based education for young women. "When mothers send their daughters to college, the [father/brother/male kin member] starts complaining, 'Why did you send her? She's going to flirt, to fill her tummy and then who's going to look after her. I'll kill you.' And that scares the women."[40] Young women internalize these discourses, aware too that distinctive clothing and surnames expose them to racial abuse. Nevertheless, a tiny share of sonala from wealthier households with progirl attitudes continues to university, a share in line with rates for indigenous women nationally.[41]

Warmikuna's access to education differs from Tsáchilas' due to uneven development and racialized postcolonial patterns of social abandonment, as well as variable impacts of male bias in households. From the mid-1980s the increasing number of women attending and completing primary education reflected state oil revenues and social policies.[42] Following provincial and national trends, the majority of warmikuna in their midthirties or younger have complete primary education from a village school.[43] Older cohorts were impacted more by internal colonialism; half of women over forty could access primary education solely in nearby canton capitals, meaning few received schooling.[44] However, interviewees' male and female children accede in equal proportions to primary education, reflecting the cash transfer program, which makes school attendance a condition. Nevertheless among Kichwa young women a bias against girls' *secondary* education remains in force, although this is less pronounced than among Tsáchila sonala. More male than female children receive some secondary education (42.9 percent and 31.5 percent respectively). Overall these patterns generate lower overall years of education for warmikuna in comparison with menfolk (4.5 years and 8.38 years, respectively, based on interviews) and nonindigenous women (see map 2.2).[45]

Gender, race, rural location, and low incomes generate qualitatively different schooling experiences. Asked about factors shaping educational

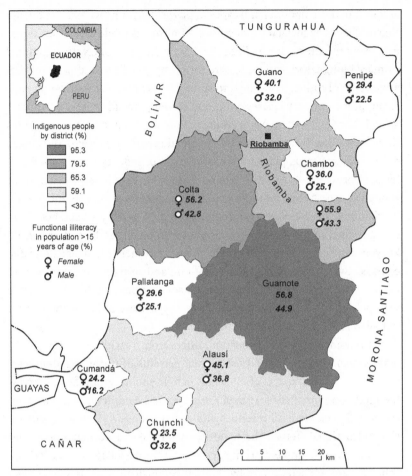

Map 2.2. Chimborazo province: indigenous population by district and gendered illiteracy rates, 2010. Map by the Cartographic Unit, Department of Geography, University of Cambridge.

access, Kichwa and Tsáchila indígenas mention poverty, followed by parents' lack of support (including male bias) and the illness or death of one or both parents. Although secondary schools are equally geographically distant for both groups, the majority of Kichwa girls currently pursue education beyond primary school at the nearby village *colegio*, an urban hub, or—among the poorest—at night school.[46] However, for children living in remote villages, families must decide whether to pay for irregular, costly daily transport or urban lodgings. The second of eight children, Ana completed one year of secondary education while working as a domestic in Riobamba; her younger brothers travel daily by bus to the district capital's secondary college. A few warmikuna continue education at night school while working as live-in domestic servants. Another woman told me how she gives $1 daily to her children for the school bus and lunch. With utility and transport prices rising as a result of neoliberal policies, indigenous households feel the pinch on family budgets, and older children have more precarious access to secondary education than younger siblings. With five children at school, Pilar explained, "My older children study in [canton capital] Cajabamba because going to Riobamba is too far and I don't have the money. The kids work and study."

Kichwa women's access to education is particularly obstructed during childhood by the loss of one or both parents due to death or marital breakdown. Orphans effectively miss formal education—if one parent dies, half receive no education, one-quarter receive three years, and the rest scrabble to complete primary. A father's death is particularly damaging to girls' education prospects, as widows command few means to make money and rely heavily on child labor to survive. These dynamics mean a father's death always entails a reduction or end to girls' primary education, in comparison with male siblings or children in households with a father. The death of both parents is comparable to that of a father, while the death of a girl's mother in childhood has a less significant impact on education history. Reverberating down the generations, these educational histories speak to the "political negation of life . . . who has priority to live and flourish, and who might be left to wither and die" (Tyner 2013: 702). Indigenous women are sharply critical of the poor quality of education provision and racist attitudes in rural indigenous-area schools. Ramona remembered how a quarter of a century ago, mestizo teachers "discriminated against us, they beat us, pulled our ears."

In our conversations women discussed education as an important sphere over which they felt little or no capacity to intervene, reflecting historic marginalization from classrooms and policy-making. As elsewhere in the Andes, nonstate education (known as popular education) has at times been more accessible to low-income rural groups than formal education. Progressive church-based organizations in Chimborazo provide literacy training, especially the Catholic dioceses' radio-based initiatives (Escuelas Radiofónicas Populares del Ecuador), which link with remote and older listeners. Now in her seventies, Sebastiana recounted how she and her husband listened to the radio and then shared information, countering a lack of formal education and familiarizing her with Spanish. Missionary nuns were active in Tsáchila villages in the mid-twentieth century, but no oral history remains of any popular education programs there. A recent state adult literacy program engaged a number of Kichwa and Tsáchila indígenas, who struggled to combine it with social reproduction and other responsibilities. Moreover, husbands are sometimes resistant to popular education because they are left with cooking and child care. A Kichwa woman in her forties with nine children explained, "Yes, I used to go to the literacy classes when I was single; I went to meetings too. But then I married and had children and couldn't go any more." Although welcomed by many women, literacy classes cannot compensate for other structural disadvantages.

Rural warmikuna and sonala struggle to match rising levels of formal education nationally. Historically and among older generations, illiterate women find it very difficult to get work or promotion (Almeida et al. 1991). Today schooling and fluency in Spanish raise women's capacity to protect their interests against mestizo power-holders yet do little to boost access to secure and better paid work, as rural poor-quality schooling imparts minimal skills that provide women no advantage relative to rural and urban indigenous men, let alone mestizos. Across the country, indigenous women's educational histories are changing with rising income and educational differentials and expectations regarding work. However, despite the near universal achievement of primary schooling and some Spanish fluency, younger generations are not guaranteed better work or status, as the goalposts of what counts as modern and "developed" are constantly shifting.

WOMEN'S PLACES: GENDER, RACIALIZATION, AND SOCIONATURAL RESOURCES

While chapter 1 traced the dispossession and internal colonialism in Ecuadorian development history, here Kichwa and Tsáchila women's position in these dynamics becomes the focus of attention. The relationship between land, work, and male-female control over resources varies across Ecuador's regions and ethnic nationalities due to the variable configurations of male-female relations, household structure, and inheritance patterns, rural economies and land markets, and specific usufruct rights. Kichwa and Tsáchila indígenas both experience racialized and gendered forms of control and mobility that condition their bare life, resulting in lesser command over land and resources than that of their male counterparts. The dynamics of gendered racialized dispossession also differ across these groups, suggesting that gender constitutes a crucial aspect of the dynamics and impact of internal colonization.[47] Although the vast majority of warmikuna and sonala rely on agriculture, they access less land and have less secure rights over land and natural resources than indigenous men and nonindigenous groups. Sonala's households have larger landholdings than warmikuna's, although the latter often have more economic autonomy (permitting them to hold land and run small farms independently). Yet rural indígenas, despite their differences, bear the brunt of skewed land distributions and male bias in agrarian policy and development.

Across Ecuador, one in five farmers has smallholder landholdings of under five hectares that total 1.7 percent of agricultural land, compared with 6 percent of farmers who control over 56 percent of agricultural land in holdings exceeding fifty hectares (Censo Agropecuario 2003: 10). In the Andes over four-fifths of rural households own less than five hectares of land-territory, as I also found talking to warmikuna in Chimborazo. In comparison with Andean families, Tsáchila households have larger extensions of land-territory, averaging five to twenty hectares, although these are small compared with average commercial mestizo farms.[48] In light of skewed land-territory distribution, Andean rural—especially indigenous—dwellers are smallholders, despite the adjudication of around 108 million hectares in the period 1954–1984 to Chimborazo associations that subsequently registered as comunas. In districts such as Guamote, over half of hacienda land was acquired by indigenous communities. Among the warmikuna interviewed, all have less than five hectares of land, and the majority (53.8 percent) have less than one hectare, a situation that places them firmly in the subaltern group regarding postcolonial land distribution, being reliant on small-scale sales as shown in fig. 2.1.

If indigenous women's land rights are insecure, the same is true of access to water and other socionatural resources.[49] Through gendered daily practices, Kichwa indígenas rely heavily on local firewood, pastureland, and water for irrigation and animals. Firewood provides household fuel, as other cooking fuels are too costly. According to indigenous women's elected leaders, women are actively involved in the integrated management of water, soil, plants, and animals in a holistic way as they create and manage microclimates by planting native tree species as windbreaks (Pacari 1998a; Vinding 1998), actively maintaining mutual care relations with what they consider to be more-than-human agents, part of Pachamama.[50] Gendered knowledge of landscapes and socionatural resources emerge from gender divisions of labor. Farming small, often steep, poor-quality plots away from irrigation water, warmikuna vividly understand everyday landscapes in terms of meager socionatural resources. Yet in many Andean irrigation systems, rights to water are registered to individual men, while formal registration of women's rights is uncommon (Boelens and Zwarteveen 2003; see Rodríguez 2007; Donato et al. 2007). Community problems, Andean

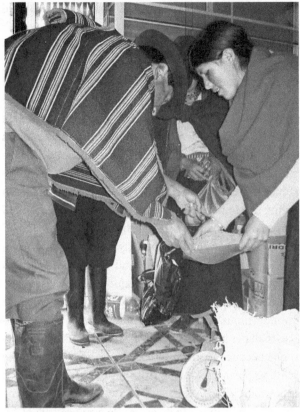

Fig. 2.1. Kichwa woman weighs out seed for sale, Quimiag, Chimborazo province. Photograph by the author.

indígenas say, include insufficient water and inadequate infrastructure for crops and women's exclusion from village irrigation committees. Indíge-nas combine a robust sense of a more-than-human socionature with politi-cal agendas of participation, justice, and redistribution, as later chapters document.

In Tsáchila and Kichwa areas, indígenas' access to wider spaces and free-dom of movement are constrained, yet the cultural meanings and specific consequences differ. Racial hierarchies and postcolonial state bias in infra-structure mean that indigenous areas are often least well served by paved and all-weather roads. Quimiag parish in Chimborazo had limited road ac-cess till the 1970s, and asphalt only in 2010. When women travel into urban centers, they are frequently demeaned on public transport in ways that draw attention to racialized-gendered bodies (Corporación Educativa Macac 1992; CEDIS 2001). Moreover, if two hours are required to get to the pharmacy or market, women have less time for organization and livelihoods. One of the starkest geographies of the divide between bare life and citizenship is that of health care provision, concentrated in urban mestizo areas and lacking quality and coverage in rural and especially indigenous-majority areas (Ecuarunari 1998: 8). Postcolonial landscapes of exclusion result in sick bodies that can barely afford to reach health care; Tsáchila communities lack clinics and pharmacies, and reaching hospitals costs the equivalent of three days' wages. In clinics, postcolonial intersectional hierarchies are reproduced by forcing indígenas to wait and not receive attention: one-third of racialized women are ignored at health centers, one-quarter are insulted, and 15 percent are treated with contempt (Luna Creciente n.d.). Rural indigenous women spend more time traveling to health centers than nonindigenous women and then wait twice as long to be seen, resulting in "more insalubrities, mortality, [and] infant mortality" (Gonzales Casanova 1965: 35; also Cuvi Sánchez and Ferraro 2000). In Riobamba, Chimborazo's capital, one woman found that "the only thing we received was mistreatment, indifference and coldness."[51] Rural low-income and racialized populations tend to lack social security, relying instead on godparents and gifts to bridge the gap between abandonment and poor-quality care. Although the majority of Chimborazo's households are in poverty, state social programs fail to reach racialized populations: free maternity care reaches a mere 3.6 percent of the province's households, subsidized preschool care 4.4 percent, mobile health clinics 4.9 percent, and free school meals 26 percent (CEPAR Chimborazo 2004: 27).

As with all geographies and mobilities, it is social relations and representations that weigh heavily on indigenous women's experiences (McDowell 1999). Gossip and social opprobrium curtail Kichwa and Tsáchila women's mobility and agency on a daily basis. Senior male kin are usually the authority figures in Kichwa households, as one woman recounted: "The men are always first with all decisions. The man lets his wife know his decision and if she says no, it's bound to create problems."[52] Kichwa warmikuna face rumors and criticisms if they spend too much time away from home or if they gather to talk in a public space with neighbors. In response, women's organizations work to establish meeting halls, although communal leaders are often reluctant to grant a building plot, still less pay for a *casa de mujeres* (women's house).[53] However, over recent years Andean rural women are

Fig. 2.2. Tsáchila woman in her kitchen. Photograph by the author.

becoming decision-makers in households and village meetings, negotiating alternative forms of decision-making and female agency (chapter 6). Kichwa women also have regular engagement with urban spaces, with the city represented as a space for education and work. By contrast, Tsáchila women are more firmly tied into extended families and village spaces and disciplined by gossip and social discourses to reduce their extravillage mobility. As Nira explained, "women start to lose confidence; there are rumors. We Tsáchila are very gossipy, saying that a woman didn't go to a jewelry-making workshop but went to see a young man." One discourse articulated by Tsáchila men and women concerns the city of Santo Domingo, viewed as a place of sexual danger for young women, as it permits contact with mestizo men—described as all-powerful and wily—who might seduce or assault them (compare Weismantel 2001).

Due to the interlocking dimensions of gender, race, rural location, and low income, indigenous women are positioned in resource geographies differentially from indigenous men, nonindigenous women, and nonindigenous men. In addition to gendered geographies of dispossession, Kichwa and Tsáchila indígenas, such as the sona pictured in fig. 2.2, are subject to social controls over mobility, public presence, and decision-making that in combination shape their lives on a daily basis.

In the colonial present, indigenous women are constituted in relations whereby "violations of [dominant] rules of courtesy, language, dress, tone of voice on the part of Indians often provokes violent verbal and physical abuse from [mestizos]" (Gonzales Casanova 1965: 35). Far from being a neutral sphere of citizenship, public space for indigenous women exposes them to racist comments and treatment, in turn informing their critique of development's failures. Extending discussion of postcolonial development, this section explores the sites and practices through which indigenous women come to understand themselves relationally as racialized subjects and different from unmarked and dominant embodiments.

Indigenous women are continuously exposed to discriminatory behavior in ways that differentiate them from indigenous men and from women and men of other racial-ethnic populations (Stoler 1995, Kellogg 2005, Garcés Dávila 2006). Indigenous women experience what Frantz Fanon calls the "epidermalization"[54] of marginalization physically and psychically through quotidian violence and sexism. Women are the first to draw attention to how they are subject to worse racial discrimination than indigenous men in daily encounters with primary school teachers, development extension workers, government officials in justice departments, city council offices, mestiza men and women, NGO workers, and merchants.[55] Andean women told me how when they sell small piles of vegetables in urban markets, consumers frequently comment in racist language about their products, hygiene, and education, reasserting racial privilege and disavowing common humanity. Away from indigenous-majority villages, women face more overt discrimination than their male counterparts, especially in provincial towns, where women's distinctive clothing, less confident Spanish, and rural clothing mark them out. In indigenous-majority Cotopaxi province in the central Andes, more women than men agreed that indigenous-mestizo relations were no better today than in the past (Arboleda 2006: 206). In my conversations in Chimborazo, women spoke movingly about how due to lack of Spanish fluency or limited schooling, they feel vulnerable in the city, hypersensitized to underlying epistemic violence. Humiliated by putting a thumbprint on a document, or unable to calculate prices at speeds demanded by consumers, indigenous women experience in direct and quotidian ways a harsh reminder of how their bodies are produced in postcolonial exclusion. Rural indigenous women are dehumanized, a denial of humanity quite distinct from the treatment awarded to market cholas (Weismantel 2001;

compare Swanson 2007). Yet, as later chapters document, indígenas' organizations politicize such experiences of racialized-gendered discrimination
in struggles against discrimination and for rights "in what she buys and
sells, and in the goods she holds" (Seminario Internacional 1992: 40; Cunningham et al. 2008; Cunningham et al. 2009).

Like indígenas across the country, Kichwa and Tsáchila women are also
subject to the racialized gendered biopolitical distinctions that operate
at the national level (chapter 1). Indigenous women's lives—and those of
their children—are routinely lost because of government decisions about
where to place health centers and staff. As a result, indigenous midwives
are often the only health workers active in remote areas and rarely receive
state support.[56] In rural poorly serviced areas, maternal and child mortality rates are considerably above national averages and consistently worse
for indigenous than nonindigenous populations.[57] Living in the Andean
community of Aulla Grande, Celia saw five of her children die and only
two sons survive. Chimborazo continues to have the high rate of malnutrition of children under five of 86 percent, a pattern similar to that found in
Tsáchila communities.

The disciplinary effects of intersections of gender, racialization, and place
also work down to the scale of the village and household, reinforcing indigenous women's embodiment in postcolonial hierarchies. Relative to indigenous male bodies, Kichwa women's bodies are accorded less significance
and value; at birth, boy children are generally more welcome and granted
more resources, values perpetuated by communal and national norms.[58]
Women marry in their late teenage years; some leave marriage until their
late twenties and then frequently are closely managed by mothers-in-law.
Men remarry quickly if widowed in order to ensure child care and reproductive work, whereas women may decline to marry again. Single warmikuna
mothers are sometimes stigmatized and blamed for pregnancy, making
them subject to violence and, at times, being forced into marriages with
older men or widowers. Single motherhood in the central Andes may also
result in women being excluded from the rights associated with being a
comuna member (comunera) (CONAIE-UNFPA et al. 2009: 42). Also in the
Andes, mothers are blamed if children do badly at school, whereas fathers
are praised for children's educational success.[59] The prevalence of intra-
familiar violence constitutes a stark reminder of the consequences of gendered power relations (chapters 5 and 6). Identifying indigenous men as the
proximate cause for indigenous women's disadvantage, however, remains

only part of female subaltern experience, as discrimination is constituted at multiple scales and in relational terms set by the colonial present. An articulate experienced national female leader explained how women become complicit in antiwomen practices: "So it's a system that society has imposed, that . . . women are for beating, that we can't get ahead. But women say, 'What a shame that it's a baby girl! Although now I'll have help in the kitchen!' But who said women are the cooks?"

As nationalist representations of indigeneity increasingly focused on cultural distinctiveness (chapter 1), so too Kichwa and Tsáchila women's embodiments were increasingly understood as cultural, although in different ways and for different reasons. Tsáchila men and women are represented as an unthreatening Other in the national imaginary, while Tsáchila women have come to symbolize the interface between postcolonial nationalism and ethnic identity. The Tsáchila nationality received central government support from the late 1970s to protect a threatened "traditional" culture for the nation. Subsequently, their leaders placed a high premium on cultural purity, setting them against state education and in favor of in-group marriage, an ethnonational politics that has women's bodies at its heart. Women's role is to reproduce culture (language, dress, knowledge) and the next generation of Tsáchila; the majority of them marry at around thirteen to fifteen years (younger than Kichwa women), and begin childbearing early, such that grandmothers in their fifties might have ten children, and twice as many grandchildren. Racialized-gendered-rural subjectivities hence suture together intimate kin and marriage relations with postcolonial national histories of creating an "indigenous slot" (Li 2000). Tsáchila statutes and communal sanctions work to police gendered embodiments, with village-level rules against women's marriage with non-Tsáchila (mestizo; in tsafiki *fetola*) men. By contrast Tsáchila men are freer to marry mestiza women and induct them into ethnic culture (for biopolitical consequences, see chapter 5).[60]

By contrast, central Andean Kichwa are represented in national postcolonial discourses as ambivalently modern, peasants on the way to becoming mestizos, although the region appears prominently in imaginative geographies as a site of large indigenous populations. Rural Kichwa women's embodiment reflects differentiated and often personalized negotiations of cultural expression, income, and strategies to avoid racism, calculations that influence women's clothing, use of kichwa or Spanish, and social interactions (Weismantel 2001; Nelson 2006). The centrality of Chimborazo to national understandings of Kichwa culture reflects the embattled racism of Riobamba's elites, as well as Kichwa serving to "represent" a stereotyped indigenous population in the mainstream imaginary.

✾

Kichwa and Tsáchila women hence share experiences of lesser access to education and livelihood resources (land, irrigation water, viable product markets, and dignified off-farm work) and of greater racism relative to the majority of men in their group. Previous research suggests that for many indigenous groups, female-male differences are greater than in the national population.[61] The Kichwa and Tsáchila counter-topography suggests otherwise. In Ecuador, the official data evidence a greater gap between indigenous and nonindigenous women's development indicators, than between indigenous men and women.[62] Ecuadorian indigenous women are much more likely to be in poverty than other groups. The counter-topography reveals that however much male and female differentiation occurs in ethnic settlements (in education, access to land and resources, lesser validation of female bodies), these differentials are qualitatively distinctive from experiences meted out to racialized subaltern subjects in regional labor markets, urban product markets, and disciplining practices of racialization. Kichwa and Tsáchila lives moreover highlight how compound inequalities force indígenas to rely on ethnic communities, indigenous men and kin, and self-exploitation. Structural forces that concatenate interlocking social differences are replicated on a daily basis, ensuring that indígenas bodies are constantly produced as less educated, less fluent in Spanish, less able to signal their modernity, less authoritative in public spaces, and less able to command regular supplies of water, sewerage, electricity, and health care. Sociospatial differentiation along these lines compounds and naturalizes stereotypes of indigenous women, just as it produces a landscape and society fractured by social heterogeneity.[63]

Gendered-raced-class intersectionality moreover arises in located configurations of modernity, indigeneity, political economies, culture, and socionatures. Despite shared experiences of racism, dispossession, limited education, and lives of hard labor, warmikuna and sonala differ because of the spaces and intersectional power relations they inhabit, arising in different moments of colonization and sociocultural accommodations to uneven political economies. Kichwa insecure peasant economies differentiate them from Tsáchila commercial production; Kichwa gender relations generate marriage and kin relations distinctive from Tsáchila ones; and the two groups are positioned differently in national postcolonial narratives about indigeneity. However, the counter-topography reveals how these factors are only three of a multifaceted set of power relations and inequalities that mold indígenas' lives on a daily basis. Tsáchila women are relatively more subordinate to male-dominated family economies and defensive ethnic identifications, bolstered by a postcolonial state interested in cultural protection. Kichwa women are relatively autonomous economic, political, and social subjects yet remain subordinate in regional racialized socioeconomies and a historically established zone of social abandonment. Hence a key difference between them comprises agency, mobilization, and organization. Kichwa women mobilize individually and in networks to make a living and protest conditions, despite long hours of work and self-exploitation. Tsáchila women by contrast operate more within kin groups, and although a few individuals network, they are the minority (chapters 3, 5, 6). Looking closely at Kichwa warmikuna's and Tsáchila sonala's relations with production, reproduction, mobility, and resources brings into focus their lives' remoteness from mestizo dreams of progress and from stereotypes about "indigenous women" found in national policy thinking. On the one hand Chimborazo's indígenas break dominant expectations about adult femininity, as warmikuna are active farmers, while public racism and social abandonment remain unacknowledged in public policy.[64] On the other hand Tsáchila women experience settler encroachment on historic territories in gendered dynamics that remain unspoken in policy debates. Although gendered-racialized in ways that match national—and global—expectations about "indigenous women," Tsáchila women are in fact highly diverse in terms of land, education, resource control, and occupations. Chapter 1 documented how single-issue models of social difference were built into development thinking and institutions in postcolonial Ecuador and were characterized by the epistemological, political, and institutional separation of gender empowerment from multiculturalism. Exploring Tsáchila and Kichwa women's lives in the round demonstrates vividly how indígenas' experiences are qualitatively enmeshed across these lines of single issue development, being inextricably coconstituted through gender and race-ethnicity, rural locations and low incomes, arising from processes that disempower them as racialized, gendered, located, and dispossessed subalterns. Rather than Ecuadorian policy's neat separation of gender and race-ethnicity, the counter-topography highlights how racialized-gendered-class-locational (as well as sexuality/social reproduction) dispossession and inequality are lived simultaneously. Interlocking dimensions of postcolonial intersectionality on daily, annual, and generational timescales shine a light on the inadequacy of single issue development as a response to social heterogeneity in postcolonial settings. Moreover, the Tsáchila and Kichwa counter-topography reveals that the experience of being an indigenous woman varies significantly through lifetimes and across ethnic group, shaped by regional political economy, and spatially-uneven expressions of postcolonial nationalism.[65] Woven through the account too are elements of indígenas' sharp critiques of their situation, critiques that move center stage in the next section.

"We Work with Our Anxiety, We Work on Our Own": Discontent with Postcolonial Development

Linked as it is to agency, counter-topography captures "the specific ways globalization works on particular grounds in order to work out a situated, but at the same time, scale-jumping and geography-crossing, political response to it" (Katz 2001a: 1216). Given daily lives molded by racism, abandonment, and exclusion, indígenas quickly come to view development not with policymakers' expectant hopes but with critical dissatisfaction. Their words bring into focus the aspects of social heterogeneity that exist beyond development's remit and understanding and which tend to subsume them into policy categories of "women," "rural," "culturally different," "indigenous," and so on. As Gayatri Spivak was the first to point out, the subaltern cannot easily be represented as a singular category without perpetuating injustices against individual women's lives, an insight echoed by Ecuadorian indígenas' critical accounts. Indigenous women's situated knowledges about development projects and broader restructuring of political economies are thus forged at the margins of development (Marchand and Parpart 1995). National narratives of development progress promise coherence and continuity, yet for racialized rural women development interventions are fractured, episodic, and uneven. Their critical perspectives reveal not only the depth of their discontent—at times, cynicism—but also reveal an important insight with profound substantive and theoretical consequences. Namely, indigenous women—due to their positionality in development—offer key insights into the limitations of development in dealing with social heterogeneity. Listening to indígenas' narratives of development provides insights into the processes behind development's limitations in dealing with postcolonial intersectionality because of its institutional, epistemological, and imaginative limits.

Indigenous women's critiques of daily apprehensions of development (or indeed lack of it) arise directly from the contexts I have described here, reflecting the intrinsically intersectional nature of disadvantage as well as the multifaceted consequences of exclusion. In a context of postcolonial abandonment, by default development does not deliver any improvement in indígenas' situation. In response, indigenous women's agendas question decision-making authority over resource allocation, call for domestic relations and divisions of labor to be recalibrated, and critique developmental project logistics and interactions. Subsequent chapters explore indigenous women's agendas in detail; I begin here with an introductory witnessing of the systematic and informed nature of women's discontent and articulacy. While critiques of development are by no means unique to indigenous women, the goal of understanding social heterogeneity in postcolonial settings prompts the following questions: what do indigenous women's unique perspectives on development tell us about the nature of postcolonial interventions? And in what ways can social heterogeneity be comprehended through paying attention to the accumulated experience of racialized subaltern women? Prompted by indígenas' insights, this section argues that social heterogeneity in postcolonial settings concerns the production of knowledge and its authorization within the power structures that shape resource distribution and policy design. Development works within authorized forms of knowledge production and application whereby indigenous women are deauthorized as interlocutors and theorists. Postcolonial development consequently deals with social heterogeneity on its own terms, with the effect of taking measures that are insufficient, inappropriate, and inadequate for female racialized subalterns.

Shaped by uneven landscapes of dispossession and abandonment, especially in Andean Kichwa areas, women's words reveal deep disappointment and cynicism with respect to development's limited scope, inappropriate framing of issues, delivery, and assumptions. Questioned about her development experiences, Gabriela, a low-income warmi in her early forties with six children, launched into her response with passion:

> The [technicians] treat it just like practice for them. Not because they are going to help or going to get better grain production, that's a lie. It's more they are going to practice, and are going to learn *from* us, peasants who plant [crops]. That's what they learn, because if I and my kin plant we haven't used [agronomists]. The community will explain how to plant this and that, but sometimes better. But they are going to give some treatments, some fumigant although that dries out the potatoes. That's what the technicians do, not because they are going to help.

And then with harvest, it's not as if the professionals are going to help! Sure, they offer, they say "we'll help," that they're practical and they know. But it's a lie. Rather they do the opposite—there in the community I tell you how many technicians, how many professionals have there been. But they haven't improved anything for us! They offer, yes, to help improve the llamas, improve lambs, but where is that [improvement]? At no time did they actually come to help with the llamas, nothing!

What appears to policy-makers and governments as a will to improve is interpreted, at one disillusioned extreme, as an active process of dismissal of indígenas' practical knowledge. A number of indigenous women angrily describe themselves as abandoned by the state and development efforts in comparison with urban centers and mestizo rural districts. According to a Kichwa woman in her thirties, "no project has come to improve agriculture, and women are too tired to go out and get a project. We work with our own anxiety, work on our own." Such interjections are then collated into demands, exemplified by this agenda from Chimborazo's rural women in the late 1990s: "We demand the recuperation of land (together with irrigation water, soil improvement and credit), the implementation of projects that take indigenous women's specificities into account and that do not add to their existing workloads and improve quality of life. We demand extra resources, and question the language of Andean communities that makes discrimination against women invisible" (ACDI-FUNDAMYF 1998: 122–23).

Other women more patiently explain the various barriers to women's agency and well-being constituted in and through existing development procedures. Sitting in her shared municipal office, a Kichwa extension worker explained how if a woman wants to increase milk production, she has to plan to buy a cow. Then, assuming her husband agrees and cosigns the application for credit, she has to improve the pastureland, despite women's difficulties in accessing support, credit, and the land itself. Finally, in this hypothetical case, she has to get irrigation water, perhaps breaking gendered norms to work at night. As the majority of rural indigenous women I spoke to made clear, existing development structures and routines do not help them take these steps. Meanwhile, interventions to support rural impoverished racialized women are severely compromised by racism and colonial presumptions that result in women's knowledge and perspectives being ignored. As a result—and in common with many rural women in the global South—Ecuadorian indigenous women experience development at one remove. Policy and state programs do not consider them to be farmers or managers of natural resources, leaving them as recipients of small, often "add-on," project components. Key to indigenous women's understandings of development then is their acute awareness of the consequences of being "beneficiaries" within highly structured forms of knowledge production in which interlocking hierarchies work to disavow and marginalize subaltern women's knowledges.

Tsáchila and Kichwa women experience development as a series of short-term, stop-start projects, which are generally characterized by little sustainability over time, and inadequate recognition of their unique insights and perspectives. In other words, in addition to the problems faced by many rural women in the global South, project structures and inbuilt policy assumptions about the intersections of gender and race-ethnicity entail specific consequences as they result in development interventions being fractured, disparate, and uneven. Agricultural and livestock technicians employed by projects are generally male and mestizo, reinforcing postcolonial embodied hierarchy and authorizing mainstream knowledge over others. Such practices arise in the context of and compound indigenous women's disempowerment vis-a-vis indigenous and nonindigenous men. In a survey in rural Andean Cotopaxi province, one in ten women said they could not participate in activities due to distance, whereas no indigenous men identified this as a problem (Arboleda 2006: 202; see chapter 3 on participatory development).

The primary reason for indígenas' discontent lies with their invisibility in rural development initiatives and lack of participation. Building on assumptions in the colonial present about gender relations and rural livelihoods, governments and agencies often allocate a secondary position in project design to women. Development policy frequently makes assumptions about women, a factor that is especially true of indigenous women, whose lives and realities are often unknown by decision-makers and agencies. As a group, indigenous women are often not perceived as farmers in policy, and this is a particularly resilient and unhelpful assumption, as indigenous women have an established role in rural and agricultural livelihoods. Rural racialized women's material labor and inputs of knowledge are hence made invisible in development's standard forms of knowledge production in census taking, public debates, and policy thinking. As noted in chapter 1, mestizo development workers frame indigenous women's concerns within a powerful Andean discourse that "knows" that a stable equilibrium exists between women and men in indigenous communities and that project benefits trickle down to all. Development policy thereby perpetuates formulations that channel and restrict the types of projects relevant to supposedly "culturally purer" indigenous women (Barrig 2006: 110). As policy documents and state programs do not consider indigenous women to "be" farmers or managers of natural resources, this leaves them incompletely or inappropriately identified.

Male-dominated state and NGO approaches interlock in some cases with communal patriarchies, resulting in restrictions on women's participation in project implementation and management.[66] Mestizo modernization policy treated women as secondary or residual in rural development, especially in DRI programs. Through the 1970s and 1980s, rural racialized women came to be known as the embodiment of backward-looking, traditional actors who were insufficiently educated to take on the task of modernizing agriculture. Hence DRI programs failed to address racialized rural women as valid interlocutors or to build a form of knowledge that took ethnoracial-gendered differences into account, nor were they pressured to do so by the National Women's Council. In major 1980s rural development programs such as DRI and FODERUMA, a Ministry of Agriculture program for peasant women "had a limited impact on the improvement of poor women's situation in the countryside (incomes and modifications of traditional gender relations)" (Cuvi Sánchez 2000: 19; also Hamilton 1998: 25). Indigenous women hence tend to interact with development at one remove and experience project interventions as episodic, small-scale, and short-term because components associated with women tend to be "additions" that result in little sustainability over time. When rural projects do incorporate indígenas, the knowledge about their situation is minimal and shot through with stereotypes forged through coloniality-modernity.

One dimension of colonial-development knowledge production is the denial of bona fide farmer status to women because of expectations about the embodied capacity and experience of agricultural field labor. The deniability of female field labor is particularly forceful in relation to indígenas, whose cumulative histories of split field-hacienda-home work and whose timeless representations as a-historically cultural, not economic, actors mean that their racialized-female-rural bodies yet again take them outside the frame of development (chapter 1). As a result, agricultural training programs are directed to rural indigenous men, although Andean women are the more constant presence in communities impacted by outmigration (Barrig 2006: 110). Ecuador's 2003 Agrarian Census found that less than 1 percent of women had received training in agricultural and livestock activities, although with high levels of male rural outmigration that training is more urgent than ever. Indígenas are quick to draw attention to these deficits in development planning. According to a female Chimborazo leader, "in agriculture and livestock farming women are those who work on the land or with the animals. But unfortunately the training courses are always done for men, not with women. So this is how all governments fail! The men with the training are out of the country!"[67] Her statement draws attention to a paradox that arises in that when development fails to reverse declining security, it boosts male migration and cuts women off from resources, skills, and authority. Projects are slow to catch up with this reality by appointing women as extension workers; local "promoters" are more often men than women.[68] A mismatch continues to exist between indigenous women's inputs into rural households' maintenance and well-being and the status they are accorded in projects and programs. Hence, although women make up a large share of the country's foodstuff producers, their national importance is neither recognized nor valued.

Represented as racialized homemakers, indigenous women cannot easily access credit independently, a constant refrain of complaint from Andean women. In addition to impacting access to health care (Wade 2009: 33; also chapter 5), such attitudes inform financial institutions' dealings with them (CONAMU 2004: 37). In part indigenous women are less likely than indigenous men and nonindigenous women to be legal titleholders to land and so lack collateral required for loans (Cuvi Sánchez 2000: 23). Dominant postcolonial assumptions about marital relations also surprise indigenous women, who become frustrated at what they perceive as costly, time-consuming procedures that require the husband to be the primary household decision-maker.[69] As Andean women consider themselves to be producers and economic agents, they cannot understand these strictures. Chimborazo women frequently told me about unsuccessful credit applications; three-fourths of them reported being turned down for credit from standard financial sources.[70] Brought up by her grandmother and with incomplete primary education, middle-aged Concepción told me: "The problem is credits and things because they don't want to approve us women [for a loan]. Why? Because I'm not living with my husband but I don't have a divorce. So they don't give me a loan. We make an effort there for nothing." Ecuador's major rural development program provided credit via the BNF but made no provision to overcome postcolonial expectations about marital interests. Instead the BNF reproduced gender-biased dynamics by permitting husbands' sole signature on male applications while demanding a husband's signature or power when women applied for credit.[71] In this context it comes as no surprise to note that only 3 percent of rural female-headed households nationally are perceived as credit-worthy.[72] Sonala in interviews foresaw few alternatives to bank credit, speaking of credit as something managed and controlled by husbands and formal institutions, not a resource for themselves. By contrast, Andean women were familiar with informal savings and credit clubs known as *cajas de ahorro* or *cajas solidarias*. These cajas operate as local savings schemes managed by and for women, offering small sums requiring no collateral and paid back through informal economic activities.[73] As a result, cajas are a lifeline for indígenas, especially when they are separated or widowed, as they provide alternatives to development's standard model. Asunción spoke movingly about how she had been denied bank credit but was now organizing a caja with other women. Her words, however, highlight how feelings of marginalization and denial inform the politicization of exclusion: "Our sadness is making us go out and look for our rights. We indigenous women have the right to make demands."[74] Querying the analytical separation of development versus rights, programs versus citizenship, Asunción's words articulate a vision of agency and well-being, a decolonial reading of postcolonial landscapes (chapters 6 and 7).

Through mestizo developmentalism and beyond, government projects frequently considered women—specifically indigenous women—as worthy only of add-on and smaller scale interventions. As documented extensively across the global South, "women-sized" projects tend to be smaller in scale and scope than "general" programs that by default are oriented to men (Kabeer 1994). Moreover, small-scale "add women in" components are easily dropped if staff members leave or budgets drop. Following this trend in the Andes, rural women are offered help with home gardens (*huertos familiares*) rather than farms, or with small animals such as chickens and guinea pigs rather than cattle, decisions that perpetuate male-female inequalities in livelihood options and resources (Vinding 1998). Reflecting these gendered models, an NGO survey in Chimborazo found that village women's associations were involved in fifteen crafts projects, ten small animal management schemes, eight agricultural training efforts, four organizational initiatives, and one housing project (ACDI-FUNDAMYF 1998). When I talked to warmikuna, they recalled more training in care of cuyes than in agriculture and livestock. The CONAIE women's representative, Norma Mayo, responded angrily to this presumption, protesting, "Micro-credit, micro-project! Everything's micro when it comes to [planning for] indigenous women!" Norma's frustration speaks to how policies emerge out of postcolonial intersectionality that naturalizes female subalterns' exclusion from macroeconomic decisions and project planning (an experience common to impoverished rural women, regardless of race-ethnicity) and the biopolitical abandonment of racialized areas and subjects in the name of national development (specific to racialized rural women). National development banks, governments, and planners all make the assumption that they "know what's best" for indigenous women, a claim that is founded on coloniality's forms of knowledge production and that underpins epistemic violence against subaltern border knowledges.[75] Taking the indígenas' standpoint, by contrast, shines light on the underbelly of development, the allocation of small projects to deal with huge problems, and the dehumanization of rural female subalterns that naturalizes disproportionate marginalization. In Chimborazo, a church-based group decided that they would rather trade among themselves than with intermediaries so established a dry goods store in the provincial capital near to the markets. Staffed by warmikuna, the store represents "what we've been thinking about, talking about, becoming conscious of—gaining an identity, an economy," a woman dressed in full skirts and shawl told me, as we sat in a room behind the shop chatting.

As well as faulting interventions' bee-sting size, indígenas articulate a stringent critique of how development interventions are experienced on the ground as a series of episodic interventions at random and inexplicable intervals. In the words of Sonia, a married warmi in her early thirties with some primary education, "it would be better not to go to workshops; instead of that, we could stay working." Norma, CONAIE's elected women's representative, drawing on her knowledge accrued through hearing indígenas' anger at numerous meetings, told me: "As for development, there has been occasional support for instance in micro-enterprises and animal tending but generally these have not covered all of [indigenous] women's needs. They've been left out. There have been very few [projects] that followed through, and of course other projects failed."[76] Indigenous women are particularly vulnerable to the temporal and spatial unevenness of development interventions as NGOs move in and out of areas on the basis of short-term or unfixed budgets. For instance, an international agency organized a leadership training program for village sonala, hoping to boost women's participation in decision-making, but the project stopped after a few years (chapter 4). Lucía, a Kichwa woman in her late thirties, recounted her experience: "Yes, [extension workers] have come to give small courses to producers, but these have been really small. We understood a little, and sometimes we didn't understand anything. They only explained in Spanish. They treated us OK but when you don't understand the course it's boring. It's that some understand, others not—the older women don't understand."[77] As across the global South, Ecuadorian rural development is frequently implemented via a series of short, one-day training workshops to introduce means to improve productivity or boost animal health. Rural sonala recount that any training they received personally has come from parents and relatives rather than project staff.[78] By contrast Claudia, a warmi without formal schooling, had this to say about workshops: "Yes, the NGO people used to come and they taught us about land, about products, how to sell and harvest them. Also some technicians used to come to teach us how to work with animals." According to a CONAIE women's representative, indígenas cannot make up for lack of formal education with endless short workshops: "This money is invested or the training given, but there is no follow-through, there is no continuity."[79] Project training for village women represents temporary interruptions in a grueling routine and offers minimal impacts.

Indigenous leaders take these experiences and transform them into a critique of postcolonial development for failing to address systematic disadvantage, and they voice racialized subalterns' claims to dignity and resources.[80] The disconnection between the harsh realities of indígena lives and rural development procedures becomes not merely a question of "filling in the gaps," but a core contest over knowledge and power. Indigenous women feel that despite the workshops, the visits from agricultural extension workers, and the endless meetings, they are not being listened to. Indígenas may on average have fewer years of formal schooling than other Ecuadorians, yet their circumstances and shared discussion (especially among Andean warmikuna) give rise to insights with critical purchase on the dilemmas of difference in development thinking and practice. According to Mercedes, a woman in her early fifties who gained a primary education at night school and catechism classes, "we want . . . to converse, we want to say things. But people don't take any notice of us! We cannot talk, we cannot say anything. So that we women too are made to be afraid, not say anything. We cannot talk, all this! So out of that there is nothing! That's it. We have these problems but people don't want to understand. And that's the problem we have." As these powerful words demonstrate, indigenous women can speak and incisively identify how they are marginalized from mainstream development. Through such critiques they additionally contribute to a reformulation of what development is and might be, and they do so primarily by changing the problem, resituating development not as a technical "fix" but as primarily a contest over knowledge and meaning. Indigenous women vary in how they view development, with some being very skeptical, if not antidevelopment, while others persistently hold out hope for the next project to deliver something useful: the vast majority share harsh criticisms of where development has gone wrong.[81]

Situating development within a decolonial frame highlights how certain subjects and knowledges are validated as expert while subaltern experiences are dismissed as noise, an unfortunate but improvable challenge to development's secure ability to accumulate better thinking and practice. Indigenous women identify these epistemological challenges at the interface between development workers and beneficiaries. Previous research documents how Andean development professionals come from a tradition where development equals modernity and indigenous women represent a problem for progress.[82] Development hence creates encounters between indígenas and a group that has the authority, arising from postcolonial privilege, to draw on professional knowledge while denying validity to indígenas' understanding and extensive practical learning about development and its failures. Devised and implemented by nonindígena subjects, interventions frequently ignore the social reproductive workloads that reflect interlocking factors of male-female difference, geographies of social abandonment, and poverty, as policy-makers are poor at grasping the ways postcolonial intersectional hierarchies shape the development experiences of rural female subalterns.[83] Extension training via workshops assumes that women can find free time to attend. In scheduling the number, timetables, and frequency of workshops, development workers neither consider women's workloads nor provide child care, as both aspects are outside development's thinking. Without these provisions, projects risk increasing women's workload without taking away any existing commitments.[84] According to an indigenous woman employed in the national electoral agency in 2010, "a comparison between indigenous and mestiza women is that mestizas can just go to meetings and participate but that we indigenous women stay at home because we live far away. So that is how we end up being denied."[85] In some cases, women have to travel to workshops using irregular and costly transport from remote areas, which in turn contributes to less regular involvement in decision-making and resource distribution. Moreover, not attending meetings reinforces women's disconnection from development, in ways that legitimize and obscure their broader invisibility in postcolonial development. In rural indigenous-majority Cotopaxi province, men outnumbered women two to one among those who knew about the provincial development plan (Arboleda 2006). In this case and others, participatory development not only lulls development staffers into a false sense of security about their knowledge of the situation

(Mosse 1994) but moreover naturalizes policy's shorthand and incomplete knowledge of social heterogeneity and the diverse interests that entails.

Intrinsic to women's articulation of their situation is the foundational principle that their public presence in development is legitimate and non-negotiable (Phillips 1995). They claim the right to use public space freely, the right to gather and move without gossip or spousal disapproval and to take part in public decision-making. Whether in communal meeting halls or on public transport, indigenous women wish to be free from a disciplinary gaze (see Fanon 1986 [1952]). In community decision-making, women may attend in large numbers, but their voices are muted or silenced, resulting in male-biased decisions. According to a Tsáchila female community leader, "sometimes, the husband says, 'you're not going to a meeting; you have to do your household chores.' " So the woman does that; in most cases women don't go to workshops." Similar male attitudes are encountered in Andean areas, although rural public cultures in Chimborazo grant increasing validity to women's gatherings, especially when they generate household incomes. Women meet among themselves or with a woman's representative of the local federation, generating energetic and voluble debates. Nevertheless, women struggle to establish independent semipublic spaces to meet and coordinate (chapter 6). On the slopes of Chimborazo mountain, Nitiluisa women's association worked for years to collect the resources to build an independent permanent "women's house," where they organize craft production and hold meetings. Likewise in Nizag, southern Chimborazo, women have a craft center in part funded by NGOs.

As these cases demonstrate, indigenous women's priorities and interests are not always identical to village men's. Indígenas' meetings frequently find them talking bitterly about "overwork" and the deliberate ignorance about their domestic contributions. In the words of one woman, "the responsibilities of the house should be shared, in agriculture, in the care of animals too. We both have two hands; men could help to wash, to cook" (quoted in CEDIS 2007a). In highland Cotopaxi province, two-thirds of indigenous women said they had no time to participate in community activities, whereas only one-third of indigenous men complained of this limit (Bourque and Warren 1981; Arboleda 2006: 202). Although these issues are not unique to indigenous households, postcolonial racial hierarchies exacerbate indigenous women's lack of time and the daily grind of dealing with uneven postcolonial public infrastructures. These dynamics have a direct impact on indigenous women's responses to potential development projects. An NGO ecotourism venture in Guamote district, Chimborazo, proposed that younger women become cooks, whereas the women wanted to become guides and managers, while older women rejected work as cooks as yet another task in already long days (Burbano and Silva 2008).

Indigenous women's practical knowledge about how development works suggests that policy representation of female indigenous subjects as unmodern and antiprogress misrepresents their agency, situated knowledges, and capacity for incisive critique. Indígenas turn the tables on development, suggesting that it is not subalterns who are to blame. They also dispute exclusion from decision-making in rural projects, arguing that participation in design and planning would allow women more oversight and better outcomes. Building on the complaints articulated by village women through hard-won experience, a group of female leaders condense these complaints into systematic critiques. According to Magdalena Aysabucha, the women's representative for the Andean federation Ecuarunari, "so we need women to generate their own resources that would grow according to their knowledge. This would be to the benefit of the entire community, even the country as a whole. Because [women] see that they are capable and can expand their knowledge, and that they're completely able to go out and become organized, not live submissively in the communities, discriminated against, and not taken into account by society."[86] Contesting the representations of femininity, organized indígenas claim a public role in decision-making with respect to households and regional political economies. "Now we're getting to know our rights as women. We're not just for carrying; we're in the process of changing and gathering strength."[87]

As subsequent chapters trace, subalterns are articulate critics of the underside of development, drawing on direct marginalization and epistemic violence. Confronting technical knowledge with decolonial perspectives, indigenous women probe the limits of ethnodevelopment and GAD, suggesting that neither has captured social heterogeneity sufficiently. While overcoming indígenas' problems of geographical distance and cultural and language issues requires time, money, and risk-taking from development (Meentzen 2001: 3), the thrust of indígenas' critiques goes much broader, to highlight how their understanding of development is not acknowledgeable within existing policy thinking. In this respect, indígena leaders recognize that development attempts to engage rural women in agriculture without fully considering the implications of postcolonial social heterogeneity. Norma, CONAIE women's representative, again: "A path has been opened where we women are working within development. But however much support has been given—economic, education, training—although that money has been spent, there hasn't been any follow-up. We've seen communal banks, small and large animal care, but all this hasn't covered everything that indigenous women need because they have been abandoned."[88] Whereas policy offers seemingly all-encompassing single issue frameworks, indígenas experience development as fractured and inappropriate, a disconnection between need and offer. In their agendas, they suggest measures to address interlocking exclusions and contradictory visibility/invisibility. For instance Chimborazo's equality plan, arising through efforts to bring indigenous women into local agenda-making, calls for local government to take into account indigenous women's specificity in relation to development (PIO Chimborazo 2005: 18). In a diversity of settings, women's groups and leaders stress how development has to recognize diversity *within* diversity and has to create flexible nonstereotyped understandings of male-female and ethnic-regional difference in development and political life (Palacios 2005). Whether under mestizo modernization (the main focus of this chapter) or neoliberal and multicultural measures (discussed later), women creatively rethink development and address marginalization. However, even when resources are awarded in participatory ways for indigenous women to draw up their own projects, they often face an uphill struggle. When UNIFEM's Andean office called for proposals, indígenas' organizations responded with enthusiasm and innovative projects.[89] Overall, women's organizations have the knowledge base to propose ways to protect strategic and practical interests, yet they often lack the public authority and command over resources to realize them. In the words of a Kichwa woman, indigenous women have "this right to go out, to know how to read, write, to learn . . . to see with our own eyes what to do. So we know what to do and how to do it." Through their embodied and situated knowledge, indígenas map out their own counter-topography (Katz 2001a), which reads their situation from an Other positionality to generate a series of demands increasingly drawn from a language of rights and decolonization.

Conclusions: Geometries of Power and Essentialism

Indigenous women are struggling against, reformulating, and reworking the relations of disadvantage they face in development. Indigenous women's emergent grassroots critique of the inappropriateness, marginalization, and homogenizing tendency of policy informs their call for social diversity to be considered more systematically across multiple scales of development. Indígenas' experiences of and responses to exclusion provide them with both a unique perspective on development processes and an object lesson in grassroots mobilization. Throughout the Andes and Amazon in recent years, women and men have organized to identify the infrastructures of exclusion that result in poor development outcomes for indigenous women and girl children. As CONAIE's Norma points out, development promises resources and involvement yet does not tackle the gendered racism indigenous women experience nor does it address exclusions arising from postcolonial inter-sectionality. Indígenas' situation is shaped by primary school teachers, de-velopment extension workers, families and husbands, state officials, and merchants and draws them into a colonial present that compounds their relative disadvantage while reproducing the hierarchies that create racial-ized, rural female subalterns as relatively less developed. Women of diverse ethnic populations mobilize to seek greater decision-making power over processes that span rural settlements and nation-states, and they contribute to international protections of indigenous and women's rights. In other words, indigenous women are *agents* in development and in communities. However constrained they find themselves in relation to urban and monetized economies, indigenous women also express agency and resistance in subtle and diverse ways. The processes shaping Kichwa and Tsáchila women's lives "link different places analytically" (Katz 2001a: 1230; Bhavnani, Foran et al. 2003). Although they face distinct possibilities and limits on agency, women's situatedness in uneven landscapes of exclusion continuously inform their in-sights and critiques and generate a postcolonial difference. Trinh Minh-ha argued that the global North pictured thirdworldwomen through the "co-lonial difference." What this chapter suggests is that diverse organized Ecuadorian indigenous women are beginning to articulate what we can call a "postcolonial difference," a vision of development generated from subal-tern experience. This vision speaks, necessarily, of postcolonial hierarchy and abandonment yet additionally imagines a decolonial reading of social heterogeneity founded on justice and rights.

Living in Punín village, Chimborazo, Juana T. tells us, speaking in kichwa, how women in her village established a savings-and-loan association, thereby extending our understanding of the indigenous women's daily struggles described in chapter 2.

> Bueno, Dios solo pagui nishpa, bonito experiencia, parlukuna. De repenteka chayashun chay experienciakunaman. Tukuylla kaipi tiyakukkunaman ama nishunchik kamachik sakirishunchik, sino ashakunallapish kallarinkapak, nachu. Siempre, ñantaka ima shinatak paskashun, sino purishpa. Ña shukkuna purikpika, chaitaka ña maijantakshi purishka nishpaka ña katinchiklla, ñachu. Shukkuna katikpika, kaipi ñanmi tiyan layachin nishpaka ña katinchiklla. Chaipika ña ñan sakirin nachu. Shina laya kanchik. Ñuka organizacionmanta ashituta parlasha.

Well God bless you. There's a beautiful experience, with lots to discuss, perhaps we can get to that. To all those women present today, we should say that we'll begin—how are we going to open up a route unless it's by walking, taking steps? Anyone can start, and then there'll be others to follow, isn't that true? I'm going to share a little about my organization.

I am from Punín that little town; it's not like other places, the life is different. We are indigenous yes, but with other customs. So we plant tree tomato, tomato, vegetables, greens in greenhouses; that's what we plant. How plentiful they are! Shining and big to take to the market. Above all we do this to sell, so we fumigate every two weeks and we make it produce as fast as possible. We harvest everything but sometimes we win and sometimes we lose. What happens in our pueblo? There are women who have operations; they get cancer of the uterus, of the blood. Cancer everywhere, in the kidneys, liver! All the women are ill and got operations; some poor women died. Why is there disease? Because they work in the greenhouses fumigating, there's lots of heat and that's how they work.

On the other hand, we just eat chemicals without stopping, no? We still take tomatoes, lettuce in the truck, and in return we bring back soft drinks, crisps, bread and noodles from town. And in other places, we end up consuming chemicals and all because we're thinking about making money, having a pocket full of cash, buying a car every year. Nothing else.

You could go to this village and perhaps you'd go for a walk around. They're building lots of houses, more than in the city, fancy houses full of marble. And what's happened to people? They are damaging their health and life. My parish is divided into the lower, middle and upper sectors. The people in the lower sector now don't want to speak kichwa, they're embarrassed to recognize themselves as indigenous. They say they're *campesinos* [peasants] and not indigenous. In terms of clothing the people of my age accept wearing indigenous clothes, but the younger ones reject it, and prefer to put on mestizo clothing. So that's how we leave behind good things and we don't follow custom and things seen from another angle. We should value what is ours. It's what we used to say, but now we don't have time. I thank you very much and salute you, thank you, God thank you for your time and coming to listen.

For my part, I don't like . . . Working every day in a glass-house, they pay $30, $10, or $20. They say that they don't want to lose this amount of money and now they don't what to shepherd the sheep and lose time. If we have our organization, we have a caja solidaria [savings-and-loan association] for women. I was really behind that caja solidaria. Why? Because we all need credits to plant, to buy fertilizer, to buy the seeds—people need more credit. When you go to the bank they ask for lots of paper, guarantees, but not everyone can be a guarantor if they don't have a house in the city, a car and are on a wage sheet. To ask for all of this, we thought that having the money in a caja solidaria between ourselves we wouldn't waste time, because we shouldn't be looking for papers, we shouldn't be walking around begging the guarantors. We would have our own savings to get loans. So that's why we make the effort and have meetings once a month, meeting from three till six o'clock. So I have to watch the time and that's how I can go and irrigate, or fumigate or other things.

In this way, uniting ourselves we've been working for a few years and now we can distribute the savings. My thinking is that if this organization didn't have sufficient money it couldn't divide the money. If the money's to be divided up they needed $100,000, $80,000—that would be enough to divide. I was against that, saying that if we divide it up everyone would just get a bit, but if you want to divide it then do it. But wanting to have funds, we decided to leave $10, in all $3,000 as a seed-fund. Now we're happy, we administer this money and we have three thousand [dollars] and we'll go on accumulating. So, with this experience I think that in the city you could also do this. You know that in the city you can't even go to the bathroom if you don't have ten cents, isn't that the truth? So there you could create a caja solidaria perhaps with migrants; we've already started as migrants and we've come quite a long way. So there are people from Licto, Flores, Cebadas, Punín, and San Luis who have been following the caja solidaria. At the beginning we put in $10 at 3 percent, but in the last discussion we had, we saw that it was very little and that there was no profit. If everyone puts in $1,000, we have $20,000 and we have enough to offer credit. So our children, who are studying, can be managers, secretaries, whatever they want.

If we don't meet, we can't talk about our problems and sometimes talk about the fiestas, customs and whatever. United we share our suffering, look out for the ill, we converse and learn. If we are alone in our house we can't learn. We don't concern ourselves with our neighbor; we don't know if he is ill, down, injured. We don't know and we don't visit. But the organization is for expressing solidarity, no? If someone is suffering, if something happens, we can give support, visit, and meet up for whatever reason. If not, everyone is going to live and to die, without it mattering if others eat or not, are suffering or not. So we're not building the kingdom of God. These are my words, thank you. Let's go on, not working only for ourselves but to open up paths for our children, for our grandchildren of our children. Yes, this path is not easy as there are spines, stones, challenges, falls—everything. But even by falling we are staying on the path, and we'll walk! This is what life is like. To all of you, thank you.

Chay shimikuna ñukapak kan. Dios solo pague, katishun wichiman.
Mana ñukanchikmanta rurashpa, sino ñukanchik wawakunamanta,
ñukanchik wawakunapak wawakunapak, shamuk ñetukunapak ñanta

paskashpa katishun. Ari ñanka mana facilchu kan, ñanpika tiyanmi kashakuna, rumikuna, trompiezokuna, urmanakuna, tukuy tiyan. Pero urmashpapish mana sakirinchikka. Sakirisha, mana jatarishaka, mana. Jatarishun, sinkurikushpapish jatarishun, purishun. Shinallatak kash-kaka kawsaipika. Dios solo paguichik tukuikuna.

_____

THREE

Crumbs from the Table

Participation, Organization, and Indigenous Women

What we would change is the organizing of women, of men—
organizing and working together to get ahead. In whichever community,
wherever, we get ahead by being organized and working on everything.
If we don't organize—then nothing! We cannot get ahead when we're
not organized in communities with directives, with comuneros. First,
you have to organize well to move ahead, for work or whatever; if not,
there are problems.

—GABRIELA, KICHWA-SPEAKER, EXPERIENCED FARMER, EX–DOMESTIC
SERVANT, AND MEMBER OF VILLAGE ASSOCIATION IN PUCUPALLA, QUIMIAG
PARISH (2011)

Participation is development's unalloyed good, a cornerstone of projects
designed to award a degree of oversight and leverage to beneficiary populations. Yet in a postcolonial context of social heterogeneity, who is to participate? And on what grounds can they articulate their demands? Treating
participation as a fundamentally political question of contestation and interests (Hickey and Mohan 2004), this chapter explores participation—in
various sites: namely ethnodevelopment, GAD, civic oversight of public
services—and participation's antimony, organization. If development
routinizes participation among its beneficiary target populations, what
happens to organization? While participation rests on understandings
of consensus and governance, how does it interface with activism and

resistance? These concerns are prompted by indigenous women's working in, and practical engagement with, participatory projects that under certain conditions and junctures facilitate strategic networking. Indigenous women's organizations experienced an explosion in numbers, reach, and influence through the late twentieth and early twenty-first centuries. From the early 1980s Andean women began to query exclusion from male-dominated ethnic federations. From that point, the trajectory of women's mobilization and organizational capacity was astonishing, accelerating from regional and local associations and representation to active participation in the Indigenous Uprisings and to an active role in a formal continent-wide network within two decades.[1] In this context, the chapter contributes to critical accounts of participatory development while situating this technology firmly within a postcolonial frame that parses the distinction between citizen and beneficiary, between participation and resistance. Participation becomes a practice by which knowledge is created (Mosse 1994), but in this case a process of knowledge construction comes to be retooled by subalterns for their own purposes, even as development's restless search for new frameworks outflanks political organization.

Participation in development is always constructed in relation to particular social groups who are to be "brought into" the fold of development, a process that, however implicitly, requires an understanding of the category (poor, rural, women) or subjects called to participate because of particular social qualities (undemocratic, marginal, voiceless, disempowered). In this sense, the codification of participation has an institutional function of promising to overcome subdivisions, seal a consensus, meld a provisional community onto a postcolonial situation, in which the unacknowledged—and unacknowledgeable—reality of social divisions, political contests, and divergent interests are to be papered over in the name of a greater good (Bhabha 1994: 43; Mosse 1994; Cornwall 2003; Kapoor 2005; Blaser 2009). Scholars of development document the on-the-ground social fractures that become immediately apparent in participatory mechanisms of gender, class, race-ethnicity, rural locations, and even more distant rural locations (Chambers 1997). The dilemma of participatory development is hence the question of which social identity provides the most cohesive basis for intervention. Although it is now a universal technology, participation has a colonial genealogy, being "an artifact of plural cultures, articulated at the interface between the organizational cultures of development agencies and the imperial cultures that shaped the very notion and practice of 'development'" (Cornwall 2006: 79). In critical analysis, participation has been interpreted as a technique with which to create autonomous, self-organizing subjects and channel energies in ways that divert attention away from dismantled welfare systems and depoliticization. Under neoliberal impulses to create a distantiated form of a desirable conduct of conduct (Rose 1996), the "passing of the stick" under participatory development becomes a means by which subjects become responsible for their own development, a procedure that absolves power-holders of a duty of care. As this chapter demonstrates, however, while some spaces open up, postcolonial legacies continue in play, operating through the norms, discipline, and meanings of social hierarchy and postcolonial power, which are often stubborn and not easily overcome except through further organization and political action to disrupt the stability of community, of consensus. So how does development and its understandings of social heterogeneity in the context of participatory projects mesh or clash with indigenous women's processes of organization and critiques?[2] This question becomes particularly important as Ecuadorian indigenous women's political organization predates development's deployment of participatory mechanisms in its current format.

It is a truth widely accepted that the participation of indigenous women in projects—as with other marginal beneficiary groups—is a crucial step toward inclusion and voice, even if insufficient on its own. Andean female leaders argue "there is no development without women's full participation," while development experts express the view that "development means promoting women's participation" and "many projects don't achieve the real participation of indigenous women" (Meentzen 2001: 32, 36). As attested in interviews and indigenous movement meetings, Kichwa women—warmikuna—in Chimborazo are widely supportive of the principle of participation and what they view as its counterpart, organization. Building on previous chapters, the chapter explores the ways development projects move from identifying an axis of social disadvantage through to operationalizing an understanding of social difference and its consequences, evaluated along the continuum from depoliticization through to participation. The analysis of participation deepens this book's argument that development's understandings of social heterogeneity often smuggle broader understandings of social relations into single-issue-focused projects, which in turn impact named beneficiaries and especially subalterns. Programs and projects that otherwise have little in common now endorse participatory objectives, as illustrated by a maternal health program, a rural development program, and an ethnodevelopment project discussed here. Comparing three programs demonstrates how stakeholders hold often diverse implicit understandings of the "rules" of intersectionality—that is, how male-female difference works out in indigenous societies, or how poverty and gender trump racial difference—such that participatory development programs tend to essentialize one framing of the issue over others. While such essentialization is rooted in development's tendency toward depoliticization and technical reductionism, it suggests that further questions need to be asked regarding how one interpretation prevails over another. If these implicit influences of intersectional thinking are to be examined critically, would the politicization of social heterogeneity make a difference in the outcomes of participatory development?

Chimborazo has experienced numerous interventions since the early twentieth century, and the on-the-ground examination of successive projects brings into focus the ways development projects "read" regional social realities and projects' means of addressing problematic aspects of social difference. A site of successive waves of social development projects to address extensive poverty, often involving rural—including indigenous—women, Chimborazo province has the lowest human development index of Ecuador's provinces (0.533). Just over half its population is employed in agriculture (women and men), and indigenous people are a majority in four cantons (Guamote 95 percent, Colta 79 percent, Riobamba 65.3 percent, and Alausí 59.1 percent in the early 2000s).[3] Moreover, exceptional levels of social organization exist, with unprecedented higher levels of organization in rural areas than in urban areas, largely based in comunas. The numbers of civil society groups and associations boomed between 1975 and 1991, and today one-fourth of Ecuadorian regional groupings of grassroots organizations are found in Chimborazo province.[4] Chimborazo also has one of the highest densities of development institutions in the country, with 178 public and private institutions in the province by 2007, including eighty-five NGOs and thirty-seven public institutions.[5] The three participatory interventions discussed here comprise maternal and child health care under the Free Maternity Services Law (Ley de Maternidad Gratuita y Atención Infantil of 2006), a development project for rural women in Chimborazo (1994–1998), and the nationwide ethnodevelopment project PRODEPINE (1998–2002).

Civic Oversight and Neoliberal Technologies of Development

Participatory development has a long history embedded in colonial forms of governmentality, although its parameters, rationales, and discursive framing of who is to participate, and for which reasons, have inevitably shifted over time. In this respect the 1990s was a key period; the New Poverty Agenda, promoted by multilateral development agencies, brought together the themes of civil society and active citizenship, the management of social risk (that is, increasing the security of the poor through developing their capacity to cope, mitigate, or reduce risks), and coresponsibility/comanagement (Molyneux 2006: 429–30). Neoliberal development began to identify an increasingly differentiated social field, in which subpopulations were distinguished according to the variable risk of problems. Accordingly, "development projects . . . (externally) define certain groups as being at risk of or actually suffering certain problems (e.g., gender inequality, environmental degradation, poverty and the like) and invite them to administer the solutions (externally) offered, that is, invite them to participate" (Blaser 2009: 450). Another feature of the New Poverty Agenda has been the use of women and development (WAD) approach to "integrate women" into development rather than emphasize their empowerment (Molyneux 2006). The three interventions discussed here each originated under the umbrella of the New Poverty Agenda, although the nature of participation and the relative emphasis placed on active citizenship, risk, and coresponsibility varied.

In 2006, the government introduced free maternity and child health care, a move celebrated by gender policy professionals and others as a major step forward in providing key resources to low-income groups. In line with neoliberal audit culture and civil participation objectives, health care services were to be monitored by members of the public in order to ensure that principles of no payment at the point of delivery, quality of services, and access to information were adhered to. The Law affirmed: "Every woman has the right to free quality health care during her pregnancy, birth and after-birth, as well as access to sexual and reproductive health programs. Likewise, free health care will be provided to newborn infants, and girls and boys under 5 years, as part of the responsibility of the state" (article 1). Universal free attention from medical service during pregnancy, birth, and after-birth and for young children was designed to benefit women as childbearers and mothers. The program was couched in a policy tradition of "maternalism," with a highly gendered construction of the moral figure of the mother (Molyneux 2006). Mothers in this way were, as users to be offered health services, in a partial response to postcolonial abandonment. The program's colonial present was implicit in its aim to pay special attention to "the geographical areas with the highest rates of maternal and infant deaths and the most economically deprived areas" (LMGAI 2007: 20), that is, internal colonies with their racialized populations.

In this health care model, the participation of civil society in local oversight committees was central. Local governments were required to consult regularly with civil society representatives gathered in "management committees" (*comités de gestión*), comprising mayors and health representatives as well as peasant/indigenous and women's representatives. In addition, "user committees" (*comités de usuarios/as*) were established to ensure citizen coresponsibility and monitoring of the law's application. Primarily consisting of women (and men "interested in the well-being of the population") who used or were likely to use these services, the user committees were to be formed in every parish and canton, and registered with the National Women's Council CONAMU. Working in a voluntary capacity for no remuneration, user committees' five to nine members were expected to undertake broad-ranging and detailed documentation of community health needs, explain services to the community, participate in district working parties, inform medical staff about resource needs, denounce staff who broke the law, provide a quarterly report, coordinate in educational activities, and—finally—inform the nearest health center of maternal deaths. To coordinate these numerous and diverse tasks, the committees were to meet once a month (CEDIS 2007b).

Despite efforts by indigenous women's allies and various rights-based local and national NGOs to publicize the provisions in the law and to encourage indigenous women's involvement in committees, the take-up has been limited. For instance, one graphic pamphlet oriented toward rural and indigenous women informed them about the program in the context of a rights-based agenda around sexual-reproductive rights, women's citizenship participation, and the "defense" of women's rights (see fig. 3.1) (CEDIS 2007b).

In Chimborazo, women of diverse race-ethnic groups highlighted in 2005 the need to implement publicity campaigns relating to the maternal and infant program, as well as protection from sexual violence (PIO Chimborazo 2005: 21). In Chimborazo—as in Santo Domingo—indígenas do not take part in the oversight committees largely because members are recruited, and meetings are held, in urban centers. According to my interviews, indigenous women are rarely consulted or involved in oversight committees, for a number of reasons familiar from the previous chapter, namely insufficient distribution of information, uneven landscapes of accessibility, and racial hierarchies. In one focus group warmikuna talked articulately about the failures of mainstream health clinics but were unaware of their right to participate (CAMACHH focus group, July 2009).[6] In Chimborazo civil oversight committees operate largely in urban areas and draw primarily on mestiza women

Fig. 3.1. Pamphlet encouraging indigenous women's participation in civil oversight committees for maternal and child health services. Photograph by the author.

with time and resources to become involved. Parish volunteer user committees are registered with the National Women's Council yet fail to recognize the gendered, location, and income constraints faced by indigenous women if they wish to participate.[7]

Due to its frames and presumptions, citizen oversight precluded incorporation of indigenous women's knowledge and experiences into health practice. Indigenous women's participation hence operates as low-cost surveillance technology in which they would be recruited into extensive time-consuming data collection with no avenue for suggestions to improve practice. Instrumentalizing women's cooperation, this civic coresponsibility nevertheless establishes a clear distinction between types of information required by/useful to the state and women's alternative knowledges, documentation of which is of no interest. While the program allows for recording health staff's racist treatment of patients, there are no established mechanisms to permit that knowledge to change health care services, as indígenas' knowledge remains irrelevant to that audit culture. Neither does documenting health care failures leave room for witnessing women's difficulty of traveling from internal colonies to clinics or rural health services' understaffing and underfunding. Given the ways participation in civic oversight is structured in contexts of postcolonial intersectionality, racialized rural women are often excluded from effective participation.[8]

Indigenous women in everyday conversations, repositioning maternal and infant care in the broader context of health provision, query the criteria by which certain services are provided at no cost and others have to be paid for (CAMACHH focus group, 2009). They draw attention, too, to the postcolonial geographies of abandonment that result in indigenous areas having the lowest health budgets. For instance, Chimborazo province systematically lacks medical personnel, as Guamote district has only 1.25 medical staff for ten thousand inhabitants. Against participation as neoliberal technology, warmikuna in Chimborazo deploy forms of organization that draw on notions of inequality, rights, and justice. Refuting the notion that participation equals oversight committees, their provincial equality agenda calls for "campaigns of information and diffusion of the Maternity Law, Childhood and Adolescent Code, [as well as] Law 103 [against gender violence], and information on sexual and reproductive rights, and on quality and cultural understanding of the provincial health service" (PIO Chimborazo 2005: 21).

User committees, as the policy that established them outlined, presume the participation of active citizens partaking willingly in the governmentality of public services through which the national community benefits. Assuming a national consensus, the system of civic oversight established in Ecuadorian health care speaks to an imagined homogeneous—or at least nondiscriminatory—nation. Yet, as previous chapters have argued, the postcolonial nation is riven by interlocking hierarchies of difference that cut across the formation of consensus and the pursuit of a single goal. Unlike previous development programs, which drew heavily on value-laden and highly descriptive—and prescriptive—qualities associated with beneficiary subjects (chapter 1), the maternal and infant health system reworks developmental coloniality to resituate development within a larger and largely imagined community, the nation-state. Yet due to the sociospatial specificity of practices through which citizenship is constructed, racialized female subalterns cannot meaningfully participate in this imagined community as civil society participants (see Chatterjee 2004). Consequently, indigenous women are always already positioned at one remove from the possibility of partaking fully in participatory mechanisms, participation's routines being incompatible with rural geographical locations and heavy workloads, while it assumes the existence of an open public sphere. As noted, indigenous women are notable by their absence in oversight committees, as the elusive promise of involvement in the nation-state is thwarted by barriers of class, racism, distance, poverty, and—most crucially—lack of authority. Although racialized impoverished and rural women are targeted by this program, they are reproduced again as passive, unknowledgeable beneficiaries, unable to convey their understanding of inequality and exclusion and how to tackle it. In relation to maternal health care, indigenous women organize outside the parameters foreseen by state policy, taking grievances to grassroots women's organizations and ethnic rights federations. Moreover, indigenous women's organizational networks resituate maternal and infant health in a broader agenda of sexual and reproductive rights, the scope of social rights, and the legacies of internal colonialism (chapter 5).

Empowerment and Rural Women's Participation

Gender policy has, since its inception, been concerned to ensure women's participation in development, whether through liberal measures to bring women into development in order to mimic men's situation or GAD's emphasis on empowerment and women's right to rework development around female concerns (Kabeer 1994; Rathgeber 2000). By the late 1990s, one-twelfth of Ecuadorian "gender" projects were directed at ethnic minority women. An early assumption that women would automatically be given a voice and choice through the very methods and practices deployed was quickly shown up as naïve, prompting recognition of the contradictions between the two agendas of participatory development and GAD (Cornwall 2003). The contradictory dynamics of gender, participation, and indigenous women's positionality can be explored through the case of the EU-funded Chimborazo rural women's project (1994–1998).

This project utilized an empowerment interpretation of gender policy in order to bolster women's participation and their autonomous income-generating capacity. According to the project directors—a European female GAD expert and a male Ecuadorian agronomist—the objective was to support traditional organizations, especially women's associations. Despite being under the gender-unfriendly Ministry of Agriculture,[9] the project adopted a clear agenda of creating women-only organizations and establishing spaces where women could participate in decision-making about the development required, while also recognizing rural women's overwork and contestations around women's mobility. The project worked in three districts: the largely indigenous counties of Alausí and Guamote and the more mestizo county of Chunchi, all among the poorest areas in the province.[10]

The beneficiary population to be included in the project was rural "women," as female and economic actors, by default including indígenas and rural mestizas, and its objective was to create women-only spaces where women would decide on income-generating projects. "The project was for women, for women to seize. They had to get organized and they did, in communities and cantons."[11] In this sense, the project "handed over the stick" to beneficiaries—a participatory goal lauded initially by Robert Chambers (1997). The project tackled rural peasant poverty through the "promotion and/or strengthening of socio-organizational capacity of traditional organizations, especially women's associations; [to] support the installation of basic infrastructure to benefit women and their families, to alleviate their daily tasks and create more time for other economic and social activities; to collaborate to put in place small productive projects to benefit women and their families; to promote savings committees and popular credit" (von Sigsfeld and Avalos 1998: 6–7).

To foment grassroots organization, the project established local women's associations to design and then implement small productive and infrastructure projects, such as bakeries, a cooking gas depository, a small shop, and a flour mill. With the goal of economic and political participation, women were to manage the projects and were required to join local women's groups in order to become beneficiaries.[12] Women became familiar with organizing and leading meetings, how to hold different roles in the organization, and how to participate in public, women-only debates. "In the meetings, we all participate. First we're the coordinator, president, secretary, vocal and vice-president. Then we all participate, not just those who know how to read and write, but all of us so that we can improve."[13] In indigenous-majority areas, the Kichwa language was used in meetings, thereby facilitating warmikuna's inputs and contributions. By the project's end, some 6,500 rural women across 180 communities were involved. Although projects were extremely small-scale, with no impact on regional political economies, they nevertheless began to provide women with a space in which to organize (see fig. 3.2).[14] Women became increasingly visible as public actors, expanding the broader recognition of the rights to "voz y voto," or voice and vote. Speaking in Tixán community in September 2009, Claudia told her story:

I was president of the women's association; we had a lot of women—up to eighty-five or ninety. We did workshops; we bought [sewing] machines. We also looked after sheep. But after that I left, another president came in and we've become a little less organized, we haven't

Fig. 3.2. A "women's house" (*casa de la mujer*), constructed in 1997 by the EU rural women's project, Chismaute village. Photograph by the author.

worked so much. I would like to keep working; I want to support this project. Also my husband supports me, tells me to go to the meetings. He helps me work with the women; he's not like other husbands who beat their wives so they don't go to the meetings. (Claudia, forty-five years old, who had no schooling before adult literacy classes)

Working alongside female facilitators, many of them kichwa-speaking, women's groups discussed the kind of project they would prefer and then decided on how to plan and implement it. As "resources came specifically for women and they could make decisions," Ana Maria explains: "it was our project and men couldn't get involved. So there were results from this project; experiences remain. Women were trained, became more agile with things, because until the project women were submissive. They didn't know what it was to talk [in public]." In the village of Achupallas, for example, women insisted on productive projects to protect traditions, such as back-loom weaving, whereas villages near the main road decided to sell prepared foodstuffs. Many communities chose to build latrines, reflecting the lack of sewerage services. Beyond these choices forged under postcolonial abandonment, village groups were also the channel through which to promote female-oriented training in rights and organization, features welcomed by many women. Discursively, the project framed empowerment as a process of overcoming low self-esteem (chapter 4).

In wake of women's burgeoning political skills in negotiation, organization, and leadership, the village associations networked in order to push for a level of regional coordination unanticipated in the original design. Organized women, in particular those in indigenous-majority Alausí and Guamote districts, founded county-level organizations and an interdistrict gas distribution enterprise. Indígenas perceived grassroots associations as a useful tool and quickly established twice as many credit groups as Chunchi district's mestiza women and over three times as many "women's houses" (casas de la mujer) as mestiza women (see fig. 3.2) (von Sigsfeld and Avalos 1998: 22, 23). According to participants' testimony, the EU project came at a conjuncture when resources and public legitimacy provided a boost to indigenous women's own dynamics: "The project arrived at a time when we were getting ready to organize but we weren't finding the route"; "We understand that there is a greater strength in the organization, and we women are able to maintain our organizations" (von Sigsfeld and Avalos 1998: 36). Toward the end of the project, female village associations were acting independently of project promoters, taking meetings out of facilitators' hands (compare Kapoor 2005: 1207). Naming activists in Andean indigenous movements, Dolores explained: "Perhaps from now on, women can go on organizing, creating more capacity and a space, no? I would say that would be an additional space for women, making them equal to men, but not just the men. Before, we [indigenous] men and women were undervalued [desvalorizados]; we were just ordered around by the mestizos. That's how we lived before. Thanks to God, to Leonidas Proaño, Manuela León, Dolores Cacuango who fought for women, fought for indigenous people, this gave us the strength to organize men and women, so mestizos didn't just use us."[15] In narratives such as this, indigenous women write a genealogy of Chimborazo organization that speaks to its postcolonial context and its diverse, often subaltern, contributors. Nearly twenty years after the project started, one of my key interlocutors, herself formerly a project facilitator, said, "Yes, it was worth it and helped a lot, also in terms of women's decision-making. All of this was with the organization around women's rights, organizing as women. So we got a lot out of it, and the NGOs taught us and supported us. So that strengthened us considerably." An internal project evaluation confirmed that women's networks and organizations were "undoubtedly one of the most important achievements of the project in the sense that women's voices and participation, leadership and negotiating capacity are recognized and respected not just in the communities but also in the local and regional power structures and institutions" (von Sigsfeld and Avalos 1998: 8).

A major influence on women's organizing was male attitudes, as women's associations and independent businesses were perceived as a disruption to the village-level "consensus" that disciplines women. In Chimborazo, persuading men of the importance of female decision-making was a long and arduous process. Male comuna leaders were generally highly resistant to women's separate associations and women-only projects. A female promoter received physical threats from men for organizing groups, which she countered with good humor and persistence: "Even if they hit me, insult me, I'm not going to do meetings with men, only [with] women," she told me. As another woman recalls, "so then the men began to understand and let the women come and do the projects. And seeing that they were doing the projects, they also helped and gave space to women. The women became presidents of organizations, secretaries. So we elected a complete committee, and we registered the organization with CONAMU. So the [women's] organizations were strengthened." Despite ongoing resistance and jealousy from a number of men, village women fought for public presence, a task that continues today, as documented in later chapters. "We women have the right to work; it's not just men who have that right to work. We women have the right to get ourselves anything. When they don't take our organizations into account, they say that women aren't worth anything. 'Why are they coming? They don't know anything!'" (Rosero Garcés and Reyes Ávila 1997: 78).

Looking back over a decade, the indigenous women originally involved as facilitators and participants in the Chimborazo rural women project have mixed views about its legacies. They treat it as one in a series of learning opportunities through which to gauge the pros and cons of projects. While on the one hand they recognize that it contributed at a key moment to the leveraging of legitimacy and visibility for women's organizational efforts, some indígena leaders now view the project as flawed in its framing of knowledge and voice. In Ana Maria's view, "this project came in with mestiza women's ideas to support us with four components: savings banks, infrastructure, businesses, and production. Four fixed projects. So we [local, warmikuna] promoters had to work with that, and say 'OK, that's what being offered, accept it or not,' with a kind of strange imposition. So people had to accept it. There was no consultation [with us beforehand] and that's just how it worked."[16] Rather than accept the project's consensus definition of women's interests, indigenous leaders reinterpret the project retrospectively as the outcome of postcolonial geopolitics, an intervention in which the participating community was one defined by mestiza feminism and not necessarily responding to indígenas' needs and interests. Such an evaluation speaks primarily to a learning process in part forged through that project. In this sense, indigenous women punctured "the myths about female solidarity [between female fieldworkers and local women] and general community-minded selflessness" (Cornwall 2003: 1335).

Another retrospective criticism from indigenous women was the insufficient follow-on support for small businesses, which often collapsed after the project's exit. The ongoing problem of development's stop-start periodicity (discussed in chapter 2) plagued the EU project, as noted by a former promoter in one of our regular conversations: "We had a county-level business in Alausí and Guamote. They were fine but then when the project finished, there was no economic support for the women and so now it doesn't work. A lot of it is about the lack of support from institutions, the authorities, even if it's just for the women's bus fares or subsistence so now the women cannot come down to parish and canton meetings." Businesses were expected to be up and running within four years, before being left to the vagaries of uneven development.[17] Looking back at the project, women articulate critiques of its failure to provide sustained dignified incomes and work and to alleviate heavy domestic labor. Relatedly, villagers fault the project for assuming that all local women had identical interests and skills, so they recall disliking the forced choice between a single village enterprise and nonparticipation. In this sense, indigenous women today continue to raise the issue of social heterogeneity as the basis for their main critiques of this participatory project.

During the EU Chimborazo project, indigenous women participated actively in ethnic rights movements, as voters and as protestors against government corruption and economic collapse. In elections, the province's citizens voted for a provincial government led by an indigenous prefect, who had formerly held the position of mayor of Guamote canton, the poorest and most indigenous in Chimborazo. Taking participation into the sphere of citizenship and shifting the practices and spaces through which citizen voice was heard (Hickey and Mohan 2004), the provincial government introduced participatory budgeting, a move that served to distribute resources to marginalized rural populations and bypass provincial power elites. In the participatory budgeting process, practical measures were taken to ensure as broad an inclusion as possible by selecting and training bilingual facilitators, ensuring equal participation by district and gender, holding consultative workshops in 124 rural communities, and holding workshops with women, children, and municipal employees to hear otherwise silent voices (Ramírez Gallegos 2001: 60–62; COMUNIDEC 2008). At the initiative of the indigenous prefect and indigenous and mestizo staff, social spending rose to unprecedented levels (40 percent of annual budgets), while considerable sums went into irrigation and roads.[18] Driven by growing awareness that poverty had increased in the province (Ramírez Gallegos 2001), indígenas alongside male counterparts used the ballot box to ensure social heterogeneity and rural racialized-gendered voices would contribute to a different kind of consensus. Warmikuna Rosario and Violeta summarized the situation for me during our conversations.

> Ñuka partimuntaka, maska kay organizacionmanta yaikushkakani, ashtawanka plantación, crédito, agriculturata trabajana, menos de interés. Ñukanchik kashna campomanka ima usia jataripi, waira jatarikpi, chai paikunapak préstamo kushkaka paikunapakka ganancia, ñukanchikpakka chaika perdida sakirin.

> For me, as an integral member of this organization, we need above all larger farms, we need work in agriculture, and credit at lower interest. In our fields, we have drought and wind, so we only lose, whereas others have profits. (Kichwa speaker Rosario, who is in her late forties and has no education, Guamote)

> I would like women to work together in the community, to collaborate, to look after animals to get ahead. (Violeta, who is in her late thirties, was orphaned when young, received minimal primary education, and is now a farmer and mother to five children under fifteen years)

Participation and Ethnic Community: Ethnodevelopment, Social Capital, and Gender

As chapter 1 discussed, ethnodevelopment emerged in the 1990s as a developmental approach to inequalities along lines of racial-ethnic difference. Firmly embedded in neoliberal governmentality yet seized on as an arena for indigenous agency, ethnodevelopment was soon put into operation in Ecuador via the flagship PRODEPINE project (1998–2002), which aimed to generate locally appropriate projects through participatory mechanisms, backed by regional teams of professionals who themselves came from the target population. Given its poverty and large indigenous population, Chimborazo became the site of numerous PRODEPINE local projects.

One of the most important development projects under the auspices of the country's indigenous development council (CODENPE) was the

indigenous and Afro-Ecuadorian development project PRODEPINE,[19] conceived to address indigenous peoples and Afro-Ecuadorian poverty and
exclusion by means of organizational strengthening, income generation
through production and credit, cultural recuperation activities, regulariz-
ing land titles and rights to water, and rural extension work. The project
was described by its architects as a participatory project "with its antenna
well set to know the demands and change required,"[20] devolving decisions
about the design and scope of local development plans to community-led
consultative processes facilitated by a small group of indigenous and black
development professionals. In addition to a preeminently participatory format, the working philosophy of PRODEPINE incorporated a sense of the
diverse social field in which it was operating, characterized by "differentiated needs, demands, rights—collective and individual—of indigenous and
Afro-Ecuadorian men and women."[21]

Despite the diversity of Ecuador's indigenous nationalities and pueblos
in terms of their cohesiveness, social dynamics, and fractures, this particular ethnodevelopment project came together around the notion of a cohesive ethnic community that was assumed to work together under traditional
authorities—presidents of comunas, leaders of local associations—on behalf
of an ethnic collective, a form of indirect rule in which "certain functions and
powers were delegated to traditional leaders and institutions" in an imposed
moral order (Cornwall 2006: 66; Radcliffe and Laurie 2006). In this moral
community, female-male difference did not represent a significant axis of
concern. Because of participatory principles, the director argued in an interview that the "incorporation of gender won't mean a drastic change."[22]
Such assurances speak more to ethnodevelopment's faith in ethnocultural cohesion than knowledge about distinctions between participation and gender
agendas. Despite ethnodevelopment's argument that mainstream development fails to take indigenous difference into account, "there was a tendency
to make invisible the participation of women in activities distinct to those
ones they were traditionally assigned to, despite an explicit interest in integrating them in the development process" (Larrea 2002: 9). "Points of tension between participatory and 'gender-aware' approaches to development
arise from—and produce—rather different ways of engaging with issues of
gendered power" (Cornwall 2003: 1326). Nevertheless, once the ethnodevelopment project had been designed and implemented, gender experts in
the National Women's Council, in conjunction with multilateral agency support, worked to recast the project's management of female-male difference
(Radcliffe et al. 2004).[23]

The project was designed without consultation with indigenous women, so their participation emerged only after the project was in operation. In part this was couched in the language of the culturally specific social capital present in indigenous—and to a lesser extent, black—settlements; as the project director again clarified in interview, "PRODEPINE is based on an important social capital that evokes consensus, agreement, and respect."[24] Encoding "normative assumptions about women" (Molyneux 2002: 177), PRODEPINE worked from the principle that women were primarily family oriented, and via the family, fully incorporated into the ethnic population. Moreover, the model of indigenous femininity was one that involved productive activities only when domestic commitments permitted. In this sense, women were perceived as beneficiaries on behalf of ethnic households—"to solve an economic problem that they've had in their house," according to the project director.

Ethnic social capital relied, too, on the gendering of community, the naturalization of ethnic women's commitment to communal interests (Molyneux 2002; Andolina et al. 2009). That women were to be subsumed into ethnic communities came in large part from policy's uncritical and largely ungendered accounts of social capital yet acquired real purchase on the ground in indigenous areas of Ecuador precisely because it seemed to fit seamlessly with the postcolonial landscapes of raced, gendered, classed exclusions of internal colonialism. Building on existing moral interpretations of racialized women, PRODEPINE enrolled women into ethnic organizational strengthening via small-scale cajas solidarias, local self-managed associations run by and for women as a mechanism to distribute credit. Nationally 547 cajas solidarias were established involving some 14,022 female beneficiaries.[25] According to the national director, "we have chosen women [to work in the cajas solidarias] because they are the people with a greater sense of responsibility, and greater permanence in the family, domestic space. And they have demonstrated a lot of interest and responsibility."[26] Women's interests were represented as equivalent to those of the ethnic community, a naturally domesticated subject whose primary goal was to nurture ethnic improvement. Although cajas solidarias were relatively new institutions, project endorsement drew on long-standing nationalist representations of primarily feminized internal colonies combined with expectations of ethnic social capital. Dealing with female-male difference through this moral framing of community and consensus, the program treated women as "additional" participants whose gender characteristics were secondary to ethnicity. In this sense, the project resembled WAD's incorporation into development on the terms of masculine power, rather than participation and GAD empowerment (Rathgeber 2000).

Yet Chimborazo's warmikuna quickly found that male-female difference in ethnic communities gave them grounds for dissenting opinions. According to village women's interviews, the credit stream via women's cajas was insufficient, as it amounted to around one-fifth of funding allocations to local development projects.[27] As an indígena recalled, "women just go to the credit unions with two, three thousand [dollars], up to a maximum of only $5,000, depending on the number of organized women there were. Whereas the men. . . . Look! They managed projects of $40,000, of $50,000, $80,000—there is always this inequality!"[28] Moreover, women complained of higher interest rates.[29] Local projects under PRODEPINE auspices generally replicated the previously noted tendency for short-term, small-scale projects (chapter 2). A woman in her forties and with two young children recalls that her women's group received money for a small animal project and workshops on how to care for the animals. However, another woman remembered that the women's association business selling guinea pigs to nearby urban markets collapsed, leading to the dissolution of the women's organization.

> We were looking after guinea pigs. With the sales we had money in the bank, but that's gone now. PRODEPINE helped us a lot but it left; it's gone. I think it changed its name. When other women came in they got rid of the [old] organization, there was bad coordination. The cuyes died and they were lost, so now there's no women's organization. (Sonia from Hospital Gatazo, in her early thirties and married with young children)

> They gave us money; a female friend helped us as she knew someone in PRODEPINE. Then some technicians came to give workshops to train us and then we began to work with cuyes. Yes there were female technicians, who gave us workshops on cuyes. (Laura, fifty years old, who received no schooling, as her father died, and who now has a small farm)

> Our women's association received a little from PRODEPINE (now it's CODENPE). They helped us and with that we've managed to keep going. Cent by cent, little by little we get on. (Elvira, a widow in her late forties with four grown children)

As well as exacerbating male-female differences in rural responsibilities—undermining the social neoliberalism's coresponsibility—it also undermined rural livelihood security and misrepresented male-female difference in rural locations.[30] What's more, indigenous families were assumed to be cohesive and stable, reflecting a standard multilateral agency model of an altruistic and heterosexual household (Bedford 2005; Bergeron 2011). Consultants drafted in to address the gender aspects of the project reported in relation to the central Andes that the model of a male head-of-household and breadwinner persisted (Aulestia 2002: 6). As well as downplaying intra-household gender relations, such models ignored class differentiation be-tween households in the short-term ethnodevelopment projects. Gender and class intersectionality meant that wealthier households contracted labor from poorer households, fracturing a notion of ethnic community, as wages were one-third lower inside villages than outside.[31] Meanwhile women increasingly relied on paid labor but were in no situation to com-mand it, as they were more likely to be among the less well paid (inside and outside villages) and did not have the social authority to consistently access assistance. Finding herself in precisely this situation, a warmi com-plained bitterly about how people "don't help out anymore." Given limited funding, women's organizational efforts were oriented toward dealing with occasional household expenses, such as buying school shoes for children, without envisioning a step-change in organizational or economic capacity.

In practice, assumptions about ethnic community were pushed to their limits, entailing profoundly gendered and racialized consequences. In Chimborazo, ongoing male outmigration and increased female responsibil-ity for agricultural production and community management demonstrated the fluid, multisited, and "stretched out" nature of ethnic social relations, as well as their interdependence on complex itineraries of household mem-bers. Chapter 6 addresses the political consequences of these dynamics for indígenas' citizenship practices; suffice it here to note how project precon-ceptions about ethnic institutions—including households—as preexisting naturally reproduced social relations bolstered interventions, a framing of social heterogeneity with profound gendered and class consequences (Radcliffe and Laurie 2006). For a female leader in the Ecuarunari federa-tion, "with PRODEPINE we didn't see any development; no reduction in impoverishment. Rather, it increased."[32]

Nevertheless, women's cajas solidarias rode a fine line between participa-tion in the name of ethnic community and an enduring boost to female sub-altern organization and visibility. In Chimborazo I encountered widespread appreciation of PRODEPINE's granting of legitimacy to women's organi-zations, and—more patchily—resources for income generation. For one indígena, then a technician in the project's Chimborazo office, the credit associations "helped women a lot," especially where community opinion supported organizational efforts: "What worked really well with PRODEPINE was the execution of the productive projects, because that had a lot of work. And also the development plans, and valuing local and regional organizations. That was the positive impact."[33] Since PRODEPINE finished, cajas solidarias have continued to exist, not least in Chimborazo, and women continue to work with them in ways that augment local agency and wider networking. Straddling the divide between economic and political activity, the cajas are embedded in forms of communication, political practice, and knowledge production that female subalterns, on the basis of evidence in Chimborazo, continue to find useful. Although women remain highly critical of their marginalization from political arenas of decision-making at multiple scales from villages through to the national ethnic rights movements, they can make those critiques in part because of the political spaces opened by the cajas and the financial and small-p political authority and voice they grant (chapter 6).

Despite indígenas' largely shared experience with indigenous men (chapter 2), ethnodevelopment raised persistent issues around female-male differentiation in and beyond ethnic communities. Coming to terms with this, women in the central Andes became acutely aware of the ways ethnic participation justified female exclusion. Against the romanticism of "the idealized . . . married couple, the family [and] symmetrical complementarity between male and female," a center advocating for indígena rights argued instead that their own "existing information . . . demonstrates diversities, contradictions and differences in roles assigned to women" in indigenous areas (Centro Maria Quilla 1992: 57). During PRODEPINE, too, women expressed their reservations to the one staff member appointed to address gender, an Andean indígena with considerable leadership experience. After the project's close, she told how "the local development projects weren't as participatory as one thinks. Women who participated in the projects . . . did not have a voice when defining the project's implementation."[34] They may have signed up for community projects, such as a Kichwa woman is doing in fig. 3.3, yet they were not in a position to shape them. In a similar vein, the Ecuarunari women's representative argued forcefully, again after the project's end, that the project sent most funding to organizations over which women had limited command. The dominant political figure of ethnic authority hence remained largely masculine. Adding to their knowledge about development, indigenous women honed their critiques of PRODE-PINE while building forms of organization that more closely matched their

Fig. 3.3. A Kichwa woman signs her name on an official document. Photograph by the author.

agendas. Hence, although PRODEPINE replicated the features of participatory projects across the global South (Mosse 1994) that consistently sideline women's equity and voice, the project validated forms of organization that—however inadvertently—served as sites for knowledge production by and for indígenas. Through their critiques, indigenous women profoundly challenge policy assumptions about social consensus and community that participatory development relies on for its moral authority. Instead of community and consensus, indigenous women speak about diversity within diversity (Palacios 2005), drawing attention to the irreducibility of social heterogeneity and the entanglement of power and difference where they seem to be most absent (Blaser 2009). While indígenas did not go as far as separating from male-dominated ethnic rights movements, they did nevertheless use the resources available to establish and build organizational structures that would support agendas for recognition of female-male diversity within ethnoracial diversity.

In the early 1990s a diverse group of warmikuna meeting in Chimborazo gave a sharply accurate assessment of how indigenous women were positioned in the panorama of development efforts. "Among the multifarious state agencies giving support to rural groups, we find that in reality there is only one dedicated explicitly to indigenous people and none concerned with indigenous women's situation."[35] In none of the projects rolled out across Chimborazo through the 1990s—maternal health, the rural women's project, or ethnodevelopment—were indigenous women, at the province or at a national level, involved from the start in its design, planning, and implementation (see Cornwall 2003). However, the three projects did vary in the degree of flexibility granted to grassroots initiatives and recognition of social heterogeneity. In this sense participatory development is "unstable and susceptible . . . its slippages render it vulnerable to re-interpretation, diversion, hijacking" (Kapoor 2005: 1218). For instance, indígenas mobilized through the rural women's project to establish regional organizations, an element unforeseen in the original project brief. Each intervention moreover conceptualized the participating community and the moral valence of participants in quite distinct fashion. The maternity law centered the maternal subject as an active citizen while the rural project sought to empower women and the ethnodevelopment project mobilized an ethnic communal subject. Despite these variations, it is also clear that racialized women's organizational energies—independent of development's will to improve—found some synergy first with associations established under the rural women's project and then the cajas solidarias funded via ethnodevelopment.

Comparing the three programs further reveals dimensions of how postcolonial development engages with social heterogeneity, uncovering postcolonial development's tendency to rely on ready-made social models of how core social institutions "work," even in hyperdiverse postcolonial settings. In a policy focusing on one dimension of social heterogeneity, such as ethnic group poverty, development thinking calls on strong understandings of the social group—community—through which the problem (impoverishment, lack of voice, inadequate health care) is to be addressed. However, the comparison between projects highlights how the drive to consensus flattens out social heterogeneity, such that an originary interpolated community (rural women, ethnic group, citizens) is promoted while crosscutting dimensions of social hierarchy are suppressed. Participatory development may be so deeply entangled in different stakeholders' desires that it makes attending to postcolonial hierarchies and social heterogeneity even more difficult (Kapoor 2005). Consensus is manufactured instead around the (postcolonial exclusionary) nation, (racially unmarked) women, or the (masculine) ethnic group. Furthermore, in order to shore up the consensus required, participatory development called on beguiling simplifications that constructed powerful images of homogeneous communities. For example, although PRODEPINE was ostensibly premised on ethnic *diversity*, in practice it understood female-male difference as a secondary dimension across all fourteen nationalities. The rural women project flattened out differences between mestiza and indígena situations, while the health oversight scheme denied the distinction between citizens and subalterns in public arenas. As in mestizo modernization (chapter 1), participatory policy relied on a stereotyped maternal figure to stand in for female differentiation. These implicit "rules" of intersectionality—commonsense and uninterrogated models of social landscapes—in turn underpin colonial frameworks that permit development to assume that it knows about male-female difference in indigenous groups, or the irrelevance of race-ethnicity to a women-only project. Whereas GAD and multicultural policy are institutionally separated and engaged in defensive struggles to protect budgets and personnel, this chapter examines how in their social neoliberal mechanisms of participation these two policy approaches share implicit agendas to build a consensus around a single line of social difference, in part through downplaying and silencing social heterogeneity. Comparing Chimborazo's participatory projects from warmikuna's perspective brings home abruptly how policy consistently fails to recognize female-raced-rural-poor subjects as a group around whom development consensus could be forged. Nevertheless, participatory development contains contradictions that give rise to questioning among "beneficiary" subpopulations who, in the case of Kichwa women, came to understand directly the need to organize outside development's terms. That indígenas could construct contingent and local forms of consensus, participation, and organization was hence beyond the vision of Ecuadorian participatory development.[36]

Social Neoliberal Politics of Vulnerability and Culture

Through the 1990s, Chimborazo experienced participatory development projects that called on (indigenous) (female) (rural) subjects to become enrolled in a community forged through consensus. Since then, however, social neoliberalism's antipoverty agenda has moved on in a number of ways. The first decade of the twenty-first century saw the continued rise of organized indigenous women, yet their participation in development's design and management remained nonexistent, in part due to ongoing colonial hierarchies. However, this period also saw a reconfiguration in the meanings of social difference, as from the midnoughties, the indigenous development council, CODENPE, committed to promote women's human rights, while the CONAMU gender council pledged to promote indigenous and black rights and integrate a "gender and intercultural perspective" into social policy to ensure basic social service provision in predominantly indigenous and black areas (CONAMU 2004: 52; Cunningham et al. 2008: 102).

During this period of social neoliberal promotion of participation as self-help and active citizenship, Ecuadorian national policy brought the category of indigenous women into visibility in ways that in fact emphasized their lack of agency.[37] Policy debates that touched on themes of social heterogeneity turned from participation and toward a concern with vulnerability and a recast meaning of cultural difference, as illustrated by these words in a speech given by the minister of social well-being: "In the geography of poverty and marginalization in Ecuador, it is the indigenous peoples who experience its most marked expression, as in their territories we observe the highest levels of poverty and exclusion. Indigenous children and women are the first to die in Ecuador" (Corporación Educativa Macac 1992). Likewise, the 1996 National Social Development Plan identified indigenous women as one of a number of vulnerable populations that deserved a high priority in policy. Indigenous women—bundled together with other discrete social groups— were represented as doubly discriminated against and particularly at risk. "First, social projects for women belonging to highly vulnerable groups, such as rural, ethnic, and migrant women, female heads of households and girl children are highlighted. This decision is based on the need to make these sectors more visible to prioritize policies that pay attention to the most discriminated women and girls. [Vulnerable groups] suffer a double discrimination. This is the case for indigenous and black women, heads of households, rural women, migrants, and girl children, among others" (Secretaría Técnica del Frente Social 1998: 134). To overcome vulnerability, the plan recommended economic solutions, offering entrepreneurialism as the route to reduce risks of poverty and discrimination, suggesting special employment programs (although the special features remained undefined), support for indígenas' economic activities (again, without describing what these might comprise), and strengthening links between banks and intermediary loan organizations to improve access to financial services.[38] The plan thereby foreclosed any consideration of power and intersectional hierarchy (especially among policy-makers [Kapoor 2005]) or the question of how to incorporate indigenous women's visions and ideas into project design and management. Identifying vulnerable subjects may not be new, yet the economic routes out of vulnerability reflect neoliberal readings of social heterogeneity, as primarily a question of risk and defenselessness. The Plan proleptically identified development subjects—the "vulnerable"—who were constructed as agency-less and whose conditions elicited and required intervention. Like participatory development, the discursive construction of "vulnerability development" depoliticized social relations of power and difference while reemphasizing in target populations' association with abjection. In other words, policy identification of vulnerable subjects did not flag up development's failings, its flawed logic and limited legitimacy, but rather pinpointed at ever more granular scales the *social qualities* of the subpopulations to be targeted.

These dynamics were also configured within a global colonial politics of feminism characterized by gulfs between policy-makers and racialized subalterns. While seemingly aware of third world/minority female beneficiaries, gender professionals arguably continue to identify third world females as "victims" in a global comparative frame (Kapur 2002). With indigenous women identified as a vulnerable group in the country's social agendas, CONAMU's gender policy-makers kept their distance, creating ad hoc and limited connections with indigenous women. After the Beijing Conference, where first nations' women made one of their first international statements, the National Women's Council maintained minimal contact with Ecuarunari women.[39] According to CONAIE's women's representative,

> regardless [of Beijing] we indigenous women were truly not taken into account inside CONAMU. You'll know that through CONAMU we're seeing the coordination of women I would call mestiza, urban and not rural. So practically through workshops, in forums where I participated, I realized that CONAMU also was an institution where, I would say, money accumulated for women—for indigenous, Afro women, mestizas, with organized women. Despite this [potential] however, there wasn't any opportunity to become established in CONAMU. And I personally have been fighting CONAMU so that they help [indígenas'] organizations and strengthen them, because there wasn't that support. So the struggle for me is that we indigenous women haven't been taken into account—they used our name, they've spoken in the name of indigenous women. But we haven't seen any benefit, we haven't had any success. Because if we indigenous women had been in CONAMU, I think that we would be in other spaces.[40]

Although indígenas sought to participate in public policy formulation, the scope for participation remained firmly circumscribed by postcolonial hierarchies. As a result, policy continued to be based on knowledge produced within colonial hierarchical framings of social difference, to the exclusion of subaltern knowledge.

> There are other institutions of government for example CONAMU a state authority where we indigenous women would like to be represented and benefit from. But there isn't [representation]. If we get in there, it's because we have to vote for such and such a government in the elections. . . . Recently, CONAMU presented me with these marvelous things they'd done—Reports on Ecuador 1995–2000, a regional conference, blah, blah—but in reality for indigenous women, we have nothing. No end to poverty, to segregation, whatever.[41]

Moreover, the policy approach to feminized racial-ethnic vulnerability through this period turned into a specific institutional intervention targeted at the CODENPE indigenous council, rather than inclusion of indígenas per se. In Ecuadorian gender policy, culture was increasingly resignified in terms of intercultural dialogue between diverse cultures, none of which was privileged relative to others such that culture came to signify both racial difference and its denial (Stolcke 1995; Wade 2009). Interculturalism hence advocated national cohesion, the ultimate participatory consensus that was to be forged through practices of mutual respect and dialogue between diverse cultural groups, all shorn of power and relational hierarchical positions. Framed in this way, it appeared logical to leverage gender policy into institutions for indigenous peoples, as the complex power dynamics between indigenous masculinities, indígenas, and gender policy professionals were so consistently downplayed in interculturalism. Rather than acting in a way consistent with racialized female subalterns' agendas, these interventions perpetuated (post)colonial racialized gender politics. The National Women's Council's 2004 Plan for Equal Opportunities (PIO in its Spanish acronym) brought together goals of female economic autonomy with a statement on how to frame indigenous women's position: "It is perhaps in this context [of economic autonomy] where cultural and intercultural rights acquire greater importance [and include] gender identity, as well as ethnic belonging, age and class; the right to freedom and free expression; to knowledge and its use; to cultural heritage and women's historical legacy; to cultural and artistic expressions and feminine aesthetics; the development of spirituality and cosmovisions" (CONAMU 2004: 31–32). In the Plan, cultural diversity became the policy rubric through which to attend to social heterogeneity and indigenous women. This policy approach uprooted cultural diversity from its history of conquest and racialization and represented Ecuadorian society as a rainbow nation of diverse traditions and ways of being. Policy in this sense foregrounded cultural difference as a something separate from considerations of social heterogeneity, which continued to be organized via single issue development organized around regimes of women's and racial-ethnic rights. The National Women's Council defined interculturalism as diversified relations between cultures—named as indigenous, Afro-Ecuadorian, and other groups—based on dialogue, consensus, and respect, the goal being "sensitivity towards differences between (fe)male one and (fe)male another" without the loss of cultural identity (CONAMU 2007: 12).[42] Indigenous women were represented as occupying specific cultural settings and as holding collective rights that did not preclude the recognition of women-specific rights (CONAMU 2004: 31–32). National diversity was formulated in intercultural gender policy as "a series of particularities that determine the salience of gender in different ethnic groups" (CONAMU 2007: 8). While celebrating interculturalism's relevance for all, CONAMU focused ultimately on (racialized) cultural difference (dominant groups' gender relations were not considered) and vulnerable female subjects. As culture was figured as a backdrop to vulnerability, the existing PIO gender policy continued in force as CONAMU policy assumed responsibility to act on behalf of indigenous and black women, a move familiar across the global South.

Concern for national consensus and removing conflicts "between cultures" (CONAMU 2007: 12) underlay policy readings of social heterogeneity. Intercultural gender policy in this respect wrote participatory development yet again, calling for civil action to step into always-already demarcated subjects and spaces. Under the postcolonial terms established in Ecuador, the nature of participation for gender policy-makers was to be distinctive to indigenous and black women's participation. Technical staff were to participate in professionalization and project design, while racialized women were cast as passive recipients of information and attendants at meetings (CONAMU 2007: 15–18; compare Richards 2004 on Chile). Again, these differentiated roles linked back to postcolonial intersectionality, representing female indigeneity as unable to articulate their own interests because of the power of patriarchal ethnic cultures. According to one development worker, "personally I don't agree [with collective rights] because they have a strong patriarchal function, and are highlighted by the indigenous nationalities. And no, they come into conflict with women's rights, very strongly. I think OK, this is a challenge but if you don't put women's individual rights first, or if you don't work concretely with interculturalism to ground collective rights, this—from my point of view—would not result in much."[43] To pinpoint the arenas in which gender policy was to establish individual rights, vulnerabilities were identified through statistically disaggregated information (CONAMU 2007: 15; also chapters 4 and 7). Intercultural gender policy replicated participatory development's discursive and practical tendency to downplay the role of power-holders in managing this intervention (Kapoor 2005).

❉

Throughout this period, racialized female subalterns continued to document and critique how their experience disrupted any singular solidarity with women or with ethnic communities. Increasingly mobilized as elected leaders at provincial, national, and international levels, "indigenous women achieved proposals based around their own difference, their demands, and as a result generated visibility such as in the Women Leaders Training Schools [Escuelas de Formación de Mujeres Líderes]" (Palacios 2005: 335). In her UNIFEM office, a former ethnic leader and now development professional spoke to me of how, in addition to questioning male ethnic authority, "the other new theme is that indigenous women began to question urban women about why they hadn't included us." Focusing specifically on gender policies around vulnerability, Maria continued, "and we really have to be included. We have to look at the issues and have a debate about interculturalism" in ways that incorporate indígenas' distinctive definitions of interculturalism, that place female-male dynamics within the heart of indigenous claims to dignity and respect.[44] As in the past, indigenous women have worked independently of state gender professionals to systematize their knowledge and formulate independent perspectives on how to pursue agendas for change. The CONAIE women's office held a series of workshops with female regional leaders from across the country to discuss the concept of gender, which generated heated debates. Without subsuming themselves into a homogeneous and race-blind category of "women" or a gender-blind category of "indigenous peoples," these representatives and leaders steadily—and in diverse ways—worked toward a conception of what it might mean to have meaningful organizational strength as raced-gendered-poor-mostly rural people in a hyperdiverse society. At a meeting at CONAIE's Quito headquarters, an Andean leader argued:

> It's not a question of going with the women who do gender and follow them . . . No, I think that we have to try. . . . Well, the problem is to

keep that related to indigenous women. In our case, it's not as if we have to put ourselves in with another [group]. . . . And we're also talking about women's rights, which mean maintaining family equilibrium as a woman. That's it! Maintain equilibrium as a woman in the [ethnic] community . . . I think that's it—the identity word, that men and women [have] egalitarian participation, in a comuna, of women and men on the basis of rights.

An Amazonian woman leader then noted how women get sent to "participate" in meetings, arguing instead for women's own decision-making power. A different Andean leader interjected, "In the end, political participation is not just among women; [it's about] economic questions and women's rights. From our point of view, we talk about rights—us! Women's rights—that's interculturalism! And I think that being indigenous we want to deal with the indigenous theme." Unlike CONAMU's top-down models of gender participation, indígenas defined interculturalism to include women and men in diverse nationalities on the basis of indígenas' rights. As Klenk has suggested, "it is exactly this lack of connection to (or perhaps refusal of) an implied 'backward' identity that can complicate undifferentiated concepts of 'women' and the 'Third World,' by illustrating the complex ways in which categories of development language are appropriated in the negotiation of multiple identities, subjectivities and material realities in specific development encounters" (Klenk 2004: 65). At the meeting, women noted their battles with ethnic male leaders over gender politics but advocated egalitarian participation in antiracist public spaces and the broader insertion of indígenas' agenda not just in "female" concerns.[45] Regarding ethnodevelopment, indígenas systematically queried why raising female issues were labeled as betrayal of ethnic consensus and why women persistently lost out to male counterparts. These viewpoints also came to the fore in Chimborazo, where a focus group complained bitterly of how few women received CODENPE grants.[46]

Unlike the lack of participation that indigenous women feel with respect to CONAMU, female indígena leaders generally feel that CODENPE is relatively more open to their participation. A leader, for instance, explained to me as we talked in her office how "in recent years there's been participation inside CODENPE by women to achieve public policies on how to carry through . . . and demand that policies are implemented. So in relation to these public policies that were designed by some female colleagues and some men, I also presented the National Agenda which united issues from CONAIE's three parts, the Coast, Sierra and the Amazon."[47] Through these forms of participation—negotiated as far as possible on women's terms—indígena leaders were involved in discussions that moved away from tropes of vulnerability and toward indígenas' validation as policy-making interlocutors. A female indigenous development council employee summarized the process:

> One aspect of CODENPE's work was a cooperation agreement with ex-CONAMU.[48] . . . with three achievements from that collaboration; inter-institutional training, so women from CONAMU talked to women from nationalities and pueblos about what gender is, as this term is resisted in our territories. Because these talks were between women distant from indigenous territories and indígenas, we talked about interculturalism, diversity, and what is understood by complementarity. We [also] had an exchange of personnel, especially of people working on women's issues. Then we systematized information on indigenous women's situation; that's being revised now. And the other thing was the proposal for a gender unit in CODENPE.[49]

Overall, although highly skeptical about gender mainstreaming, indigenous women were willing to endorse "development with identity" as long as it continued to listen for arguments about the existence of female-male difference.[50]

Conclusions

The Equality Plan for Chimborazo province, entitled "Women of Chimborazo Constructing an Equal Opportunity Plan," was published in January 2005.[51] The Equality Plan resulted from a process of consultation with indigenous and mestiza women and highlighted, alongside economic and sexual-reproductive rights, the issue of participation. Pointing to how "in the 1990s numerous women's organizations surged into existence and gradually defined their objectives," the document foregrounded the need to strengthen women's groups even further. As in other spaces created by indigenous women, the emphasis was on rights, specifically the right to be integrally involved in governance and decision-making at every scale from villages through to the nation-state, in ways that illustrate the widespread vernacularization of rights discourses (Merry 2006; see chapter 6). In stark contrast with gender policy's cultural turn, the Chimborazo agenda positioned indigenous—and other low-income and rural women—as organized political actors in decision-making. Although they struggle to participate as equally authorized interlocutors in provincial politics, indigenous women continue to be active spokespeople for subaltern agendas of organization that exist beyond the scope of participatory development.

Nevertheless, despite a carefully polished veneer of inclusion, it is becoming increasingly clear that participation is about power-holders renouncing responsibility, a form of social abandonment retooled for neoliberal times, "a complex play of absence and presence that creates an appearance of autonomy" (Blaser 2009: 446). Hence for indígenas, participatory development has been an empty promise, regardless of the community in which they have been asked to participate. As abject subjects in postcolonial hierarchies, indigenous women are identified with risk—of gender inequality, of poverty, of poor services—yet they are consistently brought into programs and projects predefined as participatory, becoming ciphers for autonomy. On the ground, participation is a technology that replicates the politics of abandonment familiar from internal colonialism—offering rural impoverished communities the "opportunity" to build their own latrines, just as the state fails yet again to do so. Participatory rationalities so permeate understandings of moral and social duty that blame adheres to subjects for failing to avail themselves of the autonomy and choice it holds out to them. And yet . . . participation inevitably raises profound questions about organization and resistance, as in a global postcolonial geopolitics of difference, participation reverberates with underlying anxieties about the failures of neoliberal democracies (Kapoor 2005). Indigenous women's grassroots networking reveals how organization and resistance operate in the complex field of social relations and power that continues prior to, in and around, and through participatory technologies of development.

The Chimborazo case demonstrates that at a local level, participatory development becomes entangled with, and works its complex power in relation to, forms of organization whose origins and trajectories are unrelated to what is foreseen in development project work-plans. Despite this most nominal and instrumental of participatory endeavors, however, warmikuna—and elected Kichwa regional and diverse national leaders—consistently disrupted the consensus that is so naturalized as the cornerstone of participation. Interrupting public debates to draw attention to the existence of diversity within diversity, indígenas point to the heterogeneous interests of subjects—poor, indigenous, rural women—recruited into participatory development. Through organizations that span village associations to regional women's representatives and networks and to national and international links, indigenous women find the means to forge a critique by forcing a comparison between participatory development and citizenship rights.

One component of indígenas' agendas is their demand to be the "entes y ejecutoras de los proyectos"—projects' subjects and executors.[52] Indigenous women remain nearly universally excluded from these roles in development. Moreover, they were further marginalized as development reconstituted itself around tropes of vulnerability, which cast certain subpopulations as almost beyond the capacity to participate. These understandings of social heterogeneity hence reorient the issue away from the governing subject and focus again on the vulnerable subaltern, obscuring racialized, gendered, and spatial forms of power. The rationality of "development of social vulnerability" makes intersectional hierarchies even less graspable in policy thinking, as it denies the possibility of recognizing a postcolonial difference and reveals once again participatory development's retooling for new circumstances. Since 2006, the malleable word "participation" was resignified as "citizen participation" in Ecuador's 2007 constituent assembly and 2008 constitution. This chapter reminds us that participation's reinterpretations are deeply invested in notions of community and consensus that have consistently denied the humanity and political presence of female racialized subalterns. Yet throughout participatory development, diverse indigenous women pushed at the boundaries of community by undercutting consensus and articulating agendas for organization that begin from postcolonial social heterogeneity.

———

FOUR

Politics, Statistics, and Affect

"Indigenous Women in Development" Policy

An indigenous woman doesn't have any possibilities and only eats
through the sweat of her brow. It's worse when she's forgotten by
her country and governments. For these reasons I ask for an office
of indigenous women, where we can learn how to develop ourselves,
where our needs and customs are respected.

—DOLORES PUMISACHO, FEINE FEDERATION REPRESENTATIVE FROM COCOTOAG
PARISH, SPEAKING AT THE NATIONAL MEETING OF INDIGENOUS WOMEN, HELD IN
RIOBAMBA (1990)

During the mid- to late 1990s development's understandings of social
heterogeneity were increasingly fractured and, as noted in the previous
chapter, increasingly focused on subjects thought to be at-risk subpopulations.
In this context, Dolores Pumisacho's call here for indigenous women to have
a specific development institution is understandable. As this chapter demonstrates, however, the coming into being of a development category of "indigenous women"—a designation of social heterogeneity that remains in scare
quotes here to mark its removal from the complex lives of diverse racialized
women—did not fulfill indígenas' agendas for change. This new beneficiary category represented a new moment in development's continuous reimagining
of social heterogeneity, emerging at the conjuncture of three coterminous
problematics—democratization, statistical designations of risk, and a neoliberal politics of affect (Comaroff and Comaroff 2001). For development to

acknowledge the category of "indigenous women" entailed first "identifying deficiencies that need to be rectified. . . . The bounding and characterization of an 'intelligible field' appropriate for intervention anticipates the kinds of intervention that experts have to offer" (Li 2007: 7). Identified as a group whose levels of participation in democratic procedures were disproportionately low, ethnic minority women were envisaged as leaders-in-the-making. In parallel, just as social neoliberalism had generated discourses about social vulnerability, so, too, it became increasingly imperative to identify in accurate ways the populations most at risk, a process that generated ever more detailed information about subpopulations. Of particular interest is that the statistical overlap of female gender and indigenous ethnicity vulnerabilities resulted in "a mass of facts" about indigenous women's poverty, lack of schooling, and underemployment. The third strand turned on the problematic of affect, with "indigenous women" coming into development visibility in relation to a perceived lack of necessary proactive embodied agency. In overlapping ways, each arena provided a diagnosis of "indigenous women" that informed and justified programs and projects. In these terms the category of "indigenous women" entered into and reoriented the way development was done and by whom. In this sense, "there was [not] a kind of person who came increasingly to be recognized by bureaucrats or by students of human nature but rather . . . a kind of person came into being at the same time as the kind itself was being invented. In some cases, that is, our classifications and our classes conspire to emerge hand in hand, each egging the other on" (Ian Hacking, quoted in Chakrabarty 2002: 87).

Although justified as a response to need and an improvement on previous thinking, development's shifting lenses of visibility were also the (mutated) outcome of grounded and contested efforts inside and outside of development's institutions to make claims on resources and procedures (Ferguson 1990, 1999). The "indigenous women" category was not a universal truth but emerged through engagement with subaltern actors and social mobilization responding to uneven postcolonial landscapes in Latin America. Hence, in addition to tracing the genealogy of "indigenous women" development, this chapter documents racialized female subalterns' engagement with, retooling of, and contestations around the technical renderings of their problems. While "indigenous women" policy seemingly spoke to intersectional agendas in development, a close reading of policy frameworks informed by indigenous female leaders and village women highlights the policy's failure to address the relational and power-drenched intersectionality found in postcolonial societies. From a marginal position in postcolonial hierarchies, indígenas appropriated and disrupted the meanings and allotted roles awarded them in global-national development policy to pursue agendas for change. Indígenas' interventions in policy-making meetings and political platforms and in village settings shine a critical light on development's current social heterogeneity agendas, by articulating a definition of what it might mean to be a "developed woman" (Klenk 2004).

Emergent Visibility: Indigenous Women and Political Governance

As I traveled by bus between Kichwa and Tsáchila villages, and Quito, talking to indígenas and then to agency staff, regional leaders and civil servants, I was increasingly struck by a paradox. Everyone talked about indigenous women as political actors, yet the frames used to talk about political action were distinct, indeed incompatible; it was like talking about two separate groups. Since then, I have come to see this paradox as a function of two strands of knowledge production, one emerging from indígenas' agency and the other linked to development "making up people," that is, using modern governmental techniques of creating categories that create order and administration, state regulation and distribution (Hacking 1986; Chakrabarty 2002). Categorization and regulation respond to the recoding of "dividing practices," reestablishing lines between full and marginal citizens (Rose and Miller 2008: 98–104). As seen in chapter 3, neoliberal governmentality of development responds to risk and vulnerability by focusing on abject populations who require intervention to produce self-actualizing subjects. Examining "indigenous women" in development policy throws light on how neoliberal management of the social constitutes categories of racialized female subalterns. Moreover, reading these policy interventions in light of indígena critique highlights the political field within which subaltern productions of knowledge dispute the construction of social subjectivities and of citizen agency. These two strands depart from different objectives, vocabularies, and rationalizations of the problems underlying action, coming into contact via grounded practices among specific women. "Indigenous women" frameworks depoliticize indígena positionality by recoding political agency in terms of a performance of active citizenship, a performance driven by neoliberal logics and designed to supersede a bundle of vulnerabilities (see Rose and Miller 2008). Indígena women confront this depoliticization head-on, rejecting policy representations of incapable or abject subjects, and reclaim the possibility of an Other form of citizenship and political subjectivity.

As in Chile's adaptation of gender policy to Mapuche indigenous women (Richards 2004), the "indigenous women" schema was designed to adapt and extend existing GAD approaches to a new target population, "indigenous women." Policy frameworks emerging in the UN Decade for Women (1975–1985) preceded and framed indigenous rights and the UN Decade for Indigenous Peoples (1995–2004). As noted elsewhere, global gender policy has tended to "add women in" to prior policy, exemplified in WID approaches (Rathgeber 1990: 495). Adding women in hence meant incorporating the category of "indigenous women" into a target beneficiary population and excising the power dynamics of racial discrimination, indigenous masculinities in postcolonial hierarchies, and internal colonies in uneven development. As postcolonial writers note, this move was not innocent, as policy's will to improve "indigenous women" arose from neoliberal spheres of knowledge, among gendered actors embedded in postcolonial hierarchies. Whereas urban, whiter and wealthier women activists and policy-makers had gained visibility and authority through Latin American democratization, they viewed "indigenous women" as socially distinctive and vulnerable subjects, for whom indígenas' unique postcolonial positionality was of no relevance. The racialized-classed and urban context for Ecuadorian mainstreaming and institutionalization shaped the postcolonial context in which the recoding of "indigenous women" as a potential beneficiary group could occur, the social meanings of the category molded into a technical tool. As noted in chapter 3, neoliberal policy began to differentiate among fragmented marginal populations, attuning responses to the social qualities perceived to exist in each subgroup. In Ecuador, "indigenous women" became a category that, although linked to vulnerability, also became linked to political concerns, as abject subjects with limited or problematic access to political decision-making and formal representation. In neoliberal governmentality encouraging self-enterprising citizenship, "indigenous women" were seen as deficient in civil and political rights. In this pumped-up participation, "indigenous women" were to learn how to behave in public life according to modern standards associated with progress (Chakrabarty 2002); "Indigenous women" in this context were "gradually, progressively, really and materially constituted through a multiplicity of organisms, forces, energies, materials, thoughts, etc." (Foucault 1980 [1977] quoted in Hacking 1986: 97). In development's beguiling simplifications, the "indigenous women" category was invested with particular social qualities and psychic dispositions that had material consequences for development's institutionalization and indígenas' spheres of action.

In Ecuador indígenas and other subalterns had been excluded from formal political representation through interlocking legal and political cultural means. They had been barred by illiteracy from exercising their voting rights until the late 1970s; citizenship in Ecuador had hence been substantively bound up with the privileges of urban locations, masculinity, nonracialized status, and secure incomes. Indeed the first NGOs working with indigenous women prepared manuals on rights and citizenship. For example, in the late 1980s community-based extension workers began to promote indígenas' electoral turnout, especially among illiterates, describing voting procedures and encouraging participation (Campos and Salguero 1987: 113; see fig. 4.1). In Peru as in Ecuador, NGOs and grassroots religious organizations sought the involvement of "indigenous women" in community and wider affairs through village associations, assuming a synergy between enhancing the participation of "indigenous women" and deepening democracy. "Indigenous women" were coded as backward subjects moving seamlessly into modern citizenship; such interventions were "to be nothing short of changing the lives of indigenous women in an ample spectrum of matters" (Oliart 2008: 4).

Beginning in 1994, the UN agency for women, UNIFEM, pressed for the greater civic engagement of "indigenous women" and girls on the basis of gender equity and human rights (UNESCO 2008). Following the 1995 Beijing women's conference, "indigenous women" as a development concern gained momentum as the UN supported extensions to the leadership and advocacy skills of "indigenous women." From the late 1990s, this PRO-LEAD program aimed to create "a critical mass of women leaders for the new century." Meanwhile in Ecuador, the PRODEPINE ethnodevelopment project was viewed as "an obvious entry point for promoting women's leadership, empowerment and participation in political and economic life." In the late 1990s and early 2000s, the IADB in parallel advocated "the visibility, leadership and participation of indigenous women in decision-making and development programs in the region" (IADB 2002). The momentum to raise the leadership capacity of "indigenous women" seemed unstoppable as multilateral governmentality aimed to induct the presence of "indigenous women" in state-centered formal decision-making arenas where historically they had been absent. Following the first continental meeting of indigenous women in Oaxaca, Mexico, in 2002, the IADB program introduced a regional Andean project for Colombia, Ecuador, Bolivia, Peru, and Venezuela "to strengthen indigenous women's participation in political processes at local, regional and national levels" (IADB 2002, 2004; BID n.d. [2004]; also Blackwell 2006). Under the rubric of social inclusion,

PARTICIPACION POLITICA
DE LA MUJER

Fig. 4.1. An NGO pamphlet encourages indigenous women to vote, Ecuador, 1987.
Campos and Salguero 1987: 137.

the Andean program funded organizations with experienced female leaders from diverse ethnic groups, and the program was extended after 2003 (IADB 2004; see Rankin 2010).

The social meanings and aspirations for "indigenous women" emerged from GAD's and ethnodevelopment's epistemological and institutional denial of postcolonial intersectionality, regardless of neoliberalism's reorientation to social difference (Lemke 2001). Rather than examine how indígenas' location in internal colonies reduced possibilities of opportunities in leadership, programs for "indigenous women" demanded burdensome administration, including the legal registration of local organizations. Each requirement filtered out grassroots groups and favored more NGO-ized and networked women, excluding the poorest and least well-connected indígenas. In one staffer's words, "it's a good program but what with all the terms of reference, the demanding administrative requirements—they're so strict! Women have to make so much effort to get out of the *selva* [jungle], spend money they don't have getting a tax registration, a bank account." Given women's daily grind of work and impoverishment, the few indígenas who did reach more senior leadership positions achieved exceptional educational and professional careers, characteristics that effectively rendered them unrepresentative of the vast majority of indigenous women even when they maintained close networks with ordinary indígenas (Cervone 1998; 2002; Santillán 2008; Radcliffe 2010).

"Indigenous women" programs understood leadership and political participation as referring to formal political office (BID n.d., 2004), thereby ignoring racialized women's grassroots social movement politics around poverty, domestic violence, reproductive health, and literacy (Arboleda 1993; Oliart 2008). The "indigenous women" category was, instead, sutured to prior national and global institutions for justice. Indígenas were encouraged to "strengthen knowledge of the UN human rights system and the means to protect their human rights" (IADB 2004: n.p.),[1] thereby sidelining community and indigenous justice mechanisms (see chapter 6). A consultation with eight women from Bolivia, Ecuador, Colombia, and Peru defined program priorities and strategies, resulting in an international relations and diplomatic framing. In addition, training included themes of conflict resolution, political and civic awareness, law and political processes, strategies of negotiation, and techniques for public speaking, whereby "indigenous women" were to become exemplary neoliberal multicultural "indios permitidos" (authorized indigenous) (Hale 2002; Richards 2007) firmly removed from the "anti-community" (Rose and Miller 2008: 98) associated with indigenous activism. Political personhood (Staeheli et al. 2004) of "indigenous women" constituted problem-solving in conflict-ridden societies, with enhanced skill sets, active citizenship, and interests aligned with democratization. "Indigenous women" were to change; political and social systems were not. In this vein, CONAMU intercultural policy advocated "strengthening women in indigenous and Afro-Ecuadorian sectors by technical-political training, to ensure women leaders are able to intervene in the political sphere" (CONAMU 2007: 14).

"Indigenous women" were additionally brought into being through performances of leadership whose parameters were established through the "forces, energies, materials" always-already endorsed in dominant political behavior, even as they "added in" "indigenous women" (also Schurr 2013). Program documents repetitively mentioned a small number of globally renowned female indigenous leaders, including "Guatemalan Rigoberta Menchú, a Nobel Peace Laureate, and Nina Pacari, former Minister of Foreign Affairs in Ecuador" (IADB 2004). Such references to Menchú's and Pacari's formidable political careers, summarized in donor material, admonished "indigenous women" for a lack of self-actualized propulsion to leadership.[2] By contrast, indígenas' conception of leadership was generally not bound up with individual role models. Life-history interviews with largely Kichwa Andean indigenous leaders suggests that indígenas construct and maintain leadership forms with extensive, emotionally and politically significant friendships that permit them to take elected office while encouraging younger and less experienced women to begin networking (Radcliffe 2010). In contrast to "indigenous women" policy's individuating disposition, regional and national indígena leaders spoke of horizontal social networks. For CONAIE's women's representative, "the political aspect is about how we can get on with practicing, how our *compañeras* can be trained to become new leaders."[3] Talking to rural sonala and warmikuna about aspirations highlighted the gulf between their political experience and policy's ambivalent celebrations of Menchú and Pacari (chapter 6).

While empowerment goals lay at the center of "indigenous women" policy thinking, its genealogy in gender mainstreaming reproduced the will to empowerment in a colonial frame, "fixing and freezing differences into [impermeable] divisions" (Chakrabarty 2002: 95) between "thirdworldwomen" and modern female subjects with full citizenship (Minh-Ha 1989; Mohanty 2002). Departing from an empowerment agenda, the IADB approached ethnic and cultural diversity from the global postcolonial context of gender policy, as did UNDP and UNIFEM. The IADB's Gender Mainstreaming Action Plan 2003–2005 coordinated *gender* equity measures to tackle the "cumulative disadvantages and discrimination faced by indigenous peoples, Afro-descendant groups, persons with disabilities, poor women and persons with HIV/AIDS" (IADB 2001; see chapter 3). The UN Task Force on Indigenous Women (created in the 2004 Permanent Forum) was requested "to integrate and strengthen gender mainstreaming in the work of the United Nations system that affects indigenous people, while highlighting the roles of indigenous women and the urgent need to address all the forms of discrimination that they face" through a three-year program in Latin America, Africa, and Asia (UN DESA 2007: iv). Program documents regularly attributed the inarticulacy of "indigenous women" in public spheres to "traditional" culture that did not endow women with the requisite cultural and political attributes for empowerment. Gabriela Vega, IADB chief of GAD sustainable development policy, said, "The characteristics associated with a good leader, such as speaking in public, being articulate and taking initiative are not qualities traditionally taught to women and, on many occasions, women exclude themselves in certain indigenous populations" (IADB 2004).[4]

The difference of "indigenous women" was thus constituted through postcolonial characterizations of raced-female-poor subjects as socially wanting in relation to political modernity. Building on prior postcolonial interpretations of heterogeneity, the new policy framework combined neoliberal interpretations of abject subjects with colonial readings of indigenous nonmodernity and gender bias, an example of "dynamic nominalism" (Hacking 1986) thoroughly grounded in postcolonial hierarchies. Inevitably it reflected processes of knowledge production from locations of power and privilege, unconnected with indígenas' realities. Always already embedded in global power relations (Alexander and Mohanty 1997), this policy locked together a surface attention to social difference with Latin American colonial readings of female indigeneity to produce a solution, namely an individualized subject unmoored from ethnic culture affiliated with modern formal politics, in which, as Bhabha notes, colonial power cannot be acknowledged. While seemingly offering "indigenous women" rights and justice, these were preemptively situated in a metropolitan epistemology of liberty (Povinelli 2005). These colonial dynamics can be further explored in an INGO project to encourage sonala's leadership.

"INDIGENOUS WOMEN" POLICY IN ACTION: TSÁCHILA WOMEN AND LEADERSHIP

From the early 2000s, a European INGO project for Tsáchila women's leadership copied many of the features of global "indigenous women" leadership policy. At the time, IBIS, an organization with long experience of working in Latin America with indigenous populations, had a formal mandate for gender equality across all its projects; in Ecuador it assisted CONAIE's political program in response to a recent law establishing electoral quotas for women. (On the quota law, also see chapter 6.)[5] In this context, IBIS viewed "indigenous women" in Ecuador's coastal indigenous groups as at risk of political exclusion and requiring intervention. A consultancy document noted how "Épera, Tsáchila and Awá women had impoverished places of representation, and have nearly zero intervention in regional and national decision-making."[6] Moreover, "decisions are taken by consensus, but [Tsáchila] women's voices are barely heard, only "yes" or "no" in reply to specific questions. Although levels of participation appear high, these spaces are merely formal" (Almeida 2007b: 56), implying that women were unable to influence public debates (Mosse 1994). Although the holy grail of participatory development—consensus—was present, it was deemed to be the wrong kind of consensus for women. By comparison, sonala discuss how lack of formal education disqualifies them from public debate. Talking to warmikuna visiting from Chimborazo, a Tsáchila sona told us all how "we aren't educated, we don't have training. So sometimes we sonala are afraid, we think we'll speak badly, make mistakes."[7] The policy proposed to "add" "indigenous women" "in," enlarging GAD to integrate the "indigenous women" category with "the concept of empowerment [adapted] . . . to the context, expectations and demands of coastal indigenous women" (Almeida 2007b: 58).

Yet IBIS was to find itself operating in the name of female empowerment at cross-purposes with the nationality's own agendas, which spoke in the name of culture. A decade earlier, the Tsáchila all-male Governing Council, including the elected governor, had created a Women's Commission, arguing that "women sustain, promote and transmit culture through the family" (Comisión de Mujer y Familia Tsáchila n.d.b: 3). According to oral testimony, the women's commission had little material or political impact on village women. Years later, Julia, one of my Tsáchila interviewees, recalled, "Sure, there was a female leader. I think one was called the Women's Commission which worked a little but failed. She couldn't do the project and I don't know what happened." When IBIS's project was rolled out, place-specific understandings of the very "matter" of "indigenous women" initially created the basis for project interventions yet ultimately scuppered the project. The reason revolved around incompatible interpretations of the link between indigenous femininity and culture: whereas policy saw "indigenous women" as being "freed" from culture, the male Tsáchila leaders viewed women as integral to cultural reproduction. At the project's start, these differences were not yet apparent: the Tsáchila council coordinated with IBIS for thirty women to learn leadership skills from each other and through regional exchanges. Local project staff found women eager for "the strengthening of the Women's Commission, . . . motivation workshops, re-valorization and self-esteem, and scholarships for professionalization. Women also consider workshops on collective rights and women's rights to be important to combat mistreatment" (Almeida 2007b: 51). Having identified the kind of "indigenous women" sought, the program proposed "to convert Tsáchila women into the fundamental axis of the nationality's development, through a real democratic exercise . . . and make them into actors with openness towards planning for community development."[8] At the same time the Tsáchila Governing Council created a new position of women's representative (*dirigente de las mujeres*), "a female leader to be considered a member of the Council of Tsáchila Governance with equal powers and rights" (Comisión de Mujer y Familia Tsáchila n.d.b: 3), requiring a change in the Tsáchila statutes. The Governing Council was to select the women's representative from among candidates put forward by each Tsáchila comuna, each candidate presenting a proposal and the best proposal granting one woman three years to carry it forward. Although a women's representative was appointed during the IBIS project, the post remained unfilled during much of my fieldwork.

Illustrating "indigenous women" policy, the IBIS project sought to eradicate culturally driven barriers to women's self-esteem, with a view to ridding sonala of timidity in public life. A former participant, Cristina, explained her interpretation of the project sitting on her porch as her children played in the yard: "Well Denmark [i.e. IBIS] supported us quite a lot because many women were timid, ashamed. This is what I tell you Sarah, ashamed because before, women never were in a dialogue like I'm doing now, no. We never had dialogues because we were timid—timid of expressing ourselves, timid about speaking, timid to share [our thoughts]. I think that we used to be afraid, afraid of speaking, yes of speaking. I was like that—it made me frightened. I said to myself, "What do I do?' " As Cristina's account makes clear, "indigenous women" considered themselves in relation to the lack of the requisite attributes for modern political personhood. Sonala came to see themselves through the lens of individualized agency. For a few sonala, this framework permitted them to rework relations with husbands and community members, with lasting impacts. According to one participant, "at the start my husband was against it, but then he supported me and this gives me strength." In the local press, male leaders proclaimed, "Women don't feel marginalized now, nor are they afraid. And this is positive."[9]

Despite uneven gains, the project replicated the tendency for indigenous women to receive short-term, easily terminated programs. According to a onetime women's representative, now in her early twenties, "we wait for days for projects like the one with IBIS-Dinamarca. And they told us to wait, for a few months, but that was it." In part the project ended due to conflicting interpretations of sonala's role in ethnic politics. Many spouses and male leaders viewed this program as guaranteeing cultural protection, whereas policy-makers effectively encouraged women to reconsider their interests as not consonant with ethnic culture. Each side subordinated sonala's interests in giving voice to interlocking exclusions and creating gendered-raced political subjectivities (Spivak 1993). In light of this standoff and constraints on sonala agency, the initial project focus on "indigenous women" was retooled as "youth" outreach, a switch that resulted in predominantly male participation (Tsáchila Informe 2006), reflecting the deep ambivalence of male villagers and the Tsáchila governor toward the project's female empowerment goals.[10]

The Tsáchila women's program illustrates how expectations about political personhood infused policy attention to social heterogeneity in ways that reembedded policy in a global colonial disavowal of (the "wrong kind" of) culture, just as it normalized technologies of the (gendered, modern) self. At the same time, while these programs represent classic examples of developmental governmentality, examining them in a postcolonial frame brings into focus the disjunctures between subaltern and policy objectives and how policy gets refounded on unquestioned colonial readings of (cultural) difference. According to these presumptions, difference can be read directly from the "indigenous" label as can indigeneity's intersectionality with gender, to give the policy-relevant category of "indigenous women." Not only did these embedded understandings of social heterogeneity come to specify the group to be addressed through projects; it also informed development's understandings of how each individual "indigenous woman" behaves in the modern political sphere. The merging of liberal and colonial conceptions of the self occurred in advance of project design and regardless of village male opposition.

LEADERSHIP BY INDÍGENAS FOR INDÍGENAS: ECUARUNARI WOMEN'S LEADERSHIP TRAINING SCHOOL

A very different project with enduring consequences for indígenas' voice, authority, and political agency is the Dolores Cacuango Women's Leadership training school (Escuela de Formación de Mujeres "Dolores Cacuango"), which builds on indígenas' understandings. The training school, initiated and supported by CONAIE's Andean affiliate federation Ecuarunari, is organized by indígena women for indígena women (Palacios 2005; Figueroa

Romero 2012). Combining feminist consciousness-raising with systematic instruction in public speaking, the training school works from existing practices of indígena political engagement. In this sphere, indígenas learn to build subjectivity in terms of self-respect as "dignified, valuable [subjects] deserving of success" (Shrestha 1995; Veloz 1997). Funded by a consortium, including the Norwegian bilateral agency, IBIS, and CODENPE, the training school provides women with the opportunity to discuss economic development, education, health, political and territorial rights, and environmental questions.[11] So successful has the leadership training school model become that various ethnic and peasant organizations have replicated it.

Training school "graduates" make up a substantial share of local female political candidates and activists in local and regional associations and ethnic federations, marking "one of the most significant achievements in recent times," according to an indigenous evaluation of local government (ICCI 2001: 5).[12] The school supports indigenous women's design and management of projects in which culture, femininity, and empowerment acquire meanings forged from their critical knowledges. One training school graduate, Ana Maria, now an elected councilor in Chimborazo, describes her experience: "I have a lot of confidence thank goodness, as I really trust the [indigenous] prefect and because of my language. I say to people, "let's do this, that; let's plan that," to benefit people [in Chimborazo]. So I get going [me desenvuelvo], sometimes more than my boss! As [development workers] don't understand kichwa, I attend people in our language, as it's much easier to make them understand. People come to find me, or I go to them. The provincial council works with participatory budgeting, so people have to decide in parish or district meetings, on the projects." Articulate and well-connected, Ana Maria embodies a political learning process arising from women's networks and ethnic civil movements.[13] "Culture" in the training school represents a resource rather than an obstacle, creatively reworked in autonomous indígena-only spaces. Although not without resource limitations, the school's capacity to enable women to gain broad-ranging information that cuts across indigenous cosmology, international law, and planning has been associated with the creation of grassroots networks and the resignification of indígena public presence.

❋

"Indigenous women" hence came into visibility in the context of broad debates around democratization, decentralization, and electoral quotas. The "indigenous women" category came into development already lacking the attributes of the modern political subject, whose embeddedness in culture elicited interventions to recode subjectivity in liberal, universal terms. An implicit catalogue of women's lack—of experience, role models, cultural background, and confidence—provided the (unacknowledged/unacknowledgeable) premise on which this group would be realized materially. Reiterating global postcolonial moves, the "indigenous women" category arguably gained force from GAD's construction of culturally different femininities and its advocacy of global empowerment agendas. While women in Tsáchila and Kichwa districts sought to retool elements of this agenda, their critical engagement was not enough to challenge the fundamental direction of the invented "indigenous woman" category.

Statistics and Risk: Getting to Know "Indigenous Women"

Once problematized in the frame of participation and gender mainstreaming, the category "indigenous women" had to be described, sorted, and classified in order to bring into focus its members' development lack and to clarify the administration of interventions. At the turn of the twenty-first century, policy-makers began to lament the scarcity of accurate and sufficient statistical information on "indigenous women." According to one international policy document, "unfortunately there are still few statistical data differentiated by gender on indigenous peoples" (Meentzen 2001: i). As throughout the postcolonial South, statistics provided the basis for ruling, a means of bringing into being subjects that, once enumerated, elicited specific interventions (Chakrabarty 2002). "Indigenous women" were hence constituted through neoliberal administration not merely as political "deficiencies to be rectified" but also as a "fuzzy" category that acquired ever sharper means of enumeration to codify and distinguish it from other needy populations. As in leadership agendas, GAD provided the initial frameworks through which information collection occurred, so in Ecuador the National Women's Council, CONAMU, gathered data to address "discrimination against women in *pueblos* and nationalities, and Afro-Ecuadorians in access to work, resources, education, health and heritage" (CONAMU 2004: 52). Although indígena representatives recognize the contribution of detailed, accurate information in tackling disadvantage, they incisively critique the mathematical premise and statistical comparisons through which "indigenous women" came into visibility.

"Indigenous women" policy was genealogically linked to a gender framework of social difference, a historical impetus that had ramifications through statistical concerns. Disaggregating gender statistics by ethnicity emerged in lockstep with the "indigenous women" category's growing policy visibility. Despite acknowledgments that statistics are poor at capturing women's lives, the primary concern remained a technical one of improving statistical accuracy (Calfío and Velasco 2005). "Indigenous women" were to be made knowable within specific parameters that rendered them subject to technical interventions (Li 2007). A precedent was set in the mid-1990s as agencies began to calibrate risk factors for maternal mortality, poverty, and so on. The Chimborazo Project for rural women, for instance, designed a methodology that combined qualitative and quantitative data in consultation with village women.[14] Not only did "indigenous women" come into visibility as a particularly at-risk population (chapter 3), statistical information coded the situation of "indigenous women" in ways that reified the value-laden and qualitatively distinctive nature of their abjection and risks.

Through the 1990s, a comparative understanding of social heterogeneity was widely used by gender planners who sought to identify how much poorer rural female-headed households were relative to male counterparts (Secretaría Técnica de Frente Social 1999; Cuvi Sánchez and Ferraro 2000). Policy documents started to make statements such as "Indigenous and black women have fewer opportunities for education and training, but they are also discriminated against for their ethnicity" in employment (CONAMU 2004: 35; 2006). A flurry of statistical collation revealed that Ecuadorian rural women's work had been systematically underrecorded, a data problem that indirectly focused attention on how indigenous women's labor was particularly difficult to capture with existing measures (Cuvi Sánchez 2000). In turn, CONAMU carried out a comparative statistical survey of mestiza, Afro-Ecuadorian, and indigenous women's hours of work. Gender-based (in effect, women-only) analysis stressed data objectivity, producing discrete measurable indicators related to institutionalized facets of life (education, hospital services and earnings) (Paulson 2000: 9). In social neoliberal targeting of at-risk groups, an emergent concern was to channel resources at needy groups, as human security (in addition to state security) became the biopolitical lens (Thomas 2001; Duffield 2007).

As leadership programs for "indigenous women" gained momentum, quantitative data were collated in ways that highlighted male-female differences in multiethnic populations. In 2003, a CEDAW committee highlighted Ecuador's need for "strategically disaggregated data by gender that makes clear the ethno-cultural and age-related diversity in the country" (CONAMU 2004: 7). Where census or statistical information was lacking, policy-makers sought out other sources. "We cannot count on sufficient reliable statistics and we have to be content with qualitative information from the indigenous women consulted."[15] Indígenas' extensive, detailed and nuanced nonstatistical knowledge of development interventions—and their varied outcomes—was hence positioned as second-best, discounted as less reliable, reflecting postcolonial knowledge production more broadly (Mignolo 2000). The close juxtaposition of statistical data work and educational characteristics represented "indigenous women" as a problematic and internally undifferentiated mass of subjects. In this way a set of "stylized facts" (Cornwall et al. 2007: 13) began to attach themselves to the category of the "indigenous woman," who thereby was increasingly abstracted from historic-geographical contexts. Indígenas were not immune to quantitative narratives. Cristina, who had been involved in IBIS's leadership project, explained, "so we were in training for nearly a year and now, Sarah, we women aren't afraid. Sure, there are still some who are timid who didn't participate in this training and workshops. Around 20 percent, yes, around 20 percent are like that. But 80 percent we're really pretty advanced already." That Cristina should link percentages and empowerment is consistent with "indigenous women" policy in its postcolonial enumeration of at-risk populations.

Although "indigenous women" were statistically configured in a comparative frame with nonindigenous women, indigenous men, and so on, there was also an underlying impulse to knowledge about "indigenous women" as social beings. In implicit comparison with racially unmarked women, "indigenous women" were more vulnerable, the causes of which were sought in statitistical correlations. Hence in education, "indigenous women" had a "deficit" relative to nonindigenous women in secondary and higher education in 90 percent of cases (UNDP et al. 2005: 3; compare Calla 2006). Where "indigenous women" were subdivided, it was to identify subjects even more at risk along a gradient of vulnerability. Ecuadorian state policy documents associated older rural indigenous women with exceptionally high illiteracy rates (CONAMU 2004: 32). The "indigenous woman" category became ever more associated with vulnerability, triggering "protectionist, even conservative, responses from states" (Kapur 2002: 6) and NGOs. CONAMU was prompted to intervene to deal with "ethnic girls and adolescents' security, the elimination of threats to their physical, psychological and sexual integrity, [freedom] from double discrimination, commerce, servility, slavery and exploitation, as well as access to education, health and recreation" (CONAMU 2004: 53).

Whereas previous rounds of gender policy had animated critiques of patriarchy and racism, the at-risk, statistical rendition of "indigenous women" unmoored their postcolonial disadvantage from interlocking power dynamics and presented it as an additive set of risk factors that resignified indígenas' positionality in terms already established in global and national development thinking.

Along with development's approach to social heterogeneity in other moments, this apparently modern anxiety is rooted in the colonial present. As statistically defined "indigenous women" emerged into clarity, anxieties concerning them as a boundary marker between tradition and modernity reemerged and reworked power relations found in earlier Ecuadorian history (Muratorio 1994). Edward Said notes how colonized populations came to be known to Orientalist discourses through the urgent collection of information (Said 1993).[16] Colonizers' knowledge about subjected populations reflected power over them as much as a concern to fix identities. In late twentieth-century Latin American development, "indigenous women" prompted similar concerns that were managed through the avid recompilation of a mass of facts. Moreover, national coloniality and its demarcation of subjects with variable attachment and claims on the nation became the wider background against which statistical work was done, an affective and historically embedded social heterogeneity, the unacknowledged and unacknowledgeable underside of developmental statistics.

It is precisely around such issues that indigenous women contest statistics-based policy. In an office with posters celebrating indigenous activism, Magdalena, an elected Andean leader and women's representative, told me in frustration, "The international indicators really annoy me. With all due respect to the UN or the MDGs, but they really annoy me because sometimes we indigenous women are not taken into account. We know that there is a huge budget out there [in international development] that just defines us as folklore or as a symbol of indigeneity [folclor y logotipo indígena]. . . . So we're not in agreement with these indicators."[17] Rejecting an "at risk" label, indígenas view themselves as agents capable of providing information about their lives' harsh realities as well as analyzing the processes underlying disadvantage. Where, they ask, are statistics on indígenas' election to local political office, any measure to contextualize the "exceptional" leaders Nina Pacari and Blanca Chancosa? Where is the qualitative information compiled by women through direct experience? Magdalena, in her inimitable way, dissects the ongoing associations between indigeneity, "problems," and power-knowledge underpinning Ecuadorian development. Although statistical knowledge of "indigenous women" bypasses questions of culture and difference, Magdalena shows that leaves in place stereotypes that reproduce the colonial present. The denomination of "indigenous women" is always-already constituted in relation to postcolonial hierarchies of race-place-income.[18]

While "indigenous women's" statistical representation constitutes an image of an aggregated abstract subject with neither individual nor collective dimensions, the leadership agenda by contrast pivots around hyperindividualized figureheads. The paradox is explicable only with reference to the colonial continuum through which the policy agenda of "indigenous women" defines its objective, namely moving an undifferentiated subaltern mass far from modernity toward an individual political agent working toward liberal representation.

Individualization and Self-Esteem: The Paradox of Cultural Essentialism

The challenge is a double one; on the one hand, to provide tools of knowledge not only on organization and parliamentary procedures that can strengthen the culture's own institutions to resolve their concerns and conflicts. But also to create, invent and work collectively with women in activities—traditional and non-traditional—in order to promote self-valorization and the construction of self-esteem, activities which offer a new horizon of understanding and feeling to each activity, in whichever area of life women are.

EDITORIAL INTRODUCTION TO ES COMO LA LUNA NUESTRO PENSAMIENTO: TESTIMONIOS E HISTORIAS DE MUJERES DE CHIMBORAZO, PROJECT DOCUMENT FROM THE DEVELOPMENT PROJECT FOR RURAL WOMEN IN CHIMBORAZO (1997)

A third, but by no means last, strand woven into "indigenous women" development and its framing of social heterogeneity concerned the necessity of transforming a traditional affective disposition associated with indigenous subalterns into a modern form of subjectivity. In a word, "indigenous women" lacked self-esteem. Policy pinpointed low self-esteem as the reason for low political participation rates and minimal take-up of leadership of "indigenous women." The trope of low self-esteem indexes women's lack of proactive embodied agency contextualized in relation to neoliberal entrepreneurialism and liberal individualization, as well as to unremarked postcolonial characterizations of indigeneity and social difference. Emerging during social neoliberalism, the will to increase self-esteem of "indigenous women" is closely tied to neoliberalism's cultural politics (Foucault 2008). In neoliberal technologies of the self, boosting self-esteem has "as its goal . . . a new politics and a different social order. It promises to solve social problems by heralding a revolution—not against capitalism, racism, the patriarchy, etc., but against the (wrong) way of governing ourselves. . . . 'Self-esteem' thus has much more to do with self-assessment than with self-respect, as the self continuously has to be measured, judged and disciplined in order to gear personal 'empowerment' to collective yardsticks" (Lemke 2001: 202). Yet, as I shall show, the instruction to self-discipline was not merely neoliberal as it coded self-esteem of "indigenous women" implicitly as a problem of indigeneity, whereby program injunctions promised a fully realized universal subjectivity in which cultural difference was rendered irrelevant (compare Povinelli 2005). Reading "indigenous woman" policy as a postcolonial social neoliberal intervention hence suggests a will to improve that has been repurposed in the neoliberal colonial present.

Developmental concepts of self-esteem—together with indigenous women's active re-working of its meanings—was brought home to me in discussions about the EU-funded Chimborazo rural women's project and its legacies (chapter 3). Willing an improved psychic realm, the project sought to create solidarity networks among the province's rural women as a means to transmit the soft skills of self-confidence. According to a staffer, "in effect the theme of women's self-esteem, combined with the [elements of] organizational strengthening and entrepreneurial capacities, was the *principle aspect* of the project. In other words, the work on women's self-esteem—or what we called "empowerment"—was the starting and end point of all program actions."[19] This project was not alone. Through the 1990s and beyond, Ecuadorian development for indigenous populations included the objective of changing the affective disposition of "indigenous women." In the Andean province of Cañar, a milk project combined production and organizational training of "indigenous women" with the goal of raising self-esteem (Ávila Inga 1996). Female networking and consciousness-raising permeated the women's movement and feminist *encuentros* (meetings) (Goetschel et al. 2007). By the mid-1990s, the concept had entered the capillaries of development thinking and practice in ways that suggest it was used to differentiate between, not agglutinate, women. Female NGO workers characterized "lack of self-esteem" as a structural limit on Amazon Kichwa women's public and productive roles (Lilliott 1997). The national PRONADER project appointed a gender expert to adapt themes of self-esteem, as well as land and technical training, to meet rural women's needs. During the 1990s Ecuadorian GAD programs understood prowomen interventions along a continuum from empowerment to low self-esteem, one that mirrored postcolonial intersectional hierarchies.

Parsing the acquired meanings of personal self-confidence in this postcolonial context through Frantz Fanon's insights suggests that this mapping out of abjection onto racialized women is no coincidence. According to Fanon, the psychic violence of colonialism articulated through the colonizer's gaze makes the subaltern "feel responsible for my body, my race, my ancestors" (Fanon 1986 [1952]: 112; Memmi 2003 [1957]) and hence lacking agency.[20] In Ecuador, the indigenous subaltern subject historically acquired a strong association with lack of self-esteem, a quintessentially modern quality defined relationally. In the 1950s Ecuadorian public debate advocated action to address Otavalo indigenous peoples' "self-valorization . . . through economic improvement" to overcome the "inferiority complex and submission" displayed in subaltern-elite interactions (Prieto 2008: 177). In the 1960s, a trainee social worker blamed women's problems in Chimborazo on an ethnic "inferiority complex" and women's removal from a feminized domestic sphere (Espín 1965; see Maldonado-Torres 2007). In midcentury mestizaje, acculturation and modernization were to occur through transforming personal conduct, a disciplining of the racialized body whereby "acculturated Indians overcome the inferiority complex [and gain] an individual and collective confidence" (quoted in Prieto 2008: 179). Whereas elite racism remained unproblematized, development assumed a role in molding affective capabilities to bring its beneficiaries up to the valued, modern disposition of self-confidence. In trying to understand social heterogeneity in the midcentury, development professionals noted that "passive submission" and an "apathetic rejection" of opportunities often hampered progress (Bromley 1977: 38).

Policy for "indigenous women" hence arises in relation to these postcolonial dynamics of power and difference. The policy visibility of "indigenous women" emerged partially from psychic differentiation between a complete modern subject and a dejected subaltern, as in the EU development worker's quote earlier. In the postcolonial oppositional categories that underlie and energize development frameworks (Said 1993), the individual pole of embodied autonomy is distinct from the yet-to-be-modernized incipient individual whose behaviors, outlook, and capacity for change are subordinate to culture (Povinelli 2005; Minister of Social Well-Being, quoted in Memorias del Seminario Nacional n.d.; Peredo Beltrán 2004: 62; UNESCO 2008: 12). As feminist scholars also note, self-esteem constitutes a form of disciplined individualization bound up with metropolitan and racialized postcolonial connotations (Mohanty 1991; McEwan 2009). Gender policy offered "indigenous women" the opportunity to move from "culture" and toward self-identity as women, an interpretation of social difference grounded in globally structured liberal feminism, in which staff act as enlightened helpmeets for thirdworldwomen (Baaz 2005; Cook 2008). Moreover, framing the needs of "indigenous women" as a problem of confidence reified ethnic culture as the primary cause of female marginalization, perpetuating an image of "a truncated third world woman who is sexually constrained, tradition-bound, incarcerated in the home, illiterate and poor" (Grewal and Kaplan 1994; Volpp 2001).[21] Policy representations of "indigenous women" hence rearticulated GAD's global coloniality and blame on indigenous culture in policy that seemingly addressed social heterogeneity and affect.[22]

By contrast, indígena activism attempted to tackle both social neoliberal and postcolonial injunctions by resignifying the meanings of self-esteem in a politics addressing racism and gendered violence. The founder of CONMIE, Ecuador's indigenous women's confederation, Teresa Simbaña, cathects self-worth to struggle against colonial dehumanization: "There was a time when we had to recognize that a woman was a person, at least with regard to self-esteem, that she was a worthwhile person, that she was a human being. . . . To train her in human rights, women's rights, collective rights. So it was very important that women could reclaim their rights, could feel that really they are mistreated in all aspects" (Simbaña 2003: 3). Self-esteem was respatialized away from an individualized psyche and toward a subaltern situated within interlocking racial and gendered hierarchies, a connection elided by "indigenous women" policy. Moreover, as Teresa makes clear, indígenas contest the separation of development from citizenship. At the Chimborazo training school, women linked self-confidence to demands for sexual and reproductive rights as part of a multiscalar decolonial politics (CEDIS 2007b). In Chimborazo's EU rural women's project, grassroots indígena promoters used the concept of self-esteem to rework relations between culture, women, and men: "Women studied self-esteem and today in meetings when we want to motivate women, we're always using the term. 'Value yourselves, like yourselves, love yourselves!' Because before in the indigenous world, we would say 'although he beats you, although he kills you, he's your husband,' or that 'women were made to be mistreated, beaten.' But since I was a girl I never agreed with that saying."[23] Indígenas also consistently raise critiques of racism, questioning the postcolonial hierarchies that reduce their interests to a cultural problem.[24]

※

The "indigenous women" development approach seemingly offered a form of intervention for female racialized subalterns, paying attention to problems of political presence, visibility, and agency. As in other development approaches, however, the "indigenous women" policy framed female subalterns' social difference in ways that were already understood within social neoliberal and human security readings of social heterogeneity, and—in unacknowledged ways—inflected with colonial difference. "Indigenous women" policy reelaborated core understandings from social neoliberal attention to risk and vulnerability, while retrieving a colonial discourse around self-esteem and subaltern abjection. Despite indígenas' extensive mobilization in and beyond Ecuador, development thinking at the turn of the twenty-first century represented "indigenous women" as abject ciphers of ethnic culture who still needed to be made into individual democratic moderns. In part this reflected shifts away from agricultural development goals and toward formal democracy, away from universal programs and toward neoliberal views of socially fragmented societies (Shrestha 1995; Chakrabarty 2002; Chatterjee 2004; Duffield 2007; Rose and Miller 2008). In Latin America, too, a form of governmentality eager to parse distinctions between rebel and permitted Indians was no doubt also at work (Hale 2002). Yet throughout these policy shifts, indígenas remained astute critical commentators and active in mobilizing for an Other politics.

Indigenous Women as Development Experts

In development we don't want to have people coming to construct us, but for us to do development from our own proposals, from the organizations. Because what happens with the NGOs and organizations? I'll tell you. It's already worked up, everything is worked out—it's like a book that's already written. And so why do they call on indigenous women? It's only to justify what's already done. We don't agree with this kind of development because it doesn't come from indigenous women, but it comes in already designed. But we do agree with a form of development that we drive from our organizations. That's what I wanted to tell you. Because from the organizations comes peoples' feelings, the various—many!—concerns, demands, and from us too come proposals—ours, to do them ourselves.

MAGDALENA AYSABUCHA, ELECTED WOMEN'S REPRESENTATIVE,
ECUARUNARI INDIGENOUS FEDERATION, SPEAKING IN MARCH 2009

I want proposals for development to come in from the provinces and to be discussed at the very highest level, so that they go into the [national] development plan.

DELIA CAGUANA, ELECTED WOMEN'S REPRESENTATIVE, CHIMBORAZO FEDERATION, SPEAKING IN 2010

What we need to do is to exercise our rights as women in conditions of equality with men, and as indigenous people in relation to nonindigenous groups.

ROSA MARIA VACACELA, INDIGENOUS WOMAN EMPLOYED IN THE SENPLADES DEVELOPMENT SECRETARIAT, SPEAKING IN MARCH 2010

Delia and Rosa María were speaking at a workshop on indigenous women and public policies, convening fifty indigenous women and ethnic representatives from around the country, with CODENPE staff and advisors. Although their politics, priorities, and attitudes to development-led change differ, Delia's and Rosa Maria's interjections highlight important dimensions of the politics around indigenous women and development in the second decade of the twenty-first century. Indígenas have learned from a variety of interventions to articulate critical perspectives from a marginal location in development, as illustrated by indígenas' deep engagement with questions around interculturalism and gender. Informed by subaltern understandings of postcolonial hierarchies, women are alive to these critiques, as leaders of ethnic rights and indígena networks and through direct embodied learning from harsh material realities in uneven postcolonial development. Indigenous women's insights into power, difference, and culture begin from a critique of power relations to which they are subjected daily. Responding in part to these critiques while also seeking to channel them into an agenda, CODENPE convened a meeting at Baños in March 2010 with the aim of discussing public policy and social spending from indigenous women's perspectives. In such arenas, indígenas speak back to development and thereby resignify participation, agency, and (self-)knowledge according to their experiences of postcolonial heterogeneity.

Through their networks and elected representatives, indígenas repoliticize the category of "indigenous women" while exploding development's certainties about how to approach social heterogeneity. Leaders express their wariness of liberal feminism's lack of attention to racial hierarchies and historic failure to acknowledge ethnicity and gender as intersecting forms of oppression in the Ecuadorian context. Such criticisms are most commonly voiced by leaders prominent in the late 1990s, such as Nina Pacari: "We belong to a people, a collective entity, and as such the struggle of indigenous women is different from that of the women's movement. It is a struggle as peoples in which men and women demand to be recognized as peoples, to be recognized as collective subjects of rights and, as such, for state and society to recognize the specific rights that correspond to us" (Pacari 1998b). Similarly Vicenta Chuma, an older Ecuarunari leader, distanced herself from GAD agendas. "The western system attempts in many ways to give a purely feminist content to indigenous women's struggle, supporting training and leadership projects on models of self-evaluation, and coercive proposals about domestic violence" (Chuma 2004: 3; also CONAMU 2007: 6). A number of indígena leaders criticize gender mainstreaming that prioritizes male-female differentials over other axes of power. An indígena leader explained: "The nonindigenous women's movement . . . has replicated mestizo society's unequal relationship with indigenous people. They continue to think that indigenous women cannot come up with our own proposals, and in this sense they try to talk in our name. . . . We indigenous women demand that NGOs and mestiza women's organizations not seek to manipulate us nor speak for us. If they want to support us, it must be based on our reality and dynamic" (Tene 2000: 211, 223). Andean indigenous women call for alternative conceptualizations of gender relations and power. Challenging the strands of feminist discourse that assume nonwestern minority cultures are more patriarchal than western liberal cultures, indígenas distinguish between ethnic patriarchs, a male but feminized subaltern produced by colonial power (see Fanon 1986 [1952]), and men's diverse attitudes and practices in communities and organizations. However, indígenas continue to disagree with men who seek to speak on their behalf, even if they have more nuanced understandings of indigenous masculinities than does policy.

In meetings in Quito and Andean villages, groups of women argued that gender is not the only way to think about power. At the same time, many acknowledge that the term is useful in certain contexts as it might leverage particular types of support for rights language, and thereby flexibly resignify the term. Indígenas are acutely aware of the (post)colonial politics of GAD and debate the validity, reach, and implications of gender as a political concept. Although there is no universal agreement, indígenas find the term good to think with. One definition was offered in a policy meeting by a female CODENPE employee, "What is gender? From the perspective of researchers who are not from here, but from western countries, they say that it's all the practices, symbols, representations, norms and social values that society elaborates around anatomical and physiological differences of sex. It's very distant. Although these ideas come from other societies, Ecuadorian society takes responsi-

Fig. 4.2. Federation of indigenous women's associations, Quimiag, Chimborazo, 2010. Photograph by the author.

bility for reproducing it and this becomes the model for indigenous populations."[25] Whereas a state employee might argue for the indigenous development council (CODENPE) to take gender more systematically into account, local community activists speak about interculturalism and rights. Building on her mobilization with Quimiag village women (see fig. 4.2), Delia organized a project to improve decision-making power around women's rights, the plurinational state, and prior informed consent for megaprojects.[26] Although not using the language of "gender," she was clear that indígenas' concerns have to be placed front and center in development debates. At a village meeting I heard a national male leader query her focus on informed consent, but Delia was adamant that this issue had wider resonances than resource extraction conflicts. For her, it was a fundamental question of female voice and authority at multiple scales—how were women to be full agents if they did not have systematic information, the right to reflect on information and then come to a decision without coercion?

In a national workshop among indígena leaders where several women had development experience, a senior Andean leader mused out loud: "So we need to validate something that makes us indigenous women. If we say equality between men and women, or 'equality and space,' that might work. We have to start from ourselves [indigenous women] as we talk about rights—political, economic and so on—rights of women, and also of interculturalism, rights of [indigenous] peoples."[27] Although holding varying views due to personal and regional histories of activism, indígenas generally downplay or avoid using the term "gender" on its own. In Amazonian Sucumbíos province, indígenas joined a multiethnic group behind an agenda for health, economic security, education, and political participation and against violence (Movimiento de Mujeres de Sucumbíos n.d.). Warmikuna organizations in Chimborazo prepared an agenda that interpreted women's rights as encompassing participation, leadership, decision-making, sexuality, violence, and indigenous justice systems.[28] Neither document used the word "gender." In contrast to development's focus on culture and psychology, indígenas' agendas turn on issues of racialized and gendered power. According to a young indígena intellectual, "it is time to change relations of power, subordination and oppression that indigenous women experience on a daily basis. . . . Gender violence is expressed in physical, sexual and psychological violence, but also at the structural level of the racist and exclusionary society in which we live. For example, when we go into the city they call us 'dopes,' 'maids,' 'indias' etc." (Santillán 2008: 115). In this analysis, postcolonial violence is multifaceted, historically rooted, and geographically specific. Indigenous women sidestep the affective discipline of neoliberal development policy that seeks to boost confidence in the public sphere. Instead they seek to create a space for the decolonization of affect and new public spaces. In the words of a continent-wide statement, indigenous women declared "the need to work for the recuperation and strengthening of self-esteem and cultural identity in order to take on our right to act and have decision-making capacity" (Mandato 1 Cumbre 2009: 4). When faced with unrelenting racial discrimination and class privilege, indígenas come to understand their positionality in relational terms as a function of a powerful act of silencing. Waiting to be seen at a public hospital, ignored in stores, or asked to come back later at the mayor's office are all experiences that generate an embodied sense of postcolonial hierarchies (Prieto et al. 2005; see also chapters 1 and 2). Opaque bureaucratic requirements, racist comments, and offhand dismissal of their queries maintain the exclusionary power relations that deny indigenous women an authoritative voice in public discussion. For one leader, Maria Huacho, "in this sense we are working for social change, because racism is definitely there. Recently there hasn't been much, but before yes there was racism to an extreme—bad treatment on the buses, in the workplace. . . . We don't just want respect only as a person; we want respect for all of my companions" (Huacho 2003: 8). Challenging "the disenfranchisement due to racism and the legacies of colonialism" (Volpp 2001: 1217), indígenas blame racism in postcolonial hierarchies, not ethnic culture, for cumulative disadvantages; discriminatory practices, and not affective dispositions, for women's marginalization.[29]

Indigenous women are "attentive to the micro-politics of context, subjectivity and struggle as well as to the macro-politics of global economic and political systems and processes" (Mohanty 2002: 501, quoted in Martin 2004: 26), a form of knowledge that informs their vision of how development might be done on their terms. The UNIFEM Andean program on indigenous women's access to justice picked up these themes of racial discrimination, and the need to strengthen collective and individual rights and to begin with indígenas' own proposals (Cunningham et al. 2009). The program to fund indígenas' proposals, UNIFEM's program director and former indígena leader Maria said, "found out that women showed a lot of interest, many proposals. Unfortunately, we don't have the funds to respond to so many proposals. I've always said that indigenous women have to be the projects' core executors."[30] Indígenas' knowledge about development hence implies the need for systematic change in priorities and funding streams. Yet indígenas continue to demand sufficient information about and participation in projects to ensure their expertise is incorporated (also Meentzen 2001: 50). Where the coherence of indígenas' proposals does get recognized, they become articulate spokespeople for types of development that challenge postcolonial exclusion and inequality. Indígenas' politics simultaneously negotiates male-female and non/indigenous hierarchies, consistent with struggles for strong and mutually embedded collective and individual rights.[31] Female leaders articulate this framework not because of ethnic movement reluctance to endorse "gender programs," but as indigenous women learn from women-related development projects how social heterogeneity and power interlock and require mobilization against colonial interpretations of male and female indigeneity.

In Ecuador, indigenous women have come to an understanding of how collective and individual rights are mutually beneficial and key to their interests (see Van der Hoogte and Kingma 2004). At a public policy meeting, an indígena state employee argued, "Yes we want collective rights; we have to struggle together. But also we women have to become knowledgeable about individual rights, so that there is justice for women and men."[32]

Other women present nodded in agreement, although they had volubly disagreed with this same woman on other points. Such perspectives have also been placed in written agendas where representatives call for strong indigenous women's rights to be embedded firmly within recognized collective territories (Mandato 1 Cumbre 2009; CONAIE Women's Office 2010). Despite the hurdles caused by postcolonial geographies of exclusion, the UNIFEM program assisted diverse associations to pursue projects designed, managed, and implemented by women. The same program moreover recognized indígenas' expertise, appointing several women to professional development positions, including the Quito-based program director and two others in Bolivia and Guatemala. In comparison with "indigenous women" development, UNIFEM permitted a reordering of development's governmentality away from leadership, vulnerability, and affect and toward women's knowledge, justice, and rights.

Given their diversity, indígenas inevitably disagree about the mechanisms and priorities for change. Whether to work with a historically exclusionary nation-state generates heated discussions. Some women leverage CODENPE to encourage local governments to listen to women; a few are willing to work in central government institutions they associate with proindigenous agendas, for example, Rosa Maria, quoted earlier. As a female minority within an indigenous minority of state employees, female subaltern bureaucrats often receive opprobrium for working in the state while many women remain highly ambivalent about the gains of doing so. Other indígenas mobilize in grassroots and provincial ethnic rights groups, preferring to work in civil society associations for development aid and political space. For a small number of women who work in multilateral development agencies, they hope to tackle cooptation and facilitate local associations: "We work with the indigenous movement, with women's organizations, and with the state."[33] Yet other women, particularly from the Amazon, demand a radically decentered polity in a plurinational model.

Despite highly diverse perspectives on the state and development, Ecuadorian indígenas currently broadly agree about the need for their voices and presence to lie at the heart of public and policy debates (see Phillips 1995; Meentzen 2001: 50). Unwilling to speak via experts, the state, indigenous men, or women's movements, indígenas advocate the systematic involvement of their own representatives in project design, implementation, and self-management. To bring their voice to public policy priorities, indígena leaders prepared a series of agendas that were often provisional and frequently contentious in and outside their organizations. In 2010, the CONAIE women's office issued an agenda, Agenda Política y Estratégica de las Mujeres de los Pueblos y Nacionalidades Indígenas del Ecuador (Political and Strategic

Agenda of the Women of the Indigenous Peoples and Nationalities of Ecuador). After months of consultation across the country, the Agenda put down in writing a series of demands and concerns from indígenas from diverse populations. Likewise, a guide to indígenas' inclusion into local government incorporated women's views on male-female relationships, questions of interculturalism, and modified gender planning (Andrade 2009). These agendas provide the backbone for discussions around rights to education, culture, politics and participation, land and territory, sexual and reproductive rights, and economic rights. Arising from indígenas' political practice of close ties to grassroots constituencies and horizontal leadership styles, the agendas articulate grassroots women's demands for wider publics and high-level policy formulation.[34]

Conclusions

Emerging from gender policy's engagement in social neoliberalism, the development policy for "indigenous women" was entirely consistent with millennial capitalism's treatment of gender, race, and income as "indices of identity, affect and political action" (Comaroff and Comaroff 2001: 293). Reiterating social neoliberalism's technical specification of vulnerable groups, the "indigenous women" policy identifies one at-risk subpopulation through a stereotyped and fixed set of qualities. To the extent that "indigenous women" policy aims to bring racialized subalterns into development as if they were somehow still "outside" it, the approach replicates WID's essentialization.[35] These policy frameworks continue to have resonance at multiple scales in Ecuador; meeting the Millennium Development Goals in Chimborazo was to occur through leadership training, electoral quotas, information management, and promotion of women's "associationism" (ODM Chimborazo 2007: 91). While "indigenous women" development promises attention to social heterogeneity in terms of gender and ethnicity, the policy's genealogy and working practice demonstrate the continued and interlocking powers of western gender thinking and postcolonial hierarchies and constructions of indigeneity. Through indígenas' critical eyes, "indigenous women" policy reveals yet again development's problematization of nonmodern subjects and its failure to tackle postcolonial intersectional hierarchies and address its colonial presumptions. The statistical "indigenous women" category sanctioned colonial "objectivity" and became implicated in epistemic violence, disregarding indígenas' critical and diverse embodied knowledges. Under this rubric, human beings are not presumed to be equally "finite and needy," in Onora O'Neill's words, as gendered-raced subalterns are presumed to be "victims" as defined by metropolitan observers (Kapur 2002).[36] Together, these polyvalent sitings and sightings of "indigenous women" perpetuate a colonizing move, justifying treatments and interventions defined by the powerful (Marchand and Parpart 1995). Although no longer a mathematical or geometrical understanding of intersectionality, policy language represented indígenas as fixed within the "indigenous slot" (Li 2000). The "indigenous women" policy thence did not address the forms of exclusion affecting indígenas nor nor did it engage with indígenas' unwillingness to renounce ethnocultural affiliations, even during their pursuit of strengthened rights as racialized, female subalterns.[37] The genealogy of "indigenous women" policy connects to colonial epistemologies that systematically elide the power relations that distinguish indígenas from other women. A counter-topography highlights how indígenas' experiences and critical knowledges emerge in place-specific articulations of policy, gender relations within subaltern groups, and forms of indígena agency across multiple scales. Although policy perceives a single gendered politics within the indigenous slot, comparisons across indigenous populations reveals the nonessentialized, grounded, and historical nature of the interests, needs and gendered subjectivities of "indigenous women." By generalizing about indigenous masculinities, policy moreover misrepresented the constraints under which indígenas operate.[38]

From a critically evaluated colonial present, indigenous women voice their dissatisfaction with policy approaches that claim to speak in their name. A decolonial story can hence be told about neoliberal governmentality, and challenge mainstream meanings of "indigeneity" and "ethnic women" and their qualities with the possibility of generating new subjectivities unforeseen in policy planning. Indígenas' contestation of development's content and meaning arises directly out of embodied and reflexive understandings of the costs of racialized-gendered-uneven development. Women make critical interpretations of GAD's postcolonial inflections, making new definitions of what a developed woman might be, largely through becoming a critical interlocutor. As such, Ecuadorian indígena leaders do not reject gender approaches a priori but situate them in a global postcolonial horizon that shapes policy on female-male difference. Without succumbing to the view that global policy is universal in its applicability, indígenas reinterpret collective and individual rights as mutually constitutive and equally necessary. Beyond these critiques, too, an incipient decolonizing vision can be discerned, addressing how diversity within diversity might be conceptualized. Subalterns of postcolonial development are, despite efforts to reduce them to mere bodies, multidimensional subjects who consistently exceed developmental representation and logics and contest how female subalterns can be categorized, known, and managed.[39] In postcolonial intersectionality, Ecuadorian indigenous women illustrate how subalterns can become *critics* of development, informed, coherent, and politicized in their alternative interpretations. In their diversity, indigenous women's perspectives echo what Ella Shohat (1998: 52, 13) terms the "mobile cohabitation of differences," a reconfiguring of social heterogeneity around relational qualities, powerful inequality, and the validity of local embodied knowledges.

During an exchange visit between Kichwa and Tsáchila women, women began speaking about the processes of political organization, while we sat at an open-sided patio in Chiguilpe village. Delia Caguana, at the time the elected women's representative of COMICH, an indigenous federation affiliated with CONAIE, rose to speak about how crosscutting relations of race-ethnicity, religion, and gender inform indígenas' politics in Chimborazo.

"Y nosotros trabajamos más en fortalecer la economía, es primero que hombres y mujeres tenemos que tener tierras. Porque eso es la nuestra economía porque si no tenemos ni tierras ni agua, no podemos como sobrevivir, no se puede como producir, no se puede vivir."

"And we work more to strengthen our economy. That's the first thing because we men and women must have land. If we don't have land or water, we can't survive, we can't produce, we can't live. So we've said we must have land, animals, wheat, and products because without this people die of hunger. Our struggle has been for that. In the 1990s, the indigenous movement in Chimborazo was strong, with meetings of over ten thousand indigenous people. We stopped all the governments; there were some that really manipulated indigenous people. In Chimborazo, we indigenous are a majority, especially in Alausí, Colta, Guamote, and Riobamba districts. In other districts, there are more mestizos. But in those four districts, we had demonstrations and everything. Every moment of struggle, we were there, but women were always marginalized. Or rather, only in the marches were women at the front; it's always been like that. So we stopped and asked, why does it have to be like this? Because when there was a problem, like when the police come, they'd say 'Women in front!' But why aren't the men in front? We fought over this, as women were just used during the Levantamientos [Uprisings], but we weren't being taken into account—just men, men, men. So this year, we finally succeeded—now, there's a greater number of female councilors, and a mestiza woman became prefect [provincial leader]. There are also parish councils with women, and female *teniente politico* [chief administrative officer at canton level]. So our struggle was for women to be taken into account, that it isn't just fine words, but that they're really listened to. That's been our struggle.

"Another thing, around four years ago there were a lot of women dying, their husbands were assassinating them—they beat them, they killed them. And no one said anything! Even when there was a *comisaría de la mujer* [police office for domestic violence issues], there were plenty of things there but no respect [for indigenous women]. So in the past year . . . well, since I was elected as women's representative there was, well, almost like a Levantamiento against the men. Why? Because there wasn't any respect for women; they were killed, there was a little bit of indigenous justice, and nothing—the man went free! And the children were abandoned with the grandparents. And seeing this, in 2009 when there was a killing, we women rose up to say, 'We're going to see about this! How would you like it if a man beat you, killed you?' They're not going to leave it alone. See, so many women are dying and that can't go on. So we reported it to the media, the women's *comisaría*, to human rights organizations. And mobilized like that, we made all the men learn how to respect us. And we spoke with mayors, with the authorities, some listened, some didn't want to, [saying] 'But they're just feminists.' It wasn't that—we were defending women's lives. And we succeeded; there haven't been deaths in 2010, 2011, no women's deaths. It's gone down a lot because we did a campaign; we had marches against machismo, and against femicide, the killing of poor women. So that was a tough struggle in Chimborazo.

"Also, in Chimborazo there's another indigenous movement, a provincial one of evangelical indigenous people, which is called COMPOCIECH, and another called FEINE, a national organization, with some people affiliated with them. So Chimborazo has some problems with religion, and the weakening of organizations. Why? Because of religion people don't want to work together; before we were just together, but religion divided us with everyone struggling for themselves, for their gods. And on the other hand, they [evangelicals] don't like mobilizing and demonstrations for water, for land—nothing. Unfortunately we haven't had an indigenous governor [i.e., appointed by national executive] in Chimborazo, unlike you [Tsáchila] here, with your governor [elected governor of the Tsáchila nationality]. We've just had mestizos after mestizos, who discriminate against indigenous people and don't strengthen our organizations.[1] . . . So, talk my compañeras!"

—

FIVE

Women, Biopolitics, and Interculturalism
Ethnic Politics and Gendered Contradictions

Previous chapters have highlighted how coloniality established forms of power over indigenous populations and their enclosed spaces of abandonment, shot through with gendered divisions of labor. Under modernity-coloniality, hegemonic discourses normalize urban mestizo subjects in part through representing indigenous groups as characterized by large families and uncontrolled fertility, discourses in turn echoed by state policy implying rural women have more children because they are less modern than enlightened urban women. National progress is thus understood in relation to masculine and feminine embodiments in ways that naturalize understandings of racial-ethnic difference and processes of biological-national reproduction. In the second half of the twentieth century, state policy and elite discourses continuously aligned indigenous women to development through a narrative about population and reproduction, a biopolitical reckoning that associated racialized female bodies with central dilemmas about interventions for improvements in well-being (Foucault 2008; Selmeczi 2009; Butler 2011). As in other postcolonial contexts, Ecuadorian gendered sexual-reproductive relations become a transfer point of power that works to establish and maintain racial hierarchies and gender power within and across ethnic divides (Anthias and Yuval-Davis 1992; McClintock 1995; Young 1995; Stoler 2002; Wade 2009). Postcolonial intersectionality works through reproduction and state biopolitics concerned with sexuality, reproduction, and intimate relations that together make material and meaningful wider understandings and dispositions of power, difference, and affect (Yuval-Davis and Anthias

1989; Alonso 1994; Wade 2010). As Alonso notes, "because constructions of gender and sexuality have been key for the formation of ethnic and national subjectivities and collectivities, the technologies of bio-power wielded by the state have had differential consequences for men and women, heterosexuals and homosexuals, for ethnic minorities and majorities" (Alonso 1994: 386). Informed by Foucault's work on biopolitics and governmentality, postcolonial scholarship shows how the state regulates sexuality and reproduction differentially across genders, races, and classes, bringing into being a naturalized hierarchy. In this way, interventions in the field of sexual and reproductive health (SRH) generate a dilemma of difference, as these issues are implicitly and inherently racialized (Wade 2009: 214) and as in practice interventions necessarily engage with diverse bodies' interactions across a field of postcolonial hierarchies.

The biopolitics of postcolonial intersectionality bring power relations down to the scale of the body, linking identities to bodies, thereby naturalizing routine exclusion. In pathbreaking work, Nira Yuval-Davis and Floya Anthias (1989; Anthias and Yuval-Davis 1992; also Butler 2011; Sylvester 2011) identified key ways by which women are interpolated into ethnic and national boundary-marking through biological and social reproduction: as biological reproducers of ethnic group members; by marrying in-group; by having children who reproduce ethnonational boundaries; and as ideological reproducers of ethnic identity (McClintock 1995; Stoler 1995; on Ecuador, Radcliffe 1996). Colonial and postcolonial Latin America has subjected indígenas to each of these ethnoracial boundary-marking powers, whether in rape by whiter, more powerful men (Curiel 2007), through to state promotion of mestizaje's whitening agendas, or in celebrating mestiza maternal roles. By contrast, indigenous women's narratives and experiences highlight diverse, regionally specific and ethnically differentiated engagement in and response to state-led biopolitics and postcolonial reproductive imperatives.

Focusing on Tsáchila and Kichwa women's diverse positions under postcolonial technologies of sexual and reproductive health, the focus here on sexual-reproductive issues deepens previous chapters' analyses by examining how attempts to adapt health policy to make it "culturally appropriate" perpetuate colonial reifications of social heterogeneity, to indígenas' detriment. Juxtaposing women's critical reflections on postcolonial development with institutional and grassroots analysis of policy design and implementation highlights the construction of SRH as it occurs at the crossroads of social neoliberalism and an indigenous anticolonial demographic politics. Indigeneity, femininity, poverty, and rural locations constitute powerful frameworks of social heterogeneity, shaping projects and informing women's struggles over the meanings of intercultural health policy, which position women at the heart of pronatalist ethnic agendas. Kichwa and Tsáchila indígenas' engagement with contemporary biopolitics occurs through the prism of marginalization under Ecuador's assimilatory biopolitics of mestizaje, which is premised on the desirability of whiteness and which continues to inform everyday discourses and practices of exclusion. In the late twentieth century, intercultural health policy responded to indigenous movement mobilization in relation to a neoliberal multicultural field.[1] Ecuadorian indigenous rights movements define interculturalism as mutual learning from and respect for diverse cultures in a heterogeneous society, although they recognize that interculturalism neither fundamentally shifts the terms of postcolonial power nor establishes a plurinational-intercultural state on the basis of principles of heterogeneity, decentralization, and autonomy (Walsh 2009a, 2009b: see also chapter 7). Rather, intercultural public policy and practice exemplify what postcolonial critic Homi Bhabha terms a "third space," where resistance to dominant biopolitics can be enunciated, albeit on terms established under neoliberal multiculturalism. Emerging from a critical dissection of colonial binaries (colonizer, colonized; self, Other), Bhabha's concept of third space explores the internal contradictions and inconsistencies of forms of colonial representation that, because of subaltern agency and resistance, give rise to new creative possibilities, representing neither the exoticization of minority cultures nor a simple celebration of cultural diversity (Bhabha 1990, 1994: 38; Sharp 2003: 64; on Latin America, Warren and Jackson 2003). In the terms set by the postcolonial nation-state, which remains an adversary and an interlocutor, intercultural public policy offers ambivalent material and imaginative space for indigenous professionalism in the fields of health, education, language use, and justice (Rose 1995).

In the context of these different gendered-racialized biopolitical projects, warmikuna and sonala critically rebut the postcolonial presumptions built into maintaining SRH policy. In addition, their intersectional knowledges insert into indigenous movement agendas a unique gendered perspective that extends intercultural policy approaches in decolonial ways. As in participatory development, indigenous women address sexual and reproductive issues from a distinctive positionality, reflecting neither liberal paternalism nor ethnic movement anticolonialism. Although often masked by state and social movement discourses, indigenous women come to an understanding of their bodies within a set of parameters defining "what kind of subject one can become within a particular framework of imaginaries of difference" (Valdivia 2009: 539). Postcolonial intersectionality shapes reproduction and sexuality, whereby Kichwa and Tsáchila women become marginalized from quality health care and life (first section). Indigenous health agendas work against postcolonial abandonment, whose material effects are explored in relation to Tsáchila women (second section). Intercultural sexual reproductive health policy brings together issues of culture and ethnic politics and carves out for itself a model of social heterogeneity that indigenous women dispute, as they experience the policy's consequences in ways that work against their agendas to meld collective and individual rights (third section). Women's critical interventions look toward decolonial agendas regarding biopolitics and sexual-reproductive politics.

Indigenous Women, Health Rights, and Biopolitics

> The subject of development biopolitics . . . often appears thin, dull-eyed and sickly or thin, bright-eyed but deficient. . . . The man is the standard stick figure, the one to deal with in the main. The woman is the stick figure with breasts that feed too many children—she is all bio and little else.
>
> CHRISTINE SYLVESTER, "DEVELOPMENT AND POSTCOLONIAL TAKES ON BIOPOLITICS AND ECONOMY" (2011)

In Ecuador's mestizaje biopolitics, indigenous women's bodies can neither be knowledgeable nor capable of authorized words; rather, indígena wombs function as condensing points for national anxieties about progress and improvement and the management of social difference.[2] Although state biopolitics is focused on maternity, the nature of health services operates in ways that perpetuate racialized differentials in population well-being, and through a systematic deafness toward indígenas' concerns. The powerful meanings that accrue around their bodies in turn inform national development approaches in ways that are largely unacknowledged. State and elite discourses consistently demonize indigenous women as the least modern in the heterogeneous country, attributing their reproductive behavior to educational and attitudinal deficits. These representations downplay the parallels between indigenous and other women. On average, indigenous women first marry or cohabit and have their first child at similar ages to mestiza and Afro-Ecuadorian women, and have an ideal family size of 3.2 children, close to the national average of 3.1 children.[3] In other words, indigenous women become the point around which anxieties about social heterogeneity—femininity, racial-cultural difference, and distance from national norms—

congeal. On this basis, indígenas' identification as unmodern subjects becomes the defining trope in SRH services.[4]

Given power-laden attitudes to elite and subaltern demographics, it is not surprising to find that health provision so markedly disadvantages racialized populations in Ecuador.[5] Two-thirds of the country's population lack access to public health care, while three-fourths have no health insurance. Arising from the sociospatial exclusions associated with internal colonies and uneven development, rural and low-income populations lack effective command over state provision of quality reproductive health services and care, as nine in ten health staff and beds are in urban centers (Montenegro and Stephen 2006: 1863; Camacho et al. 2006).[6] Intersecting exclusions of gender, income, and place of residence strongly shape access on the ground: state-sanctioned prenatal care is three times more frequent among nonindigenous than among indigenous women (Larrea et al. 2007). Indigenous-majority internal colonies have exiguous health coverage: in three predominantly indigenous Andean areas in 2007, 40 percent of women received no antenatal care largely because of their poverty (29.5 percent), received inappropriate information (15.2 percent), and had to travel to distant clinics (13.6 percent).[7] In Andean and coastal indigenous households, family members assist at home births. Francisca, a teenage mother from impoverished and poorly connected Guamote canton, recounted how her father helped with her home birth. Previous research has highlighted Andean women's active choices in birthing at home, citing a series of exclusionary attitudes and practices in state clinics (Visión Mundial 2007: 94–96; Baeza 2011).

As family planning programs cost up to double in rural areas (Terborgh et al. 1995), indígenas must make expensive, time-consuming and work-disrupting journeys to nearby towns to attend clinics.[8] Once indigenous women enter hospitals, a provincial indígena leader exclaimed, "I would say that the [staff] lack training in human relations, in knowing indigenous women's rights."[9] The lack of state reproductive health services is particularly notable in the Amazon region. In Sucumbíos province, over two-fifths of women of diverse race-ethnic origin currently have no access to state-sanctioned health care during pregnancy, resulting in one of the country's highest rates of maternal mortality, an experience shared by Shuar women in central and southern Amazonía. In Amazonian Orellana province, one in seven rural indigenous women attended clinics.[10] Recent figures confirm the persistence of horrific rates of indigenous maternal mortality—Chimborazo province had maternal and infant death rates in 2004 of 85.6/100,000 births, compared with the national average of 56.4/100,000 live births (Ecuador MSP 2005). Threaded through these geographies of neglect are the social attitudes of health sector decision-makers and staff, who frequently treat indigenous women's knowledge of birth, health care, and pregnancy with disdain.[11]

Despite policy-makers' assumptions that women in indigenous communities do not discuss SRH, this contrasts with my experience of Andean indigenous leaders who organized well-attended workshops on sexual-reproductive rights where warmikuna and sonala talked openly (also Canessa 2012 on Bolivia). Women in Andean rural settlements express clear ideas about an ideal number of children, while in workshops warmikuna from Amazonia and the Andes reported that in their view "an excessive number of children" was undesirable (Corporación Educativa Macac 1992: 57; Rens 2003: 98). Kichwa and Tsáchila indígenas are highly conscious from direct experience of the discrimination, cultural snobbery, and poor-quality service in clinics. Alienated in quotidian plays of nonrecognition (Fanon 1986 [1952]), indígenas are more likely to give birth at home than other mothers. As a Tsáchila sona explained, "there isn't a medical dispensary, nothing of that kind in our community. What we have to do is hire a car or truck to take us to the hospital. But at night that costs $30 and by day $25; there isn't a bus."[12] Many women also prefer to consult community midwives, whose extensive experience and social standing enable them to provide a dignified and sensitive service. Women articulate a diverse set of knowledges about SRH, some of which are tied to ethnocultural differences and embedded in informal networks between women. In the Andes, village midwives are frequently the nodal point and source for knowledge, although women additionally acquire information from friends, personal experiences, and development workshops on SRH issues. In light of women's hinterland of Other knowledges, they are informed of a wider set of options regarding family planning than those envisioned by state services. Hence, among a number of midwives, health care draws on nonwestern ontologies where more-than-human earth beings work together with expectant mothers in rural landscapes to ensure well-being.[13] Listening to indígenas suggests that, at least among warmikuna, women have a wider frame of reference than those sanctioned by the state, which often treats indígena midwives as unskilled birth attendants.

Reflecting the state's biopolitical neglect of rural and poor indigenous bodies, the geographies of maternal care compound the gulf between on the one hand inaccessible and discriminatory state services and on the other women's practical skills and social networks that acknowledge them as worthy of care. Women face particular difficulties in accessing state maternity services, due to poverty, poor rural provision, and health professionals' attitudes. However, income differentiation in Tsáchila communities makes a mark. Cristina, now in her forties, was able to pay for transport and the maternity hospital twenty years ago: "My children were born in the clinic, all three of them at the Santo Domingo maternity hospital." Inequities in health service provision compound lifelong disadvantages for many racialized low-income groups. In the Andes, rural warmikuna continue to work hard throughout pregnancy, often failing to receive adequate nutrition. Moreover, for Andean women hospitals are often associated with maternal deaths rather than life-saving treatment, according to COMICH's former health representative.[14] In combination with uneven provision of sanitation, these factors underwrite rural areas' infant mortality rates, which are 70 percent higher among indigenous than nonindigenous populations, while chronic malnutrition affects twice as many indigenous children under five years.[15] Among Chimborazo-based women, one in ten had experienced the death of at least one child, including two women who each had lost four infant children. In this sense, racialized landscapes of neglect come to bear directly on indígenas' bodies and communities. Regional geographies of social abandonment impact indígenas' bodily well-being in distinctive ways: Amazonian petrol in internal colonies generate "accidental spills of toxic waste in indigenous territories that cause cancer, abortions and other illnesses [with] a direct impact. . . . In this case, women's rights as individuals are violated as well as their collective rights, as the toxic wastes damage their territories" (CONAMU 2007: 6). Indigenous women point up the invidious position they come to occupy under postcolonial governmentality of population and reproduction. Due to the state's failure to overcome exclusionary practices, Ecuadorian indígenas face disproportionate risks in childbirth: a major continental study reported that remote communities recorded maternal mortality rates of 250/100,000, over three times higher than the national average (compare Agamben 1998; Sylvester 2006; compare Table 5.1).

Among Kichwa women interviewed, the average age of marriage or cohabitation was just under eighteen years, compared with the husband's average age at marriage of midtwenties (no equivalent data was available on Tsáchila). Listening to women reveals the diverse logics and contextual embeddedness of subaltern knowledges, which inform astute insights into postcolonial biopolitics and indigenous women's response to western medical options, in the context of personal circumstances. In Chimborazo,

TABLE 5.1 Sexual and reproductive practice, knowledge and providers by race-ethnicity, Ecuador, 2004

Sexual-reproductive issue	Indigenous women (%)	National average (%)	Mestiza women (%)
Knowledge of contraceptive pill	53.6		92.5
Contraceptive use		72.7	74.7
Use of pill	47.2		13.5
Sterilization	3.5		25.7
Contraceptive source			
Health Ministry & public	46.2	35.6	35.5
Nonprofit provider	14.6	15.1	15.1
Commercial provider	37.5	47.2	47.3

Source: Adapted from CEPAR ENDEMAIN 2004. (CEPAR ENDEMAIN uses categories of white-mestizas, indigenous groups, and "other" women, making Afro-Ecuadorian women invisible.)

women were familiar with a range of family planning methods, notably more so than Tsáchila women.[16] An economically secure woman in the unusual position of having rural insurance, Gioconda recounted, "I just used an IUD. I wanted to have my tubes tied but my husband didn't want that, saying that he didn't want an operation. I got it from being affiliated to the Seguro Campesino, and so it didn't cost much. I just have to have an annual check."

Other women relied on natural remedies, together with what was generally described as "taking care" with their husbands.[17] In her midforties, Gabriela, who has six children, described how "we just take care of ourselves [with her partner], the two of us. I haven't had—what is it?—planning, just natural remedies. There are natural remedies and also taking care with the calendar method." Unprompted, a warmi told a group of Tsáchila and Kichwa women and men that "now I don't use chemical pills any more—just plants." A number of women in Chimborazo had caesarean hospital births, so were advised against more than three pregnancies.[18] Although a "western" policy, several women expressed a strong sense of agency around this form of fertility control. Laura, a fifty-year-old with no formal education, said, "I can't have any more children because I already had three caesareans and also I had my tubes tied." Asked about her husband's response, she explained, "My husband works quite far away, and comes home two weeks a month. I don't see him much but I don't have problems with him."[19] For Mireya, a twenty-two-year-old woman with primary education, "my husband and I haven't talked about it because I had a caesarean with my first daughter. So I can only have three children, then I was tied." Other women continue to lack access to appropriate information, reflecting social attitudes as much as availability. A thirty-year-old Andean indígena with primary education, Petrona attributed a neighbor's death to an IUD, an interpretation bolstered by her older husband's reluctance to inquire about family planning options. Overall, women's take-up of western contraceptive methods was very variable, depending on women's age and level of education, socioeconomic security, and husband's support rather than ethnicity and "cultural" attitudes. Contraceptive take-up among warmikuna remains relatively low; among interviewees, two-fifths talked of contraceptive use, half reporting that they used contraception, including natural remedies, and half reporting that they did not.

Married young indígenas often find it difficult to access relevant information on sexual-reproductive issues to make informed choices due to taboos, low-quality public education, and lack of services. According to surveys, indigenous teenagers and young adults are much less likely than mestiza and other women to have information on periods, sexual relations, pregnancy and birth, or HIV-AIDS (30–50 percent less likely) and considerably less likely to get information on contraceptives (over 60 percent less likely) (CEPAR ENDEMAIN 2006). In comparison with Kichwas, Tsáchila women marry earlier, yet in each group women with larger families are pitied. The Tsáchila women's representative, herself married with no children, explains, "Yes, they marry young! At thirteen, twelve years old they are with a husband. At fourteen they're already with a child and after that there is no improvement for women; they're stuck." Rather than perceiving large families as a development problem however, she frames it as a problem in the context of heavy workloads: "I know women with eight [children], sometimes people have up to twelve. So I would say that it's a shame because people fill themselves with children and they can't manage at home, so they suffer a lot." For other women, the question is not family size per se but the contextual circumstances of household and services. In this vein, a Kichwa woman said, "Before, our mothers used to have quite a lot of children. My mother for example had nine children. So I didn't want to have nine kids! How would I get them education, food? So now you can wait five or ten years to have children."[20]

As Florinda, orphaned young and with limited formal education, told me, "I walked along behind [my husband], carrying a baby and with another

Fig. 5.1. Kichwa woman with her children, Chismaute. Photograph by the author.

in my tummy. I wasn't worth anything, just working and suffering." Her family comprised nine children.

The trend is toward smaller family sizes among Kichwa and Tsáchila indígenas, becoming closer to nonindigenous women's family size. However, the intersectional dimensions of rural location, low incomes, and racially structured health services intervene to shape the experiences of family planning and outcomes. Despite living in Chimborazo's poorest district, Maria, now in her midtwenties, had decided to have two children. Among thirty-three Kichwa warmikuna interviewed, average family size was 3.8 children, yet numbers varied across the generations; whereas twenty-year-olds had two children on average (2.14), women in their thirties had 3.2, in their forties 4.92, and in their fifties five children, on average (see fig. 5.1). Women over forty were most likely to have seen one or more child die.[21] Given the ubiquity of racist discrimination, one can speculate how much desire for smaller family sizes might be influenced by an aversion to subjecting one's children to racism. Among Kichwa and Tsáchila groups, single motherhood is not necessarily considered a social stigma, although women rather than men are blamed. One in ten Chimborazo warmikuna were single mothers, either with a single child resulting from rape or—in one case—an affair with a secondary school teacher.[22] Unusually, a monolingual warmi straightforwardly explained that she had children by several men, none of them a husband. Systematic research undertaken by indigenous organizations notes that single mothers are sometimes forced to marry older men or are excluded from comunera rights (CONAIE et al. 2009: 42).

Learning from life experiences, a number of older women advised against early marriage and childbearing. Married at seventeen and now in early middle age, Concepción explained, "My husband left me with six children, without money, without food, without a house. So I went to work all by myself. So now with my kids I advise them that they should work and only have children [and] husbands later, get a house [first]." Speaking as a warmi, she argued that reallocating household labor was the primary goal: "We can't make a woman do everything, or we don't make her equal to the husband. When there is no agreement about this, then there's no equality among the children, the next generation" (discussed later). Tsáchila and warmikuna indígenas expressed concern about having children soon after marriage; as a Kichwa woman explained, "I said to my husband 'How are we going to have children one after the other?' I had my daughter almost immediately [at twenty years old]. So I said, 'In these difficult times, how can we go on having so many children? Better to take care.' My husband also said that would be better, we'll take care. We didn't go to the clinic but we just took care between us two." Her comments suggest rural warmikuna have to consider the material contexts for childbearing. In several cases, decisions were made without reference to the state's medical provision and were based on women's knowledge of nonclinical family planning and discussion with husbands. A young Tsáchila woman discussed the matter with her informal partner: "We'll see how many children we want. We've thought about having two or three at most. As one child is very . . . I do know where to go [for contraceptive], but I haven't gone there yet."[23] In thinking through maternity and family, warmikuna take into account structural vulnerability and lack of material options. Yet they then often lack access to the means to realize plans. As in the foregoing quote, household poverty is often cited as the primary factor in decisions about family size—by force of circumstance, women limit themselves to two or three children due to education and housing costs. Gioconda said, "It's because of inheritance; you can't get ahead with too many children." Violeta, a thirty-year-old warmi with five children, narrated how she and her husband had "decided to have children, but now we don't want more because we don't have enough money for education." For a Tsáchila woman in her midforties, "Well life is hard, having to pay for food and school every day! So we can't have many children; that's why

I only have three. But the truth is that in my case I don't really know about contraception. I've never used it because with my last child I had problems. So now I can't get pregnant. But there are other women who use contraceptives like injections, pills, and calendar and—what's it called?—the rhythm method."[24]

As these cases make clear, aspirations for children's education frequently inform women's attitudes to family planning. Younger and wealthier Kichwa and Tsáchila indígenas take up options framed as modern and urban interventions, despite the cost. Nancy, a land-poor Kichwa woman married at eighteen, told me: "Yes we used family planning. Rather before we didn't know about taking care of ourselves naturally, so I had my tubes tied when I was twenty-eight in Riobamba. It cost me one million sucres, which is now $40 but then was a lot of money. But we were thinking that if we have more children, we wouldn't have enough for schooling. Now that we don't have sufficient land, tomorrow or later what are we going to live on? So we thought that and arranged to use contraception." Higher levels of formal education are associated with the use of private sector SRH options. Now studying at university, Nira, a wealthier Tsáchila woman in her twenties, explained, "Yes I use CEMOPLAF [a private SRH organization]. I go to checkups regularly and I negotiated this with my husband. He agreed and wasn't so negative; he's a good person. I don't want children yet; I want to be a professional and then . . . !" Although mestizo biopolitics appears to influence spousal discussions, poorer women do not have the same options as wealthier households. Pilar, a poorer mother of five children in Chimborazo explained: "We didn't plan [our family]. First we decided to have three children—my husband even said that. But when I wanted to have my tubes tied it cost a lot of money. . . . He nearly hit me because it was a lot of money, and told me, 'Let's leave it, we'll have the kids, I'll work and I'll look after you.' So we had two more, then he died and left me with five children." Frustration at the sheer cost and its equivalent in hours of low-paid work reminds us that Andean households struggle with interlocking exclusions.

Situated in postcolonial intersectional hierarchies, indígenas develop a means of thinking about sexual-reproductive health in ways that acknowledge indigenous men's role, unlike state policy, which tends to focus disproportionately on subaltern women. Like indigenous women in Guatemala, Peru, and Bolivia (Meentzen 2001: 41), Ecuadorian racialized women criticize family planning projects for ignoring men and their position in these dynamics. On the few occasions when mestizo biopolitics acknowledges men, it relates to ethnic patriarchal barriers to sexual and reproductive health.[25]

Men often accompany their wives to clinics, which is interpreted in mainstream discourse as a means to control women's choices. That women might seek support from partners to face derogatory treatment from health staff is not considered. In interviews, indígenas narrated the importance of cross-cutting factors behind male attitudes, and women's testimonies spoke about engaging husbands in sustained discussions—at times over years—to come to decisions about family size. Now in her late forties, Aurora explained, "By then we had ten children and [her husband] went to look for family planning. Exactly! But when we had only five, six children I wanted to get contraceptive but he didn't want it. He didn't know or understand, and he was annoyed; he didn't want contraception."

Eventually the couple went to the parish clinic, where Aurora received a free tubal ligation. Generally, Chimborazo women suggested that adult indigenous men know little about pregnancy control, although they are key to decision-making. For this reason, women—particularly Andean women—consistently lobby for male participation in intercultural SRH workshops, as I saw in Chimborazo. In the central Andes, family planning often remains an issue for male involvement in decision-making, not necessarily solely for women.[26] Warmikuna explained that some men are firmly opposed to female use of family planning measures. Yet indígenas spoke in terms not of unilateral male resistance arising from ethnic culture but of personal circumstances. Maria Petrona, after completing Hispanic primary education, married an older, divorced man, who—although supporting her political participation in village meetings—was reluctant to adopt modern contraception: "Well my husband was married, then he divorced and got me [me cogió a mí]. So he's older and that's why he hardly helps in these issues. Otherwise, thanks to him, he has supported me in whatever else . . . But in family planning no, he doesn't want it. He says 'you're still young.' "

In another case, a husband backed his wife's election as village secretary but procrastinated about family planning against his wife's wishes, only acceding when he "became tired." In the meantime, Aurora had borne ten children after marrying at seventeen years old. In another case, Florinda married at sixteen after one year of schooling and now, with nine children, says, "No I didn't use contraception when I was with my husband. I said I didn't want to have children, and wanted to get contraceptives. I already had four children and didn't want more. But he said, 'You want to go with other men, so you don't love me anymore. So that means you'll have to work on your own.' He left me at home with the babies and went off with a fifteen-year-old girl. So I was stuck." Where disagreement arises, warmikuna explain it in terms of male sexual jealousy that colors decisions about the use of contraceptive methods. Yet at the same time, indigenous women mention factors such as highly racialized and uneven health care provision in shaping their experience of reproductive and sexual rights. Whereas national development discourse highlights merely the fact of indígenas' fertility, careful survey data suggest that over a quarter of indigenous women's pregnancies are unwanted, compared with under one-fifth among mestiza and other women (CEPAR ENDEMAIN 2006). In Amazonian areas, the percentage of unwanted pregnancies was found by qualitative research to be higher among indigenous than nonindigenous women; nearly half of all pregnancies were identified as unwanted (Goicolea et al. 2008).

An intersectional account of postcolonial biopolitics with Kichwa and Tsáchila women suggests the interlocking factors behind unwanted pregnancies and poor health outcomes. Rural indígenas highlight the factors of poverty, uneven provision, health professionals' attitudes, and spousal relations as proximate factors that come together in contingent ways to shape individuals' options at various points over the life course.[27] Rejecting postcolonial national discourses that make them the problem, Tsáchila and Kichwa women identify the problem as the harsh costs of exclusion and lack of dignified care. The postcolonial difference that they thereby articulate draws on their experience of epistemic violence within and across multiple scales from households, villages, regions, and the nation-state, in order to speak back to the colonial difference that views them as exceptional. In this politics of postcolonial difference, indígenas resituate relations of race-sexuality-gender not as universal abstract policy issues but as power-inflected, located, and uneven realities in which they claim a right to be heard.

Indigenous Movements and Intercultural Agendas

In the early twenty-first century Ecuador, as happened across Latin America, shifted development policy to interculturalism, seeking to inflect mainstream arenas of health, education, and development with more culturally sensitive attitudes toward and relations with multicultural social realities (chapter 1). In the context of neoliberal cultural and political projects, this policy focus committed the state to "foster interculturalism in its policies and institutions according to principles of equality, and the equality of cultures" (Comaroff and Comaroff 2001; Walsh 2009a: 5). As it marked a moment at which Other forms of knowledge were acknowledged and selectively validated, interculturalism represented for indigenous movements an institutional and epistemological arena in which to forward agendas previously excluded from development thinking. While this arena was inevitably contained within neoliberal governmentality, interculturalism permitted subaltern indigenous and Afro-Ecuadorian participation in program design, delivery, and management, albeit in limited and highly conditioned ways. In intercultural health measures, social heterogeneity was framed in relation to diverse (cultural) forms of being and knowing, whose interests were to be devolved to comanaged institutions with indigenous and Afro-Ecuadorian involvement. Sexual and reproductive health issues in this sense were linked to racialization, and not gender inequality.

In this respect interculturalism constitutes a third space where elements of disparate agendas are brought together and articulated in new ways to forge new forms of governmentality (Bhabha 1990; Hall 1990). On the one hand intercultural health operates within neoliberal multicultural understandings of at-risk populations, as discussed in chapter 4, but is also inflected by an anticolonial biopolitical agenda informed by border knowledges and the bare life meted out to racialized subalterns (Fanon 1986 [1952]; Mignolo 2000; Sylvester 2011). In Ecuador the third space of intercultural health prioritizes the national indigenous movements' principles of nondiscrimination in service delivery and hybrid indigenous-western health practices, alongside an ethnic biopolitical agenda. As in previous development policy, the intercultural agenda constructs social heterogeneity in ways that entail specific consequences for indígenas and the operationalization of development practice, due to underlying postcolonial assumptions and power. In other words, third space is not gender neutral, as it situates racially marked subaltern female bodies at the heart of contests over belonging, rights, and difference.

Before turning to discuss Ecuador's intercultural health policy on its own terms, it is worth pausing here to explore the ways one indigenous rights movement formulates a biopolitical agenda, as this informed the understandings of social difference that were brought into intercultural SRH policy and practice. From the mid-1990s, CONAIE thought at length about demography, reproduction, and racial-ethnic difference in ways that distinguished it from elite and state agendas premised on the value of whiteness.[28] With the UN Population Fund, CONAIE held a series of workshops to bring together indigenous groups' views on population and on sexual and reproductive issues. The discussions emphasized how poor health outcomes for large numbers of indigenous citizens resulted from discriminatory resource distribution and severe inequalities in access. Postcolonial hierarchies were

Fig. 5.2. Illustration from the cover of a CONAIE document representing women's reproductive role. CONAIE-UNFPA 1994.

blamed for the uneven development of state health services, resulting in "indices of disease, deaths, and malnutrition [that] are a true reflection of the exploitation of which we are the victims, while women suffer disproportionately high rates of infant mortality" (CONAIE-UNFPA 1994: 111–12). Women's affective connection to children was highlighted, downplaying men's visibility as parents and echoing movement discourses on mothers, particularly in calls to reduce the disproportionately high indigenous maternal mortality rates.[29]

Ethnic movement critiques of a political system that normalized social abandonment prompted the national confederation to draw up an agenda for boosting subaltern population with an explicit objective of countering ethnic genocide (see Stavenhagen 1986). Pursuing pronatalist logics, CONAIE argued strongly against "the family planning program being developed by the government because it means the disappearance of our pueblos" (CONAIE-UNFPA 1994: 111–12; Stavenhagen 1986). Family planning services were criticized for providing inadequate information on potential health risks and causing birth defects. As the hinge between fertility and ethnic population growth, indigenous mothers were exhorted to persuade daughters to avoid abortions (CONAIE-UNPFA 1994: 120). In these ethnic agendas, the proper type of sexuality was normatively constituted as heterosexual and reproductively oriented, while women were described as health and literacy promoters, organizers of family livelihood, and prime users of traditional medicine, associations with indigenous femininity that are vividly represented in fig. 5.2.[30] Under this anticolonial and pronatalist rubric, confederation documents drew distinctions between a pre-Columbian idyll of health and ethnic autonomy against a process of colonial disarticulation resulting in "alcoholic husbands and sons, [some of] whom visit prostitutes."[31] Social heterogeneity was represented in terms of two culturally distinct and historically rooted biopolitical systems, with male-female differences in knowledge and roles accorded a secondary role. At the same time as these debates in Ecuador, the UN Permanent Forum on Indigenous Issues urged governments and UN agencies to "fully incorporate a cultural perspective into health policies, programs and reproductive health services aimed at providing indigenous women with quality health care, including emergency obstetric care, voluntary family planning and skilled attendance at birth."[32] In the first decade of the twenty-first century, the indigenous development council established an office for "Women and the Family," signaling its intention to place women firmly within questions of reproduction and, more implicitly, sexuality, while downplaying liberal feminist interpretations of gender.[33] Echoing ethnonationalist struggles across the world (Yuval-Davis and Anthias 1989), Ecuador's main indigenous movement viewed women as the means to achieve an indigenous renaissance through reproduction, thereby countering genocidal decline. In summary, ethnic movements' anticolonial agendas awarded a central symbolic importance to health and indigenous women's reproductive capacities. Pronatalist agendas hence placed ethnocultural difference within a global and national frame arising from grounded histories of genocide and dispossession, rather than in relation to ahistorical tradition (Chua et al. 2000).

Outside CONAIE's offices and official documents, such biopolitical imperatives to protect indigenous mothers and boost ethnic populations hold real material and discursive force, as women informed me in Tsáchila settlements. For this small indigenous population increasingly impacted

by mestizo urban growth and agrarian land grabs, the issue of ethnic survival brings together a highly emotive articulation of biopolitical interests
and indígenas' reproductive capacity. In conversations with Tsáchila leaders,
villagers, and commentators, fears about population and cultural decline
were a recurrent theme. In many interlocutors' minds the risk of population
collapse was to be solved by measures to regulate marriage—a commonly
voiced desire was to have village women bear indigenous children. These
narratives were often traced back to the first state-recognized Tsáchila governor, who was known to be a traditionalist keen to enforce the strict marriage rules. From the time of the state's recognition of Tsáchila comunas, the
nationality's statutes included written guidelines dealing with what is called
"group purity." Under these statutes, article 5 establishes that "children
of parents of the [Tsáchila] group are accepted as community members [if
they] contract marriage with persons of the same group. Those who do not
observe this stipulation will be expelled definitively from the group, as it is
imperative that the group's purity be preserved, along with their authenticity
and survival" (Velástegui 1984: 84–85).

The statutes also make traditional clothing and hairstyle prerequisites
for ethnic group membership, providing visual markers of ethnic embodiment. The social outcome of such governmentality is women's marriage
during adolescence and immediate childbearing.[34] Petrona explained: "I
experienced it directly in such an unjust way. I married at seventeen years
old—very young, no? Because in those days parents told you, 'M'hija, marriage is like this, M'hija, get ready to get married.' For the culture, not always,
but the first thing they want is for you to find a husband, fearing that we
would commit the error of marrying or falling in love with a mestizo man.
They call anyone distant from our culture mestizos. So our parents' interest
was in having us marry very early." As her narrative makes clear, Tsáchila-
mestizo marriages are a fraught area, especially with urban and commercial
encroachment. In 2008, the governor restated the principle that any Tsáchila
marrying mestizos have to leave not just the village but the ethnic group.
His statements carefully avoided distinguishing between women and men.
However, in practice and in comuna statutes, the policy was implemented
in a gendered way as it was entangled with commonsense understandings
of Tsáchila women's social qualities, and mestizo men. Sonala are widely
viewed as vulnerable to seduction by mestizo, non-Tsáchila men, who are
interested in land. Tsáchila Peripa village recently amended its statutes to
explicitly regulate women to avoid further encroachment on ethnic land
and culture. Under these statutes, women marrying mestizo men lose in-

heritance land rights and community membership. By contrast, Tsáchila men's marriages to mestiza women are not problematized, as women are expected to adopt ethnic clothing and reproduce ethnic culture (Radcliffe with Pequeño 2010; Ventura 2012). The underlying social qualities attributed to indígenas shape biopolitical imperatives while impacting female education opportunities, which in turn compound women's reliance on village resources and social ties. "The majority of people here say that girls are going to end up pregnant if they attend secondary school [in nearby Santo Domingo town]. And that it's only important to be able to sign their name and then they must stay at home doing domestic tasks."[35] In discussions, sonala made it clear these pressures were not timeless tradition but a political, economic, and legal conjuncture of racialized and gendered exclusion, a function of interlocking factors of urban growth, land grabs, and ethnocultural assimilation.

As illustrated in the Tsáchila case, ethnic biopolitical agendas entail profound consequences for female subjects experiencing the most marked impacts of intersectional postcolonial hierarchies. Consequently, ethnic rights demographic-SRH agendas have profound implications for female and male indigenous subjects.

Intercultural Health Policy—What Spaces for Indigenous Women?

As indigenous mobilization opened up spaces in the state for the creation of hybrid public policy to reflect their agendas, so an intercultural biopolitics came into being, a policy arena that reflected neither the platitudes of mestizo biopolitics nor anticolonial ethnic demands. As this hybrid third space emerged, intercultural health policy and practice represented and treated indigenous women in ways that reflected a pragmatic compromise between neoliberal multicultural exigencies and the indigenous impulse to protect mothers and children. "Third space displaces the histories that constitute it and sets up new structures of authority, new political initiatives, which are inadequately understood through received wisdom" (Bhabha 1990: 210–11). While this is not the place to detail the operation of intercultural health, the intercultural sexual and reproductive rights arena offers an illustration of the internal differentiation of the subaltern category, and how social heterogeneity goes "all the way down." Although neoliberal multiculturalism acknowledges cultural differences, the hierarchies on which they rest— gender, race, and sexuality—remain firmly in place (Wade 2009: 217–18). As this section shows, the incorporation of "subaltern" agendas into development does not "solve" the issue of social heterogeneity.

Broadly speaking, the intercultural health agenda demands the ending of uneven geographies of health service provision and the recalibration of colonial hierarchies between western and subaltern medical practices.[36] Yet these policy principles quickly showed how health care services were mired in colonial stereotypes around indigenous women. In this case social neoliberal representations of vulnerable populations informed global intercultural health policy that pictured indigenous women as vulnerable victims of poor care provision. Policy also celebrated traditional medicine and ethnobotanical knowledge, both associated with women's role in ethnic divisions of labor.[37] Melding these global policy agendas with Ecuador's ethnic movement agendas resulted in the foundation in 1999 of the National Health Directorate of Indigenous Peoples (DNSPI). The directorate's goals were to provide health professionals and workers who would understand indigenous cultural values, to create complementary medicine, and to recognize cultural diversity. Although hampered by financial restrictions, patronizing attitudes, and lack of political will, intercultural health attempted to provide indigenous populations with sexual and reproductive health services by hybridizing western and indigenous approaches. In this respect, the DNSPI advocated teaching three "sexuality systems" to indigenous groups—scientific, ancestral, and church. The directorate also emphasized the need for family planning services to be organized according to the cultures of the country's fourteen nationalities and so embarked on an extensive research project to collate data on nationalities' sexual and reproductive attitudes.[38] Under neoliberal precepts, the research preceded allocation of responsibility for services (Blaser 2009), a context where social heterogeneity became the infrastructure for an emergent administration. The DNSPI eventually assumed responsibility for treating at-risk residents in rural parishes with over 60 percent poverty with a team of traditional health practitioners and community workers as well as bilingual and bicultural health workers (Terborgh et al. 1995; Ecuador 1996: 162). Intercultural health policy characterized then "neither a disciplining nor a normalizing society, but instead a society characterized by the fact that it cultivates and optimizes differences" (Lemke 2001: 200). Reproducing development's colonial thinking, intercultural health policy could not challenge uneven development and racism but created new racializations, as intercultural health provision in Chimborazo became equated with indigeneity (Baeza 2011: 57).

One key component of DNSPI agendas was family planning, alongside maternal and child health programs, and for this it successfully garnered international investment for sexual-reproductive health workshops from the late 1990s. One important site for these workshops was provided by indigenous women's civic organizations. Workshops brought village women into a public arena to talk about topics previously embedded in private social networks and Other knowledges. According to interviews in Chimborazo, indigenous leaders enthusiastically took up educational efforts to respond to female concerns and interest in information. According to a young indígena promoter who organized workshops in the late 1990s, "speaking about sexual-reproductive health was—my god!—like speaking about a fantasy. Women never knew how to start talking about it" in public.[39] In Chimborazo, workshops funded first by the EU and then UNFPA provided women with varied sexual and reproductive health information, and endorsed traditional midwives' knowledge, while informing women about the cost and availability of various services.[40] Speaking directly to indígenas as valid and interested interlocutors, the workshops I attended in Chimborazo were conducted in kichwa and engaged indigenous women and a few men as equals.[41]

However, although indigenous women welcomed information, their position in wider patterns of exclusion and social abandonment remain the prime determinants of their biopolitical situation. Participation in information-sharing networks could not in itself overcome uneven development or compensate for assaults on indigenous livelihoods and income. Indigenous women fared poorly under general and intercultural health policy. Maternal mortality among indigenous women rose by a third after 2001 (Ecuador MSP 2005). In 2012, ministerial documents noted that interculturalism was not working, as "methods and strategies were insufficient to respond to young indigenous people in terms of cultural specificities," and that "young women and men do not access SRH except in emergencies or—in the case of women—pregnancy" (Ecuador 2012: 40). Indígenas' poverty, racialization, and abjection in postcolonial hierarchies remained yet again outside the factors to be considered in policy that focused excessively on their bodies and reproduction.

Indígenas Rework Interculturalism: Adding Women's Agenda

As the case of Ecuador's indígenas illustrates, the subaltern category is irredeemably and continuously riven by different interests, positionalities, and politics. In the subaltern category of indigenous peoples, indigenous women work to define a political, specifically female, critique of intercultural policy and practice. In Ecuadorian ethnic politics—as across many Latin American countries with powerful indigenous movements—the voices and actions of indigenous women are struggling for the recognition of "diversity within diversity" (Palacios 2005; Hernández 2008; Suárez and Hernández 2008). As discussed later, indígenas are critical of how female-male difference is brought into intercultural development policy and so organize to articulate an indígena-specific perspective from within mixed-gender ethnic rights confederations. As a result, sexual and reproductive health issues constitute a core strand of organized Ecuadorian indigenous women's struggles to raise awareness, improve treatment, and secure resources. In this politics, women do not parrot anticolonial masculine positions or views on sexual-reproductive issues. Instead the intercultural third space represents for them a space that is "fragmented, incomplete, uncertain and the site for struggles for meaning and representation" (Law 1997: 109). Opposed to a voluntaristic return to "traditional" knowledge, Andean women remain vociferously critical of deficiencies in health services, particularly in relation to sexual-reproductive issues and sexual violence, thereby positioning space, class, and gender alongside racialization as factors to be considered in policy.[42] Indígenas articulate their interests in SRH informed by their understanding of social heterogeneity from the margins. Indigenous women thereby disrupt the notion of a singular subaltern set of interests in development, and they bring situated knowledge to bear on the institutional and politicized biopolitics that lies between mestizaje and indigenous pronatalist politics.

Women frequently become involved in ethnic politics through roles associated with health and well-being and hence their activism was key to the institutionalization of intercultural health care. In village councils women are widely accepted as elected representatives for health issues, which in turn become gendered as female in local, provincial, and national organizations. In Chimborazo a warmi told me, "We women are concerned about our children and if the schools call us, we women go to represent them. And at home too it's the mothers."[43] Yet health agendas can also authorize women's political interventions; particularly in the Andes, women are elected into village leadership for the health portfolio, an entry point into otherwise male-dominated decision-making spheres.[44]

In seizing SRH issues as their own, women's networks in Chimborazo sought to create a space to discuss reproduction and sexuality openly and circulate information on SRR. Through regular workshops bringing together scores of women (along with male partners and children), leaders gave presentations and answered questions in public, where the working assumption is justice and transparency. The workshops I attended in Chimborazo provided village women with core information about family planning and health choices in a setting that encouraged discussion among women and between spouses. Indígena leaders stressed to me how, in comparison with previous decades, women no longer giggle with embarrassment. Leaders also sought to rework the meanings of female-male difference within households and thereby challenge a singular anti-colonial ethnic politics. In Chimborazo, accessible pamphlets and public meetings were used by provincial women's representatives to change public attitudes toward the birth of a son (historically welcomed with a party) and a daughter (associated with fear for her suffering). The same pamphlets explained conception and the factors determining a child's gender.

Although liberal feminism at a global scale assumes that ethnic minority men succeed in pressing more children on spouses, younger Kichwa indígenas clarify that they gain authority to decide family size, in part because of the discussions they have held at indígena workshops. Despite marrying at sixteen years and having two children within two years, Lucía, now in her late thirties, explained how she and her husband "decided together; we decide nearly everything together." A twenty-year-old with primary education, Marta explained how she and her husband decided to have two children to play together, but no more. A warmi in her thirties who had attended the indigenous women's training school, Gioconda, explained, "Yes we have contraception. We have four children, and before when we had two children my husband said that's enough. But I still didn't want to go to the doctors. But that's why I have only four children, he wanted two but not me." Younger Kichwa indígenas appear to be recasting ethnic pronatalism as an issue of healthy, nurtured offspring through negotiations with spouses, although as will be shown here, impoverishment and male resistance continue to play a role in some cases.

Indígenas coordinated across women's directorates in local, provincial, and national indigenous federations, together with the National Council of Indigenous Ecuadorian Women (CONMIE), to create support networks and autonomous spaces in which to systematize their concerns and agendas. From the mid-1990s, multiethnic groups of indigenous women across the country demanded the provision of free maternity treatment, training courses in western and traditional medicine, funding for alternative community health programs, laboratories for natural medicine, support for traditional midwives and healers (yachaqs), and training for women in infant care and community pharmacies (CONAIE-UNFPA 1994: 112; also Ecuarunari 1998: 8). In Chimborazo, training for village women in leadership and human rights began to include modules on sexual and reproductive rights, repositioning them neither as wombs at the service of ethnic agendas nor as vulnerable subjects for postcolonial condescension.[45] In addition, women called for the provision of training courses in nutrition and for indígena representatives to work with officials on maternal-child projects, natural medicine, and family planning and thereby incorporate their knowledges into institutional practice. Likewise, Kichwa indígenas called for the full implementation of intercultural health through increasing health coverage, affordable medicine, and diverse participation, hence addressing uneven investment and spaces of abandonment. In interviews, warmikuna regularly highlighted their command of robust and practical knowledge around childbirth and healing, "which we have practiced for centuries," as noted by a midwife at a Riobamba workshop. Women thereby denaturalize and hence politicize their expertise over health care in childbirth in ways that disrupt ethnic movements' appropriation of female knowledge. At the regional and national level, female subaltern representatives began to position themselves as knowledgeable actors whose viewpoints were valid in policy debates. Speaking at a national workshop, a provincial leader spoke out angrily: "I think we have to apply our principles—that's what the [intercultural] policy says. Otherwise it's as if our [intercultural] institutions exist only sometimes, or they follow whatever is modern or western. But why the hell have we fought for this to go on in the same way?"[46]

Such interventions sustained pressure on public policy, interjecting women's priorities and knowledges into the process. Alongside cumulative grassroots actions, women pursue sexual and reproductive rights through ethnic rights organizations, although they often face resistance from male leaders.[47] From the mid-1990s, indígenas' national networks politicized postcolonial exclusion through calls to be treated as autonomous and respected decision-makers over women's health and sexual and reproductive rights. Their agendas hence politicized the boundary between development and citizenship, using a vernacularized language of rights and justice (Chatterjee 2004; compare chapter 6).

Contingent combinations of female activism, a mobilized sense of entitlement, and opportunities for shifting practices have given rise to dispersed initiatives across the country. The multiracial Sucumbíos women's movement established its own intercultural center for maternal and child health, which arose in the context of a proposal for "intercultural maternity" (Garcés Dávila 2006). Putting racial discrimination under the spotlight, the movement demands "sensitization of health personnel attending women" and advocates a less hierarchical staff-patient relationship.[48] In Chimborazo, sustained grassroots efforts in workshops and through women's leadership led eventually to higher-than-average rates of female—particularly indígena—participation in local oversight committees associated with the Maternity Law (compare chapter 3). In the indigenous majority Guamote and Colta districts, nine in ten committee members are indigenous women. In Guamote, too, women coordinated with NGOs and local government to raise women's involvement in SRH projects from zero to 30 percent.[49] Across these examples, as noted by an activist who has long worked with indigenous women, "it is significant that women are discussing the need for families to take contraception on board. This would require support from outside actors through the creation of spaces for women's greater involvement, and community reflection together with a gender perspective on problems and possible solutions" (Garcés Dávila 2006: 113).

Moreover, a number of local initiatives demonstrated the possibility of positive synergy between intercultural agendas and indígena positionality. One scale for action consisted of municipal and provincial government. Organizations achieved a historic agreement with the Chimborazo council and ten local mayors on the basis for women's rights. The agreements included a commitment to "promote networks of services to guarantee the integral treatment of women, fomenting the exercise of sexual and reproductive rights," and for municipalities to "promote programs to increase the quality of health care for women in all phases of life, recognizing their sexual and reproductive rights."[50] Women's networks in the province ensured the inclusion of sexuality, taboo, and the importance of bilingual health staff into various provincial policy documents, for example the *Agenda de Equidad de Género de las Mujeres Kichwas de Chimborazo* (Gender Equity Agenda of Kichwa Women of Chimborazo). Nevertheless, despite this pressure, intercultural health delivery largely remained disdainful of indígenas' knowledge, as health workers failed to acknowledge them as equal interlocutors with relevant skills, power, and insight. Medical staff continued to discriminate against racialized women, calling them "Marias" and "dirty." Behind an intercultural veneer, indígena women recounted to me the lack of improved services in rural clinics and the continued hardscrabble for money, social isolation, and damaging treatment the clinics represent.

Gender violence represents one issue around which indígenas articulate a trenchant critique of SRH policy and practice. According to indígena representatives, sexual jealousy and domestic violence are woven through and into debates around SRH and have to be confronted systematically without demonizing indigenous "culture" or adopting liberal feminist perspectives that reinforce postcolonial stereotypes (Pequeño 2009). For many female

Fig. 5.3. Kichwa-language pamphlet informing indigenous women about rights to a life without violence.

leaders, gender violence is an issue that cannot be contained within intercultural health institutions, as it requires a more systematic, interinstitutional response primarily informed by women themselves (see for example the pamphlet excerpt in fig. 5.3). Hence leaders focus on transforming behaviors and attitudes while strengthening systems of justice accessible to women. According to existing research, male sexual jealousy can be the reason men offer for physical violence among diverse ethnocultural groups, especially in contexts of male migration and female leadership (Cayapa et al. 2000; Muratorio 2002; Segura Villalva 2006; CEDIS 2007a; Movimiento de Mujeres de Sucumbíos n.d.)—an insight confirmed for me in interviews with women who raised this issue without prompting.[51] Mercedes, a warmi in her early fifties who completed primary education as an adult, told her story: "How I suffered with my husband! He shouted at me, beat me and insulted me. I was alone, crying and suffering. Then recently I've come out of the house, getting advice from other women, listening to the workshops."

Among sonala, I encountered a greater reluctance to speak openly about violence (and some local commentators argue that marital violence is culturally unacceptable), although women do speak frequently of men's "jealousy" of women. Violeta, a monolingual tsafiki speaker with no formal education, explained how she wished "husbands would change their jealous attitudes . . ." While acknowledging that these factors are exacerbated by insecure livelihoods, national indígena leaders condemn the impunity of the few men who use violence. To strengthen their hand, leaders take strategic recourse to national surveys that reveal the extent of violence against indigenous women (as for instance to raise the profile of a gender analysis of SRH issues in the intercultural health directorate) while remaining acutely aware that such statistics tend to reproduce the nationally popular stereotype of violent, culturally atavistic indigenous cultures and masculinities (PAHO 2003; CEPAR ENDEMAIN 2006; interview, Cristina Cucurí, CEDIS, Riobamba, 2009). Framing violence as the outcome of wider social hierarchies and discourses that devalue lives and make bodily harm and killing banal, indigenous leaders work to publicize the judicial impunity of feminicide, adolescent pregnancies, and rape, as activists have done in Ciudad Juarez, Mexico (Wright 2001).

As this implies, indigenous female leaders increasingly break the public silence that surrounds the issue of gender violence, thereby expanding the remit of intercultural policy in ways that disrupt both developmental understandings and ethnic movement agendas. Rather than reading indigenous bodies as available for state interventions to control fertility or for ethnic pronatalist politics, indigenous women bring to public attention the ways racialized and gendered power at the bodily scale operates to disempower indígenas. Whether by publicizing the coercion involved in village sexual relations or the impunity enjoyed by violent men, indigenous women's networks question the ways reproductive sexuality and gendered embodiment are crosscut by intersectional power. At the same time, indigenous women train their sights on the complacencies of intercultural policy, calling for men to participate in SRH workshops and education initiatives. Leaders encourage young women to empower themselves by continuing a college education even if that means commuting to the city, thereby shifting the focus away from communal "protection" for young women as in Tsáchila villages. Another avenue for contesting grassroots biopolitics is the intercultural justice system. Leaders work to ensure that when violence, including rape, occurs, women have local, timely, responsive, and culturally attuned recourse to sanctions and protection (Pequeño 2009). In Chimborazo, indigenous justice systems on the ground have created a public arena in which women—leaders and villagers alike—name and sanction crimes. During a workshop held in Tixán village in southern Chimborazo for rural men and women, women volubly brought into the discussion their knowledge of cases of rape, other types of violence, and disputes over paternity. Through verbal interventions, warmikuna forced the male federation leaders present to listen at length to problems that had not been on the formal agenda. At the regional scale, programs supported the insertion of a clause on women's rights into local statutes governing indigenous justice in Cotacachi and Sucumbíos, and nationally women lobby the intercultural health directorate to deal with gender violence.[52] Their perspectives address dimensions of social heterogeneity—family position, class, rural location—in ways that speak to lived experiences and possible solutions.

However, a theme less acknowledged in public statements is older generations' complicity in violence against women. In our conversations, warmikuna told how older household members, particularly mothers-in-law, at times condoned spousal violence. After marriage, many young women share housing with their husband's family, making mothers-in-law key influences on workloads and spousal relations. Joaquina, in her early forties with six children, described a common situation: "Sure, mothers-in-law have a lot of influence. They think that we're wandering around half asleep [i.e., not working], and then make the husband beat us," although she then turned the tables, saying that mothers-in-law "are drunken, sleeping in the street." By contrast, Magdalena, a young woman with a tired face from an especially poor household, highlighted male resistance to family pressure: "At home, there are discussions with my mother-in-law—that she doesn't want to see me, saying that I'm not for her son. She tells me to leave; she doesn't want to see me. She makes a lot of problems. Luckily, thank god, her son doesn't listen. She tells him that he has to mistreat me, that it would be good to beat me, that he should get rid of me. She says that I'm poor with nowhere even to drop dead." Her testimony draws together poverty, a resilient masculinity, and daughter-in-law status to explain the outcome of household negotiations, factors that emerge in other accounts. Marta used a government housing grant to relocate away from her parents-in-law: "I was living in the country with my husband mistreating me, and that's what my in-laws were telling him. I lived with them for eighteen months; there was no money. My in-laws mistreated me. Then I got . . . my own house in Riobamba with the housing bond; it's very different now." Through these critiques, indígenas remind us of the proximate contributory factors of kin relations and household structures in creating inequality.

Another strand of activism against gender violence is a rights framework. Through the vernacularization of rights discourses (Merry 2006) women

Fig. 5.4. COMICH-UNIFEM poster against domestic violence, in COMICH office. Photograph by the author.

speak of their right to equal treatment to men and to state protection from violence. During fieldwork I encountered these narratives in Chimborazo and not among the Tsáchila, hinting at the spatially uneven extent of activism and the regional dynamics of police-civilian relations. Kichwa indígenas speak about their rights to renegotiate female-male household relations.[53] Rather than refer to complementarity or Andean culture, women drew on a rights discourse articulated by regional and local leaders to speak against complacency regarding indigenous female-male relations (as exemplified in the COMICH poster in fig. 5.4). After years of violence from an older husband, one woman from a small village in southern Chimborazo spoke to me in these terms: "Before, women weren't valued at home and there's still machismo among some women, some men. So there's no understanding. Before, women were mistreated like anything. Now when anything is said, they make a statement [to the police]. So for me that's a right. In everything, we women have rights equal with men. When there's comprehension in the communities and the right to participate, we all have rights. That's how I think we should go forward." Gioconda attended the Dolores Cacuango training school, combining that with farming and raising four children. In Chimborazo's SRH workshops and women's networks, women like Gioconda increasingly reject the Andean platitude that violent practices and attitudes are somehow part of indigenous "culture," instead arguing that they are "negative acts that affect women, families and the community in general," in the words of CONAIE's women's office agenda (CONAIE Women's Office 2010).

In this way, indígena leaderships reinterpret interculturalism away from ethnic maternalism and liberal feminism's blithe use of cultural diversity and toward centering indígena women's experience and analysis. Using the framework of rights in ways that blur the boundary between development and citizenship, representatives lobby for the consistent and meaningful inclusion of women's rights and justice into public policy. Moreover, indígenas articulate a distinct critique to liberal feminists as they question the validity and singularity of the meanings of culture and interculturalism, and feminism's capacity to address intersectional positionality. Building up from autochthonous notions of well-being in reproduction, indigenous women's vision of intercultural health and biopolitics represents a distinctive gendered political interjection into intercultural third space (Rose 1995).

Conclusions: Third Spaces and Gender Resistance

While issues of sexuality now inform scholarly accounts of development (see, among others, Peake and Trotz 1999; Chua et al. 2000; Lind and Share 2003; Lind 2009), the discussion of sexual rights in relation to the politics of intercultural development aids a deeper enquiry into sexual-reproductive issues in contexts of postcolonial intersectionality. While sexuality and development literature largely focuses on rights to services and recognition and diverse sexualities, a grounded account of how programs become embedded in postcolonial hierarchies reveals the importance of colonial biopolitics in shaping program design and implementation. Ecuadorian indigenous women's experiences also highlight the ways subjects at the bottom of postcolonial hierarchies experience and then voice critiques of such programs. Despite efforts at interculturalism, the Ecuadorian case confirms a wider point that neoliberal multiculturalism since the 1990s has "not undermined the sexualized images attached to racialized categories" (Wade

2009: 216). Postcolonial elites' association of indigenous populations and women with a problematic fertility and mortality profile still permeates Ecuadorian policy on sexual and reproductive health, while the denial of validity to racialized rural populations as equally deserving of care has justified uneven geographies of provision. In this sense, SRH issues in development are inextricably entangled in the power relations of social heterogeneity. Indígena subalterns in the Ecuadorian case are subjects caught in a web of exclusion and difference, whose wombs represent a core point of contention between the postcolonial nation-state and ethnic rights movements.

Beyond domestic postcolonial relations of intimacy (McClintock 1995; Stoler 2002), the emplacement of indigenous women within postcolonial biopolitics highlights the coeval significance of sexuality in the intersectionality of race-gender-nation and the colonial legacy that shapes the nature of indigenous women's citizenship and rights. Women's access to health care and bodily well-being relates not solely to racial exclusion and state neglect, but also to the emergent space of intercultural policy and practice in which, due to the persistence of coloniality, indigenous women are again positioned as stereotypical docile bodies. Interculturalism—an uneasy compromise between neoliberal multiculturalism and ethnic rights agendas—represents for indígenas no unitary alternative to racial marginalization, no simple arena of cultural harmony. Their contests over the content and meaning of intercultural policy and practice means that interculturalism "refuses to settle down . . . [being] simultaneously structured by intersecting geometries of power, identity and meaning" (Pile 1994: 265, 273). On the one hand indigenous women reject the argument that all "indigenous women 'want to have children' and that family planning is 'outside their culture' " (Goicolea et al. 2008: 96). Yet neither do they feel impelled to reject ethnic cultures to pursue individual sexual and reproductive rights promoted by Ecuadorian GAD policy-makers. Sexuality and reproduction become a key part of indigenous women's struggles for rights, as they comprise "the aspects that most affect indigenous women at a personal level, in family relations, and in participation. They are barriers to knowing and exercising our rights and the right to a life without violence" (CONAIE Women's Office 2010: 14).

SIX

From Development to Citizenship
Rights, Voice, and Citizenship Practices

Through a critical account, subaltern agency in rethinking development has been documented in the previous chapters, which have shown how indigenous women contest the boundaries between development and citizenship and challenge the discursive and material construction of beneficiary subjects as lacking both authority and knowledge. The postcolonial difference in indígenas' accounts reveals the means by which female racialized subalterns rupture the dominant assumptions about social heterogeneity, and contextualize a new understanding of development in relation to postcolonial intersectionality. This chapter turns to focus on the nature of indigenous women's agency to shift the nature, content, and meanings of development. In an array of diverse acts of citizenship, what scope do women at the margins of postcolonial societies have to reconfigure the relation between formal and substantive rights (Holston and Appadurai 1999; Isin and Nielsen 2008)? And how does the innovative vernacularization of rights inform a reworked hybrid form of citizenship and make rights real for indigenous women? In relation to the widely established distinction between beneficiary subalterns and rights-bearing citizens (Chatterjee 2004), indigenous women's acts of citizenship are found to be tightly bound up with development and welfare procedures, yet they also contest that marking off of citizenship and rights.

Dressed in her Sunday best, Sebastiana packed her small bag with her ID card, an extra shawl, and a mobile phone. I had invited her to take part in an exchange between Tsáchila sonala and Kichwa warmikuna at the end of my research, as in interviews and meetings women were always asking about each other—how do they do things differently on the coast? How do warmikuna take up leadership positions? So we had decided on a small-scale exchange between a few women to learn about and talk directly with village women in each location. Hence Sebastiana's packing. Yet she was also carrying something that proved much more significant during our exchange, namely her critical evaluation of what it means to be an indigenous woman and in turn what that positionality entails for rights and citizenship. Throughout her life, Sebastiana has practiced citizenship in ways shaped through interlocking hierarchies of gender, race, place, and income, marital status and agrarian livelihoods, situating citizenship as "a field of interaction where multiple axes of difference, identity and subordination politicize and intersect" (Dietz 2003: 419).

Citizenship practices are thus firmly embedded in and reflect the postcolonial social relations and spaces documented here. In the colonial present, indigenous women cannot take citizenship as a series of agentive acts for granted, as they frequently come face to face with its incomplete and partial operation, and because their citizenship practices are systematically denied equal authority. Drawing on their words and experiences reveals the ways that indigenous women come to think of themselves as citizens through a series of small daily acts. Rather than a closed, fixed property of political personhood, citizenship can be viewed as embodied, repeated, and practiced through quotidian actions and in an interconnected set of local and informal spaces and practices of citizenship (Staeheli et al. 2004; Holston 2009; Staeheli 2011). Indigenous women's political action in social movements is rightly celebrated and documented extensively, yet most Ecuadorian racialized female subalterns never join social movements or stand for official political office, although they are members of rural comunas, carry ID cards, and vote in local and national elections. In this sense the "relationships, practices and acts that construct, regulate and contest citizenship are more important than the status assigned to individuals. In this way, citizenship is always in formation, is never static, settled or complete, and identities or subjectivities as citizens are similarly unstable" (Staeheli 2011: 398–99). Indigenous women—through repeated exclusion from, or only partial realization of, the practices through which citizenship might be achieved and subject to marginalizing discourses that undercut their authority as political actors and fully rights-bearing citizens—"make do," improvising a form of citizenship in the exiguous spaces available. At the same time they practice this improvised partial citizenship, however, they become vocal critics of the forces that produce content-less citizenship. Dispersed sites of indígena agency have been mentioned in previous chapters, including the Dolores Cacuango women's training school (see chapter 4), village women's associations, and an individual woman's reworking of domestic relations. Yet questions remain about the extent to which these sites can act as catalysts for change at a wider scale and fundamentally reorient development and citizenship, beneficiary, and agent.

Practicing Citizenship through Development and Welfare

At first sight, indigenous women's interface with citizenship appears entirely set within the parameters set by the institutions of development, in ways that separate them off as subjects from full citizenship status and in routinized ways that excise them from agency (Chatterjee 2004; Hickey and Mohan 2004). In Ecuador one banal item sutures development to citizenship—the identity card (*cédula*), whose meanings and uses differ according to whether one is an impoverished rural or comfortable urban dweller, a mother or a widow. In other words, social heterogeneity is key to the ways boundaries between development and citizenship are articulated. One of the most routine citizenship practices for Ecuadorians is the procedure of getting and carrying an identity card to show to state officials. As racialized female rural dwellers often on low incomes, indigenous women find themselves deploying the card for primarily development-related activities and interactions. Subaltern interfaces with these cards that index citizenship-development relations are inevitably grounded in postcolonial dynamics of state formation and ethnic difference.[1] Relations of coloniality mediate between the state and some indigenous populations, as civil servants are unwilling to award cards to people with identical names, something that particularly affects Tsáchila women. Overall sonala are less likely than Andean warmikuna to have cards; women blame the state information systems, the state's failure to recognize Tsáchila naming practices, which result in the repeated use of a small number of names, and insufficient action against identity theft.

In internal colonies, the ID card becomes the vector between subalterns and a resource distribution system, not a passport to full standing and dignity. A bilingual warmi just turned thirty, Virginia, told me: "I use [my ID card] for everything; it's useful for everything. They ask for it at the school. Sure, we have to show our card, all the time, every month." Carrying it with them at all times, most Ecuadorians memorize their card number, as it is used frequently in numerous bureaucratic procedures, yet access to cards reflects postcolonial landscapes of exclusion. Within living memory, Tsáchila and some Kichwa women did not have these documents. Rural indigenous women are still least likely to have an ID card, in comparison with other Ecuadorians (CONAMU 2004: 38). Nevertheless, as development and welfare schemes have incorporated indigenous beneficiaries, so women's holding of cards has become largely routine. Reflecting the card's role, younger women today get one in anticipation of development interventions to facilitate banal official procedures—as did, for example, Rosita, a seventeen-year-old sona living with her extended family. Ana, a single Kichwa mother living with her parents, applied for a card after her thirteenth birthday in order to set up a savings account. An unmarried warmi living with her widower father and six siblings, Juana remembers how in her early twenties she received a card in order to register official ownership of a land plot. Tsáchila women associate the card with bureaucratic procedures: "The ID card is really needed to . . . to do any business, papers and all that" (Cristina, forty-six years old). Whereas younger women take it for granted, older generations remember a time when they only received a card after marriage. Women in their sixties and older remember when women were not asked routinely for ID cards (their husbands were). Different cards are now issued for minors (under eighteen years), who have to show their cards on buses in random police checks. Younger warmikuna associate their eighteenth birthday with getting an adult card.[2]

Relationships with state institutions mediated by ID cards provide insight into the material and embodied nature of development-as-it-interfaces-with-citizenship. The state uses ID cards and lists of names to target benefits and development at individuals, as cash payments or resources are only distributed if women's names are on an agency computer system. For instance, low-income women with school-age children and babies have to show a card when collecting the human development bond, a CCT scheme for child health and education. However, the cards are firmly embedded in postcolonial social difference. Cards indirectly reveal much about holders' social backgrounds and, by signaling certain social qualities, can influence the treatment received from officials. The level of formal education achievement is indirectly marked on the card, which carries a thumbprint, a cross, or a carefully crafted signature. Concepción celebrated the completion of literacy classes with a renewed card, a major achievement for a woman in her forties with six children: "So I went to get an identity card but I didn't know how to read or write, or not well. So now in banks and stuff my signature's there . . . it's valued. Yes, with literacy programs I got a new ID." As Concepción suggests, cards are not neutral badges of national identity but reflect materially the kind of person one is and thereby shape the nature of substantive citizenship experienced.

Moreover, the effectivity of ID cards is bound up with intimate power relations that profoundly impact indígenas' ability to act as autonomous agents. A minority of women noted that their husbands held their cards, restricting their autonomy with respect to development-citizenship. Marta, a young woman from Chimborazo, recounted to me: "My husband keeps it. He looks after it, puts it with his own card." The Tsáchila women's representative was adamant that husbands frequently store their wives' cards, although no woman mentioned this to me directly. Moreover, marital status is indicated on the card and shapes the types of development resources women can access, so when status changes, cards should be amended. Cards identifying women as married limit the access of separated women to resources and their decision-making powers, as in applications for credit to buy or work land. For separated women unable to afford divorce, a card indicating their married status effectively blocks women from accessing formal financial institutions. Andrea, a middle-aged warmi living in an unformalized relationship, was only able to get credit from an informal credit union run by other village women, where marital status was irrelevant. In the district of San Juan, Sebastiana, an older woman who had separated from a violent husband twenty years earlier accessed credit only after organizing a caja solidaria. When I met her one day in Riobamba market, she told me excitedly, "Yesterday I went to the office where they told me I'm now divorced! So I got a new ID card." Lack of status, resources, and links to legal advice all compound indígenas' limited agency to keep their official cards linked to changing life circumstances. As these two cases illustrate, it was largely women's organizational agency and creativity that permitted them to overcome barriers. In this way, indigenous women vernacularized new forms of economic citizenship, recalibrating the relationship between ID cards and substantive rights.

The ID card's context-specific linkage to resources, dignity, and recognition is further exemplified by the fact that it links to contingent development resources (bank loans, child-related benefits) rather than universal welfare. For subalterns reliant on informal economic activities, ID cards have done nothing to grant labor and social security rights.[3] In this respect the card represents no linkage with forms of universal support; although required to show a card to gain work, indigenous female employees find that it does not guarantee social security coverage. Married and single young warmikuna narrated how they worked as domestic servants without an ID card. A warmi in her late twenties with primary education, Lisa said: "I was only fifteen years old when I was in Quito. My bosses didn't pay social security; I just had to get an identity card to have an [official] document, never for the security."[4] Working as a manual laborer in commercial agriculture likewise required ID yet again did not guarantee social security registration.[5] In these circumstances, the historic weakness of central state welfare provision intersects with the low value accorded to indigenous women's embodied labor to generate an empty category of citizenship. Among sonala, none were registered with social security, although they mentioned anecdotally other women so covered. In summary, the majority of Kichwa and Tsáchila indígenas have access to the most quotidian marker of development-citizenship, although it provides only exiguous and uneven access to rights and resources, being profoundly embedded in postcolonial dynamics between the state and subalterns.

Practices of Community Decision-Making: Membership and Authority

The smallest political community in which indigenous women have a stake is the comuna, whose membership, procedures, and decision-making roles were established by national legislation in the 1930s.[6] The comuna was created at a time when the central nation-state was concerned to modernize village politics and induct indigenous peasants into political citizenship. As such the comuna law framed social heterogeneity in classic paternalistic colonial terms as leading to "the intellectual, moral and material improvement of community members" whereby racial subalterns would become rights-bearing subjects through practicing citizenship at the local level (quote from Lucero 2008: 71–72; also Becker 1999; Prieto 2004). Comuna membership in turn grants rights to participate in regular meetings where decisions about development are taken and elections of village representatives occur. Although Andean communities were the first to be formed under the legislation, Tsáchila villages did not become comunas until the early 1970s. Today community structures remain highly significant as the grassroots basis for wider civil society organizations and formal political structures. In recent decades, comunas have provided enabling structures and facilitated ethnic mobilization (Yashar 2005). Chimborazo alone has over five hundred comunas, especially in the most indigenous parts of the province; 85 percent of canton Colta's population, 93 percent of Guamote's, and over half of Alausí's population are found in these jurisdictions (COMUNIDEC 2008). The 1937 law explicitly includes women as comuna members, required—as are men—to elect village representatives even if not expected to become representatives themselves. On-the-ground gendered meanings and practices, however, condone widespread female exclusion, although indígenas use a variety of means to rework and resignify local decision-making. Hence the comuna becomes the site of struggles between different political visions that operate simultaneously.

As in the case of other rights frameworks, the 1937 comuna rights have been vernacularized across villages in diverse ways that frequently result in women's less secure voice in village affairs and second-class comuna citizenship. In our discussions, indígenas narrated how they continuously faced problems because women's status in comunas is frequently misunderstood and unclear, particularly regarding their status in decision-making. In Tsáchila areas and across Chimborazo, comunas use a variety of criteria to establish membership, including inheritance of usufruct rights from an existing comunero (i.e., member), adult status, or upon marriage. In some Kichwa communities, women and men become members after they marry or when they reach thirty years old if still unmarried. According to Soledad, a warmi in her midtwenties with two preschool children, "you don't need land to be comunero. I've been a comunera since I married—I wouldn't have been if I hadn't married and helped at mingas [comuna work parties]." Warming to her theme, she continued, "You have to help out in the community with any communal work. We are part of the community and have to support and help." By contrast, Mireya became a community member in Chimborazo at eighteen, as this marked her adult status, although she had married at fifteen. Younger women, especially when single, are frequently excluded from membership, as Julia, a married sona with complete primary education, explained: "There aren't hardly any women included in the list of comuneros, no. The only people on the list are the [community] founders in the original papers. So sometimes, some men are not on the list."

As noted in chapter 2, the intersecting dynamics of gender, ethnoculture, and marital status in postcolonial hierarchies reduce sonala's comuna land access and thereby marginalize them from the political authority constructed within comunas. In yet another pattern, in one community, a woman registered herself and her Tsáchila husband when they felt ready at nineteen years old.

Just as marriage can be a route to community membership, so can widowhood and divorce. A twenty-nine-year-old warmi, Teresa, recounted, "In the community the comuneros are almost all men. The names on the list are all theirs but when husbands die, widows become comuneras. So there are no unmarried young comuneros—they belong because of their parents." As Teresa suggests, kinship and household status play a large role in shaping access to village decision-making arenas, especially among younger and married women. A divorced, middle-aged, monolingual (tsafiki) sona, Violeta, decided to register as a comunera to formalize rights over her father's land. Among one Tsáchila village's female comuneras were three widows, one single mother, and six sonala in informal partnerships with mestizo men.[7] In a different situation, a sona and one Andean warmi each explained how the end of a partnership might also end comunera status.

Junior status may entail comuna responsibilities without corresponding rights. Younger women in Chimborazo told how they contributed to work parties and attended village assemblies without the benefits. Unmarried for the most part and daughters of comuneros, indígenas' discussion reveals the extent of their contribution. An unmarried warmi in her midtwenties and third of eight siblings, Gina recalled her attendance at fortnightly meetings on her mother's behalf and less frequent mingas. Beatriz, also young and unmarried, said, "No I'm not a comunera but my father is. I go along on his behalf, going to meetings, courses, elections, and mingas." Asked if she will become a comunera in due course, she said, "We're not obliged to but I guess that we children will."

In common parlance, being a comunero or comunera grants rights to "voz y voto"—a voice and a vote—in local affairs. Yet indígenas rarely feel that they have an official or socially sanctioned right to voz y voto. Despite different ethnic social relations and development histories, Tsáchila and Kichwa women told remarkably similar stories about marginalization. Village assemblies use local languages but despite this, exclusionary political cultures are what deny women authority to speak. Consequently men are more likely to speak in comuna discussions, and despite male encouragement of Kichwa and Tsáchila women, women's interjections are less extensive and less authoritative than men's. If asked to speak up at a village meeting, Tsáchila women say that they are not confident about speaking publicly. Many sonala indeed expressed doubt about whether wives actually have voz y voto. In Tsáchila settlements, men outnumber women at meetings one to fifty, so when women turn up when their husbands are ill or away, women have limited experience and are seen as temporary members.[8] Cristina explained, "Some women are not comuneras but they come to represent their husbands. Now we participate but I would say some are shy; they just come to listen. We just speak in tsafiki in meetings but if the authorities come we speak in Spanish." In areas of Chimborazo with male outmigration, women say that they attend monthly assemblies "on husbands' behalf," a representation that preempts expression of women's own interests. Indeed in Kichwa areas women often constitute the majority of participants, but their contributions are often muted and deprecated (Bourque and Warren 1981). Nevertheless, Kichwa meetings generally have higher levels of female participation than Tsáchila villages. Nancy, an Andean woman in her thirties, expressed it articulately: "Some women speak but not everyone . . . there are apprehensions. I don't think there should be, as I believe we all have ideas. . . . Well, in the community among ourselves we women talk. But when they say to us 'Go to a meeting,' we don't want to. It's also that perhaps husbands don't give women time to go out, or the women themselves don't want to go." Those without formal membership feel particularly unable to articulate proposals in meetings, as explained by Carmen in Chimborazo, "Yes I go to assemblies sometimes but then it makes . . . it makes me nervous."

In large part, the practices of citizenship at the scale of the comuna are structured through crosscutting inequalities that work to restrict women's acts of citizenship and political voice. Tsáchila and Kichwa women explained lesser female participation by noting the heavy loads of work and time commitment involved in social reproduction and care. As a Tsáchila leader explained, "women don't go to meetings because sometimes women have to do stuff at home, look after the kids, all that. So [the man says], 'I'm going to the meeting.' This is what happens most of the time." Sona Julia explained, "Well, I hardly go to the meetings; I don't attend because I have to be at home cooking; there's no time." Likewise, Andean women complain that domestic and reproductive responsibilities limit the chance to participate, as for example did Sonia, a married woman in her early thirties with two young children. The material realities of women's double burden of difficult physical work are undeniable, although village meetings can represent a space where women can rest and talk among themselves. Nevertheless, a number of Chimborazo women did intervene, more than sonala did. Gabriela, who described herself as a comunera, explained, "When it's time to demand something, yes I know how to make the demand. I ask to speak and I speak. There are some women who speak, but then others are quiet, listening."

In part, constraints on women are bound up with power relations around gender, sexuality and embodiment, highlighting how local biopolitics and male-female relations influence indígenas' positionality and make a qualitative difference to their political acts. Julia explained that many Tsáchila men are "jealous" of women who attend public meetings and hence try to restrict their participation. In southern Chimborazo Joaquina, a Kichwa-speaking woman in her forties who is separated from a violent husband, recalled as we sat in the corner of a village meeting: "My husband sent me to meetings, but some husbands mistreat their wives; sometimes they hit them hard. Sometimes my husband beat me, but now I'm OK." Andean indígenas additionally identify specific masculine behaviors that undermine women's practice of village politics. Concepción, also in her forties and now separated, said, "No way did my husband let me to go meetings! Only he knew about it. I didn't even know about the church organization. I couldn't!" Similarly a widow living near Lake Colta, Chimborazo, with five children, explained how some men "just want to be giving orders; they just want us to be at home." Younger women pick up quickly on these attitudes and come to expect them, as shown by a single, primary-school-educated seventeen-year-old sona who, when I spoke to her in her family's cooking area outside the house, took it for granted that husbands are jealous of women going to a meeting.

Despite these normalized attitudes, a number of leaders and village women say that men are supportive of wives' local practices of citizenship. Unprompted, they spoke in ways that compared welcome male support and unwelcome controlling masculinities. Married for over a decade, a warmi told me, while we sat in the shade of a village hall, how her husband supports her participation in assemblies and women's meetings; "We talk about it," she said; "he isn't jealous or anything."[9] An older, uneducated woman highlighted the range of spousal attitudes in her Andean village: "My husband supports me—he's very good. My husband isn't bad like some others who beat their wives so they don't go to workshops. My husband tells me to go to meetings, participate and get women together." Although husbands' attitudes are crucial for women's realization of local citizenship, men in key civil positions can also serve as facilitators. A warmi, now middle-aged and long married, was encouraged by a priest to attend meetings. In Chimborazo, Catholic pastoral organizations have often promoted women's participation in community meetings and to deem themselves equal to husbands. In some comunas, elected male leaders promote women, giving them confidence to stand in village elections. In certain Tsáchila communities, individual men encourage female participation, although women continue to feel afraid, as they are subject to jokes and distrust from many men (interviews 2009; Almeida 2007a: 78).

As noted, the comuna entails obligations and responsibilities as much as rights and representation. Although women have only partial, poorly defined rights to political voice, their obligations are widely discussed, well understood, and strictly enforced.[10] According to Soledad, a married warmi with two school-aged children, "Yes we go out to clear the road, the irrigation ditches, to do community work in small groups. If not, the community obliges you to pay a fine set in the statutes. You have to pay five dollars, ten dollars, depending on how easy the work is; the harder work is $20. Who's going to want to pay that and stay at home?" As Andean female rural laborers earn under $10 per day, these fines represent significant loads on household budgets. Even if unsure about their status as comuneras, women perceive a strong social pressure to contribute to work parties. According to Magdalena, an Andean woman in her twenties, "Well no, I'm not really a comunera but I always go to the works. I'm obliged to be available." Sometimes unmarried and noncomunera women undertake communal work, as in Lisa's case, participating after a stint of domestic service in Quito.

In the areas of Chimborazo affected by male outmigration, wives stand in for absent husbands. Gioconda, a mother of four children, explained her situation: "I participate in meetings, in mingas for the school, for water supplies and in assemblies. When we don't, we have to pay a lot. If my husband's not here, I go." In Chimborazo, village political cultures make it acceptable for spouses to represent each other at assemblies, but work parties generally require both to attend, as Renata noted, as her young son played around her feet. Widows of course do not have such flexibility, being expected to attend all meetings and mingas or face the same fines as married couples, a factor prominent in discussions in Chimborazo.[11] Older women's responsibilities are set by practice and precedent, resulting in an uneven set of rights and obligations as women become less able to do hard physical labor. According to an Andean widow in her forties, "it depends on the village— sometimes they say widows have to help in the minga, sometimes they don't. In my village when people reach their 'third age' they aren't allowed to work anymore." A widow in her seventies, who spent her life fighting for women's rights, remembered when women had no "voz y voto" but contributed to minga obligations and paid the same fines, despite women's lower wages. Sebastiana remembered how "women didn't have the right to speak in the meetings. But the community used women for the mingas. I went to the minga [as a separated woman], or had to pay the same as the men—this was when there were sucres, not dollars. And in the meetings, women didn't have the right to speak or hold women's meetings. But I organized women so that we could speak out."

The comuna hence represents a site for political acts that constitute local citizenship and is recognized as such by indigenous women, who also have direct experience of the interlocking factors that devalue and marginalize their contribution. Although facing compound disadvantages and exclusionary village-level practices, the comuna constitutes for the majority of women a space where they acquire a sense of political personhood and familiarity with political acts, some of which can be a launchpad to further political action.

Stepping into Public Life: Becoming Village Leaders

Despite a marginalized comuna position, the indigenous women I met were generally in favor of local, elected representatives making decisions—in the *cabildo* (village council) as well as regular village meetings. In addition to their formal politics, comunas offer spaces for civil society organizations, including women's groups.[12] Although these grassroots organizations are often established by various development actors, including NGOs, the state, and international agencies, indigenous women conceive and use them as a practical and knowledge-producing arena in which to familiarize and apply forms of substantive citizenship. Despite originating in standard GAD and participatory development, village organizations may in some circumstances contribute to furthering indígenas' expression of interests and pursuit of political change, especially in Andean areas in comparison with Tsáchila villages. Forms of local decision-making and resource collection hence represent a crucial—albeit small-scale and restricted—site where indígenas contest the boundary between development and citizenship, between subaltern and citizenship status. In this sense they develop what anthropologist James Holston calls "insurgent citizenship," forms of political practice that challenge and transform the political status quo (Holston 2009). Through regular engagements with development decision-making and political acts, village women's groups vernacularize rights discourses in practices and acts that challenge the breach between development assistance and subaltern agency. Indígenas—especially younger, wealthier, and formally educated women—could thereby challenge postcolonial intersectionality at a number of scales. "After the project finished in the community, there was nothing, people became disorganized, thinking that someone would give them something. So we women—I was just a young woman, *huambrita*, we saw that the organization was dying. So we began again to say, no this isn't good and that we have to create community cajas. And we began with ten people, then twenty, thirty . . ."[13]

Throughout the later twentieth century, state, NGOs, and Catholic Church development projects encouraged the formation of women's groups at the village level. Today in the Ecuadorian Andes these women's groups, composed of forty to one hundred women, now represent a taken-for-granted social infrastructure, especially since the 1980s, when indigenous movements and female leaders promoted their creation and registration.[14] One estimate calculates that Chimborazo currently has over two hundred credit unions embedded in village women's organizations, while in one Colta parish all but two of sixty-four communities have a women's association. While not necessarily tied directly back into leadership projects (chapter 4), the mixed origin of village associations continues to underpin their ambivalent role on the cusp of development and citizenship. Whereas in some cases they function primarily as civil society mechanisms to cheapen the delivery of resources, in other cases they are "extending the rights of inclusive citizenship" (Hickey and Mohan 2004: 20). In a development guise, associations function as low-cost social engineering mechanisms through which to provide limited resources to beneficiary populations. In this case, unpaid civil society leaders—including a number of indígena women—assist associations' applications for small-scale development funding and facilitate coordination with development technicians, liaising between villagers and development resources.[15] Chimborazo's provincial representative for indigenous women, for instance was highly energetic in this type of initiative, informing female villagers about development opportunities and helping them get assistance. One of the beneficiaries, Concepción, explained: "Thanks to the Cooperative '4th of October' and to our women's leader, they helped us and we're working with this loan. We bought some cows and we're improving with that. Now thanks to the women's representative, the [NGO] technicians did this to motivate everyone . . . They approved us outcast women [botadas mujeres]. . . . Since 2006 we've been working with quinoa."

Such action does not guarantee quick or easy access to means for changing livelihood and political recognition. Gioconda worked for six years to bring a Japanese aid project to her village association in Chimborazo. In landscapes of postcolonial exclusion, indígenas come to rely on associations for key resources. Yet these associations also constitute a space in which women gather in public to debate concerns and priorities, which in turn are carried forward by elected leaders to higher level organizations. Associations are thus highly ambivalent, lying on the knife edge between tyranny and transformation (Hickey and Mohan 2004).[16] In some respects contra to neoliberal practices (Gershon 2011), Andean associations under favorable circumstances facilitate informal learning, prompt consciousness-raising, and provide women with verbal and political tools to challenge biased communal governance and exclusionary public cultures. Primarily associations offer a space in which to compare experiences and articulate critiques: "If we don't meet, we women can't talk about our problems and sometimes talk about fiestas, or other things. Meeting together we can share our suffering, look out for the sick; we can talk and learn. If we are just at home we can't learn. In some villages, we're not worried about our neighbor, we don't know if she is unwell, down, harmed. We don't know and we don't visit. But the organization is there to bring us together [solidarizarnos], no? If someone is suffering, if something happens we can all give support."[17]

Indígenas recall occasions when they spoke out for the first time, having been muted in other village meetings. According to Elvira, a widow from near San Andres, Chimborazo, "women speak in our meetings. For example sometimes I continue talking. Sometimes other women say to us, 'You must speak, say what you think.' Whether we can or not, we have to speak out. Some learn how to speak." However, mutual encouragement in local spaces was not something I encountered or heard about in Tsáchila communities, and this situation arguably reflects the contingent role of ethnocultural difference and geographies of postcolonial development in shaping indígenas' agency. According to Concepción, an older warmi, "Yes I speak in [women's association] meetings, or if there are things I don't understand I ask questions. We make ourselves participate. If we are shy, we can't talk; if we're shy we either talk badly or keep quiet. Now we're getting ahead when we go out and organize and that gets rid of our fear, our shyness."

One workshop I attended in southern Chimborazo began with a video of the Levantamientos uprisings before discussing indígenas' central role in political protest (see Palacios 2005: 320–23) (see fig. 6.1). Meetings might bring women up to date with international human rights conventions, or explain which institutions are in place to protect indígenas' access to justice. These sites and practices become a route through which to inform and politicize women. A Kichwa grandmother in her late thirties, Liliana, who had work experience in the coast city of Guayaquil, explained: "Among ourselves we get organized, so they don't mistreat us in those ways; we get involved." Women's narratives confirm other research that suggests women's associations are political spaces independent from comuna councils.[18]

Practical experience and involvement in women's emergent networks combine to facilitate wider political roles for some indígenas, as the visibility and authority they command in women's groups gets translated into

Fig. 6.1. Kichwa women watch a film of the 1990 Indigenous Levantamiento (Uprising), Tixan. Photograph by the author.

elected office at the comuna level. "In diverse grassroots organizations such as water groups, producer associations, or cooperatives, women's participation is visible and, moreover, it is in these settings that many of them gain recognition and become leaders" (Palacios 2005: 320). Chimborazo communities have between one and three women elected to a village council, while Tsáchila comunas have a small but consistent number of elected female cabildo members. Moving into village positions often begins with nominations for the least important roles (*vocal* and secretaries). Starting as *vocales* (organizers), women in subsequent years can be reelected to positions such as women's or health representatives, but in a few cases as village treasurer or president. Progression through these "grades" is not automatic, however, nor is it related to Andean ritual positions in which post-holders take on ever more senior sponsorship roles. Rather, women accrue practical political skills and knowledges if they go through a series of community positions, influenced more by male outmigration and local practices of leadership than development interventions and "ethnic culture."

Women's comuna-level office-holding is shaped, as always, by gendered expectations working in interaction with local political cultures and attitudes about social hierarchies and thus reflects significant and sustained efforts to rework prevalent understandings of gender, ethnicity, and authority. Warmikuna recognize that they are participating due to male migration but seize resulting political opportunities. Speaking in her village in economically vibrant Colta, Antonia said, "Women have come into the leadership this year replacing their husbands, because sometimes men have to migrate elsewhere. That's when we women replace them," echoing Lisa, who lives in the mountainous eastern area of the province. As well as "migrant wives," widows also frequently take on more formal elected roles in village cabildos, at times mentioning directly that there is no husband to disapprove.[19] Whether as vocal, secretary, or village president, women view participation as a process of learning to act politically. Mercedes, now in her late forties and married with ten children, spoke of her accomplishments: "The experience of being [comuna] secretary, as they say, is that when you don't know what to do, it's bad. But then you go along and then it seems OK, as you begin to learn things, to go out and about." Asked if she would like to be in the cabildo again, she said, "Well if people choose me, then sure. If people don't vote for you, there's no way," but she is very conscious of community disapproval of her political work: "They elected me first as secretary, and then they came to speak to me saying that I was going out, leaving the house, the children. It just takes one person to demoralize everyone."

Given the deeply ingrained political cultures that undercut women's political legitimacy, the practices of standing for election, holding a recognized post, and promoting changes in local decision-making constitute significant reworkings of local citizenship practice. In addition to caring for six children, Concepción told me proudly how "in the community I'm vocal and in the irrigation committee too. I go around [ando despierta], telling people about meetings." Echoing women in similar positions, Concepción feels valued for this work. "As vocal I have to help the leaders, communicating with wherever, Riobamba, Quimiag. And the mishus [mestizos] have to speak to us first, because we organize the meetings with the cabildo," as does Maria Petrona, who is twelve years her junior and has younger children. Growing confidence with the practical embodied knowledge of local leadership brings women to understand themselves in transformed ways. With complete primary education under her belt, Andrea told me modestly of how she was elected as leader because of her thinking and problem-solving skills, which she loves practicing.

Political and organizational skills come to the fore in some cases, overcoming male resistance and granting women public authority. Women with extensive community leadership experience speak passionately about the potential for change embodied in local governance. Female community presidents have become more common and accepted in Chimborazo and Tsáchila areas.[20] Sitting in the open-sided meetinghouse at the center of her Tsáchila village, Cristina summarized her leadership trajectory for me: "First of all I was vice-president after I became a comunera at twenty-eight [years old]. Then I rested for a year. One year later they nominated me as treasurer. And then I rested for five or six years, and then I became secretary again. Then after a while I was nominated to be president, two years in a row." Accumulation of political practices and experiences slowly and at a local scale contributes to indígenas' emergence from development beneficiary status to a series of practical citizenship acts.

Yet husbands and other comuna members often remain ambivalent about women's formal participation in village affairs, as evidenced by women's reports of constant negotiations with spouses and sniping from neighbors. In coastal and Andean areas, social disapproval of women-only groups is felt by different generations of women, regardless of marital status and level of formal education. Violeta, a married woman in her thirties from a small village near Tixán in southern Chimborazo, explained the constraints: "We have association meetings to work together as women. But some don't want to meet because their husbands prevent them." Furthermore, religious divisions sometimes cause warmikuna's associations to splinter, weakening organizations (see the narrative in Interlude II for an example of this pattern). Married, middle-aged Aurora struggled to hold political office while villagers whispered behind her back, spreading rumors that she could not be a good mother and serve on the cabildo, matching the experience of Mercedes described earlier. However, some villages proactively establish measures to raise the numbers of women in local political office. In one Tsáchila community, a young trainee teacher told me, as we sat outside during her break: "Men talk more, but now in the cabildo there have to be at least one or two women for equality. That's what they are working for, so that there is gender equality."

As this example illustrates, women's growing fluency in political practice has forced a new recognition of diversity into village politics. Associations and elected village indígenas provide an increasingly normalized but always political demonstration of women's interests and interventions in debates. Accordingly, local political action can provide an arena for articulating perspectives on male-female relations that differ from both neoliberal policy's maternal figure and from ethnic movements' pronatalist complementarity (chapter 5). In this sense, indigenous women create what Nancy

Fraser terms "subaltern counter-publics" (Fraser 1997), as village associations offer a new type of public space, especially in Kichwa areas. According to Mercedes, "it's to change what we have had; it's for women to go out and get training. Or to learn how to live, how to speak to one's husband or the children at home. If we don't do that, we are stuck at home, not knowing where to turn. We don't have means of thinking, talking through issues because, otherwise, most of us sit and weep. I tell my nieces—let's go to the women's association meetings! I say they have to report what happens, and not repeat rumors. And the community president, he takes no notice." Gathering weekly, women claim public space for themselves while making visible alternative forms of political culture. The acquisition of leadership skills and consultative agendas in associations in turn have incremental impacts on provincial and regional ethnic politics.

Local Government: Gender Quotas, Indigenous Movements, and Hybrid Practices

The struggle of mestiza women had results for indigenous women, for example in the vote for indigenous women. So, as a result we've been able to occupy positions of power even if they're local.

INDIGENOUS WOMAN EMPLOYED BY DEVELOPMENT SECRETARIAT
SENPLADES (MARCH 2010)

Emergent networks of women's associations and female leaders, supported in turn by some subaltern men and institutions, have over recent decades given rise to a growing group of indígena women who hold local electoral office. With the unrelated events of gender quotas in elections (1997) and the foundation of the indigenous Pachakutik party (1996), indigenous women's achievement of political office appeared for the first time to be a real possibility.[21] Quotas were, as the quote in the epigraph suggests, important yet insufficient in facilitating indigenous women's local election, as Ecuador's electoral quota law paid no attention to the postcolonial intersectional positionality of indigenous women (Cunningham et al. 2008: 54–55; Schurr 2013). Yet indígenas' representatives and ethnic organizations carried out sustained action beyond quotas to raise their formal political presence. Indigenous-controlled municipalities introduced measures that facilitated indigenous female participation, although it has yet to equal indigenous male participation.

A qualitative analysis of women's formal participation reveals the extent to which political acts of citizenship at comuna level translate into political voice at wider scales, and by what authority indígenas make their views heard. Andean indígenas become active in local formal politics through ethnic movement participation and gendered electoral quotas. Warmikuna progressively gained a greater presence in these parts of government, in marked contrast to sonala's almost complete exclusion from elected office to political bodies beyond the comuna.[22] Contrasting Tsáchila and Kichwa experiences suggests that indígenas' representation comes about through two interconnected processes—first, regional ethnic movement support for women's participation, and second, women's creative hybrid of ethnic identity and gender politics, both outside mainstream development's expectations. Despite restrictive practices in communities, women have networked to dispute local elections, which has resulted in a small but significant presence, in turn providing other women with examples of citizenship practice (see also Hernández 2002).

Ecuadorian laws on electoral quotas require political parties to ensure a minimum share of female candidates. According to advocates, quotas challenge masculinist norms and create a new grammar for action by diversifying the range of interests, experiences, and embodiments present in formal decision-making institutions (Phillips 1995; Alvarez et al. 2003). By increasing women's chances of election, quotas aim to deepen democracy by drawing underrepresented women into formal political decision-making bodies. Quotas reflect impulses toward technocratic good governance and democratization, as well as political action by the women's movement to further what feminists argue are "promising footholds" for gender equality (Goetz 2004; INSTRAW 2006; Del Campo and Magdaleno 2008). In Latin America, high-profile prodemocracy women's movements ensured widespread adoption of quotas in the 1990s, which have become publicly accepted (Craske and Molyneux 2002). Ecuador's quota law raised the numbers of female candidates over the period 1997–2004, although women have continued to be less likely to be elected than men at all levels of office (Cañete 2005). Under Ecuador's quota law, "Law 2000–1," party lists have to include at least 50 percent women, rising incrementally from 30 percent in 2000 to half of all candidates in 2006.[23] Social heterogeneity was taken into account in a minimal way, as the law established the broad goal that "ethnocultural participation will be taken into account" but did not set ethnic quotas (article 58, quoted in Vega Ugalde 2005: 173). At approximately the same time, the broadly indigenous party Pachakutik adopted a 40 percent quota for women among its candidates in 1997, an earlier and larger commitment than other parties (Terán 2004: 83–85; compare INSTRAW 2006: 124; Van Cott 2000). As with other gender policies, indigenous women remain skeptical of the degree to which a western-derived analysis of women's interests is applicable to their situation. As the CONAIE women's agenda states, the quota law and other "prowomen" laws "don't take indigenous women's specificities into account as they were devised from the perspective of *mestiza* and urban women" (CONAIE Women's Office 2010: 4).[24]

In May 2000, women composed over half of local government candidates in the indigenous-majority provinces of Cañar and Chimborazo. Local governments in Ecuador comprise parish councils (*juntas parroquiales*), municipal governments, and provincial councils, all of which saw increases in budgets and powers over recent decades.[25] Yet less than a quarter of elected officials were women of all racial-ethnic groups, because women tended to be placed far down party lists and hence did not get elected (Radcliffe et al. 2002; INSTRAW 2006). However, preliminary analysis of 2002–2006 elections across the country suggests that indígena women were relatively successful when standing for office in indigenous-majority areas, although they were most likely to be elected for the lowest level offices, namely the juntas parroquiales and municipalities.[26] Indigenous female candidates on indigenous party lists were more likely than nonindigenous women in nonindigenous parties to be elected in 2002 and 2004, although that pattern was reversed slightly in 2006. Moreover, indigenous women's electoral success was most notable in indigenous-majority, and mostly pro-Pachakutik, provinces of Chimborazo, Cotopaxi, and Imbabura in the Andes, and Morona Santiago and Sucumbíos in the Amazon.[27] Nevertheless, indigenous men continued to more likely to be elected in these—and other—provinces than indígena women, regardless of quotas.[28] Indigenous women were only rarely successful in election to more prominent positions: among candidates for mayor, women had a 0.9 percent success rate; provincial councilor, 2.6 percent; provincial deputy, 3 percent.[29] At the national level, too, between 1984 and 2004 only one indigenous woman was elected national deputy for Pachakutik (Vega Ugalde 2005: 192; compare Schurr 2013). Whereas women have become increasingly credible candidates in areas populated by indigenous residents, their wider authority and legitimacy as representatives for multicultural societies continues to be undermined by postcolonial intersectionality.

In this context, the local municipal governments that experienced the electoral emergence of indigenous-led councils were instrumental in addressing some of the barriers to indígenas' inclusion and voice. Yet women made quite clear that despite rising numbers of indigenous-majority municipal councils, there was no corresponding rise in indígena elected representatives. These 'alternative municipalities' were significant albeit highly local-ized spaces in which the meanings and reach of women's participation could be rethought. One notable case was Colta municipality in central Chimbo-razo, a largely indigenous district and small town of around forty thousand inhabitants.[30] Under the indigenous-majority authority, one-tenth of Colta's municipal budgets went to a newly established local women's office. Under the banner of "equality between men and women," women were encouraged to speak in Kichwa in public meetings. Consultation with women's organi-zations and community members generated extensive discussions during the preparation and implementation of the local strategic plan. By 2010, the provincial council had a series of initiatives widely praised by rural indige-nous women, because it provided rural subaltern women with opportunities to contribute ideas, a relatively large budget, personnel, and a clear insti-tutional structure. Two female representatives from each community were directly involved in the diagnosis of problems and policy design, drawing on the accumulated expertise of around fifty village associations. One of the most significant policy changes was a commitment to equalize minga work contributions, a policy change that resulted from a study undertaken by the local women's office.

Colta's program was relatively short-lived (thereby replicating a wider problem for rural female subalterns, see chapter 2), effectively ending when the mayor became provincial prefect and overseas funding ended. Over the longer term, however, such programs consolidate and normalize—at least in the uneven geographies of postcolonial development—the political voice and authority of female subalterns. The gains are exemplified by Ana Maria, married with school-age children, whose paid work as a development technician for the provincial council provided a backdrop to her interest in political office. When I met her in March 2009 she was busy campaigning as a Pachakutik candidate for municipal councilor in Colta, despite party officials' attempts to take her off the list. At the time she had already gained considerable experience, having been a parish vocal, then a junta parroquial councilor, and a candidate for a provincial councilor's seat (an election lost by a few votes). By March 2010, however, she had emerged victorious as a Pachakutik councilor in Colta. Ana Maria's political trajectory exemplifies the forms of agency that rework the links between development and citizen-ship to permit indígenas' greater visibility and authority.[31] Indeed village-based warmikuna in Chimborazo lauded Ana Maria for her commitment to indígena issues, such as coming and speaking Kichwa at an International Women's Day parish fair. In discussions over lunch during an ethnic federation workshop held in Riobamba town, a warmi called Agatha spoke warmly of female—and male—role models: "We thank the [male provincial] prefect who supports women's organizations. Also I thank the female councilor from Colta [i.e., Ana Maria] who supports us—she is an indigenous woman. We feel really proud of the councilor because she shows how an indigenous woman can also become an authority, and it shows us that we are capable of everything. Other women can now see that we can become authorities, and that education is important, and that age doesn't matter." A combination of supportive male leaders and a political vision rooted in consultative procedures brought about an unprecedented degree of female participation with longer-term consequences, evidencing how postcolonial intersectionality can be reconfigured.[32]

Despite these important initiatives, serious limits remain on the extent to which women can convert extensive grassroots experience in communities and women's associations into elected office. In interviews with UN researchers, indigenous women's representatives were most likely to talk about difficulties in local government than were policy-makers and nonindigenous female political actors (INSTRAW 2006: 96, 121). Indígenas' representatives were also less likely to be able to identify allies or other institutions involved in boosting their participation, reflecting skepticism about gender policy bodies and mestizo/a politicians (INSTRAW 2006: 116–20). Mestizos and men's resistance to working with a senior indígena woman who is elected as mayor or concejala (councilor) is persistent and pervasive. If they take up office, women come under constant pressure to demonstrate that they are capable and their viewpoints relevant. Echoing the damaging effect of racist and sexist jokes about Rigoberta Menchú (Nelson 1999), male and mestizo attitudes in Chimborazo obstruct elected women's actions and capacity to bring about change. One provincial leader found that "for one month, I replaced the mayor and straightaway various (male) indigenous councilors asked for holidays, so they wouldn't be managed by a woman" (quoted in CEDIS 2007a: 25; also ICCI 2001; Santillán 2008: 96).

Of the 243 comunas and local organizations in the four most indigenous regions of Chimborazo, only seven had women as presidents in 2007 (CEDIS 2007a: 25). Too frequently, women are involved solely in consultation on policy-making rather than in implementation, or authorities fail to listen to women at all. At a meeting to address this issue,[33] a woman angrily reported that "unfortunately neither the government nor our own Pachakutik authorities take women's potential into account . . . and they only get us to carry out their own marvelous ideas." Women too often remain relegated as spouses of local officials, not as representatives in their own right, experiences that indicate the consistency of colonial attribution of lesser authority with subaltern social categories, especially at supra-village scales. Their position in intersectional hierarchies continues to mean that their embodied differences are perceived as "unrepresentative" of the postcolonial nation-state, despite its (unacknowledgeable) foundation on social heterogeneity. Moreover, this deauthorized positioning is continually reinforced through the meanings around social difference that implicitly and explicitly underpin policy conceptions for quotas, consultation, and local government. Development's inability to keep racialized female subalterns steadily within its concerns, and the excessive association of indígenas with vulnerability, bolster a public perception of indigenous women as less authoritative politically and less capable in public office.

In a poor part of southern Chimborazo, the situation in overwhelmingly indigenous Guamote canton highlights both the gains and the constraints of indígenas' citizenship practices in elected office and decision-making. With indigenous leader Mariano Curicama elected as mayor in the 1990s, municipal governance shifted to a more participatory, prorural, and proindigenous model, with a self-proclaimed "indigenous parliament" and a local development committee. After 1997, and drawing on best practice from other "alternative municipalities," Guamote introduced participatory budgeting, in which female inclusion was systematically promoted. As in Colta, widespread consultation informed the municipal development plan, and women's voices were particularly sought out. "The consensus among the canton's population was for equality between men and women to be a core part of development."[34] Key in this dynamic was the creation and centrality of the first local women's organization, the Corporación de Mujeres Indígenas de Cantón Guamote (Canton Guamote Women's Organization; COMICG), which grouped together fifty-six grassroots women's associations. By the end of Curicama's first term in 2000, the local government went from having no women to an unprecedented three female councilors, one female president of the women's local organization, and a female vice-president of the indigenous parliament. By 2008 these gains were exceeded, with four councilors, one coordinator of the municipal health council, and, again, the presidency of the women's organization, while women made up one-third of local consultative committees (*mesas de concertación*). Local statutes also enshrined a commitment to encourage women's leadership, illustrating the possibility for validating indígenas' citizenship practices in local government spaces.

What perhaps was more significant about Guamote is that local women articulated a political positionality that challenged dominant understandings of social heterogeneity in Ecuadorian political culture. The COMICG organization achieved an innovative hybrid of Andean cooperation together with a reworked set of meanings around female-male difference. According to Rosario Naula, a councilor and active COMICG member, "what we bring together is something unique. We will go on working with what is traditional and what is proposed to us [i.e., gender equality] because women's participation is really important. So women have struggled as women, organizers, leaders to put forward our words, our voices, so that others hear us, including our own compañeros. That's why we participated in the canton development plan and why we speak in Kichwa in meetings" (quoted in Hernández, Larrea and Gallier 2005: 76).

In practical terms, indígenas fought to further their human rights by promoting an antiviolence statute that strengthened female access to justice in the statutory and customary systems. The resignified positionality articulated by indígenas contributed to sustained change, according to a number of sources. Colta councilor Ana María told me how Guamote continued to have a significant number of female indigenous councilors, in comparison with Alausí canton, which had no program to encourage women and only a single indígena representative.[35] Arising from direct experience of postcolonial exclusion and grassroots acts of citizenship, Guamote's indigenous women become catalysts for new directions in political practice, and their experimental approaches are communicated to wider audiences through videos, testimonies, life-histories, and leaflets (Palacios 2005; Schurr 2013). They vernacularized rights through a hybrid with local practices and understandings, without conceding a focus on their own words.

Yet reoriented practices and understandings of indígena political personhood do not necessarily create "representatives" for female subalterns as if they were isomorphic with the diverse group of indigenous women across Ecuador (Phillips 1995). Nevertheless, indigenous women in positions of national leadership in ethnic federations suggest that there are certain patterns of leadership practice that bridge the gulf between village women and the women who gain national leadership positions.[36] First, national leaders speak of the important legitimacy granted to them by grassroots support, which is sustained through long and frequent consultations with village women and regional representatives. Second, indígena national leaders are embedded in friendship and solidarity networks among senior female leaders, on whom they call for advice. Third, and unlike many male ethnic leaders, the majority of national indígena leaders expect to return to provincial, regional, and local associations rather than remaining permanently in national positions; in this sense, female leadership is experienced relationally between and across scales. In contrast to "indigenous women" programs that anticipate an individualized trajectory into ever-higher political scales (chapter 4), indígenas describe a supportive mesh of like-minded women at various organizational levels.

To consolidate gains and counter resistance, senior levels of Ecuadorian indigenous leaders have established new institutional and political spaces to support the coherence and legitimacy of indígena presence in politics over recent years. Working for wider implementation of equity measures (e.g., ICCI 2001: 48), women coordinate with indigenous organizations for the measures to facilitate their centrality in decision-making. Organizations such as CODENPE, ICCI, and the Dolores Cacuango training school produced guidelines to improve female participation, building on initiatives described earlier.[37] Drawing on successful precedents, indigenous women wrote manuals on how participatory methods, gender planning, mechanisms for municipal action, and indicators of success could provide local governments with a toolkit (Andrade 2009). The Dolores Cacuango training school forged innovative best practice measures among Amazonian Shuar and coastal populations. With support from an indígena professional in UNIFEM, a couple of indigenous municipalities in the northern Andes and Amazon devised and applied local statutes to reduce gender violence, again through a creative hybrid of culturally specific forms of authority with GAD criteria of nonviolence against women.[38] The promotion of antiviolence statutes at the municipal level was designed to ensure the full exercise of indígenas' human rights through access to both ordinary and ancestral justice. Other programs organized by and for indigenous women provided elected women with training in municipal governance.[39] Although at times ad hoc and short-term, these steps cumulatively evidence how indigenous women vernacularized notions of women's rights by hybridizing new "ethnic" and village practices and routines, and by systematically weaving together elements of indigenous politics with protections that indígenas had devised independently.

As these cases indicate, indigenous women are able to rework the meanings of political spaces and acts in certain areas and at certain levels of government in ways that move them away from development beneficiary status and toward citizenship. By means of networks spanning villages to national federations, the nature of being a female racialized subaltern has been subject to transformation in ways that rework indigenous women's politics of presence. Extending previous chapters' insights into indígenas' unique perspectives on postcolonial development, the foregoing material indicates the practices and analytical frameworks by which indígenas— especially warmikuna in comparison with Tsáchila—build and launch themselves from subaltern counter-publics. Participatory mechanisms such as women's associations play an important role in building and diversifying indígenas' acts of citizenship. Although Tsáchila and Chimborazo femininity and levels of organization differ, female comuna presidents exist in both groups. Kichwa women have a more publicly visible counter-public than sonala. Although electoral quotas assist indígenas, they do so only in indigenous-majority areas and do not provide them with public authority equal to that of nonindigenous women and indigenous men.

From Development to Rights

Rights as a political language and a means to politicize injustices have become the daily currency of Latin American social movements. Moreover, human rights frameworks have become extensively vernacularized in ethnic rights movements and in indigenous women's region-spanning, multi-scaled politics (Merry 2006), as previous chapters have documented for Ecuador particularly in the Andes.[40] The national CONAIE women's office has worked extensively to engage in international rights instruments such as CEDAW and ILO Convention 169, as well as to inform women across all indigenous nationalities and pueblos about the rights standards they endorse. Yet how does this vernacularized language of rights translate—if at all—into the practices and meanings of citizenship articulated by indigenous women in villages, among women who have no leadership position and whose political participation might be limited to a fortnightly meeting of the village women's association?[41] In order to address this question, I took to asking my interlocutors an open-ended question about how they understood rights at the end of our conversations. As might be anticipated, women expressed a diverse range of understandings of rights, yet overall their words neither reinscribe nor abandon western discourses of modernity, creating context-specific "paradoxical effects" (Dietz 2003).

Although at the grassroots, women cannot speak on the whole with the fluency of national leaders, they understand what rights represent and associate rights with specific agendas for change. The vernacularization of rights has a spread and depth as a function of interlocking subaltern exclusions, reflecting place- and time-specific articulations of interests, self-positionings, and political opportunity structures. Although when we were discussing rights one woman immediately responded that all rights were important, the majority spoke of a single one or particular set. Older indígenas, especially those without formal education, found it most difficult to define rights or link them to their lives. For instance Rosa, a middle-aged sona without schooling who had raised five children, could not say what rights were.[42] Counterintuitively, a share of younger women in their twenties and thirties also struggled to express what rights might mean. Women from the most deprived Andean and coastal districts were more likely to marry and have children young and hence were the least likely to attend meetings. Attendance at primary school did not guarantee knowledge of rights or citizenship, reflecting the poor quality of teaching and way women are actively deeducated through their adulthood. On the whole Tsáchila indígenas are less familiar with the entire language of rights, as illustrated by young married Sandra, who had just completed secondary education and who said: "The most important right is to be a citizen"; then she paused and looked around, and said, "What is it? I've forgotten everything! What else? Right to have voz y voto—that has to be it."

Nevertheless, two-thirds of indígenas I interviewed did identify one or more rights that corresponded to them individually, although this varied across ethnic groups. Only half of sonala named a specific right or defined which rights were lacking in the country. By comparison, three-fourths of warmikuna could do so, hinting at the uneven landscapes of ethnic movements and their impacts in spreading discourses of rights. Literature on indígena activism in social movements tends not to query where women's understanding of rights comes from or to distinguish between different kinds of rights. By contrast, qualitative engagement with women across two nationalities provides a picture of how and which rights are made meaningful at the village level, among indígenas who may never hold elected office or become a representative. Many Kichwa and Tsáchila women in rural districts think that rights are part and parcel of resource-led agendas and institutional contexts. For many, but not all, rights are one dimension of development, a part of the language of distribution and benefits that links to technical assistance, a general "good." Some women link rights and development projects directly. Violeta, a sona in her late fifties with no formal schooling, suggested that "before, there weren't women's rights. Now with the new governor women are receiving loans," emphasizing how rights are equated with development resources in many women's minds. In Chimborazo and Santo Domingo, grassroots women are only patchily integrated into the broader political discourse of rights, especially if they do not attend meetings,

do not participate in women's associations, and have little formal education. For all that warmikuna have begun to articulate a rights discourse,
there are others—in both ethnic groups—who are not interpolated in rights
language except in relation to development assistance. "Yes, [rights] are
great, I like them," one Serrana woman told me, while Virginia, a Kichwa
widow in her thirties, explained to me unprompted her surprise on learning that the bono payment would not be taken from her "because I have the
right to it!"

Despite ethnic activists' valiant efforts to reassure indígenas that they
are rights-bearers, in practice women continue to be subject to the ongoing
denial of personhood and full citizenship status. For a number, the interpretation of rights-as-development projects is couched in terms of livelihoods
and food security. Illustrating the suturing of rights to development resources, Mercedes suggested to me that "we have rights as women to ask for
any project, and we have rights to go out to talk about projects in whichever
meeting."[43] Articulating rights in relation to impoverishment, indígenas
view credit and assistance with agriculture and food as core rights to which
they are entitled, such as sona Elizabeth, in her midtwenties, a university
trainee teacher; Cristina, a sona in her midforties with complete primary
education; Carmen, an unmarried Kichwa-speaker in her midtwenties with
some secondary education; and Soledad, of similar age, from a low-income
runa family.

However, important distinctions arose between highland and lowland
groups: whereas sonala understood access to resources and projects to be
mediated by men, warmikuna viewed themselves as claimants to resources
in their own right. Indígenas prioritized rights differently—Kichwa and
Tsáchila both ranked women's rights and rights within the household,
though for Tsáchila livelihood rights were second in importance, whereas
for warmikuna education and indigenous rights were more significant.[44]
Kichwa and Tsáchila described women's rights in very different terms.
Whereas Andean women primarily spoke of rights to participation and voice
and secondarily about resources, sonala tended to focus on resources. A significant minority of Kichwa indígenas used the language of diverse rights
to articulate incisive viewpoints on their interests and current situation.
Aurora, a warmi with complete primary education gained at night school,
noted: "Well, we have rights. We women have rights to participate in any
meeting, do our business, to talk . . . to go out. That's what we women have
rights to." The right to participate was expressed vividly by Lucía, a married warmi in her thirties: "Yes, women go to the meetings and they talk.

Women demand their rights—as water users, their rights to assistance, so that women can do important work like men." Monolingual Kichwa speakers also stressed participation, for example Rosario, now in her forties: "My right is to participate, to live in a community, to be able to be leader, look for support, to go to offices" of state agencies and NGOs. Older warmikuna remembered that these rights to participate were hard-won, as historically they did not participate in village affairs.

Women's expression of rights in relationship to kinship and the household often linked to antiviolence agendas but continued to articulate this in ways specific to racialized female experience rather than liberal feminism. According to Nancy from Chimborazo, "the rights we have in the country would be that there's more training and workshops for women and men to stop husbands mistreating their wives." Warmikuna of all ages and educational levels spoke about how they wanted to "know what women's rights are and what we can do so women aren't mistreated," as explained by Claudia (forty-five years old, orphaned at a young age, and with no formal education). Other indígenas stressed the importance of women's rights to household resources, such as land, for example Cristina, who told me in her patio in her Tsáchila village: "We four girls had no option of having land, only the son should have land. And if they are not submissive until they marry, women's rights are not clear. I was very interested in seeing how this worked." Whereas Andean women stressed rights to training to learn more about rights, Tsáchila spoke more about individual rights to education.[45] For warmikuna speaking at federation-sponsored workshops, training and rights were intimately linked in meaning to struggles for women's rights and broader visions of political economy. For instance Renata, thirty-five years old, with completed primary education and two children, saw rights to education expanding political personhood: "Rights for women are about them moving forward, getting more, knowing a little more. That's it. Not being in the house or with the animals, but going out and getting to know more, bit by bit."

Women's discussions of indigenous rights invest them with meanings of equality, struggle, and justice, thereby resignifying the multicultural focus on culture.[46] Women of all ages and levels of education in Chimborazo referred to indigenous rights as pertaining to them, or to the fact that indigenous rights imply equal treatment to mestizos. Carmen, a twenty-year-old with incomplete secondary education, positioned herself as a rights-bearing indigenous person: "many mestizos treat us badly but there are laws that treat us the same. That is my right." Women at the grass roots view indigenous rights as something achieved through social mobilization and aimed at tackling persistent racism. Listening to Tsáchila and Kichwa indígenas talk about rights suggests a number of important points. First, the scope and nature of rights were in many women's minds, indissolubly linked to development's depoliticization and resource distribution. Second, indígenas articulate critical accounts of rights, combining rights of being women-indigenous-poor-rural in ways that reflect epistemological challenges to postcolonial intersectionality. Such an articulation of rights hence represents women's multifaceted concerns and the grounded nature of rights politicization at the margins of postcolonial citizenship.

Conclusions

Citizenship routines and practices are often taken for granted. Yet as Kichwa and Tsáchila women's experiences demonstrate, they can become fragmented and partial and subject to postcolonial power relations. In parallel with indígenas' development experiences, citizenship does not guarantee secure, recognized, and defended claims on resources and authority. From the standpoint of indigenous women, the formal features of citizenship—voting rights, representation on party lists, voice in decision-making, and so on—are paper-thin formalities that do little to challenge the multifaceted relations that block their effective empowerment and perpetuate inequalities. The rules of the game give the appearance of gender and racial neutrality, yet indigenous women's active engagement in constructing and practicing citizenship consistently reveals the breaches between citizen practices and justice, between full citizenship and project beneficiary status (compare Mukhopadhyay and Singh 2007). In this context, subaltern voices represent not a privileged, pure, or unmediated "alternative" to normal citizenship but a messy, embodied battling over the hegemonic understandings and consequences of citizenship. While this situated, content-less, citizenship has been noted previously in Latin America, tracing citizenship as a contested set of practices from the ground up reveals both citizenship's embeddedness in development governmentality and the ways subaltern agency reworks and resignifies practices as forms of insurgent politics. Indígenas destabilize liberal ideas of citizenship through reasserting claims and forms of subjectivity outside mainstream policy and nationhood. Indigenous women in this sense rework, demonstrate resilience, and organize resistance to intersecting hierarchies as expressed through citizenship practices and political theory. Their acts envisage and work toward a form of political subjectivity that speaks to sociospatial position in postcolonial intersectional hierarchies. Comprehending the unequal distribution of resources and power, indígenas' practices constitute an uneven and precarious form of insurgent citizenship (Holston 2009).

Indigenous women work under pervasive and ongoing constraints at local levels yet manage to create a rich social network alongside sympathetic organizations and indigenous men. In male-dominated political systems and cultures, indigenous women make vigorous representation of their interests and concerns (Phillips 1995: 136). Tsáchila and even more so Kichwa indígenas make citizenship in, around, and through village associations, local elected leadership in indigenous majority areas, women's training schools, extensive grassroots support, and a practical discourse of female agency (Staeheli 2011). Fixed neither by dominant understandings of female interests nor cultural agendas, indígenas' agency is expressed through a creative hybrid of tradition and newer resources (such as rights language, gender, etc.) that gives rise to unique frameworks regarding rights and social difference. Informed by their positioning in postcolonial intersectionality, Tsáchila and Kichwa indígenas do not view gender rights and ethnic rights as starkly opposed, mutually exclusive alternatives. In these innovative reworkings of hegemonic notions of citizenship, a small number of women express "a postcolonial difference" with respect to citizenship, which means turning the colonial difference on its head by articulating a vision for change that emerges from their situatedness in postcolonial intersectionality and development. In so doing, networking and transformations of meanings recast what village associations, leadership, and agenda-setting can represent in the repertoire of citizenship acts.

Rights-based development has had an extensive impact on the ways issues of social justice and inclusion can be articulated and pursued (Molyneux and Lazar 2003; Cornwall and Nyuma-Musembi 2004). Warmikuna's and sonala's citizenship practices suggest that it is not merely a question of adding a single issue dimension to rights-based approaches (such as gender or race-ethnicity) but of recognizing the relational, contingent, and power-laden ways subalterns work within and against exclusionary citizenship to pursue dignity in contexts of postcolonial social heterogeneity. As the next chapter discusses, the pursuit of dignity based on destabilizing dominant notions of citizenship involves indígenas occupying "a site of racial, gender and identity struggle connected to decolonization" (Altamirano-Jímenez 2010). In new perspectives on citizenship, indigenous women provincialize northern discourses about the (female) political subject and rethink the categories of political modernity. Although we can recognize traces of the international human rights movement, Marxism as a horizon of critique, and a certain kind of gender politics, Ecuadorian indigenous women articulate an agenda for change that is greater than the sum of these parts, a postcolonial difference emerging within and against those political categories, their agendas becoming even more distinctive in the context of constitutional change and the development agenda of buen vivir/*sumak kawsay*, discussed next.

SEVEN

Postcolonial Heterogeneity
Sumak Kawsay and Decolonizing Social Difference

As previous chapters have demonstrated, Kichwa and Tsáchila indigenous women in Ecuador bear witness to the ongoing existence of internal colonies where spaces and subjects are reduced to abandonment and bare life. Under these terms indigenous women came to represent a challenge to mainstream development, as they are viewed as "mestizas in the making," not female racialized subalterns. The hegemony of a male-head-of-household policy model compounds indigenous women's livelihood insecurities and lower intrahousehold status, perpetuating communal patriarchies. Out of these experiences, indigenous women make claims based on a distinctive political and epistemological intervention. Although active and engaged participants in ethnic rights movements—based on agendas shared with indigenous men as racialized, feminized, laboring, and disposable bodies—they also raise intersectional perspectives on their gendered-raced-located development experience. Negotiating male subaltern communitarian politics on the one hand and mestizo-family models of feminist policy on the other, indígenas propose an innovative politics of mutually embedded collective and individual rights, in relation to participation, sexual-reproductive rights, and land-territory. Challenging policy that targets social difference through an index of vulnerability, indigenous women criticize social neoliberal approaches that flatten out power in postcolonial hierarchies just as they contest participatory development's reliance on the disciplining premise of social consensus. Denaturalizing male, urban, and mestizo expectations around subjectivity and experience, indigenous women articulate a gendered-raced-located perspective on modernization, single issue development, neoliberal multiculturalism, and interculturalism. By so doing, they reposition themselves as legitimate claimants to dignity and security, centering themselves as necessary interlocutors in policy debates and political arenas. Yet indígenas' practical, embodied, and articulated knowledges are actively deauthorized by development's routines, staff, conceptions of social difference, and impulse to improve, all of which are based on coloniality's parameters, and which are defined against nondominant types of social heterogeneity. In response, leaders and village women mobilize to speak out about and dissect development's institutional and imaginative limits in relation to social heterogeneity. In multifarious political activities and agendas, indígenas demand that development and public policy recognize diversity within diversity in order to create flexible, nonessentialized understandings of interlocking racial, gender, locational, and class differences. In this way, indigenous women become creative thinkers about development and produce border knowledges that contribute to decolonization.

The contestatory engagement of female racialized subalterns with coloniality's legacies expressed through development's shifting politics of visibility continues to resonate through Ecuador's most recent development. Buen vivir policy (often translated into English as "life in plenitude" or "living well")[1] arose in the 2007 Constituent Assembly, was ratified in the 2008 Constitution, and was adopted into government policy and planning through the National Development Plan 2009–2013.[2] Resulting from "new assemblages of social movements leading to new agendas in development, citizenship and rights" (Goodale and Postero 2013: 263; also Radcliffe 2012), buen vivir development selectively draws on indigenous border thinking, making it one of the first nation-state endorsements of nonwestern approaches.[3] Continuing a critical account of postcolonial development's engagement with social heterogeneity, this chapter examines how buen vivir policy has been articulated and institutionalized and the complex responses of diverse indigenous women to policy reorientation. Tracing indígenas' agenda for development decolonization contributes to an emergent literature on gendered dynamics in postneoliberal countries (Aguinaga et al. 2011; Lind 2012; Calla 2012; Hernández and Canessa 2012). However, scholarly debate around gender justice and development often focuses on legal institutions (whether statutory or customary) (Molyneux and Razavi 2003; Goetz 2007), whereas the Ecuadorian indigenous women provide grounded accounts of an emergent perspective that goes beyond liberal notions of human rights and political subjectivity, and which calls into question many of the legislative and institutional bases of buen vivir development in practice. The chapter ends by drawing thematic and theoretical consequences regarding indígenas' border thinking for development debates and postcolonial theory.

Buen Vivir and New Developmentalism

Arising out of a strongly rights-based and social-movement-influenced constituent process, the 2008 Constitution incorporated a range of antineoliberal and prorights agendas, attempting to reposition Ecuador in the global economy while fundamentally restructuring the relationship between state, citizens, and resources.[4] Buen vivir for many observers offered a route away from technical neoliberal solutions and toward a recalibrated relation between society, economy, and nature. Measures such as the renegotiation of oil contracts and increased social spending are widely interpreted as examples of postneoliberal governance, as they overturn neoliberal goals of privatization, downward pressure on social programs, and free-market privilege. Ecuador's new political economy also features a strong role for the state in regulating labor markets, resource extraction, and galvanizing citizen participation. Hence, the country remains capitalist—and indeed heavily reliant on energy and agricultural exports—but acknowledges the diversity of informal sector economic activities and the role of caring and reproductive work and envisions a form of solidarity economy in which collective well-being, redistribution, use values, and human needs prevail. In this sense, it represents a popular pushback against the marketization of everything (Gibson-Graham 2006).[5] In this context, macroeconomic policy under state oversight is designed to release resources through which to establish a more inclusive and fairer society (Escobar 2010), in which a highly elaborate rights framework—encompassing constitutionally grounded economic, social, political, and cultural rights—creates the possibility for increasing capacities and reducing barriers to social inclusion.[6]

Constitutional rights in turn informed national development planning, specifically the National Development Plan for Buen Vivir. In the national development plan, "buen vivir" is used to refer to an environmentally and socially sustainable development objective that is strengthened and guaranteed through rights-based citizenship in which the barriers to substantive citizenship caused by impoverishment are removed. According to the plan, the goal of development is to establish buen vivir—hence, "development is the realization of buen vivir, and the construction . . . of buen vivir is what enables this new vision of human and social development" (Walsh 2010: 19).

To an unprecedented degree in the Ecuadorian context, "the concept of Buen Vivir, good life . . . is the direct relation between rights and the development model. It's a question of exercising these rights while living with dignity, without this implying an accumulation or competitive regime. Buen vivir in general includes rights and institutions that grant people the conditions to effectively enjoy human rights, the rights to live in harmony with each other and with nature, for present and future generations" (Transition Commission 2011: 23). Buen vivir development established twelve goals that encompass endogenous development, including a solidarity economy, recognition of unpaid—including reproductive—labor, cultural diversity, viewing nature as constitutive of and intrinsically valuable as social life, and environmental sustainability (Acosta 2008; Ecuador 2009; Escobar 2010: 21). With social rights at the core of the 2008 Constitution and development thinking, the state envisions not a classic or universal welfare state but a form of development justice committed to dealing with discrimination, labor insecurity, uneven development, and income gulfs.

Buen vivir's genealogy is closely associated with Andean indigenous worldviews, as well as diverse strands of left-wing politics, environmentalism, feminism, theology, and development with identity (Cortez 2011). Arising from rich conversations between environmentalists, feminists, indigenous groups, and lawyers,[7] the rights-based buen vivir agenda reflects a variety of influences from preexisting policies, amended to increase social inclusion (for example, the conditional cash transfer), subaltern policy demands (for example, measures against discrimination and racism), and socialist agendas around work and labor (for example, improved conditions for low-paid formal sector workers),[8] and so on. The minimum wage rose by about 40 percent in real terms from 2007 to 2012.[9] Ecuador's social budget saw a rise in the late 2000s relative to the 1990s, reaching the historically unprecedented amount of $40 billion. Yet, as chapter 2 noted, Ecuadorian minimal social spending was historically low and highly skewed toward certain recipients and remained at lower levels than other Latin American countries. Recent rises are spectacular in the Ecuadorian context but remain low in the regional context. Social programs, moreover, continue to be targeted at low-income groups, children, and families, and food and nutrition programs,[10] as well as the construction and maintenance of community centers, although the extent and nature of the programs often shift. In line with postneoliberal experiments elsewhere in South America, Ecuador's buen vivir agenda places the state firmly at the center of the management, regulation, and operationalization of development and political economy, and crucially as the arbiter in development disputes, as "without an efficient state development is impossible."[11] A strongly developmental state reflects the "socialism of the 21st century" agenda as well as popular demands for redistributive and egalitarian politics. In this sense, the antistate rhetoric associated with neoliberalism has been reversed, as the state assumes responsibility for redistribution and guaranteeing rights for human subjects and nature.

Given its unprecedented concern with rights and social spending, buen vivir promises transformations for those most marginalized and stigmatized by previous policy approaches. Indeed Kichwa women discussed buen vivir with me on buses and in meetings in ways that vividly conveyed their sense of connection to a more inclusive concept that, exceptionally, was granted official recognition. Kichwa women expressed perspectives on current government policy in ways that were detailed, critical, and insightful. Needless to say, however, buen vivir development faces the challenge of dealing with the entrenched institutionalization of social difference and a persistent failure to tackle colonial legacies, another dimension that indígenas were quick to identify. This chapter turns now to explore buen vivir's engagement with social heterogeneity, and indigenous women's articulation of their positionality to buen vivir development, a response that reflects neither policy formulations nor ethnic rights agendas, neither governmentality nor culture.

Buen Vivir and Social Heterogeneity

[Buen vivir development aims at] promoting social and economic inclusion with the addition of gender, intercultural and intergenerational goals to ensure equal opportunities. It is one of the most up-front policies in the country which has been put into the National Plan. And within that, we must work to make equality between men and women, as well as the plurinational state and interculturalism. Another policy talks about recognizing and respecting sociocultural diversities, [and] eradicating all forms of discrimination—whether of gender or sexual preference.

—INDIGENOUS WOMAN, EMPLOYED IN THE SENPLADES STATE
PLANNING SECRETARIAT (MARCH 2010)

Continuing a long process of recalibrating development's approach to social heterogeneity, buen vivir set in motion a set of institutional, conceptual, and programmatic transformations to address the underlying question of social difference. The national buen vivir development plan is committed to equal rights for all people, what it terms "equality in diversity," and to promoting equality, cohesion, inclusion, and social and territorial equality.

Diversity is recognized in relation to gender, sexuality, race-ethnicity, (dis)ability, generation, migrant status, and identities. Naming these aspects of social heterogeneity, buen vivir policy abolishes the historic single issue development councils (for women, indigenous, and Afro-Ecuadorians) and replaces them with a set of interrelated equality councils, charged with mainstreaming policy related to "gender, ethnicity, generation, interculturalism, disability and human mobility" (Guchin 2010: 60, 71; Transition Commission 2011: 40) and with dealing with diverse social groups, including women and men, children and adolescents, nationalities and pueblos (indigenous, Montubio, and black populations), and disability issues. Under the umbrella of the National Planning Secretariat, mainstreaming and intersectionality are to be organized intersectorally, an arrangement that places little emphasis on specialist appointments. Until the equality councils gained full legal recognition in 2014, transition commissions oversaw the policy design for each of the aforementioned dimensions of social difference, in some cases collaborating with relevant ministries. Informed by new state institutions pursuing human rights, the transition commissions became constitutionally responsible for the formulation, monitoring, and evaluation of public policy.

From the perspective of buen vivir advocates, "buen vivir is inseparable from the category diversity," as it was designed to address socioeconomic exclusion and its material and symbolic dimensions (León 2010: 106, 110). Accordingly, diversity was no longer to be associated with lack or passivity but with potential, capacities, strength, and recognition. In light of coloniality's persistence in developmental understandings of social heterogeneity, the key questions remain whether buen vivir's recognition of diversity successfully shifts powerful postcolonial social hierarchies and addresses what I have termed the second-generation challenge of working creatively with crosscutting differences. Analyzing social diversity as the product of oppression and subordination, buen vivir policy seeks to recognize and nurture individual and collective potentials, as illustrated in one policy document. "Formal and material equality are founded in the valuation of existing differences in society, which takes them into account not in order to oppress and subordinate, but rather to release potential and favor personal and collective development. This conception goes beyond understanding equality as creating assimilation or comparisons as the latter do not guarantee the eradication of discrimination" (Transition Commission 2010: 3).[12]

However, the enduring legacies of subordination in policy frameworks were not systematically considered, while each council prepared a separate equality agenda, with no systematic attention paid to intersectional policy challenges. The gender and women equality agenda and the nationalities and pueblos agenda, moreover, reveal the enduring standoffs over axes of difference, and a reworking of colonial readings of social difference. Under the 2008 Constitution, gender planning was reinstitutionalized. In May 2009, a presidential decree abolished the National Women's Council (CONAMU), and it became a "transition commission," preparing for its ultimate refoundation under the umbrella of equality councils.[13] Women's movements successfully lobbied the Constituent Assembly to recognize economies as hyper-diverse and comprising care activities, reproduction, and diverse economies, in ways that echoed global conversations about the need to reimagine capitalist economies in more diverse ways (Gibson-Graham 2006). In its working document, the gender transition commission presented a Fraserian triple agenda of redistribution, recognition, and representation on behalf of women, based on the participatory and prodemocracy goals of raising women's political, social, cultural, and territorial representation. In addition, the commission prepared background documents to inform the Buen Vivir Development Plan on gender equity and gender violence, while policy conversations began on issues of gender and ethnocultural difference.[14] Like its predecessor, CONAMU, the transition commission was largely staffed by women from mestiza, urban women's movements, although under its brief to foster civil participation in policy formulation it consulted with various groups, including representatives of indigenous groups, the disabled, and children.[15]

In practical terms, the transition commission focused its efforts on four thematic areas: institutional mainstreaming,[16] rural women, diverse sexualities, and gender violence. Regarding rural women, the transition commission continued mainstreaming work with ministries and multilateral agencies such as FAO, expecting that food sovereignty policies, the recognition of unpaid domestic labor, and government agendas to promote land distribution would combine for the successful "rehabilitation of rural women's work" (León 2009: 5). The 2010 law of food sovereignty contained no affirmative action for women, although it did place emphasis on small producers and female heads of households.[17] However, the lack of consensus in the gender transition commission scuppered attempts to build empowerment into rural policy. In the end, the Rural Women's Support Program focused on microcredit provision via cajas solidarias and measures to eradicate violence against rural women through the ordinary justice system.[18] Such steps offered little new to rural indígenas, whose microcredit organizations had already surpassed this neoliberal model (chapter 3), while activism put gender violence firmly into the interface between statutory and community justice systems (chapter 5). In this sense, the transition commission's policy for rural women continued to excise postcolonial intersectional concerns and had limited practical impact on many racialized rural women.

The commission's approach on violence and on diverse sexualities also utilized frameworks through which colonial racialized relations were reproduced, albeit on new policy foundations. In a single mention of indígenas, the transition commission working paper recommended that older women go into Hispanic schools to share "ancestral knowledge," a suggestion that reproduced colonial tropes of indígenas' noncoevalness with modernity (Transition Commission, 2011: 52). In another policy initiative, the transition commission's media campaign against gender violence illustrated the persistence of racialized thinking around indigenous masculinities. Advertisements depicted diverse racial-ethnic men from across Ecuador, and were premised on the argument that gender violence "doesn't have a poncho,"[19] an intervention that reaffirmed associations between indigenous masculinities and culturally driven violence, even as it sought to undermine the same associations. Moreover, advertisements downplayed indígenas' agency in tackling postcolonial positionality and their agendas of customary justice (chapter 5). With social difference "whitened out" in this way, the power relations of postcolonial hierarchies remained unquestioned, as illustrated by legislative measures to recognize sexual rights. Building on the 2008 Constitution, laws recognizing queer sexualities granted status and visibility to the racially unmarked (white, mestiza) subjects who are most vocal in claiming these rights, while legislative agendas failed to acknowledge struggles that are associated with racialized subalterns (also Transition Commission 2014). According to Amy Lind (2012: 541), the constitutional and policy recognition of diverse sexualities meant that "in this [policy] imaginary, LGBTTI[20] individuals are linked to progress and respectability; water [an issue that mobilized rural and racialized women], in contrast, is linked to race and poverty." In this politics, liberal individualist rights are awarded higher status consistent with colonial hierarchies, in contrast with "collective" racialized priorities concerning resources such as water. Coloniality's framing of relational values of race, gender, location, and class is highlighted in these examples. Such policy agendas are consistent with the gender transition commission's decision to firmly endorse individual rights, as—although it recognizes constitutional collective rights—its policy framework explicitly records that (racialized) collective rights should only be recognized to the extent that they do not threaten individual rights. As Karen Engle (2010) argues, the indigenous collective rights often contain provisions to limit full enjoyment of those rights—what she terms the "invisible asterix"—provisions arising from western epistemologies and geopolitical concerns that preempt indígena agendas of decolonization and self-determination.

Social policy likewise demonstrates continuity with existing colonial-modern expectations around female subjects, as buen vivir social spending remains deeply entangled in "maternalist, heteronormative understandings of the family and women's rights" (Lind 2012: 538; also Guchin 2010). In this respect, the human development bond (*bono de desarrollo humano*), a cash transfer program, was expanded under buen vivir development. As in CCT programs found across the world, small amounts of cash are paid to mothers of children under sixteen in the poorest 40 percent of the population. Under buen vivir, the monthly payment was raised in various steps from $15 to $50 (by 2014), with the number of beneficiaries and bono expenditure rising, without however "substantial modifications with respect to past" procedures, according to one report (Minteguiaga and Ubasart 2014: 87).[21] Women's access has been facilitated through diversification of access points, such as buses that run to remote villages in Chimborazo, saving women time and money going to their nearby urban center. Such measures represent a technical improvement. Under buen vivir, female bono recipients are defined as those in precarious forms of work and without a regular income, and outside social security or work-related benefit systems. Meanwhile, a socially conservative and economically instrumental use of women's time and social reproductive labor (Molyneux 2002) continues. According to a recent policy manual, mothers—whose diversity and incomparable positionalities remain unacknowledged—continue to be those "with responsibility for purchases, food preparation, care for children's health and education. The mother is recognized as the best person to administer the [bono]. It is hoped that mothers invest in their children these additional resources and improve their family's quality of life" (Ecuador 2013: 415). An implicitly racially unmarked female subject risks becoming the social referent for such policy formulations, whereas for racialized women working in agriculture or washing clothes, this policy paradigm creates as many obstacles as it removes, as Kichwa and Tsáchila women's experiences show.

Hence buen vivir policy speaks extensively about the importance of diversity and interculturalism and the need for social inclusion, and work across institutions. In the gender transition commission, however, a preexisting equality plan (the PIO) was reused, and little critical reflection was given to postcolonial hierarchies. Buen vivir's diversity hence remains embedded in ways of thinking that rely on colonial presumptions about the social. Indígenas, including the CONAIE women's office, were not party to sustained discussions about buen vivir gender policy. Ethnocultural difference was raised and not pursued, so that the commission's working document positioned indigenous—as well as black and rural—women's knowledges firmly in the past.

❋

Plurinationalism [represents] not unity in order to become western through development and economic growth. It's a unity to be what we want to be beyond reductionist, predatory and inhumane forms, and with respect for our differences. (CODENPE AECID 2011: 21)

Under the same process that impacted gender policy, the indigenous development council, CODENPE, similarly saw its remit change, shaking up its institutional structure and radically undercutting its broader legitimacy within Ecuador's development landscape.[22] As CODENPE was slated to become the National Council of Equality for Nationalities and Pueblos, its attention to social heterogeneity continued to be assigned the role of adapting policy for the recognition and rights of diverse persons, communities and pueblos, and nationalities, reflected in initiatives to devise "life plans" for each nationality.[23] In this, ethnodevelopment formally recognized the need for projects to include women, family, and intercultural concerns, as well as to deal with women's triple discrimination (in production, reproduction, and unpaid community labor) by means of increasing female participation in public policy design and providing formal and informal education and leadership opportunities (CODENPE 2010b; CONAIE-AECID 2011). The reformed council's conversations focused on four central themes: sumak kawsay (a kichwa term often translated as "buen vivir"), interculturalism, the plurinational intercultural state,[24] and the living earth, Pachamama. Each of these policy fields continuously referred back to women's central role and the need for an approach different from machismo *and* feminism. No staff were assigned exclusively to women's issues. In discussions, too, women were metaphorically linked to Pachamama, evidenced in a summary of the council's post-2008 objectives: "Codenpe has . . . new jurisdictions, but there isn't one specifically for women. However, there are those associated with the protection of Pachamama through our worldview [*cosmovisión*] and we have the guarantee of collective rights."[25] Clarifying its position regarding collective and individual rights, CODENPE declared that if there were to be a conflict between collective and individual rights, the former would be granted primacy (CODENPE AECID 2011: 86). Moreover, indigenous women have continued to articulate the problem from their standpoint in ways that replicate neither state-led development nor indigenous agendas. In light of the gender transition commission's prioritization of individual rights, the historical standoff between multiculturalism and gender politics that shaped Ecuadorian development for decades continued into buen vivir development and "postneoliberal" approaches to social heterogeneity (see chapter 1).

Development's reorientation away from neoliberal and toward broadly antineoliberal, state-led definitions of buen vivir in Ecuador reflected an attempt to rethink social heterogeneity through new forms of institutionalization, and the prioritization of interculturalism and cross-sector coordination. Buen vivir has placed great emphasis on diversity, social inclusion, and rights; both collective and individual rights have been constitutionally embedded. Nevertheless, the historical basis for professional standoffs and stubborn social categories appear to be rooted in Ecuadorian development thinking, meaning that approaches to social heterogeneity have continued to be strongly influenced by long-standing postcolonial expectations. Buen vivir development has not yet held an extensive conversation around intersectionality.

Indigenous Women and Buen Vivir Development

If neoliberal multiculturalism offered a "truncated, conditional and reluctant" recognition of difference (Rivera Cusicanqui 2012: 98), Kichwa and Tsáchila indigenous women are aware that for the first time in their lives, government policy and public debate are being discussed in terms and with components they consider to be their own, as buen vivir originates in subaltern spaces and knowledge production. As was not the case with previous development models, Kichwa warmikuna claim to have a broad understanding of buen vivir— or, as they prefer to term it, sumak kawsay—as a dignified form of living in dynamic relation with more-than-human socionatures. Unlike GAD, ethnodevelopment, or "indigenous women" in development policy approaches, indígenas have felt knowledgeable about buen vivir development. They are more than usually articulate about it, demonstrating a sense of connection to and authority about the theme. To varying degrees, the indígenas I interviewed across rural Andean and coastal regions demonstrated that they understood that some form of buen vivir is incorporated into a constitutional rights framework and, in turn, informs national development policy.

In this sense, buen vivir—and to an even greater extent, sumak kawsay—represented something that was uniquely theirs, not merely in its publicly acknowledged associations with indigenous agendas but more profoundly as a gendered-raced-rural-subaltern sphere of understanding. Unlike the deauthorization of their experience and knowledge characteristic of previous development, indigenous women feel informed and in command of the indigenous components of buen vivir. A rhetorical question voiced by an Andean leader exemplifies this standpoint: "Whose idea was the plurinational state, and sumak kawsay [their term for buen vivir]? It was ours! The indigenous peoples—us, women and men in our meetings!" Interventions like these highlight how indígenas' critical understandings of development precede and contextualize recent policy shifts, a point developed later. As Aguinaga and coauthors note, "peasants, indigenous, black, poor urban women are those who make up popular feminisms, the same women that development perceives only as program beneficiaries in a subaltern status. . . . These new feminist currents in the Andean region are not the product of progressive governments but arise out of the contradictions that emerge in specific processes of change" (Aguinaga et al. 2011: 81).

Ecuadorian indigenous women were hopeful that their long-standing demands could be met under buen vivir development. According to Monica Chují, female vice-president of the Amazon indigenous confederation CONFENIAE and member of the Constituent Assembly, buen vivir is "one of the most important and profound proposals in the context of globalization, as [it represents] a new model of development and economic growth" (quoted in Esquivel 2013: 2). Issues as diverse as land and territory, climate change, food sovereignty, indígenas' political participation, quality intercultural health and education, antiviolence measures, and solidarity and sustainable economy agendas were consonant with indigenous lifeways and politics. Before the Constitution and buen vivir plan adopted food sovereignty agendas, diverse indígenas had played an active role in defending food sovereignty through maintaining seed and crop diversity, managing local control and production-exchange circuits, and mobilizing to protect biospheres. In conversations unconnected to policy debates, Kichwa warmikuna are passionate advocates of organic production.[26] Likewise, diverse indígenas' conceptualization of work as combining unpaid and paid labor now resonates with buen vivir commitments to reward work in whichever sphere it occurs. Echoing feminist economist arguments, indigenous women also point out how dignified work means men sharing reproductive work. However, diverse indígenas do not speak with equal facility about buen vivir, reflecting their heterogeneity and uneven incorporation into the contentious politics around buen vivir. In comparison with Andean warmi-kuna, sonala knew little about sumak kawsay and government buen vivir, often mentioning specific projects such as housing bonds rather than more ambitious, wide-ranging goals. Taking another perspective were Amazon-based women who voiced sustained critiques of buen vivir's Andean origins and the need for more heterogeneous conceptions of development.

Subaltern women's interests in overcoming the social abandonment associated with internal colonies were only partially met with buen vivir. In the year buen vivir was adopted as government policy, poverty rates fell by three percentage points to 37.1 percent, and again in 2011 to 28.37 percent, down from 49.8 percent in 2003 (Ecuador 2010, ECLAC 2011). Poverty in rural areas saw a significant reduction although it remained at high levels, dropping from 71.3 percent in 2003 to 50.5 percent in 2011. According to government statistics, indigenous peoples' unmet basic needs fell from 82.2 percent to 77.2 percent between 2005 and 2010. Official data provided evidence of the racialized challenges of buen vivir planning; during the first five years of government "50,000 indigenous households . . . [were] brought out of poverty" (La pobreza indígena 2012) although rising levels of racial discrimination in the labor market affect all indigenous subjects (Ponce and Acosta 2010: 16). Combined with gender discrimination, racialized women remain firmly on the bottom rungs of informal labor markets, untouched by the minimum wage or social security coverage. Racialized female subalterns experience the unacknowledged gendered dynamics of these processes, receiving cash transfers but seeing little improvement in labor markets. Domestic service, with its low pay and limited benefits, remains a major employer, demonstrating more continuity with colonial divisions of labor than labor rights and solidarity economies because legislation to regulate domestic service has been unevenly realized. Indígenas' structurally vulnerable position hence often persists.[27] Although road-building was a government priority, indigenous women experience its impacts only patchily: "We'll have sumak kawsay when the road comes up to the community, when the heath-land is not destroyed."[28]

Women gain tangentially from material infrastructure in the shadow spaces they call home, including infrastructure for water, sewerage, electricity, schools, health centers, and roads, as long as these investments can be made without furthering the colonization of territories (Meentzen 2001: 51–52). For this reason, indígena leaders consistently press for policy implementation and action. According to the CONAIE women's representative, "from my point of view I'd say that sumak kawsay has to be implemented by the government because it's not just about talk or filling our mouths with lovely speeches about how sumak kawsay exists in Ecuador."[29] The empty promises of environmental protection were also cause for indígenas' critique. A woman representing coastal nationalities said, "The real sense of buen vivir has been lost, of the coexistence of nature and people, as women, as men."[30] The majority of racialized rural women who continue to labor on family farms perceive little impact of buen vivir's labor provisions, yet they are faced with increasingly fraught contests over resources for agricultural production (water, land, credit, labor).

After several years of buen vivir development, indigenous women were in a position to discern the extent and direction of change. In Kichwa and Tsáchila settlements, indígenas pointed out how the CCT bono combines the worst aspects of welfare and the market. Although promoted as not "traditional 'welfare,' but [not] much like 'the market' either" (Ferguson 2007: 76), the bono in its buen vivir reincarnation did not address their needs. On the one hand women continued to be monitored regarding children's health and educational milestones, yet they could not access quality health and educational services due to postcolonial uneven development.[31] Moreover, the bono was insufficient for large families, while family planning services did not address women's specific sexual and reproductive health needs, especially in Tsáchila villages. Neither could the bono match urban inflation and antirural price pressures. Educational gulfs between indigenous and nonindigenous achievement remained dismal, reflecting coloniality's geographies of poor provision and gender-racial-locational hierarchies.[32] Likewise in health, despite a stated commitment to tackling unequal access to quality care and respectful patient-staff relations, intercultural health policy in the buen vivir era replicated long-standing racializing marginalization of indígenas and their knowledge. According to a Chimborazo leader, "we haven't seen buen vivir—it's just a phrase," especially as health service staff persist in disrespectful behavior toward racialized rural women. Buen vivir also selectively continued to erase indigenous women from areas of policy where sensitivity to crosscutting lines of exclusion might be expected. The legislation on "indigenous territorial circumscriptions" for indigenous and black territorial-political autonomy noted gender issues in local elections but failed to address women's rights to land–territory. In addition, a Japanese-funded project in Chimborazo added mention of buen vivir to a participatory sustainable rural development effort without considering warmikuna's perspectives on community consensus.

In light of disappointed hopes and ongoing inequality, indígenas articulated trenchant critiques of buen vivir, thereby extending in novel directions their embodied knowledges and perspectives on development. Unlike previous policy models designed and imposed from above, sumak kawsay (viewed as different to buen vivir) represents a bundle of knowledges about relations with the earth, socioeconomic priorities, and templates for action on which indigenous women feel uniquely privileged to comment. Whereas in the past development knowledge was held and applied by professionals— including indigenous professionals in ethnodevelopment—sumak kawsay's origins and current ubiquity in public debate represent an entry point for indigenous women into an issue of widespread public concern. Whether in dismissing politicians' descriptions of buen vivir or intervening in debates about public policy, indigenous women speak from a sense of the rightness and authority of their voice in relation to other interlocutors. In the processes of vernacularizing rights-based agendas (see chapter 6), Kichwa women from their twenties through their fifties, with variable formal education and diverse livelihoods, began to mention the right to sumak kawsay. Lisa, a young Andean woman, was enthusiastic about the constitutional rights framework, yet she was outnumbered by women skeptical about the ability of a remote government to deliver material improvement. When asked about the recent political changes, most indígenas sensed that constitutional rights were based on the government's interpretation of buen vivir and not their vision for sumak kawsay, consequently presaging limited change. According to Sonia, a married Kichwa woman with one son, "for me, the most important rights would be sumak kawsay, and to have mutual understanding in a marriage, and have food for our hungry family. But the government doesn't deliver what it promises." In this way, a few village women suggest that buen vivir and sumak kawsay are not synonymous.

The CONAIE's women's representative was not willing to concede that sumak kawsay's originality makes it difficult to implement: "It's not enough that the governments or authorities say that they don't know what to do." While at times these critiques consist of indigenous antigovernment rhetoric,[33] in many other cases criticisms are voiced by village women with no political ax to grind and who express bitter disappointment in yet another failed round of development. Despite constitutional guarantees of equal access to quality services, the ongoing daily reality remains rural disadvantage, as noted in a conversation with an Andean leader: "For us now there is no sumak kawsay; the little gifts the government gives us aren't sumak kawsay. Sarah, you've seen that we don't have water for irrigating our crops."[34] Water resources, health care, and education were all arenas in which women high-lighted the gap between buen vivir principles and delivery. "We don't have buen vivir, we lack health care—we don't have medicines in the community. And the government says that health has improved for everyone. But that's not true—we don't have anything."[35]

One Andean woman, active in an evangelical ethnic organization, spoke about the lack of quality health care and went on, "It's good to hear about sumak kawsay. I would say that there's a lot of talk. It's just a phrase that's used. If we did have sumak kawsay, women would have educational grants."[36] Viewing the gender transition commission as beyond their influ-ence, indígenas focused attention on CODENPE, and argued consistently for it to recognize diversity within diversity across its actions.[37] "Our colleagues in CODENPE have to be sensitive to justice agendas, that there has to be equal-ity between men and women. If we want collective rights, we have to strug-gle together. And we women have to become more sensitive to individual rights."[38]

Buen vivir has not dampened Ecuadorian indígenas' enthusiasm for inter-national policy changes in order to clarify and empower their agendas. Ec-uadorian women network with others across the world to leverage legal and development change to address raced-classed-income-location inequalities. In late 2013, indígenas renewed their demands for the CEDAW Convention to address intersecting gendered-racialized discrimination. They called on states "to address the specific situations faced by indigenous women; the collective rights of indigenous peoples must be recognized as part of protect-ing the individual rights of indigenous persons," and suggested the UN dec-laration on indigenous peoples as a reference point.[39] At the II Continental Summit of Indigenous women of Abya Yala, held in Cauca, Colombia, in No-vember 2013, over four thousand delegates from Ecuador, Peru, Bolivia, Gua-temala, Mexico, Venezuela, Panama, Colombia, and Chile met to synthesize priorities. The meeting focused on development, how to protect human and indígenas' rights, and how to challenge racism and inequalities, resulting in a statement that noted how resource extraction, water and forest exploitation, and megaprojects continue to generate impoverishment, displacement, and the loss of knowledges and sovereignty. At the same meeting, indígenas called on ethnic rights movements and nation-states to ensure women's consistent, dignified, and authorized participation in decision-making, political office, and public policy design. Amplifying the standpoint of fe-male decoloniality scholars (Curiel 2007; Rivera Cusicanqui 2012; Galindo 2013), they further condemned what they term the rapeability of indigenous women (that is, colonial sexed-gendered-raced violence) and demanded the decolonization of Pachamama. A month previously, a smaller global group of indigenous women gathered in Lima, Peru, focused on intersectionality, intergenerational agendas, and the challenges faced by growing numbers of urban indigenous populations.[40] Three core issues emerged: women's full exercise of territorial rights; indígenas' rejection of institutional, epistemic, and domestic violence; and the urgency of sexual-reproductive rights. These meetings repositioned buen vivir/sumak kawsay not as limited to one country but as a wider agenda for subaltern populations (Declaración Piendamó 2013), embedded neither in antiglobalization politics nor localist cultural agendas but in a uniquely hybrid standpoint engaging with multiple spaces and scales.

Beyond Buen Vivir: Women's Decolonial Interpretation of Sumak Kawsay

Frequently indígenas' skeptical account of post-2008 development has been informed by their understanding that although buen vivir refers nominally to indigenous notions of sumak kawsay, government policy did not encompass the latter's full meaning and transformative potential either in its means or ends. Moreover, an expansive sense of sumak kawsay underpins women's interjections in ongoing debates about development and change. This section situates indígenas' perspectives on buen vivir, sumak kawsay, and decolonization in relation to their standpoint, processes of knowledge production, and postcolonial intersectionality. Women's accumulated knowledge gives them a sense of greater insights and a unique basis for comprehending sumak kawsay, which in turn inform their perspectives on buen vivir development.

In my conversations with diverse Andean Protestants and Catholics, farmers and off-farm workers, rural and poor urban women, a clear and articulate understanding of sumak kawsay came across. "We think of sumak kawsay in terms of food, the environment, in water, in the protection of lands and slopes. So buen vivir is something integrated. We're talking about how we all must live well, well-fed, well-educated, with our own rights, right to life, good environment, right to a good state education . . . And that we're all accepted—men, women, boys, and girls without discrimination on the basis of color, ethnicity, clothing, and language—nothing! We all have the right to buen vivir that's in the constitution; article 1 states that it's everyone's right."[41] Rural women's key role in food production and rural livelihoods, especially in contexts of male outmigration, in turn means that they associate land-territory with a gendered perspective on sumak kawsay. "And who defends the territory the most are the women in the demonstrations and the uprisings. They bring the idea that the land is not marketable, that it cannot be reduced to a commodity—that's their idea."[42] A group of low-income rural warmikuna, meeting behind a collectively run dry goods store, spoke of how women's knowledge was integral to the notion of sumak kawsay and indeed, that it predated CONAIE's adoption of the concept. After an animated discussion in kichwa among ten women, one of them translated: "We women were thinking about [sumak kawsay] before CONAIE and before Ecuarunari and the NGOs . . . Women have been thinking about sumak kawsay for a very long time. We've talked about the protection of Pachamama, care of the environment, and how we produce organic food. Also for sumak kawsay we have been working a lot on identity, valuing our own kinds of food, community ways of life, [and] organization. This is what we try to continue to do in our store."[43] Informed by a relationship of mutual care with Pachamama, racialized women are harsh critics of environmental damage caused by extractive industries. According to Chimborazo's elected women's representative, "we don't want mining to come and contaminate the rivers; we want to protect the environment."[44] In a similar vein, an indígena development professional explained, "If the government starts to agree to mining, to exploitation of natural resources, it's contradicting the rights of nature, denying the constitution and sumak kawsay itself. So that's the contradiction we have. We indigenous people understand our territory in terms of a habitat, as a space for our worldview, our life's habitat for social, natural, and economic reproduction."[45]

The elected women's representative for the Chimborazo indigenous federation highlighted the gulf between constitutional promises and changes in everyday lives: "I believe that indigenous people will have sumak kawsay when our rights are met, and we have policies for poor people, and when it isn't just written in the constitution."[46] In statements about the plurinational state and sumak kawsay, indigenous women foreground personal embodied knowledge and their status as equal interlocutors in debates.

Women with work experience in development have seen in practice how colonial difference continues to impact buen vivir development. Informed by her employment at the state planning office, an indígena voiced the opinion that sumak kawsay challenged Ecuador's postcolonial racial politics: "The white people in SENPLADES [National Planning Secretariat] don't want to talk about sumak kawsay. They resist even saying sumak kawsay! They just talk about buen vivir."[47] In this interjection and others, buen vivir is portrayed as yet another colonial move to police and manage indigenous agendas. In part this reflects widely held skepticism in Ecuador's indigenous movement, as CONAIE questioned the extent to which buen vivir could be implemented by urban, overseas-educated technocrats.[48] An Andean professional indígena working in nonstate education spoke out against the risk of sumak kawsay's depoliticization and a return to "development as usual": "It looks like we're confused, thinking that 'sumak kawsay' and 'alli kawsay' [literal translation into kichwa of *buen vivir*] are the same—it's not the same. 'Buen vivir' is [a translation of] 'alli kawsay,' it's theirs [mestizos' term]. What the government calls buen vivir is actually alli kawsay for the modern western world. But 'sumak kawsay' is the life that we see on waking in the morning; it's a life in plenitude, this life in harmony; it's life in conversation with all the Apus [mountain more-than-human agents]; it's me and everyone living with nature, eating from the land, rituals, our festivals. Eating what Mother Earth gives us; this is life in equilibrium. This life in harmony is sumak kawsay that we've lived for over ten thousand years. But alli kawsay [buen vivir] gives me the impression that it's a question of luxuries, without thinking of anything but me, arriving home to all the things the modern western world offers us."[49] Through debates, indígena leaders clarify the distinction between buen vivir and the decolonizing, anticonsumerist, rural-oriented, and more-than-human politics they associate with sumak kawsay.

Grounding a political vision in daily lives, rural Kichwa warmikuna highlight how from their perspective sumak kawsay does not correspond to existing analytical and planning boundaries that separate political economy and culture, national project and everyday livelihood. In their discussions, indigenous women in the Andes attempt to refound a set of priorities for life through recalibrating priorities. A regional women's leader articulated her understanding of sumak kawsay in relation to grassroots action. Sitting on the kerb waiting for a bus after a meeting, Delia told how she came to realize that sumak kawsay provided an unprecedented set of criteria by which to evaluate indigenous women's position and possible solutions. Galvanized by this insight, she devised a series of workshops with women across Chimborazo villages to debate sumak kawsay and how to achieve it.[50] Among the topics of discussion were women's rights and gender equality, the plurinational state, and rights to prior and informed consultation. While these items were all on CONAIE's agenda, Delia's explanation of why she had chosen these components illustrates precisely the ways indígenas creatively resignify ethnic agendas. All of these, she argued, were coconstituted alongside the strengthening of indígenas' organizations.

Women's practical knowledges and agendas are also rooted in interactions with more-than-human nature, that is, powers and agency—often beyond human control—of nonhuman beings, including mountain peaks, streams, and rocks. Andean indígenas view the living earth, Pachamama, as having extensive powers and encompassing other more-than-human agents, all of which influence their lives. As one warmi explained to me, sumak kawsay "originates in the rural communities where Pachamama makes the crops, or in foodstuffs, the environment, water, protection of land, slopes. Sumak kawsay is something integrated." Because of gendered divisions of labor in internal colonies' shadow spaces, women accrue deep knowledge and direct practice of ecosystems and socionatural resource dynamics that are simultaneously spaces of abandonment (Pacari 1998a). As such, indigenous subalterns often place more-than-human actors and forces centrally in their politics which goes beyond what was foreseen in the new constitution. The 2008 Constitution recognized nature as a bearer of rights and granted it integral respect for its vital and evolutionary processes. For Kichwa women, by contrast, sumak kawsay refers to a model of socially and environmentally sustainable life that upholds the earth's capacity to provide a balanced, equitable standard of living, and humanity's mutually dependent engagement with socionatures, whereby human social reproduction occurs in close symbiosis with living earth environments. Sumak kawsay in this sense represents a series of practical knowledges embodied by humans and more-than-humans, accumulated through indissoluble relational connections between nature and society. Accordingly extractive mining projects, the privatization of water, and the marketization of nature all act against sumak kawsay. According to Maria, a former indígena national leader, "for indigenous communities, sumak kawsay means having land, having territory. But they have to be clean, without pollution, and having unpolluted water, and that the earth produces. And well-nourished children with food produced here, educated, with health care and rights—that is sumak kawsay! That everyone respects each other, respect for one another's difference."[51] Rather than multiculturalism's thin recognition, Maria defines respect as profound epistemological recognition. Departing from this perspective, women sometimes come into confrontation with biodiversity conservation agendas such as reducing emissions through deforestation and degradation (REDD) and "green economy" initiatives (Declaración Piendamó 2013). Anthropologist Marisol de la Cadena notes how the "expansion of the political spectrum [to include more-than-human agents] may destabilize governmental categories, those population-making tools that regulate life and death in a nonstate" (De la Cadena 2010: 345). In political commentary, Kichwa women speak precisely of their relations with a more-than-human socionature in ways that epistemologically disrupt state buen vivir's rights for nature. Indígena leaders instead call on democratic states to recognize Pachamama and water as living beings and hence subjects of a broad and deep set of rights; such demands articulate indígenas' ontological difference and their challenge to modernity-coloniality's frame.

In this agenda for improvement, warmikuna prioritize an animate socionature in ways that overturn standard development approaches and also state-led buen vivir. According to indígena women, their agendas seek to shift development from being a minimal concession to respond to bare life and into a form of human and more-than-human thriving. In our conversations, a number of warmikuna made clear that sumak kawsay rests fundamentally on more-than-human assemblages whose well-being is reciprocally related to human well-being. Gathered to discuss livelihoods of subsistence and small sales, a group of warmikuna, unprompted, described this aspect of the more-than-human to me: "For indigenous people [a life force is] present in the animals, food, the fields, in the sown ground, [and] in the land. We first have to say thanks to the Pachamama, ask her authorization to start harvesting. So it's to do with all beings [human and more-than-human]. So sumak kawsay is not just about eating well; it's about living all this presence with the beings [seres] which give life to all existence" (CAMACHH focus group, 2009). Indigenous women hence stress a form of care-work and nurturing that explodes the liberal and progressive feminist conception of diverse economic activities (see Gibson-Graham 2006; León 2010), as they resituate human embeddedness in these relations alongside mutual care with more-than-human actors.

Informed by such border knowledges, sumak kawsay cuts the ground from underneath neoliberal social development by discarding policy premised on needy, vulnerable, at-risk populations while drawing inspiration from subaltern experience forged through postcolonial modernity, where life and politics are conjoined in more-than-human and human security. Andean more-than-human earth-beings can enter politics and by so doing disavow "the separation between 'nature' and 'humanity' on which [western/global] political theory . . . was historically founded" (de la Cadena 2010: 342). Whereas buen vivir granted nature constitutional rights, sumak kawsay expands the circle of political subjects with agency (de la Cadena 2010), encompassing diverse more-than-human agencies and thereby overturning the liberal premise of development as human mastery over nature and its mono-logic vision of who or what is worthy of rights. In interviews, Ecuadorian indigenous women did not self-consciously talk about Pachamama as a political agent, yet their recalibration of well-being and dignity in relation to the more-than-human marks a significant contextual response to the postcolonial exclusion to which they are subjected (for example, Anderson 2007; Sundberg 2014; Radcliffe 2014a). Since sumak kawsay rejects a liberal human-nature distinction, many indigenous women in Ecuador today align themselves with more-than-human agency, creating an assemblage of vital, political, reciprocally constituted, and needy beings, whether in an everyday way or in a contentious politics over the country's future (compare Mandato 1 Cumbre 2009). Indigenous women's distinctive and grounded ontologies offer a profound challenge to mainstream development's reproduction of internal colonies and subaltern abandonment.

Moreover, Ecuadorian indígenas remind us that indigenous more-than-human politics is inherently intersectional, in that raced-gendered-sexed subjects have different positionalities and hence political interventions to make in an expansive sumak kawsay. This reconfigured political sphere is one where indígenas are knowledgeable interlocutors, able to consider well-being in relation to the Pachamama. Their border thinking and situated-embodied epistemologies around development are inevitably shaped by legislative and constitutional changes, as this is not a form of knowledgeable critique that exists outside history or politics. Their situated knowledges highlight how buen vivir continues from indígenas' perspectives the policy formulation of modernity-coloniality's conception of social difference (and its removal from the category of nature). Whereas neoliberal multiculturalism represented "the neutralization of the decolonization impulse" (Rivera Cusicanqui 2012: 99), indigenous women's version of sumak kawsay places decoloniality firmly back on the table and situates raced-sexed-located women front and center as interlocutors, implementers, and theorizers of development. Having vernacularized a rights discourse and combined it with subaltern knowledges, a significant number of indígenas have constituted a political subjectivity that empowers them as knowledge producers and as interlocutors in development debates in pursuit of rights, citizenship, and socionatures.

> We must seek an Other model of an intercultural state, a plurinational state, for all women and men. (Mandato I Cumbre 2009)

> [Our aim is] to construct in practice an intercultural state, truly just and democratic and equitable, that generates conditions for women and

men of the pueblos and nationalities to achieve true sumak kawsay, respecting our interests and sociocultural specificities in light of development with identity. (Agenda Política y Estratégica de las Mujeres de los Pueblos y Nacionalidades Indígenas del Ecuador, 2010)

Constitutional recognition of nature's rights and buen vivir debates represent the first time in Ecuador, indeed in Latin America, that nonwestern conceptions of development have so thoroughly influenced state projects for the future (De la Cadena 2010; Cortez 2011). The decolonizing more-than-human epistemology emerges not by design or from myth but from processes whereby "historic experiences of life [are] converted into struggles and proposals" (Macas 2011: 52), forged by indigenous movements, intellectuals, and their allies. Moreover, buen vivir and, in different ways, sumak kawsay constitute a political act, an intervention designed to shift away from one regime and toward a contingently alternative configuration of rights and being, reconfiguring the terrain on which distinctions between bare life and citizenship are made (Chatterjee 2004; Isin 2012: 564). By highlighting the Orientalist origins of citizenship and development, sumak kawsay reinvents the relation between them yet inevitably remains an unfinished project (Mignolo 2000; Quijano 2000; Isin 2012), as the institutional and political context remains largely unable to carry these decolonial agendas forward.

Despite sumak kawsay's origin in agrarian interactions with more-than-human agency, indigenous women are very clear about how the scaling up and guarantee of sumak kawsay relies on the decolonization of the nation-state, another component of the post-2008 landscape of Ecuadorian contentious politics. Part of CONAIE's agendas since 1990, demands for a plurinational intercultural state aims to decolonize the state and create a polity encompassing multiple internally diverse nationalities interacting with one another through mutual respect and equality, through decentralization and autonomy. Indígena leaders are original and key thinkers in debates about the political agenda concerning the foundation of a plurinational intercultural state. Displacing racialization as the basis of power, the intercultural plurinational state involves "not simply adding or contributing diversity to an established structure . . . but also simultaneously re-conceptualizing these structures plurally and interculturally" (Walsh 2009b: 70–71; CONAIE 2010b). This agenda hence runs in an opposing direction to single issue development, and social neoliberal policy frameworks.

Indigenous women view sumak kawsay and the plurinational state as coconstituted and equally significant; if sumak kawsay provides the goals and the content for change, the plurinational state represents the institutions to guarantee sumak kawsay's realization. In their conversations about the polity, indígenas talk about state-based change in terms of multiple interacting scales that guarantee justice and nondiscriminatory public institutions. Sitting in her Quito office, the women's representative for the Andean federation Ecuarunari, Magdalena told me: "We want [sumak kawsay] in our communities and we want to wield a plurinational, intercultural state so that we're all in the same condition and we can be equally capable."[52] Reframing Amartya Sen's notion of capabilities by linking it to decolonial agendas, Magdalena forcefully highlighted subaltern agency vis-a-vis the state; as she said, "we will wield this state." In international forums too, Ecuadorian and other indígenas declare themselves fully behind the plurinational state, as in the name of sumak kawsay they "seek our model of the plurinational state for all men and all women" (Zhingri 2009: 2). Meeting in southern Peru, Latin American indígenas called for the "guarantee [of women's] active, critical and constructive participation in the exercise of their rights within a new paradigm of buen vivir and plurinational states" (Mandato 1 Cumbre 2009: 3). Whereas postcolonial citizenship recruited subalterns into limited, highly conditioned and codified spheres, and neoliberalism offered passivity and vulnerability as the conditions for inclusion of raced-gendered-poor subjects, the plurinational-intercultural state represents a horizon of active, more-than-human relational dignity and security.

In this reenergized citizenship, the CONAIE women's office encourages diverse indígenas to participate in designing and monitoring public policies in order to ensure that constitutional and planning objectives are realized, especially in relation to indígenas' political rights (CONAIE Women's Office 2010). Participation in incremental acts that build a plurinational intercultural state infuses local and transnational agendas for change. A continental meeting held in Puno, Peru, resolved that "we indigenous women must not remain passive during the implementation of government's public policies; we must be capable of intervening in them, obliging states to consult us and let us participate in all themes related to our rights" (Mandato 1 Cumbre 2009: 3). The 2013 Cumbre statement highlighted their participation in the design of public policies that required support from women's organizations and allies in international development agencies.[53] According to an indigenous female professional involved in a program that builds up from indígenas' organizations and creative responses to postcolonial development, "we're trying to encourage public policies from an intercultural angle. So there's training . . . Another theme we're working on is justice and collective and individual rights in the administration of justice. And the last theme is public policies and the state, with the goal of operationalizing the plurinational and pluricultural state."[54] In this way, indigenous women practice citizenship at multiple scales and in overlapping spheres and reconfigure mainstream understandings of gendered citizenship and justice (Staeheli et al. 2004; Mukhopadhyay and Singh 2007: 17). In this way, racialized subaltern women reformulated participation to include incorporation of diversity and social heterogeneity into public policy, arising from subaltern agency.

Nevertheless, women's heterogeneity has brought diverse interpretations of political and institutional positioning into the arena of buen vivir development. Whereas some indígenas view Ecuador's post-2008 constitutional commitments and social welfare as conquests on subalterns' behalf, others are extremely wary of buen vivir planning, seeing in it postcolonial depoliticization and stereotyping. Yet they all share decolonization agendas and take subalterns' knowledges seriously, even if they differ in their interpretations of whether subaltern interests are being met. Divergent views were aired at a workshop in Baños town, among orchid-covered slopes, during lengthy discussions about buen vivir's institutional, educational, and political dimensions. A female Shuar leader spoke out against a new type of conformity: "The Plan could be understood as a national plan for buen vivir, and that we must all be subject to a national plan. Excuse me friends, but that's a great error for us as representatives of different nationalities to commit to this. If we want to construct a plurinational country, then we'd be wrong. If we're fighting for a plurinational state, we must really divide this up—we must practice diversity and democracy" (Baños Workshop 2010: 29–30).

Rather than assuming that decolonial development is uniform, this Shuar indígena highlights the plural types of development that could arise in a plurinational intercultural state, arising from heterogeneous human collaborations with more-than-human agents.[55] Other women at the same meeting emphasized how indigenous "conquest" of the state had led to government buen vivir planning. According to an Andean woman, "someone said that the National Development Plan was not prepared from the grassroots; that's true. However the ideas in the constitution, the sumak kawsay—although it's been translated badly, although mestizos don't understand—for me, it's our struggles' objective—that conquest. Since colonial times we've raised our voices of protest."[56] Although agreeing that sumak kawsay represented a core decolonial objective, other women at the same meeting were skeptical that the state would become plurinational-intercultural under current circumstances. In this vein, a woman from the central Andes spoke out: "Take the example of the development plan presented in Chimborazo. SENPLADES came to our office to present it. 'Look at this development plan,' they said, 'this is how we want to work.' Reading and reading . . . But we didn't see the [plurinational] state in there—How is [the plan] going to strengthen the plurinational state? It's only about interculturalism . . . We have to apply the plurinational state or it's going to stay outside the game."

Moving beyond coloniality's dehumanization and avoidance of postcolonial intersectionality, indígenas' debates speak to the rehumanization and more-than-humanization of life-worlds. As sumak kawsay engages the political nature of more-than-human assemblages, it raises the possibility of rethinking the relation between collective and individual rights in innovative ways. As noted, state buen vivir gender and indigenous policy remains influenced by zero-sum understandings of collective (ethnic) and individual (gender) rights, each policy arena reasserting incompatible and irreducibly separate types of rights. Yet for indigenous women, located in the relationally worst position of postcolonial intersectionality, collective and individual rights need to be integrated in order to establish intercalated robust, just administration and guarantees of justice. Exploring rights in terms of a plurinational-intercultural state that is present—not absent—and of differentiated coherent acts of justice that do not consistently treat racialized-female-poor bodies as unworthy, indígenas thereby recast the question of collective-individual rights in ways that the Ecuadorian state and key stakeholders in the country have yet to comprehend. Moreover, indigenous women locate the core question of rights in dialogue with embodied and performative dimensions rather than written documents and abstract concepts. Rights are not merely abstract philosophical concepts; they are realized in practice, as during an indígena's dignified interaction with a female police officer. Not the text of a constitutional article from months of lawyerly negotiations but the embodied and primed mental and bodily disposition of a dominant nonsubaltern subject prepared to listen to and act appropriately to an indígena's denunciation of rape.[57]

Ecuador's public debate does not figure decolonization prominently. Nor does government policy (including gender policy) and institutionalization address decolonization, unlike the Bolivian state structure (compare Burman 2011; Calla 2012 on Bolivia).[58] Ecuadorian women from diverse pueblos and nationalities use a tone of serious critical engagement with little or no explicit mention of decolonization or depatriarchalization, although effectively they voice and pursue agendas that seek to transform raced-national-political-gendered relations in important ways and continue to struggle to achieve a decolonized state. Differences between Ecuador and Bolivia have multiple causes, relating to distinctive political cultures, distinctive histories of indigenous mobilization and state response, political-constitutional processes, and the dynamics of women's politics in each country. Nevertheless, diverse Ecuadorian indígenas are deeply engaged in reconfiguring the dynamic between collective and individual rights, and the positionality of racialized female subalterns in a more-than-human politics, thereby contributing to a political subjectivity different from postcolonial nationalism and global rebellion, as it is oriented toward a situated politics of life and dignity (Maldonado-Torres 2007: 262).

Arguably decolonization requires "paying attention to the internal dynamics of the subalterns," as well as performatively bringing decolonization into being through "our gestures and acts and the language in which we name the world" (Rivera Cusicanqui 2012: 104, 105–6). Ecuadorian indígenas' cumulative acts to bring into being a combination of more-than-human agency, a plurinational-intercultural state, and a sustained focus on race-gendered-class-locational hierarchies speaks to precisely this politics of decolonization. Indígenas feel no nostalgia for liberal divides between individualized citizenship and collective rights, between human politics and subordinated more-than-humans. Their recasting of social heterogeneity becomes a resiting of boundaries between human and nature, in the name of recognizing those subjects that were most dominated within coloniality-modernity. Decolonial citizenship remains based on rights, yet relates these to subjects whose difference does not collapse into postcolonial hierarchy. Decoloniality in action is exemplified by indígenas' disruption of the separation of (ethnic) collective rights and (feminist) individual rights (Walsh 2009b: 180; also Acosta 2008: 33; compare Gibson-Graham 2006).

Final Thoughts on Social Heterogeneity, Development, and Postcolonial Challenges

By starting from the postcolonial intersections of race, gender, location, and income that produce the contingent and precarious lives of indigenous women, this book has explored the responses of successive policy approaches to the dilemma of difference. The objective has been to examine the situation of racialized female rural subalterns as a means to analyze the way development—global, national, modernization, neoliberal, postneoliberal—treats the issue of social heterogeneity. A different starting point—Afro-Argentine urban children—might raise distinct contingent issues that Ecuadorian indígenas do not. Nevertheless, examining development from the perspective of indígenas in different contexts of development and coloniality has revealed that this is not merely an empirical discussion, as it provides an X-ray of development's blind spots and complacent readings of social difference and of the ways policy attends to subjectivity shorn of intersectional positionality. Through the genealogy of Ecuador's development history, indigenous women were either excessively visible or invisible in the metrics of projects and programs. Indigenous women were largely invisible in modernizing rural development, most gender and GAD programs and participatory development, and the specific concatenation of intersectional exclusions that characterize indigenous women were erased from development concerns, as the social categories and qualities mobilized were, according to policy presumptions, already covered and included in rural households, women, and a cohesive community. The continued invisibility of indigenous women's structural and relational position within these policy formulations speaks to the enduring power of hegemonic understandings of need, voice, and authority.

Neoliberal governmentality's capacity to work with and indeed instrumentalize social difference has been extensively noted (Lemke 2001; Hale 2002; Andolina et al. 2009; Asher 2009). Close examination of Ecuadorian development dynamics between policy and beneficiary extends this discussion in important new directions, first through a postcolonial analysis of different policy areas influenced by neoliberalism (health, participation, 'indigenous women in development,' and so on), second through the steady analytical focus on indigenous women's experiences in postcolonial intersectionality's interaction with development, and finally in its comparison of neoliberal dilemmas of difference and the "postneoliberal" policy emerging in recent years. In each case, emplacing neoliberal social policies firmly in a colonial present reveals how colonial templates and stereotypes provide enduring rules of interaction and shorthand models of gender, race-ethnicity, location, and poverty that are picked up on and retooled by neoliberal interventions. Household head, farmer, mother, and active citizen are categories not merely bound into neoliberal governmentality, powerful though this is, as they additionally rework the social expectations about embodied agency, unrealized entrepreneurialism, and conformity to existing statistical categories laid down through decades of postcolonial development. In this sense, the "market" is not a neutral arbiter able to transcend or cast aside the importance of social difference (specifically postcolonial intersectionality). Postcolonial political economies and nation-building produce hierarchically organized and intrinsically *social* markets and politics, binding together colonial epistemologies of freedom, the market, and social difference (Povinelli 2005).

Addressing single issue development approaches within a broader comparative analysis of development conception of social heterogeneity thereby reveals that single issue foci (exemplified by gender policy and ethnodevelopment) rely heavily on what I have termed "rules of intersectionality," that is, colonial-inflected assumptions about configurations of gender and household relations, or how culture encapsulates ethnic development. Taking social heterogeneity as an intrinsic problem for the will to improve permits an original analysis of single issue development (rural poverty, gender, racial inequality) by drawing comparisons across these policy fields that are so frequently considered as if they are discrete areas of scholarly and policy concern. Single issue development collapses down the internal heterogeneity of social categories, drawing frequently on malleable yet persistent colonial designation of subpopulations' qualities, dispositions, and characteristics. Whether single issue interventions seek to empower women or alleviate poverty, they call on and redeploy already-designated social categories whose characteristics are viewed through colonial eyes, with its inbuilt tendency toward "probabilistic truths and predictability" (Bhabha 1990: 87). Hence, populations associated with subaltern difference are expected to transform into modern, nonsubaltern subjects or become placed under the powerful "invisible asterix" that erases qualitatively significant social characteristics associated with subalternity. Although seeming to start from a distinct agenda, participatory development, too, referred back continuously to a homogeneously conceived social identity, which was used as the basis for forging consensus. This presumption disciplined beneficiaries around development's institutionalized categories and—in some cases—in the name of the nation-state, thereby disregarding the interlocking forms of exclusion and epistemic violence that went into the making of single issue development, and postcolonial statehood.

Moreover, differences between Kichwa and Tsáchila women are not irreducibly made by ethnic cultures, despite development's tendency to fixate on reified culture as the primary cause of indígenas' disadvantage (for example, in explaining their unwillingness to take up political leadership). A counter-topography across and between Kichwa and Tsáchila territories unpacks the differentiated outcomes for indigenous women, while bringing into focus the power of racialization, masculine bias (in ethnic populations, civil society, nation-states, and development), and social abandonment that cumulatively—in historically and geographically variable ways—exclude women from secure, dignified, and autonomous lives. Space is fundamental to this, as social relations are constituted in and through spatial relations, through and across multiple scales simultaneously. By examining the coconstitution of social heterogeneity with geographical variation across Ecuador, the account contributes to critical development geographies of postcolonial development. The counter-topography reveals how the qualities associated with femininity in different sociospaces are constituted through regional economies, forms of colonial dispossession, contingent histories of institutional presence/absence, and the unpredictable dynamics of subaltern organization. Rather than reify Kichwa and Tsáchila women's experiences as diametrically opposed forms of ethnic female experience, each inextricably embedded in ethnic cultures, the indígenas' account highlights the fractal power geometries of internal colonialism overlapping with ethnocultural distinctions (forged at the boundary between settler and indigenous, between the state and subalterns) and the category-fixing of development thinking.

Through the initial focus point of indígenas, this review of Ecuadorian development has also revealed key moments at which racialized rural women have been singled out as a high-priority target population, such as in neoliberal political agendas of "indigenous women in development," in biopolitical concerns, and in ethnic interculturalism. At these points, indigenous women entered policy remits as at risk and vulnerable subjects whose disposition and behaviors became subject to micromanagement and discourses of belonging. Maintaining a steady analytical focus on development genealogies hence provided a means by which to uncover the forms of power that push and pull racialized female subalterns in and out of policy dealings with social heterogeneity. A postcolonial critique of development's selective optics revealed how postcolonial intersectionality remained outside the purview of varied initiatives, as again and again projects and programs mobilized social models that denied and misrecognized diversity within diversity. Throughout each of these forms of development one of the most invisible dimensions continued to be indigenous women's persistent and widespread exclusion from dignified, secure, and adequately remunerated economic options.

Moreover, indígenas' direct experiences of postcolonial intersectionality inform critiques of development's failure to think about social heterogeneity outside those terms. Projects including indigenous women directly or indirectly consistently disavow diversity within diversity, instead foregrounding a homogeneous community constructed through the active suppression of social difference and the silencing of indigenous women's qualitatively distinctive disadvantages. Indigenous women are national citizens, women, and racial-ethnic subjects, yet the social qualities that development thinking associates with each of these categories in turn are qualities that indigenous women—because of their position in intersectional hierarchies—cannot lay claim to. Regarding development, indigenous women consistently request inclusion in policy decision-making in order to provide development with systematic information regarding the specificity of their positionality. In a politics of presence, indigenous women demand to be interlocutors whose social reality deserves to be considered. By erasing indígena agency, policy closes off indigenous women's subaltern power-knowledge about development.

Disillusioned by international aid's ineffectiveness and overreliance on standard procedures, some in development studies have begun to explore the value of complex adaptive systems thinking, in which blueprints and ten-year plans are overturned in favor of more open-ended, innovative strategies that build local capacities, bolster iterative learning, and create flexible, change-responsive, and incremental outcomes. Ecuador's buen vivir development illustrates well the grounded, learning-based, and open-ended process celebrated in these debates, recombining as it does local capacities and endogenous knowledges. However, what the steady focus on Ecuadorian development histories reveals is the "stickiness" of postcolonial stereotypes, colonial-era assumptions, and implicit models of social relations that perdure regardless of changes in policy headlines. Although at one level, Ecuador got rid of its single issue development institutions, replacing them with councils charged with taking into account intersectionality and multiple axes of social (dis)advantage, in practice institutional and society-wide relations lagged behind these promising visions. Development scholar Ben Ramalingam (2013) suggests that self-organizing adaptive systems break up sclerotic routines and deliver synergistic goals required in education, health, and disaster planning. The Ecuadorian case cautions against the expectation that complex adaptive systems can jettison so easily the modes of abandonment and exclusion that forge everyday realities for millions across the world. Whereas male internet entrepreneurs deploy flexible micro-systems relying on desperate individuals willing to trade their time for internet access, the entrenched postcolonial nation-state and its coconstituted lopsided society continue to put raced, rural, and impoverished individuals into precisely the position where such options for income generation appear welcome. The

issue is not to assume development can generate a positive individual freedom out of what dominant thinking represents as "a domain of habituated
nonfreedom," but rather to explore "practices of social coordination" that
perpetuate inequality (Povinelli 2005: 158, 1630).

Examining these questions through close collaborative engagement with
Kichwa and Tsáchila women and taking their interpretations and experiences seriously adds immeasurably to understanding development's treatment of social heterogeneity. Subjects most marginalized by hegemonic
developmental models of social difference query how policy thinking and
interventions come to solidify around rigid and status-demarcating subjects
and spaces. In daily lives molded by social distinctions forged through racism, abandonment, and exclusion, racialized female subalterns have come
to view interventions not with policy-makers' expectant hopes but with critical dissatisfaction, as their viewpoints reflect neither unmediated subjection
to governmentality nor containment within culture. From a position within
coloniality-modernity, indígenas criticize postcolonial development for its
uneven coverage, its systematic depoliticization, and its reduction of qualitatively powerful intersectionalities to technocratic simplifications. These
points carry implications for postcolonial theorization of subaltern experience, as they emphasize how material interests and community are not incompatible bases for subaltern political mobilization. Indígenas' agendas
provide counter-evidence to the suggestion that subalterns are necessarily
best served by class politics. In Ecuador, rural, poor, racialized females
organize around redistributive interests expressed in/through anticolonialism (with indigenous men) and through nonwestern conceptions of postcolonial femininity. Moreover, close attention to indígenas' agendas reveals
innovative recasting of what might be meant by subaltern politics, as illustrated by the simultaneous pursuit of individual and collective rights and the
ontological disruptions to politics represented by Pachamama.[59]

Postcolonial studies hence can bring from grounded ethnographic study
of the colonial present, and a focus on indigeneity, bare life, and abandonment of racialized subalterns, insights into how the very "matter" of being
human (in relation to reason, interests, affiliations, etc.) is coming under
scrutiny, from two major perspectives. On the one hand the colonial present
is forged in large part by the ways naturalized, forceful, and commonsense
discourses and practices constitute the embodied, material bodies whose
chance of acceding to security and dignity is so skewed. These discourses
and practices are sociospatial, operating at multiple scales and compounding uneven development in ways that undercut any simple theoretical or de-

velopment formulas. On the other hand postcolonial studies has much to offer in discussions about the political context and consequences of bringing the more-than-human into consideration alongside subaltern experience. As the Ecuadorian indígena case suggests, the more-than-human dimensions of subaltern experience cannot be reduced to an apolitical factor of cultural otherness. Taking the more-than-human seriously in postcolonial analysis requires recognition of its political and social copresence with subalterns, as well as a contribution to theorizing the ways policy reworks colonial hierarchy in "environment and development." As development becomes ever more enrolled in tackling the problems of the Anthropocene, so too there is an urgent need to decolonize the powerful associations between agentive nature, environmental agendas, and indigeneity that circulate in global policy.[60]

Indigenous women's situated knowledges, accumulated through direct experience, embodied and inscribed onto bodies and into quotidian relations through which they become low-cost, disposable labor, are forged at the heart of development. However, Ecuadorian indigenous women's engagement produces knowledge and reinterprets taken-for-granted political categories and concepts normalized through development's western genealogies. By overturning hegemonic conceptions of collective and individual rights, and in recasting hegemonic notions of freedom and culture (Povinelli 2005), Ecuadorian indigenous women's networks—gaining strength from ordinary warmikuna and sonala, among others—do much more than tell us about place-based ways of life. Confronting development as a problem of knowledge production, their critiques speak to the urgent need to decolonize developmental conceptions of woman, rurality, race-ethnicity, and citizenship, as well as enduring policy interpretations of social dispositions and development potential. In a wide-ranging discussion of subaltern positionality, postcolonial scholar Nelson Maldonado-Torres argues that in the sixteenth century, Fray Bartolomé de las Casas's debates concerning the human status of Indians in the Americas established skepticism and doubt at the heart of coloniality-modernity's processes of knowledge production. Henceforth European knowledge was not only skeptical about knowledge claims but also, suggests Maldonado-Torres, was organized through the colonial difference articulated around the western-subaltern binary, such that "yo conquiro" (I conquer) predates and permits Descartes's "cogito ergo sum" (Maldonado-Torres 2007). Although American Indians, aboriginal peoples, and First Nations were eventually recognized as (a different kind of) human (Anderson 2007; Lester 2012), western knowledge production based on skepticism toward subaltern knowledges became a universal and privileged form of knowing. Exploring Ecuador's development genealogy and the ways it addresses social heterogeneity and marginalizes indígenas' knowledges suggests that western skepticism underpins developmental knowledge and its treatment of social heterogeneity. Kichwa warmikuna and Tsáchila sonala permit us to take the argument further: although coloniality-modernity ensured that epistemological authority was awarded to skeptical western "universal" knowing subjects, in practice critical thinking was never exclusively theirs. Indigenous women's insights suggest that epistemological doubt, analytical enquiry, and critique are not uniquely the privilege of a subject centered in the West. From a colonial encounter, subalterns construct a parallel skepticism that, albeit arising in the entanglement of coloniality-modernity, occasionally generates alternative knowledge. In this sense, indigenous women are not merely vivid empirical reminders of development's colonial present as theorizing participants in a wider conversation about how to understand, conceptualize, and practically reconfigure citizenship, rights, and more-than-human politics. Indigenous women's critiques of development's complacencies are hence integral to a wider conversation about decoloniality, an unfinished yet urgent endeavor.

NOTES

Introduction

1. All rural interview respondents are identified with a pseudonym. Indigenous spokespeople and elected female leaders speaking in public are identified by name. Delia Caguana was a key facilitator and collaborator during the research (during which she was the elected women's representative in Chimborazo's federation, COMICH) and chose to be identified by name.

2. Given postcolonial racial hierarchies and state formation, official figures concerning racial-ethnic diversity are subject to considerable dispute. Ecuador's 2010 census questioned respondents on their self-identification: 71.9 percent identified as "mestizo" (i.e. biologically and/or culturally "mixed" populations, referring to European and indigenous ancestry), 6.1 percent as white, 7 percent as indigenous, 7.4 percent as *montubio* (coastal region peasant group, recognized as a separate racial-ethnic category), 7.2 percent as Afro-Ecuadorian (claiming varying ancestry to African descent), and 0.4 percent others. Ecuador's indigenous movement disputes these figures, arguing that indigenous nationalities account for around 15–20 percent.

3. "Development" here refers to systematic programs of intervention from diverse institutions that seek to improve living conditions.

4. To clarify, the term *social heterogeneity* is used here to refer to social distinctions arising through myriad power relations and inequalities; Silvia Rivera Cusicanqui's term "motley," or *ch'ixi* in Aymara (2012), expresses a similar meaning.

5. Foucault understood *genealogy* to refer to how ways of thinking and acting cohere over time to underpin public discourses and institutional practices.

6. Other ethnographic explorations of racialized rural subaltern women's development experiences include on Afro-Colombian women, Asher 2009; on Ethiopian Maasai women, Hodgson 2001.

7. Postcolonial work is most rewarding and theoretically generative when it engages with how ordinary people experience and respond to the uneven nature of the colonial present, in the friction between the local and the global. By contrast Vivek Chibber uses the concept of culture (defined against what he terms "psychology") without examining how these factors become contingent and

malleable and inform diverse political dispositions, struggles, and definitions of socioeconomic interests (Chibber 2013).

8. As should be clear, my approach treats neither "culture" nor "psychology" (pace Chibber 2013) as closed fixed attributes, seeing them as relationally produced across material and discursive fields.

9. The term "will to improve" is Li's (2007).

10. Key to this analysis hence is reflexive consideration of the process of knowledge production; see Dirlik (1994); Escobar (1995); Sylvester (1999); McEwan (2003).

11. *Abjection* refers to the material effects of normalizing powers of discursive practices, and in practice to degrading conditions that deny dignity to subjects.

12. In this sense, analysis keeps in its sights the discursive, performative, material, and epistemic (Spivak 1993 [1988]; McEwan 2009; Blaser 2010).

13. Women in the majority world are shaped by a series of overlapping, mutually influential economic, religious, legal, sociocultural processes, what Grewal and Kaplan (1994) term "scattered hegemonies."

14. Intersectionality has been critiqued for its undertheorization, weak attention to power, and reductionism of social identities (see, among others, Dorlin 2005; Wade 2009). By considering intersectionality in relation to postcolonial accounts of agency, power, and the radically diverse nature of crosscutting identities, I hope to overcome these limitations.

15. *Racialization* refers to power relations that attribute racial difference to certain populations in ways that naturalize race as a system of social difference. *Dispossession* can be defined as processes that result in transfer of control and ownership of assets to more powerful subjects, through force, law, or social norms.

16. *Colonial difference* refers to the epistemic validity and normalization of metropolitan knowledge and subjects, whose authority is bolstered by comparisons with the colonial Other located in the past and at a distance (Mohanty 1991; Said 1993).

17. In response, the UN advocated methodologies to make visible and address "full diversity" through disaggregated data, contextual analysis, and intersectional reviews of policy (see chapter 4 on data on gender and race-ethnicity).

18. Resulting from women's movement activism during transitions to democracy, the formalization of gender rights has had a significant impact on governance in state bureaucracies (women's ministries and directorates), in electoral politics (quotas for women), and across policy fields as diverse as education, health, and development. For overviews see Laurie and Calla (2004); Nagar (2004); McEwan (2009).

19. The term *subaltern* refers to a nondominant group whose position precludes their full humanization, authority, and voice, a condition tied particularly to colonization and postcolonial nationalism. The subaltern category is hence socially heterogeneous across time and space, and does not presume political or identity cohesion.

20. In some cases, governments create nominally nonmarket areas in order to preserve indigenous cultures and/or biodiversity in the remnants of ancestral

indigenous territories, as did Ecuador with the Tsáchila (Wainwright 2008; Li 2010; Anthias and Radcliffe 2013).

21. *Indigeneity* refers to performances and embodiments through which nonwestern subjects, spaces, and knowledges are imagined, circulated, and acted on in postcolonial settler societies (Shaw et al. 2006; de la Cadena 2010; Canessa 2012). Often indigeneity circulates between states, advocates, and development agencies without indigenous peoples' involvement.

22. Being tied to world history, race is historical, although it implies something natural and embodied (Wade 2009; Quijano 2000). Ethnicity is often closely tied to notions of cultural difference, although it may be naturalized through associating particular ethnic groups with specific biospheres and territories. In this book, the use of "ethnoracial" refers to how groups are attributed with racial and social characteristics.

23. Building on Agamben's work on bare life (Agamben, 2005), Biehl (2005) defines *abandonment* as being left to die, and the status of having no place in the social world.

24. The UN definition lists a variable conjuncture of features that might characterize indigenous populations, including occupation of ancestral lands; common ancestry; culture; language; residence in certain parts of the country. An indigenous person is one who belongs to these indigenous populations through self-identification as indigenous, and is recognized by these populations as one of their members.

25. The colonial returns today in sexualized violence perpetrated in indigenous territories (Hernández 2002; Curiel 2007; Lugones 2008; Rivera Cusicanqui 2010).

26. *Indígena* hence refers to indigenous *women*, although in Spanish the term encompasses male and female subjects. In this respect, "indígena" signals that indigenous masculinities are feminized in relation to hegemonic masculinities. "Indígenas" is also used to refer to women from more than one indigenous nationality (see chapter 4 on development policy for "indigenous woman").

27. In this sense, this book's contextual analysis, an intersectional review of policy initiatives, and a critical contextual analysis of a small number of intersectional policy initiatives, all contribute to "uncover the ways multiple identities converge to create and exacerbate . . . subordination" (Yuval-Davis 2006: 204).

28. This book does not address indigenous masculinities systematically, except to the degree that their actions and attitudes shape power dynamics influencing rural low-income indigenous women. On indigenous masculinities in development, see Bedford 2005; Radcliffe et al. 2004; Andolina et al. 2009; and in Andean countries Valdivia 2009; Burman 2011; Canessa 2012.

29. Theorized by Foucault, *biopolitics* refers to the administration and regulation of human and nonhuman life at the population and individual level, and associated forms of governance (Foucault 2008; Lemke 2001). Substantive citizenship refers to individual and group capacity to make formal membership rights into material and intersubjective gains (Holston 2009).

30. "Political society constructs persons and groups along multiple lines of identity, including gender, race, color, sexuality, class, religion, ethnicity and nationality" (Dietz 2003: 417).

31. See Okin 1999. By contrast, Bhabha 1999; Volpp 2001; Kapur 2002; Fisher 2004 all argue that these expectations are embedded in global postcolonial dynamics.

32. In this sense, Ecuador's indigenous women are similar to diverse women who strategically draw on human rights discourses in local and national struggles, in ways that disrupt liberal feminist expectations (Bhavnani et al. 2003: 12; Merry 2006). On Latin American indigenous women's activism, see Hernández 2002; Stephen 2005; Blackwell 2006; Speed et al. 2006; Hernández and Canessa 2012; on indigenous women's position on development, see AIPP Women 2012; compare Minority Rights Group 2012.

33. Ecuadorian indigenous women who attain national leadership positions in civil society movements tend to have higher than average education, and specific opportunity structures (Radcliffe 2010).

34. Poverty figures compared 1998 and 2006. Unmet basic needs rose from 80.4 percent in 2001 to 83.2 percent in 2006 (Ecuador Indígenas 2009).

35. Ecuador's 2011 HDI score was 0.720 (Ramírez Gallegos 2008). Ecuador has minimal welfare provision, relatively in the Latin American context. One in eight citizens are covered by social security, forcing reliance on extended kin and higher-income patrons.

36. Ecuador is also middle-ranking in gender inequality regarding male-female gaps in education, the economy, and political empowerment.

37. Illiteracy rates remained largely static among indigenous women, while economic studies showed poorer wage and employment opportunities compared with indigenous men and nonindigenous women. Of rural women, 95 percent are in poverty; 91 percent of indigenous women are underemployed.

38. With respect to modernity-coloniality, *decoloniality* refers to "long-term process of re-signification that is irreducible to a political-economic event" (Castro-Gómez and Grosfoguel 2007: 17), as formal political independence did not remove multiple interlocking hierarchies of racial, ethnic, sexual, epistemic, economic, and gendered relations.

39. See Marchand and Parpart 1995; Espinosa 1997; Mendez Torres 2009. Organized Latin American indigenous women drew attention to colonial assumptions in the CEDAW convention for not reflecting postcolonial intersectionality, requesting it be amended to pay attention to racial discrimination against indigenous peoples. Indigenous women and their advocates criticize the Millennium Development Goals for a focus on individuals and not groups, and for not dealing with intersecting relations of race-ethnicity and gender (Pazmiño 2008).

40. On this debate in Latin America, see Mignolo 2000; Hernández 2008; Suárez and Hernández 2008; Walsh et al. 2009.

41. Postcolonial theory uses the term *subaltern* to refer to social subjects whose existence, dignity, and survival are framed as irrelevant in postcolonial power

hierarchies yet who are capable of contingent articulations of anticolonial politics. Indigenous women in Ecuador frequently use life history testimonies to record their knowledge (see Bulnes 1990; Rosero Garcés and Reyes Ávila 1997; Sniadecka-Kotarska 2001; Coordinadora Cantonal de Mujeres de Cotacachi 2008). Indigenous spokeswomen and representatives also write narratives (De la Torre Amaguaña 1993; Santillán 2008; Velasque 2008).

42. "Ordinary" is used here in Henri Lefebvre's (1971) sense as relating to everyday life where utopian and political aspirations can crystallize.

43. On the analyst's positionality in these dynamics, see Spivak 1993 [1988]; Suarez and Hernández 2008; Blaser 2010; Hernández 2008, 2014.

44. In this contrapuntal knowledge production, no one perspective is awarded a privileged status; it emerges from my lengthy—and necessarily ongoing—process of unlearning privilege as loss, and thinking relationally across two sets of indigenous women's standpoints and knowledges.

45. I also held regular meetings and exchanges with the CONAIE women's office, Ecuador's main indigenous confederation, as well as with an advisory committee composed of indigenous representatives and a few nonindigenous women working in development and NGOs, who provided advice and support.

46. Between 2008 and 2011, I undertook semistructured interviews with national and regional women's leaders, diverse ethnic leaders, and policy-makers and other stakeholders and a detailed analysis of government and nongovernmental policy documents over the past thirty years, and I attended regional and national policy meetings. Semistructured interviews with fifty Kichwa and eighteen Tsáchila women took place in villages, during workshops (Chimborazo) or quiet periods of women's days. Focus groups were held in three Tsáchila villages with women, and I attended various ethnic federation and development workshops and meetings. Interviews were largely conducted in Spanish; three interviews were in local languages through a local intermediary.

47. Nationally, Kichwa is Ecuador's largest indigenous nationality and includes several subgroups known as pueblos.

48. Chimborazo, home to Kichwa Puruhá, has levels of poverty around 50–59 percent (Gini coefficient 0.41–0.45), while Santo Domingo province, home to the Tsáchila, is 40–49 percent poor (Gini coefficient 0.36–0.38) (Ecuador 2010).

Chapter 1. Postcolonial Intersectionality and the Colonial Present

1. These mentions of triple oppression come from Franke 1990; Kellogg 2005: 174; CONAMU 2004, 2007; and CONAMU 2004: 32, respectively.

2. Compare Richards 2004 on how Chile's National Women's Service treated Mapuche indigenous women as a group to be "added into" existing gender policy.

3. I draw on Agamben's concept of "bare life," which refers to the material and epistemological consequences of being excluded from the polity, and resulting legal and social abandonment. Here *bare life* refers to postcolonial subalterns in nation-states as nominal citizens who are abandoned in situations where law—and development agendas—are suspended.

4. On women under Spanish colonialism, see Kellogg 2005.
5. *Uneven development* in geography refers to the processes whereby economic growth and human well-being are produced in ways that inexorably lead to spatial inequality, especially under capitalist political economies (Smith 2008 [1984]; Watts 2003).
6. According to Gonzalez Casanova 1965, also Stavenhagen 1986, internal colonialism includes monopolistic relations over Indian commerce and credit, the decapitalization of ethnic communities, and the exploitation of indigenous labor through feudalism, peonage, slavery, forced labor, partnerships that deprive them of land and resources, and locking them into lower wages.
7. Indigenous forced labor was widely used for road and railway building during the early twentieth century.
8. Epistemic violence refers to the destruction of nonwestern ways of understanding the world, and the resulting domination of western knowledge in part through its claims to universality (Spivak 1993 [1988]; Foucault 1980 [1977]).
9. Fanon 1986 [1952]; Memmi 2003 [1957]. Latin American analyses of internal colonialism engaged with critiques of colonialism emanating from Africa and Asia, drawing parallels between the psychic damage of French colonialism and the quotidian violence meted out to Latin America's indigenous groups.
10. Early commentators on male-female differences in internal colonialism include Gonzalez Casanova 1965: 34–35; Romo Leroux de Morales 1975.
11. Rosero Garcés and Reyes Ávila 1997: 11; compare O'Connor 2007: 182.
12. Internal colonialism's labor exploitation and cultural marginalization were contested by indigenous and black populations. From the nineteenth century, indigenous women initiated grievances against police and hacienda owners on behalf of male relatives, and stood alongside male kin to defend rights. However, women's agency was erased from legal and historical records by the justice system and gendered assumptions about (indigenous) women's passivity. One of the most important figures in mobilizations was Dolores Cacuango (1881–1971) who, among other demands, called for the end of women's forced labor (O'Connor 2007).
13. It is interesting to speculate whether women's association with Earth Mother (see chapter 7) emerged at this historic moment, not from "tradition" but a configuration of power, difference, and protest.
14. The comunas fifty years later became the basis for indigenous mobilization against neoliberal development (Warren and Jackson 2003; Yashar 2005; Clark and Becker 2007).
15. See Bromley 1977: 37 for a statement of these expectations.
16. On racialization in Ecuador, see Cervone and Rivera 1999; De la Torre 1999, 2007.
17. Even when they existed, national plans granted little attention to uneven geographies arising from racialized dispossession, although they compounded indigenous poverty and low status.
18. Antecedents to the Andean Mission included itinerant programs of literacy and technical advice, and the eradication of fleas. On the Andean Mission, see

Junta Nacional de Planificación 1970; Ecuador Bienestar Social 1984; Alvarez Herrera 2005: 25–26; Prieto 2015.

19. In 1964, the Andean Mission was nationalized and eventually placed under the authority of the Ministry of Agriculture in its Rural Development division. The household improvement program was later taken up by the Ministry of Agriculture (Consejo Nacional de Desarrollo 1991). The women-specific part of the Andean program ended due to what was labeled the "different reality" of rural communities and limited knowledge of women's situation (Rens 1965: 49; Bromley 1977: 38–39; Alvarez Herrera 2005: 25–26; Prieto 2015).

20. The boundary-marking meanings of "indigenous women" between what was developed and what remained to be developed were hence different from the meanings acquired by the "indigenous women" category that emerged in development in the mid- to late 1990s (see chapter 4).

21. A state-sponsored book produced for International Women's Year in 1975 meshes nationalist agendas with mentions of the "Shyri princess" Paccha and two colonized women, Baltazarra Chiuza and Lorenza Avemanay, who fought against the Spanish (Romo Leroux 1975: 38).

22. Between 1960 and 1979, haciendas were broken up across the Sierra. Indigenous farmers had to buy land over ten or twenty years, becoming reliant on cash economies of agricultural sales and wage labor.

23. The phrase "uncontainable challenge" is Li's (Li 2007: 11).

24. By the early 1960s, Ecuador had an estimated twenty thousand families living as huasipungueros on hacienda estates for no wages or "an abnormally low daily wage" (Svenqvist 1979: 101).

25. Aiming to raise agricultural productivity, a second agrarian reform in 1973 remained largely unimplemented, that is, indigenous tenants with precarious land rights and landless groups often remained unaffected.

26. Between 1969 and 1981, individual shares of national wealth rose from $200 per capita to $1,600 per capita on average (Mahoney 2010: 225–26); most resources ended in the hands of urban middle classes and elites.

27. "The death of Indians was, in fact, their birth as mestizos and, only as such, citizens of the nation" (de la Cadena 2010: 347).

28. For example, pyrethrum production in Imbabura, Cotopaxi, Tungurahua, and Chimborazo, sheep improvement programs in Cotopaxi, and forestry (Junta Nacional de Planificación 1970: 5–6, 16, 18; Ecuador Bienestar Social 1984: 194).

29. Patchy development of state infrastructure did nothing to stop smallholders moving; between 1950 and 1982, the Amazon region's population grew by 277 percent, as landless Andeans risked subsistence on the agricultural frontier (Labao and Brown 1998). Currently two-fifths of the Amazon region is nominally designated as territories for indigenous populations, yet they struggle to protect land and livelihood against destructive oil extraction and settler depredations. One-fourth of indigenous territories lie in nature conservation protected areas, where indigenous populations tackle problems associated

with insecure tenure, lack of effective protection from extraction, and restrictions on land use.

30. Census data demonstrated that indigenous and peasant women were more sedentary than nonindigenous women. Nonindigenous mestiza and elite women by contrast were more likely than men to change residence between census dates (Cuvi Sánchez 2000; Secretaría Técnica de Frente Social 1998: 23; Pontón and Pontón 2008: 121).

31. De la Cadena 1995 argues that this emerging differentiation had village-level impacts for gendered divisions of labor in southern Peru. I argue that these reconfigurations had multiscalar ramifications, documented in later chapters.

32. Quotes from Ecuador Bienestar Social 1984: 165, 175. The Office of Indigenous Affairs suggested that "indigenous peoples . . . served as the basis for the generation of the majority of economic surplus during the colony and part of the republican era, their culture was violated, their possession of land was affected, and their language and organizational forms ignored" (Ecuador Bienestar Social 1984: 181). In the early 1980s, Ecuador's indigenous population was around two million citizens. On the "indigenous slot," see Li 2000; on culture's global valence, Yúdice 2004.

33. During fieldwork, there were unverified rumors of oil prospecting companies in Tsáchila communities.

34. The anticolonial Declaration of Barbados of 1971 inspired Ecuadorian groups to proclaim that "the maintenance of Indian society's cultural and social integrity, regardless of its relative numerical insignificance, offers alternative approaches to the traditional well-trodden paths of . . . national society." The Declaration was highly significant to Ecuadorian civil protests of this era (Mercedes Prieto, personal communication, May 2009).

35. On immaturity, see Li 2007: 15; on Bolivia see Postero 2006: 218; on Ecuador's folklorization of indigenous groups see Muratorio 1994, Crain 1996. Ethnic performance "conceals no presence or identity behind its mark: it is not what Césaire describes as 'colonization-thingification' behind which there stands the essence of the *presence Africaine*" (Bhabha 1994: 88). Internationally, indigeneity was accumulating a historic significance that had ramifications for the understandings of social heterogeneity in development. From the mid-1980s, international law and intergovernmental negotiations framed indigenous interests in terms of cultural rights, heading off demands for self-determination.

36. During the nineteenth century, Ecuadorian "state policies treated the woman question and the Indian problem as separate categories, overlooking indigenous women in both cases. This separation led indigenous peoples and feminists to develop very different strategies when demanding change" (O'Connor 2007: 203). However, only in the late twentieth century did this separation get institutionalized in social development.

37. Similarly in Bolivia, policy for gender and ethnic rights was administered in different institutions with mutually hostile personnel (Luykx 2000; Paulson and Calla 2000).

38. According to the World Economic Forum measures, Ecuador ranked twenty-third in the world in gender equity in 2009. This is remarkable, as a decade earlier Ecuador had been found gender inequality to have a "pervasive significance" (personal communication, Washington, DC, 1999). Ecuador ratified the Convention for the Elimination of Discrimination against Women (CEDAW) in 1981, and then established secretariats for women's issues as well as a cross-party commission in what was then the national Congress to pursue women's agendas.

39. During the late 1990s, state support for gender policy led to the creation of a stronger women's council, CONAMU, in 1997, replacing an institutionally weak directorate. In 1999 the Women's, Youth, Child and Family Commission was permanently established in the National Congress (Herrera 2003; Lind 2005). The Commission oversaw legislation in favor of women's rights among others, based on international conventions. The Ley contra la violencia a la mujer y la familia (Law against violence against women and families) was ratified November 1995. National women's machineries work most effectively when they have a clear location in government structures and authority (Rai 2003: 25).

40. *Mainstreaming* refers to the process of inserting gender awareness and equality measures into all aspects of development in order to ensure a more systematic effort to reduce male-female inequalities in development (Rai 2003: 16; Walby 2005; on Ecuador, Lind 2005). The Beijing women's conference endorsed gender mainstreaming, to tackle uneven gendered power relations, and the costs of masculinity, as well as of femininity, although mainstreaming is often co-opted and depoliticized (Cornwall et al. 2004).

41. CPME differs from other strands of Ecuador's women's movement (Lind 2005; Herrera 2003; Vega Ugalde 2007).

42. On gender policy's problematic relationship with race, see White 2006.

43. In the mid-1990s, large state projects with a gender component accounted for 7 percent of 313 gender-related projects, compared with NGO gender projects, which accounted for one-third of all projects (Saldana and Paz y Miño 1999). Of 313 projects, one-fourth were in income generation, a further one-eighth broadly developmental. Gender projects during this period reinforced an association of "gender" and a generic "women" category: women were the beneficiaries in 29 percent of projects, their organizations in 16 percent, and "Other" female beneficiaries accounted for 9 percent.

44. Quote from Herrera 2003: 15; on Ecuador, also Martínez Flores 2000; Lind 2005: 2. On depoliticization, Ferguson 1990; Cornwall et al. 2004: 4–5; Li 2007.

45. Indigenous woman speaking at a workshop on indigenous women and public policy, Baños, March 2010.

46. In the Andes, some of these meanings of complementarity make it attractive to certain ethnic agendas (see chapter 5). See critiques of complementarity in Barrig 2006, Oliart 2008. On its development consequences, see Herrera 2003; Strobele-Gregor 2008.

47. Anonymous development professional at a multilateral institution, quoted in Radcliffe et al. 2004: 401.

48. Hence neither Kichwa Chimborazo nor Tsáchila women—like many of their peers across the country—were affected by flower production.

49. Prompted by neoliberal restructuring of racial regimes, indigenous civil organizations emerged to challenge political and civil exclusion and gained widespread public legitimacy for their demands for social and economic rights (see, among others, Van Cott 2000; Assies et al. 2001; Sieder 2002; Yashar 2005; Lucero 2008).

50. International formulations of indigenous rights provided leverage for Ecuador's indigenous movements to shift the terms of engagement, while ILO Convention 169, ratified by Ecuador in April 1998, established rights to respect for indigenous cultures, livelihoods, organizations, and institutions, as well as a historic relation to lands and territory. Transnational networks among human rights groups, ethnic organizations, and northern development NGOs and bilateral agencies also played a role (Warren and Jackson 2003; Bretón 2005; Andolina et al. 2009).

51. On PRODEPINE, see chapter 3, and on intercultural health, chapter 5.

52. With relatively weak state institutionality, ambivalent elite attitudes toward neoliberalism and multiculturalism, and grassroots mobilization against harsh restructuring, Ecuadorian neoliberal multiculturalism took on specific characteristics, namely early recognition as a pluricultural and multiethnic society, blocks on neoliberal reforms, and indigenous occupation of spaces in the state (e.g., CODENPE).

53. On Latin America's shift from stratified universalism to targeted programs, see Assies et al. 2001; Molyneux 2008.

54. By contrast, Bolivia, Guatemala, and Mexico saw falls in measures of discrimination (Hall and Patrinos 2005: 5).

55. In Ecuador being indigenous raised the probability of poverty by 16 percent, second only to Mexico (Larrea Maldonado et al. 2007).

56. On the continuities between colonial interventions and postcolonial development, see McEwan 2009; Mahoney 2010.

57. "There have been perceived affinities between multiculturalism and other social or political stances [for example] feminism; given the shared perspectives on the importance of respecting distinct experiences and outlooks and on the need to combat oppression and facilitate the claims and integrity of marginalized or disenfranchised groups, feminists and multicultural positions have often been seen as compatible" (Molyneux and Razavi 2003: 15; Fisher 2004: 112–13).

58. On multiculturalism and women's rights, Okin 1999; see Bhabha 1999; Fisher 2004; Phillips and Saharso 2008.

59. Whereas Susan Okin 1999: 22 suggests minority women's subordination is largely informal and private, feminist geographers document multiculturalism's profound impacts on *public* policy and *public* cultures (Pratt 2005; Laurie and Calla 2004).

60. Later chapters examine whether development programs to promote culture inadvertently entrench gender inequalities (chapters 3 and 5).

61. Essentializing liberal feminist accounts of multicultural societies moreover downplay the influence of embedded cultural values on first world women, and deny the influence of economies, states, geopolitics, and history on gender relations (Mohanty 1991; Volpp 2001: 1195–1203; Kapur 2002; Nagar 2004).

62. On Ecuador, see Herrera 2003; global case studies in Baaz 2005; Cook 2008.

63. Demand for professional training in ethnodevelopment did however lead to the creation of transnational curricula and learning opportunities that included many women (see Laurie et al. 2005; Andolina et al. 2009, chapter 5).

64. Such households are associated with relatively high education levels, land availability, and no hacienda-type relations. However, pressures toward convergence with mestizo gender patterns can also be found in these areas, arising from segregated nonagricultural labor markets and the negative valuation of subsistence work (Hamilton 1998: 26–29; Hamilton, et al. 2001).

65. Female employee of CODENPE, speaking at a workshop, Baños, March 2010.

66. Metaphors of addition link to tropes of burden, obstacle, and weight, all metonymically associated with female "natives" in colonized territories. Associations between indigeneity, femininity, and physical labor have long provided a postcolonial index of "development." Since Columbus's arrival in the Americas, native women were "visible primarily as workers . . . [and] the kind of labor done by women became a primary index of the degree of civilization of the society in which they labored" (Maddox 1991: 228; on Ecuador, Romo Leroux de Morales 1975: 90; O'Connor 2007: 202). Moreover, viewing intersectional inequalities as additive tends to presume a foundational "core" to social difference, such as "women" in gender policy or "indigenous" and "black" groups in ethnodevelopment.

67. On Mexico, Sanchez-Pérez et al. 2006; on Ecuador, Garcia-Aracil and Winter 2006.

68. On indigenous women as culturally distinctive market micro-entrepreneurs, see Radcliffe and Laurie 2006; Richards 2007; De Hart 2010.

69. In 2006–2009, just under two-thirds of credits were given to women compared with one-third to men.

70. Feminists criticize mainstreaming for bureaucratic recalcitrance, the lack of sociopolitical will, and the failures of imagination.

71. On relations between indigenous and women's movements in Ecuador, see Lind 2005; Prieto 2005; Strobele-Gregor 2008. Through the 1980s and 1990s only a few individuals were willing and politically able to move between movements, Nina Pacari being a rare exception, contributing to gender policy in the 1998 Constitution and the indigenous movement (see chapter 5).

Chapter 2. The Daily Grind

1. "To do a topography is to carry out a detailed examination of some part of the material world, defined at any scale from the body to the global, in order to understand its salient features and their mutual and broader relationships.

Producing topographies necessarily situates places in their broader context and in relation to other areas or geographical scales, offering a means to understanding structure and process. . . . A central aspect of most topographical maps [is] the contour line. . . . This notion of topography involves a precision and specificity that connects distant places and in so doing enables the inference of connection in uncharted places in between" (Katz 2001a: 1228; also Nagar et al. 2002). Feminist geography focuses attention on how women experience highly differentiated access to public decision-making and private resources as they are situated in place-specific gendered public-private relations that combine local, national, and transnational elements (Mohanty 1999; Martin 2004; Nagar 2004, Staeheli et al. 2004). The counter-topographic approach contrasts with the testimonies collected from indigenous women leaders. Although the research methods did not systematically document greed, gossip, competitiveness, and conflicts among women, this does not mean they are absent.

2. In 2001 Chimborazo's Human Development Index (HDI) was 0.593, compared with Ecuador's equality-adjusted 2011 HDI of 0.533. Other populations in Chimborazo include 2.2 percent white, 1.1 percent Afro-Ecuadorians, and 0.4 percent "other." Tsáchila and Puruhá statistics on unmet basic needs are from CODENPE 2010b: 24. Due to Santo Domingo province's recent foundation in 2007, no HDI information is available. Recent data on the racialization of poverty is also difficult to locate.

3. Larrea Maldonado et al. 2007: 90. Poverty rates among nonindigenous women are 54.6 percent.

4. Seven percent of indigenous women are in the secondary sector (in comparison with 24.6 percent of indigenous men, 12.7 percent of nonindigenous women, and 25.5 percent of nonindigenous men). One-third of indigenous women in work are found in the tertiary, largely services, sector, in comparison with 24.4 percent of indigenous men, 76.3 percent of nonindigenous women, and 45.9 percent of nonindigenous men. Hence indigenous women are more similar in their sector segregation to indigenous men than they are to nonindigenous populations, regardless of gender.

5. In Chimborazo farms of under five hectares on average have two cows, two pigs, five chickens (Censo Agropecuario 2003: 68). On class differentiation among indigenous women in Oaxaca, see Stephen 2005.

6. By contrast, Amazon women are more likely to be restricted to agricultural and domestic work.

7. In national divisions of labor by sector, commerce is the most feminized, with over two-fifths of all economically active women (compared with one-fifth of men).

8. Indigenous women who beg and sell small quantities of foodstuffs on Quito's street corners are associated with highly gendered racialized imagery, linked to concepts of ignorance, laziness, and filth (Swanson 2007).

9. Focus group with CAMACHH women's group, Riobamba, July 2009.

10. Focus group, Gallo Rumi, Chimborazo, July 2011.
11. Founded by Archbishop Leonidas Proaño, the Escuelas Radiofónicas Populares del Ecuador (ERPE) promoted agricultural development and organic agriculture for fifty years for 3,500 families across Chimborazo and Bolívar provinces (www.erpe.org.ec).
12. A participatory survey in Cotacachi, northern Andes, found that women had an average of 0.25 hectares, mostly titled to husbands (Mujeres Campesinas de Cotacachi 2010).
13. Interview Ana Maria Pilamunga, Riobamba, March 2009.
14. Average 0.44 hectare; range 0.05–3 hectares.
15. For one in eight women, purchased land represented the only land to which they had access as orphans or children/wives of landless kin. Some land-rich women purchased and inherited land-territory, suggesting that land purchase contributes to differentiation between households. The largest landholdings are of women who inherit and buy, or who buy only (4 percent of interviewees).
16. The idea for an exchange visit emerged in discussions with women in Santo Domingo and Chimborazo, and involved the Chimborazo federation women's representative, an older Kichwa widow, a younger married Kichwa woman, and a middle-aged married Tsáchila woman. Over three days we visited two Andean villages and two Tsáchila comunas.
17. Across Santo Domingo district (before it became a province) farms under five hectares (one-fourth of farms in the district, covering 1.9 percent of agricultural land) and farms of five to ten hectares are dedicated primarily to banana and cacao production, and have no cattle, around 4 pigs, 13 chickens and an average of 4–4.6 people per household. Santo Domingo farms of over fifty hectares in size make up 15 percent of the province's farms and cover 57 percent of agricultural land. In coastal Ecuador, landownership across racial groups is overwhelmingly male; landholdings are also larger than in the Sierra, as four-fifths of households have over five hectares of land (*Censo Agropecuario* 2003: 63).
18. Ventura 2012: 44 provides similar figures: Tsáchila average household usufruct landholdings of four to fifty hectares, oriented toward commercial production of cacao and bananas, and foodstuffs such as yucca.
19. Interviews 2009–2011; Ventura 1997.
20. Based on twelve women, women's range was one to ten hectares; husbands' range two and a half to twelve. Discrepancies between the household totals, and spouses' relative contribution, arose from inconsistencies in recording all land sources.
21. See Secretaría Técnico de Frente Social 1998: 139. However, international development agencies from the late 1990s attempted to find an association between women and poverty and between indigenous women and poverty yet never obtained significant correlations (Prieto, personal communication, 2009).
22. Ana Maria Pilamunga, interview (July 2009).

23. In Andean Cotopaxi province, seasonal male migrants earned four times their wives' agricultural wage (Hamilton 1998).
24. Through the 1990s, increasing female labor market participation led to eight in ten rural women working in Chimborazo, although on average they earn less than two-thirds of male wages (ODM Chimborazo 2007).
25. Nationally, a small number of indigenous women are employed in the cut-flower industry that expanded in northern Andean Ecuador, but this does not generally include Chimborazo women. Interviewees did not mention female migration to Europe or the United States.
26. In urban areas, women's pay is only 65.9 percent of men's (García-Aracil and Winter 2006). Afro-Ecuadorian women face similar—but not identical—issues, as although they face gender-segregated labor markets, the educational "gap" with Afro-Ecuadorian men is not as great as among indigenous groups.
27. Chimborazo's migrants often work on coastal plantations and coastal cities, as well as in the southern highlands and Amazon as craftspersons and truck drivers. Localized recruitment, regional economic histories, and contingent connections between peasant and commercial agriculture generate variability in migration flows. National discourses strongly associate indigenous women with immobility in rural areas. O'Connor 2007 argues that indigenous women have been associated with rural homes and reproductive labor since President Garcia Moreno's mid-nineteenth-century government, while a recent report noted that "indigenous groups have the propensity to live in rural areas, primordially in the case of [indigenous] women" (Pontón and Pontón 2008: 121).
28. Anecdotally, one Tsáchila woman had migrated to Italy in the late 1990s.
29. Around one-fifth of Kichwa interviewees had migration experience as single women into informal urban jobs.
30. Although Tsáchila maintain diverse relations with non-Tsáchila actors, including urban mestizos, these relations are not primarily mediated by women nor involve female employment (Ventura 2012).
31. Globally female unemployment has risen faster than men's in countries based on export manufacturing, while female unemployment lasts longer than men's on average. Restructuring of economic and political relations at interconnected scales from the global through regional and national, down to local and household, inevitably shift relations between women and men, between women, and between men (Nagar et al. 2002).
32. Ecuador's inequality worsened in 1990–2001, impacting women through restructuring of labor market conditions, increased unemployment, and widening gender wage gaps. During the 1990s, rural women in paid farmwork received a third of men's wages, while craft work earned women half of men's income (Secretaría Técnica de Frente Social 1998). In 1999, surveys found that 88 percent of rural indigenous women were in (what counted officially as) work, showing higher rates than among nonindigenous women (58 percent) but lower levels than among male indigenous (94 percent) (Prieto 2005: 268).

33. In the Amazon, colonization expanded the agricultural frontier, while indigenous women's labor continued to be lower value. For Amazon and Andean case studies, see Labao and Brown 1998, Rosero Garcés and Reyes Ávila 1997: 41, Phillips 1987, Rens 2003, Garcés Dávila 2006.

34. Boelens and Zwarteen 2003 discuss the Andean situation.

35. *Midlife* refers here to twenty-five to forty years old; survey information is presented in CONAMU 2006, CONAMU and INEC 2008. In the CONAMU survey, Tsáchila and other indigenous women's hours of labor were not recorded.

36. Interview, Delia Caguana, COMICH women's representative, Chimborazo, September 2009.

37. The 2010 census registers 5.1 percent illiteracy among mestizos, 20.4 percent illiteracy among self-identified indigenous respondents, and 26.7 percent among indigenous women, demonstrating again a greater breach between indigenous and nonindigenous than between indigenous men and women. Among urban indigenous populations, gender differences also occur, although the rates of illiteracy are lower: around one-fifth of urban indigenous women are illiterate (20.4 percent), compared with one-tenth of urban indigenous men (10.3 percent) (CEPAL-BID 2005: 63).

38. Secretaría Técnica de Frente Social 1998: 49; Prieto et al. 2005; Peredo Beltrán 2004.

39. At the time of fieldwork, El Búa community had a college offering three years of secondary education.

40. Tsáchila woman speaking at Tsáchila-Kichwa exchange, Chiguilpe, July 2011.

41. Nationally 6.18 percent of indigenous women are enrolled at university, lower rates than for indigenous men (9.43 percent) or nonindigenous women (24.4 percent) (García-Aracil and Winter 2006). Nevertheless, younger indigenous women pursue higher education. Among the Kichwa and Tsáchila interviewees, three married women in their twenties currently attend university, as do their husbands. A Kichwa woman studied farm management at an agricultural technical university, and two Tsáchila pursued university teacher training (Radcliffe 2010).

42. From the 1960s, state efforts to universalize access to primary education and reduce illiteracy had notable impacts: the expansion of rural and urban education with oil-fueled national development resulted in a fall in illiteracy from 44 percent in 1950 to 11 percent in 1995 (CEPAL-BID 2005). Despite this, Ecuador's educational rates remain low relative to Latin America.

43. That is, six or seven years of schooling, which girls generally finish at twelve to fourteen years old.

44. Restricted household budgets and social attitudes then prevented this younger group from attending secondary school.

45. Interview data matches census and survey data for Chimborazo province. In indigenous districts: Guamote, 2.2 years women, 3.4 years men; Colta, 2.2 years women, 3.6 years men; Riobamba, 7.4 years women, 8.4 years men; Alausí, 2.8 years women, 3.7 years men. In Chimborazo province overall, rural

producers have 3.3 years education on average (men) and 2.4 years (women) (*Censo Agropecuario* 2003: 11).

46. According to official 2001 figures, 36.8 percent of indigenous girls aged thirteen to nineteen attend some educational establishment, compared with 45 percent of indigenous boys, and 59.6 percent of mestiza and white girls (CEPAL-BID 2005).

47. According to government surveys in the late 1990s, rural female-headed households owned parcels of land that on average were half the size of male household heads', and in poor households the ratio was 1:3 (Campos and Salguero 1987; Secretaría Técnica de Frente Social 1998). Pontón and Pontón 2008: 131 suggest that indigenous women are more likely to own land than Afro-Ecuadorian women, in part because the latter are concentrated in urban areas.

48. In Amazonia, mestizo colonization and indigenous displacement influence the dynamics between women, land, and rights. Amazonian rural households on average have access to twenty hectares, although indigenous women are vulnerable to losing land rights if they separate from spouses (Maria Andrade, interview, 2009).

49. *Social natures* or *socionatures* consist of the relations between, and the inseparability of, society and nature, and the material agency of the nonhuman world (see chapter 7).

50. Extending the concept of socio-natures (see previous note), *more-than-human* refers to the ontological difficulty of distinguishing society and nature, and acknowledges the crosscutting social and political agency of nonhuman life that, in western thinking, are placed under the category of "nature."

51. DNSPI 2003: 49; see testimonials in Rosero Garcés and Reyes Ávila 1997.

52. Unidentified woman quoted in CEDIS 2007a: 28.

53. Focus group in Nitiluisa, Chimborazo, May 2005; also Rodríguez 2007: 119.

54. Fanon 1986 [1952]. In other Latin American countries, indigenous women are subject to invasive forms of power (Hernández 2008: 6; Oliart 2008; Kellogg 2005: 176); on Ecuador, see Lind 2005; Radcliffe 1996.

55. At the five hundredth anniversary since Spanish colonialism, indigenous women spoke of how they are subject to a *machista* (patriarchal) and colonial society (Seminario Internacional 1992; also Richards 2004; Coordinadora Cantonal de Mujeres de Cotacachi 2008; UNIFEM 2008).

56. Focus groups in Chimborazo 2009, DNSPI 2003: 49.

57. In the mid-1990s two-fifths of indigenous women failed to receive prenatal care (compared with 17 percent of nonindigenous women), while three-quarters of indígenas gave birth at home. Infant mortality is 70 percent higher among indigenous than nonindigenous rural populations, with national rates of infant mortality at twenty-two per one thousand live births (Larrea Maldonado et al. 2007: 99).

58. CEDIS 2007a; interviews 2009–2011.

59. Comments made by an Andean leader at a CONAIE workshop, Quito, March 2009.

60. Whether couched in terms of protecting young women or defending Tsáchila presence, such discourses contribute significantly to household decisions about young women's formal education after primary school, as secondary schools are located in mestizo urban centers.

61. In Latin America, women's wages are 17 percent less than men's on average, but with racial-ethnic difference, that gap leaps to 28 percent (Atal et al. 2009; also Meentzen 2001: 3).

62. Female indigenous individuals stand an 89 percent chance of being poor, compared to indigenous men's 84 percent, nonindigenous women's 55 percent, and nonindigenous men's 60 percent (Larrea et al. 2007: 89).

63. According to national aggregate data, indigenous women are disadvantaged relative to nonindigenous women in income, access to postprimary education, labor markets opportunities, and the impacts of racial discrimination on life opportunities.

64. In Chimborazo indigenous men were more likely than men from other racial-ethnic groups to undertake domestic work, although by no means did they equal indígenas' contributions (Santillán 2008: 45).

65. Certain dimensions of postcolonial intersectionality are backgrounded (including class, bodily (dis)ability, household, and kin), reflecting indigenous women's research priorities (see Ehlers 2000; Stephen 2005).

66. Ana Maria Pilamunga, interview, March 2009.

67. Ana Maria Pilamunga, interview, March 2009.

68. Ecuador's long-established NGO FEPP titles land, trains peasant professionals, creates community development, and supports savings-credit yet privileges male farmers. Women make up one-third of the trainees in "female trades" such as crafts, dressmaking, and beauty programs, while their associations make up less than one-fifth of FEPP's total (Martínez Flores 2000; interview, Gloria Davila, SNV agency, May 2000).

69. In a late 1990s survey, indigenous female heads of rural households had no access to credit, compared with one in twenty male-headed Indian households, 12 percent of female-headed urban households, and one in five urban male-headed households (Secretaría Técnica de Frente Social 1998: 135).

70. In one case, a middle-aged married woman independently received US$793 credit, for which she provided a copy of her identity card and proof of voting.

71. According to my interlocutors, a wife only signs when credit is released.

72. Interview, Susana Albán, CONAMU, Quito, 2006.

73. Occasionally caja loans fund children's further education, with the hope that higher eventual salaries will permit the loan to be repaid (on cajas, see chapter 3).

74. As they unite women to talk about opportunities, cajas are an important space for women's politicization; see chapter 6.

75. Following Foucault's concept of "subjugated knowledges," Mignolo defines border thinking as new forms of knowledge "in which what has been subalternized . . .

becomes articulated as a new loci of enunciation" and the basis for knowledge production (Mignolo 2000).

76. Interview, Norma Mayo, CONAIE women's representative, February 2009.

77. On language issues, see Calla 2006, UN DESA 2007: 21; Meentzen 2001: 39. Unusually, the rural development office of Chimborazo's provincial government includes a Spanish-speaking male agronomist and the one female bilingual professional, making the latter a key interlocutor in outreach and training (chapter 3).

78. Oxfam América identified a similar critique in Peru: "A permanent criticism involved the concept of training. Two of the most widely recognized [indígena] leaders were emphatic in stating that they disagree with these workshops, because they assume that 'we don't know' and that we are untrained" (Cárdenas et al. 2011: 62).

79. Norma Mayo, CONAIE, Quito, February 2009.

80. Women's critical voices are also raised in ethnic rights forums. At one debate, an Andean female leader complained that "the indigenous federation said that they were giving a training course in my community, but it never happened" (unidentified woman, workshop on public policies, Chimborazo, March 2010).

81. Compare Meentzen 2001: 32–39.

82. This discussion builds on important work by Oliart 2008; Barrig 2004, 2006; Lilliott 1997, 2000.

83. For example Consejo Nacional de Desarrollo 1991. Research by CONAMU on women's work hours has a limited impact on development. In a regional exercise, indígenas in Guatemala, Peru, Panama, and Bolivia asked projects to use "their knowledges and specific cultural practices, and special efforts to promote indigenous women's participation throughout the entire project cycle, and to value women's contribution" (Meentzen 2001: v).

84. Andean case studies include Medina et al. 1999, *Censo Agropecuario* 2000.

85. Anonymized woman leader, speaking at an indigenous women's workshop, Quito, 2010.

86. Interview, March 2009.

87. Unnamed woman, cited in CEDIS 2007a: 29.

88. Interview, Quito, March 2009.

89. However, many women were hampered by lack of local resources and capacities (interview, Maria Andrade, formerly CONAIE's women representative; see chapter 4).

Chapter 3. Crumbs from the Table

1. Indigenous women's mobilization has an extensive literature; see, among others, Cervone 1998, 2002; Sniadecka-Kotarska 2001; on the Enlace Continental, Blackwell 2006. Hernández 2008.

2. In Ecuador, Cervone 1998: 235 argued that indigenous women hold positions of power and decision-making because of rural development. My chapter explores in depth the nature of interactions between indigenous women and

development with respect to a genealogy of participatory development and organization.

3. The HDI is a composite measure of life expectancy, mean years of schooling, and per capita national income. In 2012 Ecuador's HDI was 0.724. In comparison with other Andean provinces, Chimborazo has relatively low levels of international migration overall (5.3 percent of households had one migrant outside the country).

4. In Ecuador, an OSG (Organización de Segundo Grado) is a group of grassroots associations at a regional or local level, while an OTG (Organización de Tercer Grado) is a group of OSGs.

5. Hernández et al. 2005; COMUNIDEC 2008: 41. By contrast, Santo Domingo has seen very few social programs or interventions.

6. Similarly, Tsáchila women on the coast are unaware of their rights and feel disempowered in clinics, especially during birth (see chapters 5 and 6).

7. Interviews with Alicia Garcés, CEDIME, Quito, 2009, and Delia Caguana, women's representative, COMICH, Chimborazo, 2009; also CONAIE et al. 2009.

8. Due to Amazonian development patterns, women face particular difficulties in securing rights outlined in the maternity law. In the province of Sucumbíos, 42 percent of women currently have no access to health care during pregnancy, resulting in one of the country's highest rates of maternal mortality. Women have seven children on average, and indigenous women may start having children at thirteen years (Movimiento de Mujeres de Sucumbíos n.d.).

9. Gender scholars and professionals criticize Ecuador's Ministry of Agriculture for its ambivalent attitude toward and slow implementation of mainstreaming.

10. Guamote is the second largest district in Chimborazo and is 90 percent indigenous, 87 percent rural. Nearly 90 percent of its population is in poverty, 63 percent in extreme poverty (Bebbington 2000; Ramírez Gallegos 2001).

11. Interview with Donata von Sigsfeld, development aid worker, Quito, September 2010. For the life history of Dolores Yangol from Guamote canton, who worked through a number of development participatory projects see Cervone 1998: 39–90.

12. Women's organizations were registered with CONAMU, "so they were strengthened, and some are still working as organizations, while others have been wound up."

13. Testimony of "Maria Ana," Guamote, in Rosero Garcés and Reyes Ávila 1997: 78. The format of having a president, vice-president, etc. is set by the terms of registration with CONAMU.

14. Gloria Dávila, SNV, interview, Quito, 2000.

15. The testimony of "Dolores," cited in von Sigsfeld and Avalos 1998: 73–74. "Dolores" mentions the progressive Catholic bishop Proaño and mid-twentieth-century indígena activist Dolores Cacuango.

16. Interview Ana Maria Pilamunga, July 2009.

17. An international aid worker in the region at the time echoed these findings; "they were projects with little imagination, little capacity. And sometimes it was more of a waste than an alternative. But it did work to organize the women, and then these groups formed a corporation at the district level" (Gloria Dávila, interview, May 2000; on Guamote, see Bebbington 2000).

18. One-tenth of provincial funds was ring-fenced for groups such as single mothers.

19. PRODEPINE has been analyzed from diverse perspectives; see Radcliffe et al. 2004, Bretón 2005, Andolina et al. 2009. PRODEPINE represented 1.3 percent of overseas aid in Ecuador (Ecuador CONPLADEIN 1997).

20. Interview, Galo Ramón, PRODEPINE director, Quito 2000.

21. Informe final de la consultoría para la incorporación del enfoque de género en las metodologías de trabajo de PRODEPINE (n.d.: 4).

22. Interview, Galo Ramón, 2000. PRODEPINE's marginalization of gender is discussed in Radcliffe et al. 2004; Andolina et al. 2009.

23. In arguing for gender mainstreaming in PRODEPINE, a national democratic community was presented as the basis for consensus: "equitable male and female participation in indigenous and Afro-Ecuadorian organizations [provides] a fundamental guarantee of a democratic process of citizenship construction" (Informe final de la consultoría para la incorporación del enfoque de género en las metodologías de trabajo de PRODEPINE n.d.: 4). As in the health oversight program earlier, this frames participation as a question of national belonging and consensus and downplays entrenched hierarchies.

24. Interview, Galo Ramón, 2000.

25. Two cajas were set up in El Búa Tsáchila community, beginning a process of women's organization that continues today, although the monetary resources of the caja are largely lent out to men (not women) (field-notes, September 2008; also Uquillas 2002: 13).

26. Interviews, Galo Ramón, April and May 2000. Policy understandings of women's essential honesty and financial probity are widespread in global development. In this sense, we can add to Yuval-Davis and Anthias's 1989 famous typology a sixth way women symbolically are recruited into racial-ethnic power plays.

27. Local development projects averaged $25,000, compared with $5,000 for women's credit unions (Uquillas 2002).

28. Interview, Ana Maria Pilamunga, Chimborazo, 2009.

29. On interest rates, see Tene et al. 2004: 18. According to a PRODEPINE director, the project matched women's organizations' funds with quantities four times greater.

30. On coresponsibility in the new policy agenda, see Molyneux 2006, 2008.

31. Gangotena et al. 1980 suggest this switch to salaried work occurred almost immediately on haciendas' dissolution. In Tsáchila communities, "community"-wide collaboration is less important than extended families' stand-alone strategic economic units (Aguirre Borja 2007: 13). Tsáchila women in interviews constantly referred to comuna schisms and disagreements.

32. Interview, Magdalena Aysabucha, women's representative, Ecuarunari, Quito, February 2009.
33. Interview with female indigenous agricultural extension worker, who had worked on the EU project and PRODEPINE (March 2009).
34. Interview with Cecilia Velasque 2000, quoted in Radcliffe et al. 2004: 403.
35. The organization dedicated to indigenous people refers presumably to the national secretariat of indigenous peoples (Corporación Educativa Macac 1992: 100).
36. These points were first made by Chandra Mohanty and third world feminists (Marchand and Parpart 1995: 1–22; Mohanty 1999).
37. Compare Richards 2007 on Chile.
38. Other foci included female household heads: economic and social support programs; elimination of discrimination against girl children; data disaggregation by gender and age (compare chapter 4). The 1996 Plan also advocates including indigenous and black women in environmental decision-making and protection from environmental damage.
39. Interview with an anonymized indigenous female national leader, 2006.
40. Interview, Norma Mayo, CONAIE, January 2011.
41. Interview with an anonymized indigenous female national leader, 2010.
42. In some respects the CONAMU document drew on indígenas demands in that the document endorsed a rights-based approach and for the first time acknowledged that indigenous women view individual and collective rights as mutually complementary. The document critiqued liberal western feminism and endorsed the Durban conference commitments to consider crosscutting axes of gender, generation, and age in tackling racial discrimination.
43. Interview, GAD professional, Quito, February 2009.
44. Interview, Maria Andrade, Quito, July 2009.
45. "Magdalena" comment, workshop on intercultural gender, Quito, March 2009.
46. CAMACHH focus group, Riobamba, July 2009.
47. Interview, Norma Mayo, January 2011.
48. In 2009 CONAMU became the Transition Commission for Gender Equality, following provisions in the 2008 Constitution to reorganize the equality councils (chapter 7). Indigenous women's advocates remained skeptical, arguing the Commission was largely staffed by CONAMU femocrats (interview, Alicia Garcés, CEDIME, March 2010).
49. At the time of writing, CODENPE did not have a Gender Unit, despite interest from indigenous women leaders.
50. Such critiques are not voiced by village women but by educated, often professional, movement leader women who spend time in communities listening to complaints.
51. It also included commitments from the provincial prefect, and a pact signed by ten mayors from the province's counties. The prefect's commitment included issues not found in CONAMU's national Plan, including improvement of women's access to paid work and reduction of domestic work (through

child-care facilities), and promoting the creation of a women's leadership training school (see chapter 4).

52. Interview, M. Andrade, UNIFEM, Quito, July 2009.

Chapter 4. Politics, Statistics, and Affect

1. Other documents informing this paragraph include IADB 2002.
2. Nina Pacari is a long-standing indigenous activist and leader who served as foreign minister and vice-president of the National Congress (she was the first indigenous person in each post) and Pachakutik party congresswoman (also Hernández and Canessa 2012: 17).
3. Interview, Norma Mayo, CONAIE Women's Office, January 2011.
4. By contrast, Chimborazo women spoke of silence as a historical issue, now overcome by female organization.
5. Interview, Arturo Cevallos, IBIS Quito, September 2009.
6. Almeida 2007b: 58; on political silence and indigenous women's expression see Arnold 1997, Burman 2011.
7. Kichwa-Tsáchila exchange visit, Chiguilpe, July 2011.
8. "Women are the nationality's cultural referent, so giving more training will grant the opportunity to indirectly train every woman's family, benefitting them and converting them into the generators and multipliers of leaders" (Comisión de Mujer y Familia Tsáchila n.d.b: 4).
9. Tsáchila governor quoted in El Comercio (Quito), 7 June 2004.
10. The few projects for indigenous women in Latin America emphasize the importance of male involvement to persuade them of the relevance of women's public role (UN DESA 2007). Development studies documents the diversity of male attitudes toward female empowerment (Cleaver 2002; Cornwall et al. 2011).
11. Later regional schools were established in the coast, Andes, and Amazon (interviews, Norma Mayo, Quito, March 2009; Julio Yuquilema, CODENPE, April 2008). The Cotopaxi school was founded in 2006 with support from a European bilateral agency and Ecuadorian NGOs.
12. Other important contributors to rising female participation were the Ecuarunari federation, the indigenous institute ICCI, and the Pachakutik political party. The Fondo Indígena now also runs a continental women's training program.
13. Participation in the training school nevertheless reflects differential take-up across generations, ethnocultural groups, and political affiliations.
14. Interview with Donata von Sigsfeld, development aid worker, September 2009; compare CONAMU 2007.
15. Information on women in diverse ethnocultural groups is embedded in ethnographic and local case studies, so unsystematized statistically (Meentzen 2001: 15).
16. An impetus to knowledge is of course bound up in statecraft. On its foundation, the National Women's Council CONAMU was required to "gather,

compile, analyze and periodically present data disaggregated by age, sex, socioeconomic indicators and other relevant ones, including the number of family members with the objective of using them in the planning and application of policies and programs" (Secretaría Técnica de Frente Social 1998: 145).

17. Interview, Magdalena Aysabucha, Ecuarunari women's representative, Quito, February 2009.

18. Alternative data collecting and analysis lack institutional and epistemological support. PRODEPINE staff criticized the lack of data and in-depth case studies on more-than-capitalist seasonal economies, and the census's limitations. Data is also lacking comparing subgroups of women and men across racial-ethnic groups by location and income (Meentzen 2001: 13).

19. The material here comes from a September 2009 interview, and subsequent email communication (original capitals in email, 2011).

20. In his reading of Fanon, Homi Bhabha stresses how colonial depersonalization not only undermines "the Enlightenment notion of 'man' but challenges the transparency of social reality, as a pre-given image of human knowledge" (Bhabha 1994: 41). He hence argues that the foundational violence and trauma of colonial alienation can never be acknowledged as such, although they remain "determinate conditions of civil authority" (43).

21. Ecuadorian gender policy defined women's cultural rights as "rights to liberty, identity, expression, knowledge and their use, spirituality, cosmovision, heritage (linguistic, creative, skills, historical memory), art, protection of institutional models [which] are inseparable from the autonomy, educational quality and life of women, girls and adolescents" (CONAMU 2004: 29).

22. Compare Gayatri Spivak on how the Anglo-American individualist subject is constructed through differentiation from the "native woman" and by "saving brown women from brown men" (Spivak 1993 [1988]: 92–93; also Shohat 1998: 16; Martin 2004: 21).

23. Interview, Ana Maria Pilamunga, Riobamba, July 2009.

24. Antiracist work has only recently entered Ecuadorian public policy. A major recent report documents racial discrimination against indigenous women across Latin America (Cunningham et al. 2009).

25. Female CODENPE employee speaking at a workshop, March 2010.

26. Conversation, Delia Caguana, Chimborazo, August 2010.

27. Workshop on Intercultural Gender, CONAIE, Quito, March 2009.

28. CONAMU et al. 2005, in which antiwomen violence is explained as the result of a broad set of interconnecting processes.

29. Globally, indigenous women called for CEDAW to acknowledge racial discrimination against indigenous peoples and engage with cultural and racial diversity (INSTRAW 2006). Indigenous women become critics of international policy, for example the Millennium Development Goals, for reflecting liberal feminism and failing to reflect indígenas' specific interests (Pazmiño 2008).

30. Interview, Maria Andrade, Quito, July 2009.

31. Pace Chibber 2013, indígenas' agendas demonstrate the capacity to distinguish between community-embedded notions of collective interests and individually oriented interests. Moreover, these agendas address collective and individual rights as equally significant while recognizing that the structures in place need to be calibrated in order to deal with indigenous women's specific position in postcolonial intersectionality.

32. Rosa, speaking at Baños workshop, March 2010.

33. Interview, Maria Andrade, Quito, July 2009.

34. Interview, Norma Mayo, CONAIE women's office, Quito, January 2011.

35. The critiques leveled at WID hence provide insights into "indigenous women" policy (Rathgeber 1990).

36. O'Neill argues that universal obligations to transnational justice are needed to meet the claims of need and poverty, on the basis that obligations are held by and toward equally "finite, needy beings" (2000: 119–32, 136).

37. See Richards 2004, on Chile's indigenous women's situation.

38. In Chimborazo, a male elected official supported women's associations, allayed husbands' jealousies, publicly endorsed female participation, and guaranteed resources and legitimacy, whereas an all-male Tsáchila leadership provided limited, highly personalistic, and weak support for women.

39. Certain Marxist interpretations of subaltern experience likewise try to reduce people such as Ecuador's indígenas to proletarians-in-waiting, whose interests are exactly matched by existing political organizations.

Interlude II

1. Onetime mayor of Guamote district, indigenous leader Mariano Curicama, became prefect of the Chimborazo provincial council from 2006. In Ecuador's autonomous provincial councils, the prefect has a deciding vote in case of ties. With province-wide jurisdiction, the provincial council maintains public services, carries out public works, coordinates municipal activities, and informs the central government of budget expenditures.

Chapter 5. Women, Biopolitics, and Interculturalism

1. Hence SRR agendas represent a different register of development intervention, to "indigenous women" policy (chapter 4).

2. Two examples illustrate this. A report on Ecuadorian indigenous and Afro populations foregrounded racialized groups' fertility, infant mortality rates, and demographic structures by gender and age (CEPAL-BID 2005), while a government plan stated "the [indigenous] fertility rate is still high and the rate of infant mortality continues at higher levels than the national rural average" (Ecuador 1996: 159, 163).

3. Prieto et al. 2005: 51; Terborgh et al. 1995: 144–45, on Bolivia, Canessa 2012. In a recent survey, 82 percent of 164 mostly indigenous women in the Central

Andes reported that their first sexual experience was voluntary; 18 percent reported violence/rape (Luna Creciente n.d.: 20).

4. The quotation in the epigraph to this section is from Sylvester 2011: 188–89.
5. Ewig 2010 documents the intersectional exclusions associated with Peru's "stubborn structures of stratification" in health care.
6. Amazonian women face difficulties in securing rights due to masculine labor markets, women's limited access to land and work, and poor state service provision, which restrict reproductive choices (Labao and Brown 1998). In northern Amazonia, indigenous women have to buy medicines in underfunded health centers (Movimiento de Mujeres de Sucumbíos n.d.: 18).
7. Women without formal education were particularly likely to miss prenatal care (Visión Mundial 2007: 90–92).
8. Only one in ten indigenous women receiving family planning advice from community-based distribution schemes had used contraception previously, compared with half of women at urban clinics (Terborgh et al. 1995: 144).
9. Interview, Teresa Pagalo, CONPOCIECH, Riobamba, July 2009.
10. Officially recognized delivery attendance in urban areas rose from 56 to 81 percent between 1977 and 2006, although among rural nonindigenous women it remained largely unchanged (56 v. 55 percent), and among rural indigenous women it rose from the extremely low level of 7–15 percent (ALDHU 1998; Hooper 1998; Goicolea et al. 2008).
11. There is no evidence for forced sterilization of Ecuadorian indigenous women. In neighboring Peru, ethnic women and leaders campaigned against sterilization targets that enrolled underinformed indigenous women (Oliart 2008: 11; Lazar 2004:311 on urban Bolivia; see Kellogg 2005 on Catholic responses).
12. Tsáchila focus group, Cóngoma, July 2009.
13. CAMACHH focus group, Riobamba, July 2009.
14. Interview with former health representative in the COMICH federation, Riobamba, July 2009.
15. Indigenous children 47 percent versus nonindigenous malnutrition at 21 percent (Corporación Educativa Macac 1992: 61; Larrea, Montenegro et al. 2007: 99).
16. Among Amazon indigenous and mestiza groups, many women use traditional methods of fertility control (Goicolea et al. 2008: 98; see Kellogg 2005: 135).
17. Women interviewed who did not use "modern" contraception included those "taking care" with husbands, and a few with previous caesarean–tubal ligations. Other research notes that indigenous women prefer to receive contraception from an "outside" health worker rather than a local distributor who knows them and their families (Terborgh et al. 1995: 144).
18. Requiring quality hospitals, caesareans acquire associations with whiteness and being worthy of the nation (Roberts 2012).
19. In a national survey, indigenous women declared themselves more content than women nationally with sterilization after the operation, but among

unsterilized women, indigenous women were the most reluctant to endorse it (CEPAR ENDEMAIN 2006). Abortion is prohibited under Ecuador's Penal Code, subject to imprisonment, except when the woman's life is in danger or the pregnancy results from the rape of a mentally disabled woman. The 2008 Constitution awarded women control over their reproductive rights, and widespread public action raised the possibility of depenalizing abortion resulting from rape.

20. Unidentified woman, Ambatillo, Tungurahua, quoted in Visión Mundial 2007: 88.

21. According to interviews, women over sixty had on average five children die; those over fifty, three infant deaths on average.

22. Adoption of children by kin or others is used to regulate household size, although only one interviewee mentioned it: the daughter of a woman in her midforties, married at age seventeen with six children, was adopted temporarily by a distant cousin.

23. Kichwa and Tsáchila women are aware of locations where family planning is available, even if they do not access services. Maria Petrona explained, "Yes of course I know although I haven't gone; there's a health center in X, so thanks to them they've helped me, but not with family planning."

24. Lisa, in her late twenties, from Achupallas, explained, "My partner told me we can't have more children now. We're broke so we can't have more than two." The doctor prescribed pills that made her feel ill.

25. State surveys suggest that indígenas are more likely than other women to have partners opposed to contraceptive use. Among indigenous rural populations in Tungurahua, Imbabura, and Chimborazo provinces, one in six women stopped using contraceptives under pressure from spouses (Visión Mundial 2007: 87).

26. Interview, Cristina Cucurí, CEDIS, Riobamba, 2009.

27. Similar issues were identified among urban Bolivian Aymara women (Schuler et al. 1994).

28. This section analyzes CONAIE biopolitical discourses through confederation documents.

29. As a corollary of dire levels of provision, "1.25 children per family" on average die in infancy, while state nursery programs take children away from mothers.

30. Wade 2009; on heterosexuality in Ecuador's development, Bedford 2005; Lind 2009.

31. CONAIE-UNFPA 1994: 104 mentions men. Palacios 2005: 328–29 notes the sexualized banter that indigenous women have to negotiate in ethnic politics.

32. UN Permanent Forum on Indigenous Issues 2006: 2.

33. Interview, Julio Yuquilema, CODENPE, Quito, April 2008; compare Palacios 2005: 324–25.

34. Interviews 2009; focus groups in Naranjos and Cóngoma, July 2009.

35. Interview, Tsáchila women's representative, September 2009; focus group in Naranjos, September 2009.

36. International policy views Latin America as an experimental site for intercultural policy initiatives and praises the adoption of traditional health practices.

Ecuador and three other Latin American countries meet the ILO 169 criteria for indigenous rights to health, passing national legislation, granting access to health services, integrating traditional practices, and making provision for indigenous participation in management (Montenegro and Stephen 2006: 1866).

37. Peredo Beltrán 2004. Indigenous health literature rarely addresses gender systematically; a PAHO review identified five of fifty-three entries on women or gender; ethnobotany, indigenous self-determination, and specific ethnic groups each had twice as many entries.

38. The DNSPI, ethnic confederations, and PAHO carried out psychosocial investigations into indigenous sexualities on the premise that health rights entail the "recognition of the diversity and citizenship rights of indigenous pueblos" (Ambrosio 2000; PAHO 2003).

39. Interview, Ana Maria Pilamunga, Riobamba, March 2009.

40. Interview Delia Caguana, COMICH, Riobamba, 2009.

41. The DNSPI reported considerable skepticism about the state's intercultural efforts and in some cases, village resistance (DNSPI 2003: 21; also Corporación Educativa Macac 1992: 77; CEPAR ENDEMAIN 2006).

42. Regarding Tsáchila women, I saw no workshops or networks of female activists, although a few individual women expressed agency. According to one woman, "I quickly realized after marrying . . . well, the reality was different. And so I only lived five years with my husband. I had to do too much work in the house, the farm. And I realized that everything was bad, and as we only have one life, I said no. But for my family it was very difficult to see their daughter separated. To be a divorced woman is a sin."

43. Focus group, CAMACHH, Riobamba, 2009.

44. Catholic, national, and indigenous thinking associates women with a natural caregiving capacity. Only rarely do indigenous women come to intercultural health politics through the mainstream health system; one indígena doctor Miryam Conejo qualified as a medical practitioner in Cuba, established an independent clinic, and advised the DNSPI, becoming DNSPI director under President Correa (ICCI 2001).

45. Women thereby queried the extent to which the state and ethnic movements "oblige indigenous women to exercise maternity, as a form of social control over their bodies and sexualities" (Baeza 2011: 12).

46. Delia Caguana, speaking at workshop, Chimborazo, 2010.

47. Indígena women also took intercultural health agendas to the global scale, with the UN calling for "the roles of traditional midwives [to] be re-evaluated and expanded so that they may assist indigenous women during their reproductive health processes and act as cultural brokers between health systems and indigenous communities' world views" (Camacho et al. 2006).

48. Movimiento de Mujeres de Sucumbíos n.d.: 18–19; CONAIE Women's Office 2010: 17.

49. Interview Cristina Cucurí, CEDIS, 2009. Also CEDIS 2007c; on Guamote, Argoti Santacruz 2003.

50. CONAMU, Municipio de Riobamba et al. 2005: 15, 20. In Otavalo multiethnic female activism and an indigenous–led municipality brought traditional birthing practice into public hospitals. In Sucumbíos indígenas demanded alternative health centers in the state system and "staff from different nationalities to give better service to women of these groups" to eliminate discrimination (Movimiento de Mujeres de Sucumbíos n.d.).

51. Given the sensitivity of gender violence, indigenous women chose whether to raise it in interviews, so this account is anecdotal and not systematic (see DNSPI 2003: 23; Pequeño 2009; Hernández and Canessa 2012).

52. Regarding Cotacachi and Sucumbíos, interview, Maria Andrade, UNIFEM, Quito, 2009, 2010; also Lang and Kucia 2009. On national action, CONAIE Women's Office 2010: 19; Coordinadora Cantonal de Mujeres de Cotacachi 2008.

53. Elsewhere in Latin America, Burman 2011; Hernández and Canessa 2012.

Chapter 6. From Development to Citizenship

1. Tsáchila leaders sought out civil registration under pressure from colonizer settlement. According to Cristina who got her card over thirty years ago: "I got it when the civil registry came to the community. At that time the now-deceased [Governor] Abraham Calazacón asked for the civil registry to come and give ID cards to all Tsáchilas."

2. For example, Teresa, a single twenty-nine-year-old warmi with completed primary education, who worked as an agricultural day laborer for $8 daily.

3. During fieldwork, the Correa government introduced changes to this sector aimed at improving labor protection for domestic workers.

4. This case was similar to Gabriela, forty-six years old, who worked as a domestic and pursued secondary education as a teenager.

5. In Chimborazo, examples include Carmen, a single warmi with complete primary education, who lived from small-scale vegetable and milk production on her parents' land; and Magdalena, in her late twenties, with incomplete primary education, who sold wool and produced subsistence crops.

6. Amazonia indigenous nationalities are often organized around "centros" (centers).

7. In this village, women were permitted to remain as comuneras, although their mestizo husbands were not, to protect communal land.

8. Interview, Tsáchila women's representative, September 2009.

9. Amelia, thirty-one years old with three children. Other women quoted in this paragraph include Maria Petrona, in her thirties with four young children; Gabriela, in her midforties with six children; Aurora, in her late forties with ten children, from Achupallas.

10. According to early testimonies of national indigenous movements, "women's participation in comuna activities such as mingas, night watch, etc., is equal to that of men" (Centro María Quilla 1992: 45).

11. Examples include Aida, uneducated, married with eight children; Elvira, a widow with four grown children, who attended school for two years. The

example cited below is of a widow with completed primary education and five dependent children from Colta.

12. The Catholic Church was important in this regard, training rural indigenous women as catechists, thereby facilitating later political action. A Kichwa leader told a 2011 meeting: "Before, there wasn't a school but a nun came into the comuna and trained me as a catechist, and I became educated. So I organized meetings; there were [also] men-only meetings."

13. Delia Caguana, COMICH women's representative, speaking in July 2011.

14. The specific contributions made by such development actors are not the main focus here; see Barrig 2004, Del Campo 2012, Hernández 2014.

15. Such work entails personal costs, as female leaders undertake it in addition to long days of work as ethnic federation leaders.

16. If female leaders cannot bring in resources, it becomes difficult to mobilize village women. Faced with uninterested or hostile institutions, indígenas face an uphill battle to keep together women's agendas at the village level (e.g., Nancy, a woman in her late thirties with completed primary education who now serves as secretary of the Guamote village women's association).

17. Anonymized woman speaking at focus group in Gallo Rumi, July 2011.

18. In a survey of forty Chimborazo women's associations, the elected group president was unrelated to the village president, suggesting autonomous female leadership (ACDI-FUNDAMYF 1998: 117).

19. As in the case of Elvira, a widow in her late forties with incomplete primary education, whose cows provide a small income for herself, her widowed mother, and four children.

20. For example Maria, a married warmi in her midtwenties who lives in an impoverished Guamote village.

21. Indigenous federations and the political party Pachakutik elect women's representatives (dirigentes de mujeres) and have political party auxiliary sections for women. Pachakutik's full name is Movimiento de Unidad Plurinacional Pachakutik—Nuevo País (MUPP-NP, Pachakutik Movement of Plurinational Unity-New Country).

22. During fieldwork, only one Kichwa interviewee spoke of standing for election; she was unsuccessful the first time, successful the second time.

23. The CEDAW committee reported Ecuador's weak application of the quota law (CONAMU 2004: 7). Women's and feminist organizations campaigned for the full, constitutionally sanctioned requirement for parties to ensure women were alternate and sequential candidates (Vega Ugalde 2005).

24. Preliminary evidence suggests gender and racial-ethnic quotas operating simultaneously give racialized women more representative election results (Cárdenas et al. 2011: 26).

25. Simultaneously, the CONAMU gender council promoted gender equity measures and gender agendas in municipal policy (INSTRAW 2006).

26. TSE electoral data for elections in 2002, 2004, and 2006 were analyzed in terms of male/female candidates (identified by first name), and indigenous/

nonindigenous parties, comparing candidates with elected representatives along these criteria (compare Schurr 2013 on recent elections). Women are assumed to be indigenous (not mestiza or Afro-Ecuadorian) when they stand as Pachakutik candidates, an assumption that might not be justified. Over the period 2002–2006, indigenous women were overwhelmingly likely to be elected to juntas parroquiales (where 67 percent of indígena candidates were elected), followed by municipalities (where 29.9 percent of female Pachakutik candidates were successful).

27. This picture became fractured once Pachakutik broke its alliance with President Correa and the latter's party, Alianza País, made electoral gains in these provinces.

28. During 2002–2006, the correlation between indigenous population shares and indígenas' electoral success was positive at the provincial and canton levels (coefficients of 0.49 and 0.5, respectively).

29. No indígena women during this period were elected as provincial prefect or Andean parliament representative. See De Cotí 2011: 255 on obstacles to indigenous women's election in Guatemala.

30. On Colta I draw on local conversations with diverse informants (also Vega Ugalde 2005; Bebbington 2000).

31. In this, Chimborazo indígenas are consistent with other research: indigenous women's representatives are more concerned than nonindigenous women and gender mainstreaming staff to emphasize the importance of participation of diverse actors in local government (INSTRAW 2006: 94).

32. Colta's program won honorable mention in the III Regional Competition of Affirmative Action for Women in Local Government, for its high levels of indigenous women's involvement.

33. The workshop was coorganized by ICCI, the association of alternative local governments (CGLA), the Ecuarunari women's office, and Ayuda Popular Noruega (APN) a Norwegian humanitarian organization. "Ana Miranda" is quoted in ICCI 2001: 36–37.

34. Argoti Santacruz 2003: 15; on Guamote, where SNV, the Dutch development agency and various local Ecuadorian OSGs assisted, see Hernández, Larrea, and Gallier 2005.

35. Interview, Ana Maria Pilamunga, Riobamba, 2009. Similar perspectives were recorded at indigenous movement events (ICCI 2001: 47; Centro María Quilla 1992).

36. In 2006 and 2007, ten interviews were undertaken with indigenous women in senior positions in diverse Ecuadorian indigenous confederations, development agencies, and state offices (see Radcliffe 2010).

37. As discussed in chapter 4, indigenous women established training schools first in the Andes and then across the country (Palacios and Chuma 2001).

38. Interview, Maria Andrade, 2009; on this program, Bonilla and Ramos 2009; Andi and Grefa 2009; compare chapter 5.

39. For example, one workshop was coordinated between an NGO working on indigenous issues and the COMICH women's representative for recently elected local female representatives (interview, Cristina Cucurí, CEDIS, Riobamba, 2010).

40. On Latin American indígenas' political activism and the importance of a rights-based framework, see among others Speed et al. 2006; Blackwell 2006; Calla 2012.

41. Surveys of the Ecuadorian public document the belief that women are able to ensure rights more frequently than indigenous peoples, women 39.2 percent "nearly always" getting rights, compared with 25.5 percent "nearly always" for indigenous populations (INSTRAW 2006). No figures are provided on indigenous women.

42. In interviews, half of Tsáchila women and one-third of Kichwa warmikuna could not articulate how rights connected with their lives.

43. A similar view was expressed by Magdalena, a twenty-two-year-old warmi from a poor family with nearly complete primary education, who married at age fifteen.

44. Warmikuna's responses must be interpreted in light of research contexts, namely the ethnic movement workshops where many interviews took place.

45. Women's individual rights to study were mentioned by Kichwa and Tsáchila women, e.g., Rosita, a seventeen-year-old single sona with complete primary education, and Nancy, a warmi in her late thirties.

46. The most important right as an Ecuadorian for Elvira, a warmi with two years' formal education, was "my identity, culture! Everything demonstrates that—that's my right—we're indigenous." Likewise Elizabeth, a sona trainee schoolteacher in her twenties, explained, "For me the most important rights are to live in the [Tsáchila] communities and that they survive."

Chapter 7. Postcolonial Heterogeneity

1. As later discussion clarifies, buen vivir represents neither welfare nor a western concept of "well-being."

2. The second Plan Nacional para el Buen Vivir 2013–2017 (National Buen Vivir development plan 2013–2017) was introduced in June 2013; my discussion relates primarily to the first plan (2009–2013) as it coincided with fieldwork (see Ecuador 2009, 2013).

3. Buen vivir acknowledges and draws on sources of development thinking that were previously found in a small number of nongovernmental organizations, many of them early adopters of development with identity objectives (Andolina et al. 2009).

4. Ecuadorian postneoliberal development and buen vivir has been approached from a variety of perspectives; see Becker 2010; Escobar 2010; León 2010; Radcliffe 2012; and on wider debates, Peck and Brenner 2009; Goodale and Postero 2013.

5. Given neoliberal cultural politics, it remains an open question "the extent to which the processes under way have changed those imaginaries and desires that became more deeply ingrained than ever during the neoliberal decades— e.g. the ideologies of individualism, consumerism, the 'marketization' of citizenship, and so forth" (Escobar 2010: 8).

6. Rights are those defined by international human rights conventions and political theory, and are shaped and guaranteed in the context of the social, active, participatory, and communitarian state and of the connectivity between individuals.

7. In part due to these multiple voices, Buen Vivir was never totally coherent.

8. The "dignified salary" law required that any profitable business first distribute profit among employees, until employees' total earnings rise to a living wage or the entire profit is distributed, a measure that boosted worker pay in the formal economy and raising the share of workers with social security from under 30 percent to over 40 percent in 2007–2011.

9. In addition, the secondary school fee of $25 was abolished, and free textbooks and uniforms were provided to schoolchildren, with free lunches for primary school children.

10. The program Aliméntate Ecuador distributes basic foodstuffs monthly in rural areas.

11. However, greater state control did not entail nationalization of natural resources but renegotiated contracts and greater state oversight (also León 2010: 107).

12. The gender transition commission sent a draft law to the National Assembly in 2013.

13. Its full name was the Comisión de Transición para la definición de la Institucionalidad Pública que garantice la igualdad entre hombres y mujeres, summarized here as the Transition Commission toward Women and Gender Equality Council.

14. Interviews, CONAMU, Quito, 2010; Alicia Garcés, CEDIME, Quito, 2010.

15. Interviews, Alicia Garcés, CEDIME, Quito, 2010; Ana Lucia Herrera, Transition Commission, January 2011; also Guchin 2010: 68–74.

16. Mainstreaming activities involved the transition commission working with large ministries, and promoting gender-aware planning, for example participatory budgeting at the Ministry of Finance (interviews, A. L. Herrera, Transition Commission, Quito, January 2011; M. Andrade, UNIFEM, Quito, July 2009).

17. On recent government agricultural policy, see Carrión and Herrera 2012: 14. Food sovereignty agendas refer to the right of people to define their own food systems based on locally meaningful social relations and biodiversity, against market and corporate food production processes. Such formal commitments could not easily displace embedded expectations regarding households and rural family authority structures, as state employees dealing with land reform

relied on masculine interpretations of households, farm production, and entrepreneurialism. As previous chapters document, such mindsets exclude racialized-female subalterns.

18. Interview, Ana Lucia Herrera, Transition Commission, Quito, January 2011.

19. Interview Ana L. Herrera, 2011; also Transition Commission 2011: 49, 51.

20. LGBTTI stands for lesbian, gay, bisexual, transgender, *travesti*, and intersex.

21. In August 2009, the bono expanded its coverage and number of beneficiaries by 25 percent, mostly among mothers and older adults. Postneoliberal policy on the CCT also allows women to draw a year's bono (totaling $360) as a loan to support economic activities.

22. CODENPE saw its budget fall 2007–2010 from 0.12 percent to 0.02 percent of GDP, restricting its capacity to support development with identity, affecting Chimborazo as the third largest beneficiary province.

23. CODENPE's relationship with the Correa government became tense (Becker 2010).

24. The 2008 Constitution provides for indigenous territorial recognition and a degree of autonomy under the Circunscripciones Territoriales Indígenas (Indigenous Territorial Circumscriptions, CTIs), established under the COOTAD legislation.

25. Workshop, Quito, March 2010.

26. In Ecuador, food sovereignty initiatives build on decades of women's national and international activism, including calls for rescue and development of agricultural and nutritional systems, rejection of market-based food security and biofuel models, and proposals for agrarian reform to guarantee land. Agendas also call for communities, waters, air, forests, and oceans to be declared food sovereignty areas, free of extraction, deforestation, and industrial food production.

27. In this context, international calls for dignified work, the creation of off-farm work, and standards of equal pay gain particular urgency (Mandato 1 Cumbre 2009).

28. Interview, Delia Caguana, women's representative, COMICH, 2010.

29. Interview, January 2011.

30. Workshop in Baños 2010.

31. See Cookson 2015 on similar dynamics in Peru.

32. Census data from 2010 show that 20.4 percent of indigenous people are illiterate, compared with national averages of 6.8 percent.

33. Indigenous leaders were criminalized, extraction activities permitted without prior consultation with affected communities, and "exceptional circumstances" cited as justification.

34. Interview, Delia Caguana, Riobamba, March 2010.

35. Interview, Delia Caguana, March 2010.

36. Interview, Riobamba, July 2009.

37. For some women, this strategic alliance was influenced by CODENPE's increasing breach with government agendas.

38. Speaking at public policy workshop, Baños, 2010.

39. "Indigenous Women Call on the Committee on the Elimination of Discrimination against Women to Recognize Indigenous Peoples' Collective Rights," 4 December 2013, www.forestpeoples.org, accessed 6 December 2013.

40. Indígenas attended the UN-sponsored meeting in September 2014, the World Conference on Indigenous Peoples, to insert intersectional agendas into the post–2015 Millennium Development Goals.

41. Interview, Ana Maria Pilamunga, Riobamba, July 2009.

42. Interview, Maria Andrade, Quito, July 2009.

43. Focus group, CAMACHH group, Riobamba, July 2009.

44. Interview, Delia Caguana, Riobamba, March 2010.

45. Interview, Maria Andrade, July 2009.

46. Interview, Delia Caguana, COMICH, March 2010.

47. Anonymized woman, speaking at workshop, Baños, 2010.

48. Compare Escobar 2010: 24; Goodale and Postero 2013: 15; on recent indigenous-government relations Becker 2010.

49. Anonymized woman, speaking at workshop, Quito, 2010.

50. Conversation, Delia Caguana, Chimborazo, 18 August 2010. Delia was subsequently elected president of Chimborazo's CONAIE-affiliated federation, COMICH.

51. Interview, Maria Andrade, July 2009.

52. Interview, Magdalena Aysabucha, Ecuarunari, February 2009.

53. This included the interagency intercultural program coordinated between UNDP, UNFPA, UNIFEM and UNESCO.

54. Interview, Maria Andrade, UNIFEM, July 2009.

55. This heterogeneity is reflected in nationality-specific Plans for Life, *planes de vida* in Spanish, prepared for some nationalities, such as the Épera.

56. Anonymized woman, at workshop, Baños, 2010.

57. Rivera Cusicanqui 2012: 107 argues that indigenous women's affective work and sexuality offer particular contributions to diversity in diversity, in what she terms Bolivia's motley/*chixi* society.

58. Bolivia has a Depatriarchalization Unit in the Vice-Ministry of Decolonization and a National Gender Equity Plan, which focus diverse debates from distinct positions (Burman 2011, Galindo 2013). Bolivia's 2008 gender equality plan argues for decolonizing the concept of gender in light of pre- and postcolonial struggles by (indigenous) women to realize their rights (Estado Plurinacional de Bolivia 2008; compare Rivera Cusicanqui 2006).

59. These examples, extensively discussed in this and previous chapters, belie Chibber's (2013) attempt to put postcolonial politics back into the box of early structural Marxism.

60. See, for example, Radcliffe forthcoming.

GLOSSARY

Alli Kawsay	Direct translation into Kichwa of buen vivir
BID	Banco Interamericano de Desarrollo (Inter-American Development Bank)
BNF	Banco Nacional de Fomento (National Investment Bank), Ecuador
buen vivir	Literally "living well," a development policy and approach introduced by Ecuador in 2007
CAMACHH	Causita Mashac Chimborazo Huarmicuna, "Mujeres de Chimborazo que buscan la vida" (Chimborazo Women who seek Life), a Chimborazo-based indigenous women's organization
CCT	Conditional Cash Transfer
CEDAW	Convention for the Elimination of Discrimination against Women
CEDIME	Centro de Investigación de los Movimientos Sociales del Ecuador (Center for Ecuadorian Social Movement Research)
CODENPE	Consejo de Nacionalidades y Pueblos del Ecuador (Council of Nationalities and Peoples of Ecuador)
COMICG	Corporación de Mujeres Indígenas de Cantón Guamote (Canton Guamote Women's Organization), Ecuador
COMICH	Confederación del Movimiento Indígena de Chimborazo (Confederation of the Chimborazo Indigenous Movement)
COMPOCIECH	Confederación de Pueblos, Organizaciones y Comunidades Indígenas Evangélicas de Chimborazo (Confederation of evangelical indigenous peoples, organizations and communities of Chimborazo)
comuna	Small political and administrative unit, largely in rural areas
CONAIE	Confederación de Nacionalidades Indígenas del Ecuador (Confederation of Indigenous Nationalities of Ecuador)

CONAMU	Consejo Nacional de la Mujer (National Women's Council), Ecuador
CONFENAIE	Confederación de las Nacionalidades Indígenas de la Amazonía Ecuatoriana (Confederation of Indigenous Nationalities of the Ecuadorian Amazon)
CONMIE	Consejo Nacional de Mujeres Indígenas del Ecuador (National Council of Ecuadorian Indigenous Women), comprising women's representatives from each of Ecuador's major indigenous federations
CONPLADEIN	Consejo Nacional de Planificación y Desarrollo de los Pueblos Indígenas y Negros (National Council for Planning and Development for Indigenous and Afro-descended Peoples), Ecuador
COOTAD	Código Orgánico de Organización Territorial, Autonomía y Descentralización (Legal Code of Territorial Organization, Autonomy and Decentralization)
CPME	Coordinadora Política de Mujeres Ecuatorianas (Political Coordinator of Ecuadorian Women)
CTIs	circunscripciones territoriales indígenas (indigenous territorial circumscriptions)
DNSPI	Dirección Nacional de Salud de Pueblos Indígenas (National Health Directorate of Indigenous Peoples)
DRI	Desarrollo Rural Integrado (integrated rural development)
ECUARUNARI	Confederación Kichwa del Ecuador (Ecuadorian Kichwa Confederation)
ERPE	Escuelas Radiofónicas Populares del Ecuador (Popular Radio Schools of Ecuador)
EU	European Union
FAO	Food and Agricultural Organization, United Nations
FEINE	Consejo de Pueblos y Organizaciones Indígenas Evangélicas del Ecuador (Council of Evangelical Indigenous Peoples and Organizations of Ecuador)
FEPP	Fondo Ecuatoriano Populorum Progressio (Ecuadorian Fund for Popular Progress)
FODEPI	Fondo de Desarrollo de las Nacionalidades y Pueblos del Ecuador (Development Fund for the Indigenous Nationalities and Peoples of Ecuador)
FODERUMA	Fondo de Desarrollo Rural Marginado (Fund for Rural Marginal Development)

GAD	Gender and Development policy
IADB	Inter-American Development Bank
IBIS	Ibis Education for Development, a Danish NGO working in various countries of the global South
ICCI	Instituto Científico de Culturas Indígenas (Scientific Institute of Indigenous Cultures), Ecuador
ILO	International Labor Organization
Indígena	Indigenous person or group, used in this book to refer specifically to indigenous women
INGO	International nongovernmental organization
INNFA	Instituto Nacional de la Niñez y la Familia (National Children and Family Institute)
IRD	Integrated rural development policy
Kichwa	Indigenous nationality, comprising a number of pueblos, which include the Puruhuá of Chimborazo province
Kichwa	Language spoken by Kichwa indigenous people
Levantamientos Indígenas	Indigenous Uprisings, indigenous mobilizations with nationwide impacts
LGBTTI	Lesbian, gay, bisexual, transgender, travesti, and intersex groups and organizations
LMGAI	Ley de Maternidad Gratuita y Atención a la Infancia (Law of Free Maternity Care and Infant Care)
MDG	Millennium Development Goals, or ODM in its Spanish acronym
mestizaje	Literally mixing; demographic and sociocultural mixing of European and Indigenous descent populations
Minga	Kichwa comuna work party that calls upon residents to contribute to the upkeep of shared facilities
MUPP-NP	Movimiento de Unidad Plurinacional Pachakutik—Nuevo País (Pachakutik Movement of Plurinational Unity-New Country), a political party representing indigenous and other popular interests
NGO	Nongovernmental organization
OSG/OTG	Organización de Segundo Grado (local civic association uniting various villages), and Organización de Tercer Grado (an umbrella organization encompassing various OSGs), respectively.
OECD	Organization for Economic Cooperation and Development
PAHO	Pan American Health Organization

Pachamama	Kichwa term referring to the more-than-human agency embodied in a living earth
PIO	Plan de Igualdad de Oportunidades (Plan for Equal Opportunities), Ecuador
PRODEPINE	Proyecto de Desarrollo de los Pueblos Indígenas y Negros del Ecuador (Development Project for Indigenous and Afro-Ecuadorian Peoples)
PROLEAD	Program for the Support of Women's Leadership and Representation
PRONADER	Programa Nacional de Desarrollo Rural (National Program of Rural Development), Ecuador
PUCE	Pontificia Universidad Católica del Ecuador (Catholic University of Ecuador)
REDD	Reducing Emissions through Deforestation and Degradation policy
SEDRI	Secretaría de Desarrollo Rural Integrado (Secretariat of the Presidency for Integrated Rural Development), Ecuador
Runa	Kichwa term for people
Sona/sonala	Tsafiki terms for woman and women, respectively
SENPLADES	Secretaría Nacional de Planificación y Desarrollo (National Secretariat for Planning and Development), Ecuador
SNV	Dutch Volunteers Foundation
SRH	Sexual and reproductive health issues
SRR	Sexual and reproductive rights
sumak kawsay	Kichwa concept of life in harmony with nature; often translated as buen vivir
Tsafiki	Language spoken by Tsáchila indigenous people
UNFPA	United Nations Population Fund
UNIFEM	United Nations Development Fund for Women, now UN Women
UNORCAC	Unión de Organizaciones Campesinas e Indígenas de Cotacachi (Union of Peasant and Indigenous Organizations of Cotacachi)
WAD	Women and development policy
warmi/warmikuna	Kichwa term for woman, and women respectively
WID	Women in development policy

BIBLIOGRAPHY

Unpublished and Online Items

Aguirre Borja, S. 2007. *Propuesta de teoría de diseño para la intervención en artesanía: Caso de estudio Tsáchila.* Facultad Arquitectura, Universidad Católica de Ecuador, Quito.

AIPP Women [Asia Indigenous Peoples Pact] 2012. "Voices of Indigenous Women from the Asia-Pacific Region." Document prepared for the Rio+20 Earth Summit 2012. Asia Indigenous People's Pact.

Almeida, Milena. 2007a. "Estudio nacional interculturalizando la equidad de género: Informe final de estudio de caso." Consultancy document prepared for IBIS. Quito: IBIS.

Almeida, Milena. 2007b. "Historia oral de mujeres indígenas de la costa: Awá, Tsáchila, Épera y Chachi. Informe final de consultoría." Consultancy document prepared for IBIS. Quito: IBIS.

Alvarez Herrera, S. 2005. "Adopción tecnológica y dimensiones ambientales en un programa de desarrollo rural: Estudio de caso PRONADER-Guano." MA thesis, Facultad Latinoamericana de Ciencias Sociales-Ecuador, Quito.

Andrade, María. 1990. "Ponencia de la CONAIE al Encuentro de Mujeres Indígenas. In Memoria Encuentro Nacional de la Mujer Indígena febrero 9 a 11 1990." Conference report of National Meeting of Indigenous Women, Riobamba, Ecuador, 9–11 February 1990. Document prepared by the Ministerio de Bienestar Social and Dirección Nacional de la Mujer, Quito, 8–16.

Argoti Santacruz, L. 2003. "Evaluación de género en el proceso de gestión local de Guamote." MA thesis. Universidad Andina, Quito.

Aulestia, Ana. 2002. "Estudios de caso sobre el impacto de la perspectiva de género en la planificación participativa aplicada al desarrollo local en pueblos y nacionalidades. Estudio de caso COCIQ Quisapincha." Consultancy document prepared for PRODEPINE. Quito.

Baños Workshop. 2010. "Encuentro Nacional de las Mujeres Indígenas para la formulación de Políticas Públicas." Baños, 18 y 19 marzo de 2010. Working document. Quito.

BID. n.d. [2004]. "A liderar." Press release. Website of the Inter-American Development Bank, www.iadb.org. Accessed 16 April 2015.

Calfio Montalva, M., and L. Velasco. 2005. "Mujeres indígenas en América Latina: Brechas de género o de etnia?" Paper presented at International Seminar Pueblos Indígenas y Afrodescendientes de América Latina y el Caribe. CEPAL, Santiago, 27–29 April.

CEDIS. 2001. "Maltrato sicológico y moral por injusticia de la comercialización." Riobamba, Ecuador: CEDIS.

Chisiguano, Silverio. 2006. "La población indígena del Ecuador." Quito: INEC. www.inec.gov.ec. Accessed 28 November 2013.

Chuma, M. Vicenta. 2004. "Las mujeres en la construcción del estado plurinacional." Presentation at Cumbre Indígena, 21–25 July. Quito. http://icci.nativeweb.org/cumbre2004/chuma.html. Accessed 5 May 2006.

Comisión de Mujer y Familia Tsáchila. n.d.a. Programa: Mujer y familia. Proyecto: Participación de la mujer tsa'chila en el proceso de fortalecimiento organizativo de la nacionalidad. Consejo de Gobernación de la nacionalidad tsa'chila. Santo Domingo.

COMUNIDEC. 2008. "El Presupuesto Participativo del gobierno provincial de Chimborazo: Un aprendizaje para la democracia." Quito: COMUNIDEC [Fundación de Comunidades y Desarrollo Rural].

CONAMU. 2007. "Propuesta Para la Incorporación del Enfoque de Interculturalidad en el Accionar del Consejo Nacional de las Mujeres." Working document. Quito.

Cookson, Tara. 2015. "Rural Women and the Uneven Process of Inclusion: An Institutional Ethnography of Peru's Conditional Cash Transfer Program." Unpublished PhD thesis. Department of Geography, University of Cambridge, Cambridge, UK.

Coordinadora Cantonal de Mujeres de Cotacachi. 2008. "Propuesta de Mujeres Indígenas del Ecuador para la Asamblea Constituyente para facilitar el acceso de las mujeres de los pueblos y nacionalidades indígenas y afro-descendientes a la justicia." Quito: Coordinadora Cantonal de Mujeres de Cotacachi, UNORCAC Cotacachi.

Declaración Piendamó. 2013. "Declaration of the Indigenous Women's Summit held in De la María Piendamó." Press release from the Indigenous Women's Summit Meeting, De la María Piendamó, Colombia. www.cumbrecontinentalindigena.com. 15 November 2013.

Défaz, Jorge. 2002. "Derechos colectivos en la nacionalidad Tsáchila." MA thesis, Universidad Andina, Quito.

Ecuador CONPLADEIN. 1997. Documento del Proyecto. Comité de gestión del PRODEPINE. Quito: CONPLADEIN.

Espín, T. 1965. "La mujer campesina y el desarrollo de la comunidad." MA thesis, Pontificia Universidad Católica del Ecuador PUCE, Quito.

Esquivel, A. L. 2013. "Construyendo una relación armónica con la naturaleza." http://www.noticiasaliadas.org/articles.asp?art=6844. Accessed 16 April 2015.

Figueroa Romero, Maria. 2012. "Comparative Analysis of Indigenous Women's Participation in Ethnopolitics and Community Development: The Experiences of Women Leaders of Ecuarunari (Ecuador) and Yatama (Atlantic Coast of Nicaragua)." PhD thesis, York University, Toronto.

Guchin, M. K. 2010. "El estado ecuatoriano y las mujeres: Nuevos sujetos de la Revolución Ciudadana?" MA thesis, FLACSO-Ecuador. Quito.

Hooper, M. 1998. "Mujeres, sexualidad y VIH/Sida: La mujer Shuar en la provincia de Morona Santiago." Manuscript.

Huacho, A. M. 2003. "Entrevista a Ana Maria Huacho realizado por G. Mendez." Proyecto comparativo entre el movimiento indígena y el movimiento de mujeres. FLACSO. Quito. www.flacso.org.ec/docs/ANA_MARIA_HUACHO.pdf. Accessed 15 April 2015.

IADB. 2002. "IADB Reaffirms Commitment to Women in Development at First Indigenous Women Summit of the Americas." Press release. 3 December. www .iadb.org/news. Accessed 15 April 2015.

IADB. 2004. "Empowering Indigenous Women." Press release. 8 March. www.iadb .org/news. Accessed 16 April 2015.

Informe Final de Consultoría. n.d. Informe final de la consultoría para la incorporación del enfoque de género en las metodologías de trabajo del PRODEPINE. CODENPE. Consultancy document prepared for CODENPE. Quito.

Interview with Mónica Chují. 2013. "Women are Gradually Gaining More Opportunities: Interview with Indigenous Leader Mónica Chují." Special report in "Indigenous Women Take a Stand." *Latin American Press*, 5–6 June.

La pobreza indígena. 2012. "La pobreza indígena en Ecuador se redujo entre 5 y 10% en 5 años." Agencia Pública de Noticias (Ecuador) andes.info.ec/es /actualidad/464/html. Accessed 16 April 2015.

Larrea, S. 2002. "Consultoría: Incorporación del enfoque de género en metodologías de inversiones públicas: Informe final." PRODEPINE. Unpublished manuscript.

León, Irene. 2009. "Ecuador: La tierra, el sumak kawsay y las mujeres." www .fedaeps.org. Fundación de Estudios, Acción y Participación Social. Accessed 7 February 2013.

Lilliott, E. 1997. "Development and the Politics of Tradition: Indigenous Women's Organizing in Amazonian Ecuador." Paper presented at Latin American Studies Association Congress, 17–19 April, Guadalajara, Mexico.

Lilliott, E. 2000. "Developing Racism in Eastern Ecuador: NGOs and Indigenous Federations Negotiating Indigenous Women's Politics." Paper presented at Latin American Studies Association Congress, 16–18 March, Miami.

Luna Creciente. n.d. "Investigación de Sexualidades con Mujeres Indígenas de la Sierra Centro del Ecuador." Quito: Luna Creciente.

Memoria. 1990. Encuentro Nacional de la Mujer Indígena febrero 9 a 11, 1990. Ministerio de Bienestar Social-Dirección Nacional de la Mujer.

Memorias del Seminario Nacional. n.d. Corporación Educativa Macac Políticas públicas para pueblos indígenas en el Ecuador del siglo XXI. Report of National Meeting on Public Policies for Indigenous Peoples in Ecuador.

Movimiento de Mujeres de Sucumbíos. n.d. Agenda de las Mujeres de Sucumbíos: La Unidad Fortalece Nuestra Acción por los Derechos de las Mujeres. Nueva Loja Ecuador: Movimiento de Mujeres de Sucumbíos.

Mujeres Campesinas de Cotacachi. 2010. Aportes de las mujeres indígenas campesinas de Cotacachi a la propuesta de Ley de Tierras. Communication. Manuscript.

Muratorio, B. 2002. "Violencia contra mujeres en comunidades indígenas del Napo: Historia y cultura en un contexto de globalización." Paper presented at Ecuatorianistas Conference, 18–22 July, Quito.

ODM Chimborazo. 2007. "Objetivos de Desarrollo del Milenio Estado de la Situación 2007." AECID-CONCOPE [Consorcio de Consejos Provinciales del Ecuador] Gobierno Provincial de Chimborazo.

Plan de Trabajo. 2006. "Plan de trabajo para la creación de la unidad de género de CODENPE." Working document prepared by CODENPE-FORMIA. Quito.

PRODEPINE. n.d.. "Anexo 2: Indicadores sociales sobre la situación de las mujeres indígenas y campesinas del Ecuador rural." Quito: PRODEPINE.

Santillán, M. C. 2008. "Mujeres indígenas ecuatorianas en los espacios públicos: Roles, dificultades e incidencias políticas." MA thesis. Universidad Politécnica Salesiana, Quito.

Segura Villalva, M. 2006. "Resolución o silencio? La violencia contra las mujeres kichwas de Sucumbíos, Ecuador." MA thesis, FLACSO-Ecuador. Quito.

Simbaña, Teresa. 2003. Entrevista a Teresa Simbaña realizada por G. Mendez en proyecto comparativo entre el movimiento indígena y el movimiento de mujeres. FLACSO-Ecuador. www.flacso.org.ec/docs/TERESA_SIMBAÑA_M.pdf. Accessed 15 April 2015.

Transition Commission. 2010. "Anteproyecto de ley de Igualdad entre mujeres y hombres y personas de diversa condición sexo-genérica." November. Comisión de Transición, Working Document.

Tsáchila Informe. 2006. Proyecto de la mujer tsa'chila en el proceso de fortalecimiento organizativo de la nacionalidad. Informe de actividades programa IBIS-Gobernación Tsa'chila, meses noviembre y diciembre 2006. Quito: IBIS.

UNESCO. 2008. Information received from the UN system and other intergovernmental organizations: UN Development Fund for Women, Permanent Forum on Indigenous Issues, 7th Session. E/c.19/2008/4/Add.2.

UN Permanent Forum on Indigenous Issues. 2006. "Report on the Fifth Session (15–26 May 2006): Recommendations Specifically Pertaining to Indigenous Women and the Girl Child, Adopted by the Permanent Forum on Indigenous Issues at Its Fifth Session." Geneva: United Nations.

Uquillas, Jorge. 2002. "Fortalecimiento de la capacidad de autogestión de los pueblos indígenas y afro-ecuatorianos: El caso de PRODEPINE." Paper presented at LASA Ecuadorian Studies, Quito, 18–22 July.

Visión Mundial. 2007. Documento de Línea de Base. Unpublished report. FLACSO.

von Sigsfeld, D., and H. Avalos. 1998. "Informe final del proyecto Desarrollo de la Mujer Rural en la Provincia de Chimborazo—Ecuador." Convenio ALA 93/17. Alausí, Ecuador. Chimborazo Province Rural Women Development Project.

Zhingri, P. 2009. "Hacia la I Cumbre Continental de Mujeres Indígenas del Abya Yala: Por la vida, por los derechos de las mujeres, por un estado plurinacional y buen vivir." https://cumbrecontinentalindigena.wordpress.com/page/2/. Accessed 21 April 2015.

Books and Periodicals

Abu-Lughod, Lila. 1990. "The Romance of Resistance: Tracing Transformations of Power through Bedouin Women." *American Ethnologist* 17(1): 41–55.

ACDI-FUNDAMYF. 1998. *Mandato Político—un reto urgente para las mujeres*. Riobamba, Ecuador: ACDI [Agricultural Cooperative Development International]–FUNDAMYF [Fundación Mujer y Familia Andina].

Acosta, J. 2008. "El buen vivir para la construcción de alternativas." In A. Acosta (ed.), *Entre el quiebre y la realidad: Constitución 2008*. Quito: Abya Yala, 27–37.

Agamben, Giorgio. 1998. *Homo sacer: Sovereign Power and Bare Life*. Stanford, CA: Stanford University Press.

Agamben, Giorgio. 2005. *State of Exception*. Chicago: University of Chicago Press.

Aguinaga, M., M. Lang, D. Mokrani, and A. Santillana. 2011. "Pensar desde el feminismo: Críticas y alternativas del desarrollo." In M. Lang and D. Mokrani (eds.), *Más allá del desarrollo*. Quito: Abya Yala-Fundación Rosa Luxemburg, 55–82.

ALDHU [Asociación Latinoamericana para los Derechos Humanos]. 1998. *Conocimiento y las prácticas de salud comunitaria y reproductiva de la mujer Shuar*. Quito: ALDHU.

Alexander, M. J., and Chandra T. Mohanty (eds.). 1997. *Feminist Genealogies, Colonial Legacies, Democratic Futures*. London: Routledge.

Almeida Duque, M., M. S. Leiva, and G. De la Bastida. 1991. *Investigación de la situación del alfabetismo de la mujer campesina en el Ecuador*. Quito: UNICEF-UNESCO-FUNDELAM.

Alonso, A. M. 1994. "The Politics of Space, Time and Substance: State Formation, Nationalism and Ethnicity." *Annual Review of Anthropology* 23: 379–405.

Altamirano-Jímenez, I. 2010. "Indigenous Women, Nationalism and Feminism." In S. Razack (ed.), *States of Race: Critical Race Feminism for the Twenty-First Century*. Toronto: Between the Lines, 111–25.

Alvarez, S., et al. 2003. "Encountering Latin American and Caribbean Feminisms." *Signs* 28(2): 393–434.

Ambrosio, T. 2000. *La intimidad desnuda*. Quito: Abya Yala.

Anderson, Kay. 2007. *Race and the Crisis of Humanism*. London: Routledge.

Anderson, Kay. 2008. "Race' in Post-universalist Perspective." *Cultural Geographies* 15(2): 155–71.

Andi, Rosa, and G. Grefa. 2009. "La Ley de Buen Trato y los promotores del buen trato." In M. Lang and A. Kucia (eds.), *Mujeres indígenas y justicia ancestral*. Quito: UNIFEM, 142–46.

Andolina, R., N. Laurie, and S. A. Radcliffe. 2009. *Indigenous Development in the Andes: Culture, Power and Transnationalism*. Durham, NC: Duke University Press.

Andrade, Maria. 2009. *Guía Educativa para la inclusión de Mujeres Indígenas en los gobiernos locales alternativos.* Quito: CODENPE.

Anthias, Floya, and Nira Yuval-Davis. 1992. *Racialized boundaries: Race, nation, gender, colour, class and the anti-racist struggle.* London: Routledge.

Anthias, Penelope and S. A. Radcliffe. 2013. "The Ethnoenvironmental Fix and Its Limits: Indigenous Land Titling and the Production of Not-Quite-Neoliberal Natures in Bolivia." *Geoforum* online.

Anzaldúa, Gloria. 1987. *Borderlands-La Frontera: The New Mestiza.* San Francisco, CA: Aunt Lute Books.

Arboleda, Maria. 1993. "Ecuador: Mujeres en el poder local." In M. Arboleda and R. Rodriguez (eds.), *El espacio posible.* Santiago: ISIS, 20–42.

Arboleda, M. 2006. "Género y gobernanza territorial en Cotacachi y Cotopaxi." In Instituto de Estudios Ecuatorianos (comp.), *En las fisuras del poder: Movimiento indígena, cambio social y gobiernos locales.* Quito: Instituto de Estudios Ecuatorianos, 151–214.

Arnold, Denise. 1997. *Más allá del silencio: Las fronteras de género en los Andes.* La Paz: CIASE-ILCA.

Asher, Kiran. 2009. *Green and Black: Afro-Colombians, Development and Nature in the Pacific Lowlands.* Durham, NC: Duke University Press.

Assies, Willem, et al. (eds.). 2001. *The Challenge of Diversity: Indigenous Peoples and Reform of the State in Latin America.* Amsterdam: Thela Thesis.

Assies, W., Marco Calderón, and Ton Salman (eds.). 2005. *Citizenship, Political Culture and State Transformation in Latin America.* Amsterdam: Dutch University Press.

Atal, J. P., H. Nopo, and N. Winder. 2009. *New Century, Old Disparities: Gender and Ethnic Wage Gaps in Latin America.* Working paper no. 109. Washington, DC: IADB.

Ávila Inga, Patricio. 1996. "Sobre mis huellas: Sistematización de una experiencia de capacitación a campesinas." In SENDAS *Una frazada de colores.* Cuenca [Ecuador]: SENDAS, 97–110.

Ayala, A. 1999. "El protagonismo de las indígenas." *Mujer Fempress* 214: 1.

Baaz, M. E. 2005. *The Paternalism of Partnership: A Postcolonial Reading of Identity in Development Aid.* London: Zed Books.

Babb, Florence. 1989. *Between Field and Cooking Pot: The Political Economy of Market-women in Peru.* Austin: University of Texas Press.

Babb, Florence. 2012. "Theorizing Gender, Race and Cultural Tourism in Latin America." *Latin American Perspectives* 39(6): 36–50.

Baeza, M. P. 2011. *Maternidad indígena en Colta: Un espacio de encuentros y tensiones.* Quito: FLACSO Sede Ecuador-Abya Yala.

Banivanua, T., and P. Edmonds (eds.). 2010. *Making Settler Colonial Space: Perspectives on Race, Place and Identity.* Basingstoke, UK: Palgrave.

Barrig, Maruja. 2001. *El mundo al revés: Imágenes de la mujer indígena.* Buenos Aires: CLACSO.

Barrig, Maruja. 2004. "Mujeres andinas, movimientos feministas y proyectos de desarrollo." In I. Sichra (ed.). *Género, etnicidad y educación in América Latina.* Madrid: Morata-PROEIB Andes, 101–12.

Barrig, Maruja. 2006. " 'What Is Justice?' Indigenous Women in Andean Development Projects." In J. S. Jacquette and G. Summerfield (eds.), *Women and Gender
Equity in Development Theory and Practice*. Durham, NC: Duke University Press,
107–33.

Bebbington, Anthony. 2000. "Reencountering Development: Livelihood Transitions and Place Transformations in the Andes." *Annals of the Association of American
Geographers* 90(3): 495–520.

Bebbington, Anthony. 2004. "NGOs and Uneven Development: Geographies of
Development Intervention." *Progress in Human Geography* 28(6): 725–45.

Becker, M. 1999. "Comunas and Indigenous Protest in Cayambe, Ecuador." *Americas* 55(4): 531–59.

Becker, M. 2010. "Correa, Indigenous Movements, and the Writing of the New
Constitution in Ecuador." *Latin American Perspectives* 38(1): 47–63.

Bedford, Kate. 2005. "Loving to Straighten Out Development: Sexuality and
'Ethno-Development' in the World Bank's Ecuadorian Lending." *Feminist Legal
Studies* 13(3): 295–322.

Bergeron, Suzanne. 2011. "Economics, Performativity, and Social Reproduction
in Development." *Globalization* 8(2): 151–61.

Bessis, Sophie. 2004. "International Organizations and Gender: New Paradigms
and Old Habits." *Signs* 29(2): 633–47.

Bhabha, Homi. 1986. "Foreword: Remembering Fanon." In Frantz Fanon [1952],
Black Skin, White Masks. Trans. C. L. Markman. London: Pluto, vii–xxvi.

Bhabha, Homi. 1990. "The Third Space: Interview with Homi Bhabha." In
J. Rutherford (ed.), *Identity: Community, Culture, Difference*. London: Lawrence and
Wishart, 16–21.

Bhabha, H. 1994. *The Location of Culture*. London: Routledge.

Bhabha, Homi. 1996. "The Other Question: Difference, Discrimination and the
Discourse of Colonialism." In R. Ferguson, M. Gever, T. Minh-ha, and C. West
(eds.), *Out There: Marginalization and Contemporary Cultures*. Cambridge, MA: MIT
Press, 71–87.

Bhabha, H. 1999. "Liberalism's Sacred Cow." In J. Cohen et al. (eds.), *Is Multiculturalism Bad for Women?* Princeton, NJ: Princeton University Press, 79–84.

Bhavnani, Kum-kum, John Foran, and Priya Kurian (eds.). 2003. *Feminist Futures:
Re-imagining Women, Culture and Development*. London: Zed Books.

Biehl, João. 2005. *Vita: Life in a Zone of Social Abandonment*. Berkeley: University of
California Press.

Blackwell, Maylei. 2006. "Weaving in the Spaces: Indigenous Women's Organizations and the Politics of Scale in Mexico." In S. Speed et al. (eds.), *Dissident
Women*. Austin: University of Texas Press, 115–54.

Blaser, Mario. 2009. "From Progress to Risk: Development, Participation, and
Postdisciplinary Techniques of Control." *Canadian Journal of Development Studies*
28(3–4): 439–54.

Blaser, Mario. 2010. *Storytelling Globalization from the Chaco and Beyond*. Durham,
NC: Duke University Press.

Boelens, Rutgerd, and M. Zwarteveen. 2003. "Water, Gender and 'Andeanity': Gender Dimensions of Water Rights in Diverging Regimes of Representation." In T. Salman and A. Zoomer (eds.), *Imaging the Andes*. Amsterdam, CEDLA, 145–66.

Boesten, Jelke. 2010. *Intersecting Inequalities: Women and Social Policy in Peru, 1990–2000*. University Park, PA: Penn State University Press.

Bonilla, Inés, and Rosa Ramos. 2009. "La construcción e implementación del Reglamento de Buena Convivencia en Cotacachi." In M. Lang and A. Kucia (eds.), *Mujeres indígenas y justicia ancestral*. Quito: UNIFEM, 136–38.

Bourque, S., and K. B. Warren. 1981. *Women of the Andes: Patriarchy and Social Change in Two Peruvian Towns*. Ann Arbor: University of Michigan Press.

Brah, Avtar, and Ann Phoenix. 2004. "Ain't I a Woman? Revisiting Intersectionality." *Journal of International Women's Studies* 5(3): 75–86.

Brassel, F., S. Herrera, and M. Laforge (eds.). 2010. *Reforma agraria en el Ecuador? Viejos temas, nuevos argumentos*. Quito: SIPAE.

Bretón, Víctor. 2005. *Capital social y etnodesarrollo en los Andes*. Quito: CAAP.

Bromley, R. J. 1977. *Development planning in Ecuador*. Hove, UK: Latin American Publications Fund.

Bulnes, M. 1990. *Hatarishpa Ninimi—Me levanto y digo: Testimonio de tres mujeres quichuas*. Quito: El Conejo.

Burbano, Adriana, and Erika Silva. 2008. "Género y ambiente en Napo, Chimborazo y Cañar." In E. Silva Charvet (ed.), *Género y ambiente en el Ecuador*. Quito: Abya Yala: 301–452.

Burman, A. 2011. "Chachawarmi: Silence and Rival Voices on Decolonisation and Gender Politics in Andean Bolivia." *Journal of Latin American Studies* 4(1): 65–91.

Butler, Judith. 2003. *Precarious Life: The Powers of Mourning and Violence*. London: Verso.

Butler, Judith. 2011. *Bodies That Matter: On the Discursive Limits of Sex*. London: Routledge.

Calla, Pamela. 2012. "Luchas legales y política de las calles en torno al racismo: descentrando la patriarcalidad del Estado Plurinacional de Bolivia." In A. Hernández et al. (eds.), *Género, complementariedades y exclusiones en Mesoamérica y los Andes*. Quito: Abya Yala-IWGIA, 43–60.

Calla, Ricardo. 2006. *Mujer indígena en Bolivia, Brasil, Ecuador, Guatemala y Panamá: Un panorama de base a partir de la ronda de censos de 2000*. Santiago: CEPAL.

Camacho, A. V., et al. 2006. "Cultural Aspects Related to the Health of Andean Women in Latin America: A Key Issue for Progress toward the Attainment of the Millennium Development Goals." *International Journal of Gynaecology and Obstetrics* 94(3): 357–63.

Campos, Gloria, and Eurídice Salguero. 1987. *Derechos de la mujer indígena*. Quito: CEDIME.

Canessa, Andrew. 2005. "The Indian Within, the Indian Without: Citizenship, Race and Sex in a Bolivian Hamlet." In A. Canessa (ed.), *Natives Making Nation: Gender, Indigeneity and the State in the Andes*. Tucson: University of Arizona Press, 130–55.

Canessa, Andrew. 2012. *Intimate Indigeneities: Race, Sex and History in the Small Spaces of Andean Life*. Durham, NC: Duke University Press.

Carby, Hazel. 1982. "White Woman Listen! Black Feminism and the Boundaries of Sisterhood." In Center for Contemporary Cultural Studies (eds.), *The Empire Strikes Back: Race and Racism in Britain*. London: Hutchinson, 61–86,

Cárdenas, N., O. Espinosa, and P. Ruiz Bravo. 2011. *Building Agendas: Gender and Indigenous Peoples*. Lima, Peru: Oxfam America.

Carrión, D., and Stalin Herrera. 2012. *Ecuador rural del siglo XXI: Soberanía alimentaria, inversión pública y política agraria*. Quito: Instituto de Estudios Ecuatorianos.

Castro-Gómez, S., and R. Grosfoguel. 2007. "Prólogo: Giro decolonial, teoría crítica y pensamiento heterárquico." In S. Castro-Gómez and R. Grosfoguel (eds.), *El giro decolonial: Reflexiones para una diversidad epistémica más allá del capitalismo global*. Bogota: Siglo de Hombres, 9–24.

Cayapa, Netty, J. Quisintuna, N. Shiguango, and C. Tene. 2000. *Warmita, ayllutapash llakichikkunata jarak kamayta riksishun*. Quito: CEDIME-Konrad Adenauer Stiftung.

CEDIS. 2007a. *Agenda de equidad de género de las mujeres kichwas de Chimborazo*. Riobamba, Ecuador: Centro de Desarrollo, Difusión e Investigación Social CEDIS.

CEDIS. 2007b. *Escuela de Formación de Liderezas en la Ley de Maternidad Gratuita y Atención a la Infancia*. Riobamba, Ecuador: Centro de Desarrollo, Difusión e Investigación Social CEDIS.

CEDIS. 2007c. "Rosa, María y Sisa dan mucho de qué hablar." Riobamba, Ecuador: CEDIS-CEPP.

Censo Agropecuario [Ecuador Agrarian Census]. 2003. Quito: Instituto Nacional de Estadísticas y Censos.

Centro María Quilla. 1992. *Protagonismo de la Mujer en el Levantamiento Indígena*. Quito: Red de Educación Popular entre Mujeres.

CEPAL-BID. 2005. *Atlas socio-demográfico de la población indígena y afroecuatoriana del Ecuador*. Santiago: CEPAL-BID.

CEPAL. 2013. *Mujeres indígenas en América Latina: Dinámicas demográficas y sociales en el marco de los derechos humanos*. División de Población y División de Asuntos de Género. Santiago: CEPAL.

CEPAR Chimborazo. 2004. *Informe de la provincia de Chimborazo: Encuesta demográfica de salud materna e infantil*. Quito: CEPAR [Centro de Estudios de Población y Desarrollo Social].

CEPAR ENDEMAIN. 2006. *Situación de la salud de los pueblos indígenas en el Ecuador*. Quito: CEPAR [Centro de Estudios de Población y Desarrollo Social].

Cervone, Emma (ed.). 1998. *Mujeres contracorriente: Voces de líderes indígenas*. Quito: Agricultural Cooperative Development International.

Cervone, Emma. 2002. "Engendering Leadership: Indigenous Women Leaders in the Ecuadorian Andes." In R. Montoya et al. (eds.), *Gender's Place: Feminist Anthropologies of Latin America*. London: Palgrave, 179–96.

Cervone, E., and F. Rivera. 1999. *Ecuador racista*. Quito: FLACSO.

Chakrabarty, Dipesh. 2002. *Habitations of Modernity: Essays in the Wake of Subaltern Studies*. Chicago: University of Chicago Press.

Chambers, Robert. 1997. *Whose Reality Counts? Putting the First Last*. London: Intermediate Technology.

Chatterjee, Partha. 2004. *The Politics of the Governed: Reflections on Popular Politics in Most of the World*. New York: Columbia University Press.

Chibber, Vivek. 2013. *Postcolonial Theory and the Specter of Capital*. London: Verso.

Chua, P., et al. 2000. "Women, Culture, Development: A New Paradigm for Development Studies?" *Ethnic and Racial Studies* 2(5): 820–41.

Clark, Kim, and Mark Becker (eds.). 2007. *Highland Indians and the State in Modern Ecuador*. Pittsburgh, PA: University of Pittsburgh Press.

CODENPE. 2009. *Nueva institucionalidad del estado plurinacional*. Quito: CODENPE.

CODENPE. 2010a. *La nueva gestión hacia el sumak kawsay*. Quito: CODENPE.

CODENPE. 2010b. *Políticas públicas para la igualdad en la diversidad*. Quito: CODENPE.

CODENPE AECID. 2011. *Construyendo el estado plurinacional*. Quito: CODENPE-Agencia Española de Cooperación Internacional para el Desarrollo [AECID].

Comaroff, J., and J. L. Comaroff. 2001. "Introduction" to J. Comaroff and J. Comaroff (eds.), *Millennial Capitalism and the Cultures of Neoliberalism*. Durham, NC: Duke University Press, 1–38.

CONAIE-UNFPA. 1994. *Memorias de las Jornadas del Foro de la Mujer Indígena del Ecuador*. Quito: CONAIE-UNFPA.

CONAIE-UNFPA, Enlace Continental, and Family Care International. 2009. *Mujer Indígena: Salud y Derechos—Diagnóstico Participativo con CONAIE. Informe Executivo del Taller*. Quito: CONAIE.

CONAIE Women's Office. 2010. *Agenda Política y Estratégica de las Mujeres de los Pueblos y Nacionalidades Indígenas del Ecuador*. Quito: CONAIE.

CONAMU. 2004. *Plan de Igualdad de Oportunidades de las Mujeres Ecuatorianas*. CONAMU. Quito: CONAMU.

CONAMU. 2006. *Encuesta del uso de tiempo en Ecuador 2005*. Serie Información Estratégica II. Quito: CONAMU-INEC-UNIFEM.

CONAMU and INEC. 2008. *El tiempo de ellas y de ellos: Indicadores de la Encuesta Nacional de Uso de Tiempo–2007*. Quito: CONAMU-INEC.

CONAMU et al. 2005. *Las Mujeres de Chimborazo construyendo el Plan de Igualdad de Oportunidades: Ecuador 2005*. Riobamba, Ecuador: CONAMU-Municipio de Riobamba-CEDIS.

Consejo Nacional de Desarrollo. 1991. *Mujer y políticas de desarrollo social. Memorias del seminario taller: Reflexiones finales*. Consejo Nacional de Desarrollo. Quito: CONADE-UNICEF-DINAMU.

Cook, N. 2008. *Gender, Identity and Development in Pakistan*. London: Palgrave Macmillan.

Cornwall, Andrea. 2003. "Whose Voices? Whose Choices? Reflections on Gender and Participatory Development." *World Development* 31(8): 1325–42.

Cornwall, Andrea. 2006. "Historical Perspectives on Participation in Development." *Commonwealth and Comparative Politics* 44(1): 62–83.

Cornwall, Andrea, and C. Nyuma-Musembi. 2004. "Putting the 'Rights-Based Approach' to Development into Perspective." *Third World Quarterly* 25(8): 1415–37.

Cornwall, Andrea, Jerker Edstrom, and Alan Greig (eds.). 2011. *Men and Development: Politicizing Masculinities*. London: Zed Books.

Cornwall, Andrea, et al. 2004. "Introduction: Repositioning Feminisms in Gender and Development." *IDS Bulletin* 35(4): 1–10.

Cornwall, Andrea, et al. 2007. "Gender Myths and Feminist Fables: The Struggle for Interpretive Power in Gender and Development." *Development and Change* 38(1): 1–20.

Corporación Educativa Macac. 1992. *Identificación de representaciones sobre mujer y comunidad en grupos Quichuas del Ecuador; Informe de investigación*. Quito: Corporación Educativa Macac.

Correa, Rafael. 2012. "Rafael Correa: Ecuador's Path." Interview. *New Left Review* 77: 89–113.

Cortez, David. 2011. "La construcción social del buen vivir en Ecuador." *Aportes Andinos* (Quito) 28: 1–23.

Crain, Mary. 1996. "The Gendering of Ethnicity in the Ecuadorian Andes: Native Women's Self-Fashioning in the Urban Marketplace." In M. Melhus and K. A. Stolen (eds.), *Machos, Mistresses and Madonnas: Contesting the Power of Latin American Gender Imagery*. London: Verso, 134–58.

Craske, Nikki, and Maxine Molyneux. (eds.). 2002. *Gender and the Politics of Rights and Democracy in Latin America*. London: Palgrave Macmillan.

Crenshaw, Kimberlé. 1991. "Mapping the Margins: Intersectionality, Identity Politics and Violence against Women of Color." *Stanford Law Review* 43(6): 1241–99.

Crespi, M. 1976. "Mujeres campesinas como líderes sindicales: La falta de propiedad como calificación a puestos políticos." *Estudios Andinos* 5(1): 151–71.

Cunningham, M., M. E. Choque, D. M. Araúz, and D. Ventura. 2009. *Mujeres indígenas y derechos*. Vol. 1. *Discriminación y racismo panorama para revertirlos*. Bolivia-Guatemala-Panamá-Perú. Quito: UNIFEM.

Cunningham, M., D. Mairena, M. López, M. E. Choque, J. Reátegui, and L. F. Sarango. 2008. *Qué está pasando con los derechos de los pueblos indígenas?* Managua: UNIFEM-UNICEF-OACNUDH.

Curiel, Ochy. 2007. "Crítica poscolonial desde las prácticas políticas del feminismo antirracista." *Nómadas* (Colombia) 26: 92–101.

Cuvi Sánchez, M. 2000. "Hacía un enfoque sistemático: Las mujeres rurales y el desarrollo." In M. Cuvi Sánchez et al. (eds.), *Discursos sobre género y ruralidad en el Ecuador: La década de 1990*. Quito: CONAMU, 9–25.

Cuvi Sánchez, M., and E. Ferraro. 2000. "Mujeres rurales en las estadísticas oficiales." In M. Cuvi Sánchez et al. (eds.), *Discursos sobre género y ruralidad en el Ecuador: La década de 1990*. Quito: CONAMU, 99–130.

Dagnino, E. 2003. "Citizenship in Latin America: An Introduction." *Latin American Perspectives* 30(2): 3–17.

De Cotí, Otilia. 2011. "La participación política de las mujeres indígenas: Importantes desafíos." *Pensamiento Iberoamericano* 9: 247–62.

De Hart, M. C. 2010. *Ethnic Entrepreneurs: Identity and Development Politics in Latin America*. Stanford, CA: Stanford University Press.

De la Cadena, Marisol. 1995. "Women Are More Indian: Ethnicity and Gender in a Community near Cuzco." In O. Harris et al. (eds.), Ethnicity, Markets and Migration in the Andes. Durham, NC: Duke University Press, 329–48.

De la Cadena, Marisol. 2008. "Alternative Indigeneities: Conceptual Proposals." Latin American and Caribbean Ethnic Studies 3(3): 341–49.

De la Cadena, Marisol. 2010. "Indigenous Cosmopolitics in the Andes: Conceptual Reflections beyond 'Politics.' " Cultural Anthropology 25(2): 334–70.

De la Torre, Carlos. 1999. "Everyday Forms of Racism in Contemporary Ecuador: The Experiences of Middle-Class Indians." Ethnic and Racial Studies 22(1): 92–112.

De la Torre, Carlos. 2007. "Entre el corporativismo y las ciudadanías débiles." In V. Bretón (ed.), Ciudadanía y exclusión: Ecuador y España frente al espejo. Madrid: Catarata, 151–81.

De la Torre Amaguaña, L. M. 1993. "Importancia de la participación de la mujer en el levantamiento indígena." In Sismo étnico en el Ecuador: Varias perspectivas. Quito: Abya Yala, 71–89.

De Lauretis, Theresa. 1987. Technologies of Gender. London: Indiana University Press.

Del Campo, Esther. (ed.). 2012. Mujeres indígenas en América Latina: Política y políticas públicas. Madrid, Spain: Fundamentos.

Del Campo, Esther, and Evelyn Magdaleno. 2008. "Avances legislativos de acción positiva en Bolivia, Ecuador y Perú." In M. Prieto (ed.), Mujeres y escenarios ciudadanos. Quito: FLACSO, 275–97.

Deere, Carmen Diana, and Magdalena León. 2001a. Empowering Women: Land and Property Rights in Latin America. Pittsburgh, PA: University of Pittsburgh Press.

Deere, Carmen Diana, and Magdalena León. 2001b. "Institutional Reform of Agriculture under Neoliberalism: The Impact of Women's and Indigenous Movements." Latin American Research Review 36(2): 31–63.

De Sousa Santos, Boaventura. 2011. "Épistémologies du Sud." Études Rurales 187: 21–50.

Dietz, Mary G. 2003. "Current Controversies in Feminist Theory." Annual Review of Political Science 6: 399–431.

Dirlik, Arif. 1994. "The Postcolonial Aura: Third World Criticism in the Age of Global Capitalism." Critical Inquiry 20(2): 328–56.

DNSPI [Dirección Nacional de Salud de Pueblos Indígenas]. 2003. "Intercambio de experiencias de salud sexual y reproductiva con poblaciones indígenas." Quito: DNSPI-UNFPA-PAHO.

Donato, L. M., et al. 2007. Mujeres indígenas, territorialidad y biodiversidad en el contexto latinoamericano. Bogota: Universidad Nacional de Colombia.

Dorlin, Elsa. 2005. "De l'image épistémologique e politique des catégories de "sexe" et le "race" dans les études sur le genre." Cahiers du Genre 39: 83–105.

Duffield, M. 2007. Development, Security and Unending War. Cambridge, UK: Polity.

ECLAC [Economic Commission for Latin America and the Caribbean]. 2011. Social panorama of Latin America 2011. Santiago, Chile: United Nations.

Ecuador. 1996. Plan Nacional de Desarrollo Social: Ecuador 1996–2005. Quito: Secretaría Técnica del Frente Social.

Ecuador. 2009. *Plan Nacional de Desarrollo: Plan Nacional para el Buen Vivir 2009–2013.* Quito: SENPLADES.

Ecuador. 2010. *Agenda Social 2009–2011.* Quito: Ministerio de Coordinación de Desarrollo Social.

Ecuador. 2012. *Modelo de atención integral del sistema nacional de salud familiar, comunitario e intercultural* MAIS-FCI. Quito: Ministerio de Salud.

Ecuador. 2013. *Plan Nacional para el Buen Vivir, 2013–2017.* Quito: SENPLADES.

Ecuador Bienestar Social. 1984. *Política estatal y población indígena.* Ministerio de Bienestar Social and Oficina de Asuntos Indígenas. Quito: Abya Yala.

Ecuador Indígenas. 2009. *Objetivos de Desarrollo de Milenio estado de situación 2008. Nacionalidades y pueblos indígenas del Ecuador.* Quito: Ministerio Patrimonio Natural y Cultural-UNDP.

Ecuador MSP [Ministerio de Salud Pública] 2005. *Mapa estratégico 2005–2009.* Dirección Nacional de Salud de los Pueblos Indígenas. Subproceso de Salud Intercultural. Quito: Ministerio de Salud Pública.

Ecuador MSP. 2010. *Salud, interculturalidad y derechos: Claves para la reconstrucción del Sumak Kawsay-Buen Vivir.* Quito: Ministerio de Salud Pública.

Ecuarunari. 1998. *Propuesta política desde las vivencias de las mujeres quichuas de la Confederación de Nacionalidades y Pueblos Quichuas del Ecuador, Ecuarunari.* Quito: Ecuarunari-IBIS Dinamarca.

Ehlers, T. B. 2000. *Silent Looms: Women and Production in a Guatemalan Town.* Austin: University of Texas Press.

Elson, Diane. 1991. *Male Bias in the Development Process.* Manchester, UK: Manchester University Press.

Encalada, Karla. 2012. "Racismo en la justicia ordinaria." In B. de Sousa Santos and A. Grijalva (eds.), *Justicia indígena, plurinacionalidad e interculturalidad en Ecuador.* Quito: Abya Yala, 185–206.

ENDEMAIN [Encuesta Demográfica y de Salud Materna e Infantil]. 2004. *Encuesta demográfica y de salud materna e infantil.* CEPAR-ENDEMAIN. Quito: CEPAR.

Engle, Karen. 2010. *The Elusive Promise of Indigenous Development.* Durham, NC: Duke University Press.

Escobar, Arturo. 1995. *Encountering Development: The Making and Unmaking of the Third World.* Princeton, NJ: Princeton University Press.

Escobar, Arturo. 2008. *Territories of Difference.* Durham, NC: Duke University Press.

Escobar, Arturo. 2010. "Latin America at a Crossroads: Alternative Modernizations, Post-liberalism, or Post-Development?" *Cultural Studies* 24(1): 1–65.

Espinosa, María F. 1997. "Indigenous Women on Stage: Retracing the Beijing Conference from Below." *Frontiers* 18(2): 237–55.

Estado Plurinacional de Bolivia. 2008. *Plan de Equidad de Género.* La Paz, Bolivia

Ewig, Christina. 2010. *Second-Wave Neoliberalism: Gender, Race and Health Sector Reform in Peru.* University Park, PA: Penn State University Press.

Fanon, Frantz. 1986 [1952]. *Black Skin, White Masks.* London: Pluto.

Fellows, M. L., and S. Razack. 1998. "The Race to Innocence: Confronting Hierarchical Relations among Women." *Journal of Gender, Race and Justice* 1(1): 335–52.

Ferguson, James. 1990. *The Anti-Politics Machine: Development, Depoliticization, and Bureaucratic Power in Lesotho*. Cambridge: Cambridge University Press.

Ferguson, James. 1999. *Expectations of Modernity: Myths and Meanings of Urban Life on the Zambian Copperbelt*. Berkeley: University of California Press.

Ferguson, James. 2007. "Formalities of Poverty: Thinking about Social Assistance in Neoliberal South Africa." *African Studies Review* 50(2): 71–87.

Ferrín, Rosa. 1982. "De la forma huasipungo de trabajo a la economía campesina." In Instituto de Estudios Económicos (eds.), *Estructura agraria y reproducción campesina*. Quito: Universidad Católica, 151–202.

Fisher, L. 2004. "State of the Art: Multiculturalism, Gender and Cultural Identities." *European Journal of Women's Studies* 11(1): 111–19.

Foucault, Michel. 1980 [1977]. *Power/Knowledge—Selected Interviews and Other Writings*. New York: Pantheon.

Foucault, Michel. 2008. *The Birth of Biopolitics: Lectures at the College de France, 1978–79*. Ed. M. Senellart. Basingstoke, UK: Palgrave Macmillan.

Franke, Marfil. 1990. "Género, clase y etnia: la trenza de la dominación." In C. I. Degregori (ed.), *Tiempos de Ira y Amor*. Lima, Peru: Desco, 77–106.

Fraser, Nancy. 1990. "Rethinking the Public Sphere." *Social Text* 25/26: 56–80.

Fraser, Nancy. 1997. *Justice Interruptus: Critical Reflections on the "Postsocialist" Condition*. Cambridge: Cambridge University Press.

Fraser, N. 2008. *Scales of Justice: Reimagining Political Space in a Globalizing World*. New York: Colombia University Press.

Fueres Flores, M., C. Morán Salazar, and D. Hill. 2013. "Soberanía Alimentaria, Mujeres y su Relación con la Tierra." In M. Fueres et al. (eds.) *Soberanía Alimentaria y Mujeres*. Cuaderno Feminista 1. Quito: Instituto de Estudios Ecuatorianos, 11–44.

Fuss, Diane. 1989. *Essentially Speaking: Feminism, Nature and Difference*. London: Routledge.

Galeano, Eduardo. 1973. *Open Veins of Latin America: Five Centuries of the Pillage of a Continent*. New York: Monthly Review Press.

Galindo, María. 2013. *No se puede descolonizar sin despatriarcalizar: Teoría y propuesta de la despatriarcalización*. La Paz, Bolivia: Mujeres Creando.

Gangotena, Francisco, E. Páez, and D. Pólit. 1980. "Apreciaciones preliminares sobre la incidencia de la disolución de la hacienda tradicional en la estructura agraria: El caso Guamote." *Revista de la Pontificia Universidad Católica del Ecuador* 26: 15–92.

Garcés Dávila, A. 2006. *Relaciones de género en la Amazonía ecuatoriana: Estudios de caso en comunidades indígenas Achuar, Shuar y Kichua*. Quito: CEDIME-DED-Abya Yala.

García-Aracil, A., and C. Winter 2006. "Gender and Ethnicity Differentials in School Attainment and Labor Market Earnings in Ecuador." *World Development* 34(2): 289–307.

Gershon, Ilana. 2011. "Neoliberal Agency." *Current Anthropology* 52(4): 537–55.

Giarracca, Norma, and Teubal, Miguel. 2008. "Women in Agriculture: Introduction. In "Women in Agriculture." Special issue, *Latin American Perspectives* 35(6): 5–10.

Gibson-Graham, J. K. 2006. *A Postcapitalist Politics*. Minneapolis: University of Minnesota Press.

Glassman, James. 2006. "Primitive Accumulation, Accumulation by Dispossession, Accumulation by 'Extra-economic' Means." *Progress in Human Geography* 30(5): 608–25.

Goetschel, Ana, et al. 2007. *De memorias: Imágenes públicas de las mujeres ecuatorianas del comienzos a fines del siglo veinte.* Quito: FLACSO-FONSAL.

Goetz, Anne-Marie. 2004. "Reinvigorating Autonomous Feminist Spaces." IDS Bulletin (UK) 35(4): 137–40.

Goetz, Anne-Marie. 2007. "Gender Justice, Citizenship and Entitlement: Core Concepts, Central Debates and New Directions in Research." In M. Mukhopadhyay and N. Singh (eds.), *Gender Justice, Citizenship and Development.* New Delhi: Zubaan, 15–57.

Goicolea, I., M. San Sebastian, and M. Wulff. 2008. "Women's Reproductive Rights in the Amazon Basin of Ecuador: Challenges for Transforming Policy into Practice." *Health and Human Rights* 10(2): 91–103.

Gonzalez Casanova, Pablo. 1965. "Internal Colonialism and National Development." *Studies in Comparative International Development* 1(4): 27–37.

Goodale, Mark, and Nancy Postero (eds.). 2013. *Neoliberalism Interrupted: Social Change and Contested Governance in Contemporary Latin America.* Stanford, CA: Stanford University Press.

Gregory, Derek. 1994. *Geographical Imaginations.* Cambridge, MA: Blackwell.

Gregory, Derek. 2004. *The Colonial Present.* Oxford: Blackwell.

Grewal, Inderpal, and Caren Kaplan. (eds.). 1994. *Scattered Hegemonies: Postmodernity and Transnational Feminist Practices.* Minneapolis: University of Minnesota Press.

Groenmeyer, Marianne. 1992. "Helping." In W. Sachs (ed.)., *Development Dictionary.* London: Zed Books, 53–69.

Guerrero, Andrés. 1997. "The Construction of a Ventriloquist's Image: Liberal Discourse and the "Miserable Indian Race" in Late 19th-Century Ecuador. *Journal of Latin American Studies* 29: 555–90.

Gupta, Akhil. 1998. *Postcolonial Developments: Agriculture in the Making of Modern India.* Durham, NC: Duke University Press.

Hacking, Ian. 1986. "Making Up People." In T. Heller, H. Sosna, and D. Wellbery (eds.), *Reconstructing Individualism: Autonomy, Individuality and the Self in Western Thought.* Stanford, CA: Stanford University Press.

Hale, Charles R. 2002. "Does Multiculturalism Menace? Governance, Cultural Rights and the Politics of Identity in Guatemala." *Journal of Latin American Studies* 34: 485–524.

Hale, Charles R., and L. Stephen (eds.). 2013. *Otros Saberes: Collaborative Research on Indigenous and Afro-Descent Cultural Politics.* Santa Fe, NM: SAR Press.

Hall, Gillette, and Harry Patrinos. 2005. *Indigenous Peoples, Poverty, and Human Development in Latin America, 1994–2004.* Washington, DC: World Bank.

Hall, Stuart. 1990. "On Postmodernism and Articulation: An Interview with Stuart Hall." In L. Grossberg et al. (eds.), *Stuart Hall: Critical Dialogues in Cultural Studies.* London: Routledge, 131–50.

Hamilton, Sarah. 1998. *The Two-Headed Household: Gender and Rural Development in the Ecuadorian Andes*. Pittsburgh, PA: University of Pittsburgh Press.

Hamilton, Sarah, et al. 2001. *Gender and Agricultural Commercialization in Ecuador and Guatemala*. Integrated Pest Management Collaborative Research Support Program IPM CRSP Working Paper 01–3. Blacksburg, VA: Office of International Research and Development, Virginia Polytechnic Institute and State University.

Hart, Gillian. 2004. "Geography and Development: Critical Ethnographies." *Progress in Human Geography* 28(1): 91–100.

Hart, Gillian. 2006. "Denaturalizing Dispossession: Critical Ethnography in an Age of Resurgent Imperialism." *Antipode* 38(5): 977–1004.

Hernández, Kattya, Sissy Larrea, and Sylvie Gallier. 2005. "Entre el discurso étnico y el discurso de género de las mujeres líderes indígenas de la COMICG." *Antropología: Cuadernos de Investigación* (Quito) 6: 61–92.

Hernández, R. Aída. 2002. "Zapatismo and the Emergence of Indigenous Feminism." *NACLA Report on the Americas* 35(6): 39–43.

Hernández, R. Aída (coordinator). 2008. *Historias a Dos Voces: Testimonios de Luchas y Resistencias de Mujeres Indígenas*. Mexico City: Instituto Michoacano de la Mujer.

Hernández, R. Aída. 2014. "Algunos aprendizajes en el difícil reto de descolonizar el feminismo." In M. Millán (ed.), *Más allá del feminismo*. University of Clairmont-Editorial Pez en el Agua-Fundación Rosa Luxembourg, 183–213.

Hernández, R. Aída., and Andrew Canessa. 2012. "Introducción: Identidades indígenas y relaciones de género en Mesoamérica y la Región Andina." In R. A. Hernández and A. Canessa (eds.), *Complementariedades y exclusiones en Mesoamérica y los Andes*. Quito: IWGIA-Abya Yala, 10–42.

Heron, B. 2007. *Desire for Development: Whiteness, Gender and the Helping Imperative*. Waterloo, Canada: Wilfred Laurier University Press.

Herrera, Gioconda. 2003. "Género y estado en el Ecuador: Entre la ciudadanía y el discurso civilizatorio." In D. Capela Ayala (ed.), *Memorias del IX Encuentro de Historia y Realidad Económica y Social del Ecuador y América Latina*. Cuenca: Universidad de Cuenca, 13–26.

Herrera, Stalin. 2010. "Alternativas económicas, tenencia de la tierra y género: El caso de Nabón." In F. Brassel et al. (eds.). *Reforma agraria en el Ecuador? Viejos temas, nuevos argumentos*. 2nd ed. Quito: SIPAE, 77–101.

Hickey, Sam, and Giles Mohan (eds.). 2004. *Participation: From Tyranny to Transformation: Exploring New Approaches to Participation in Development*. London: Zed Books.

Hodgson, Dorothy L. 2001. *Once Intrepid Warriors: Gender, Ethnicity and the Cultural Politics of Maasai Development*. Bloomington, University of Illinois Press.

Hoffman, Kelly, and Miguel A. Centeno. 2003. "The Lopsided Continent: Inequality in Latin America." *Annual Review of Sociology* 29: 363–390.

Holston, James. 2009. "Insurgent Citizenship in an Era of Global Urban Peripheries." *City and Society* 21(2): 245–267.

Holston, James, and A. Appadurai. 1999. "Introduction: Cities and Citizenship." In J. Holston (ed.). *Cities and Citizenship*. Durham, NC: Duke University Press, 1–18.

ICCI [Instituto Científico de Culturas Indígenas]. 2001. *Taller intercultural de mujeres indígenas de poderes locales: Construyendo el poder local desde la diferencia.* Quito: ICCI.

INEC [Instituto Nacional de Estadística y Censos]. 2008. *Las mujeres indígenas del Ecuador: Condiciones de educación y uso de la lengua en el acceso al empleo.* Quito: Instituto Nacional de Estadística y Censos.

INEC Census. 2010. *Censo de Población y Vivienda 2010.* Quito: Instituto Nacional de Estadística y Censos.

INSTRAW [International Research and Training Institute for the Advancement of Women]. 2006. *Participación de las mujeres indígenas en los procesos de gobernabilidad y en los gobiernos locales: Bolivia, Colombia, Ecuador, Guatemala y Perú. Informe Principal.* Santo Domingo: INSTRAW.

Isin, Engin. 2012. "Citizenship after Orientalism: An Unfinished Project." *Citizenship Studies* 16(5–6): 563–72.

Isin, Engin, and G. Nielsen (eds.). 2008. *Acts of Citizenship.* London: Zed Books.

Jazeel, Tariq, and Colin McFarlane. 2010. "The Limits of Responsibility: A Postcolonial Politics of Academic Knowledge Production." *Transactions of the Institute of British Geographers* 35: 109–24.

Junta Nacional de Desarrollo. 1964. *Plan general de desarrollo económico y social 1964–1973.* Quito: Junta Nacional de Desarrollo.

Junta Nacional de Planificación. 1970. *El desarrollo del Ecuador 1970–1973.* Vols. 1–3. Quito: Junta Nacional de Planificación.

Kabeer, Naila. 1994. *Reversed Realities: Gender Hierarchies in Development Thought.* London: Verso.

Kapoor, Ilan. 2005. "Participatory Development, Complicity and Desire." *Third World Quarterly* 26(8): 1203–20.

Kapoor, Ilan. 2008. *The Postcolonial Politics of Development.* London: Routledge.

Kapur, R. 2002. "The Tragedy of Victimisation Rhetoric: Resurrecting the 'Native' Subject in International/Postcolonial Feminist Legal Politics." *Harvard Human Rights Journal* 15: 1–37.

Katz, Cindi. 2001a. "On the Grounds of Globalization: A Topography for Feminist Political Engagement." *Signs* 26(4): 1213–34.

Katz, Cindi. 2001b. "Vagabond Capitalism and the Necessity of Social Reproduction." *Antipode* 33: 709–28.

Kay, Cristobal. 1998. "Agrarian Reform in Latin America: Lights and Shadows." *Agrarian Reform/Reforme Agraire* [FAO] 6: 8–31.

Kellogg, Susan. 2005. *Weaving the Past: A History of Latin America's Indigenous Women from the Pre-Hispanic Period to the Present.* Oxford: Oxford University Press.

Klenk, Rebecca. 2004. "Who Is the Developed Woman? Woman as a Category of Development Discourse." *Development and Change* 35(1): 57–78.

Labao, L., and L. Brown. 1998. "Development Context, Regional Differences among Young Women, and Fertility: The Ecuadorian Amazon." *Social Forces* 76(3): 819–49.

Lang, Miriam, and Anna Kucia (eds.). 2009. *Mujeres indígenas y justicia ancestral.* Quito: UNIFEM.

Larrea Maldonado, C., et al. 2007. *Pueblos Indígenas, desarrollo humano y discriminación en el Ecuador*. Quito: Abya Yala-Universidad Andina Simón Bolívar.

Las tsachilas se alistan para ser lideresas. 2004. *Comercio* (Quito), 7 June.

Laurie, Nina, R. Andolina, and S. A. Radcliffe. 2005. "Ethnodevelopment: Social Movements, Creating Experts and Professionalising Indigenous Knowledge in Ecuador." *Antipode* 37(3): 470–95.

Laurie, Nina, and Pamela Calla. 2004. "Development, Postcolonialism, and Feminist Political Geography." In L. Staeheli et al. (eds.), *Mapping Women, Making Politics*. London: Routledge, 99–112.

Law, L. 1997. "Dancing on the Bar: Sex, Money and the Uneasy Politics of Third Space." In S. Pile and M. Keith (eds.), *Geographies of Resistance*. London: Routledge, 107–23.

Lazar, Sian. 2004. "Education for Credit: Development as a Citizenship Project in Bolivia." *Critique of Anthropology* 24(3): 301–19.

Lefebvre, Henri. 1971. *Everyday Life in the Modern World*. London: Penguin.

Legg, Stephen. 2007. "Beyond the European Province: Foucault and Postcolonialism." In J. Crampton and S. Eldon (eds.), *Space, Knowledge and Power*. Farnham, UK: Ashgate, 265–89.

Lemke, T. 2001. " 'The Birth of Bio-Politics': Michel Foucault's Lecture at the Colège de France on Neoliberal Governmentality." *Economy and Society* 30(2): 190–207.

León, M. 2010. "El 'Buen Vivir': Objetivo y camino para otro modelo." In I. León (ed.), *Sumak kawsay/Buen Vivir y cambios civilizatorios*. Quito: FEAPS, 105–23.

Lester, Alan. 2012. "Humanism, Race and the Colonial Frontier." *Transactions of the Institute of British Geographers* 37: 132–48.

Li, Tania M. 2000. "Articulating Indigenous Identity in Indonesia: Resource Politics and the Tribal Slot." *Comparative Studies in Society and History* 42(1): 149–79.

Li, Tania M. 2007. *The Will to Improve: Governmentality, Development, and the Practice of Politics*. Durham, NC: Duke University Press.

Li, Tania M. 2010. "Indigeneity, Capitalism and the Management of Dispossession." *Current Anthropology* 51(3): 385–414.

Lind, A. 2005. *Gendered Paradoxes: Women's Movements, State Restructuring and Global Development in Ecuador*. University Park, PA: Pennsylvania State University Press.

Lind, A. (ed.). 2009. *Development, Sexual Rights and Global Governance: Resisting Global Power*. London: Routledge.

Lind, A. 2012. " 'Revolution with a Woman's Face?' Family Norms, Constitutional Reform and the Politics of Redistribution in Postneoliberal Ecuador." *Rethinking Marxism* 24(4): 536–55.

Lind, A., and J. Share. 2003. "Queering Development: Institutionalized Heterosexuality in Development Theory, Practice and Politics in Latin America." In K. Bhavnani, J. Foran, and P. Kurian (eds.), *Feminist Futures: Re-imagining Women, Culture and Development*. London: Zed Books, 55–73.

Lindqvist, Sven. 1979. *Land and Power in Latin America*. London: Penguin.

Loomba, Ania. 2005. *Colonialism/Postcolonialism*. London: Routledge.

Lucero, José Antonio. 2008. *Struggles of Voice: The Politics of Indigenous Representation in the Andes*. Pittsburgh, PA: University of Pittsburgh Press.

Lugones, María. 2007. "Heterosexualism and the Colonial/Modern Gender System." *Hypatia* 22(1): 186–209.

Lugones, M. 2008. "Colonialidad y género." *Tabula Rasa* (Bogota) 9: 73–101.

Luykx, Aurolyn. 2000. "Gender Equity and Interculturalidad: The Dilemma in Bolivia Education." *Journal of Latin American Anthropology* 5(2): 150–78.

Macas, Luis. 2011. "Diferentes vertientes para un nuevo paradigma de desarrollo." In G. Weber (ed.), *Debates sobre cooperación y modelos de desarrollo*. Quito: CIUDAD, 47–60.

Maddox, L. 1991. "Bearing the Burden: Perceptions of Native American Women at Work." *Women: A Cultural Review* 2(3): 228–37.

Mahoney, James. 2010. *Colonialism and Postcolonial Development: Spanish America in Comparative Perspective*. Cambridge: Cambridge University Press.

Maiguashca, L. 1987. "Empleo y relaciones campo-ciudad en Santo Domingo de los Colorados." In S. Pachano (ed.), *Políticas agrarias y empleo en América Latina: Memoria del seminario*. Quito: Instituto de Estudios Ecuatorianos-ILDIS, 81–94.

Maldonado-Torres, Nelson. 2007. "On the Coloniality of Being: Contributions to the Development of a Concept." *Cultural Studies* 21 (2–3): 240–70.

Mandato 1 Cumbre. 2009. *Mandato de la I Cumbre Continental de Mujeres Indígenas de Abya Yala*. Puno, Peru: 1 Cumbre.

Marchand, Marianne. 2009. "The Future of Gender and Development after 9/11: Insights from Postcolonial Feminism and Transnationalism." *Third World Quarterly* 30(5): 921–35.

Marchand, Marianne, and Jane Parpart (eds.). 1995. *Feminism, Postmodernism, Development*. London: Routledge.

Martin, Patricia M. 2004. "Contextualizing Feminist Political Theory." In L. Staeheli et al. (eds.), *Mapping Women, Making Politics*. London: Routledge, 15–30.

Martinez Cobo, Jose R. 1983. *Study on the Problem of Discrimination against Indigenous Populations*. UN Commission of Human Rights, Subcommission on Prevention of Discrimination and Protection of Minorities, 36th Session. Final Report. Geneva, Switzerland: United Nations.

Martínez Flores, A. 2000. "Uso del género en las ONG de desarrollo rural." In M. Cuvi Sánchez et al. (eds.), *Discursos sobre género y ruralidad en el Ecuador: Década de 1990*. Quito: CONAMU, 71–97.

Mayoux, Linda. 2001. "Tackling the Downside: Social Capital, Women's Employment and Microfinance in Cameroon." *Development and Change* 32(3): 435–64.

Mbembe, Achille. 2003. "Necropolitics." *Public Culture* 15(1): 11–40.

McCall, L. 2005. "The Complexity of Intersectionality." *Signs* 30(3): 1771–800.

McClintock, Anne. 1995. *Imperial Leather: Race, Gender and Sexuality in the Colonial Conquest*. New York, Routledge.

McDowell, Linda. 1999. *Gender, Identity and Place: Understanding Feminist Geography*. Cambridge, UK: Polity.

McEwan, Cheryl. 2003. "Material Geographies and Postcolonialism." *Singapore Journal of Tropical Geography* 2(3): 340–55.

McEwan, C. 2009. *Postcolonialism and Development*. London: Routledge.

McIntyre, Michael, and Heidi J. Nast. 2011. "Bio(necro)polis: Marx, Surplus Populations and the Spatial Dialectics of Reproduction and 'Race.'" *Antipode* 43(5): 1465–88.

Medina, G., et al. 1999. *Género y páramo*. Quito: Abya Yala.

Meentzen, Angela. 2001. *Estrategias de desarrollo culturalmente adecuadas para mujeres indígenas*. Unidad de Pueblos Indígenas y Desarrollo Comunitario. Washington, DC: IADB.

Melamed, Jodi. 2006. "The Spirit of Neoliberalism from Racial Liberalism to Neoliberal Multiculturalism." *Social Text* 2(4): 1–24.

Memmi, Albert. 2003 [1957]. *The Colonizer and the Colonized*. London: Earthscan.

Méndez Torres, G. 2009. "Miradas de género de las mujeres indígenas en Ecuador, Colombia y México." In A. Pequeño (ed.), *Participación y políticas de las mujeres indígenas en América Latina*. Quito: FLACSO, 53–71.

Merry, Sally. 2006. "Transnational Human Rights and Local Activism: Mapping the Middle." *American Anthropologist* 10(1): 38–51.

Mignolo, Walter. 2000. *Local Histories/Global Designs: Coloniality, Subaltern Knowledges and Border Thinking*. Princeton, NJ: Princeton University Press.

Mignolo, Walter. 2005. *The Idea of Latin America*. London: Blackwell.

Minaar, R. 1998. "Género dentro de un discurso étnico: El ejemplo del movimiento indígena en el Ecuador." In G. León (ed.), *Ciudadanía y participación política: Memoria del Simposio*. Quito: Abya Yala, 69–80.

Minh-ha, Trinh. 1989. *Woman, Native, Other: Writing Postcoloniality and Feminism*. Bloomington: Indiana University Press.

Minority Rights Group. 2012. *State of the World's Minority and Indigenous Peoples*. London: Minority Rights Group.

Minteguiaga, Amalia, and Gemma Ubasart. 2014. "Menos mercado, igual familia: Bienestar y cuidados en el Ecuador de la Revolución Ciudadana." *Íconos* 50: 77–96.

Mitchell, Kathryne. 1993. "Multiculturalism, or the United Colors of Capitalism?" *Antipode* 25(4): 263–94.

Mohanty, Chandra T. 1988. "Under Western Eyes: Feminist Scholarship and Colonial Discourses." *Feminist Review* 30: 61–88.

Mohanty, Chandra T. 1991. "Cartographies of Struggle: Third World Women and the Politics of Feminism." In Chandra T. Mohanty et al. (eds.), *Third World Women and the Politics of Feminism*. Bloomington: Indiana University Press.

Mohanty, Chandra T. 1999. "Crafting Feminist Genealogies: On the Geography and Politics of Home, Nation and Community." In E. Shohat (ed.), *Talking Visions: Multicultural Feminism in a Transnational Age*. Cambridge, MA: MIT Press, 485–500.

Mohanty, Chandra T. 2002. "'Under Western Eyes' Revisited: Feminist Solidarity through Anticapitalist Struggles." *Signs* 28(2): 499–535.

Molyneux, Maxine. 2002. "Gender and the Silences of Social Capital: Lessons from Latin America." *Development and Change* 33(2): 167–88.

Molyneux, Maxine. 2006. "Mothers at the Service of the New Poverty Agenda: Progresa/Oportunidades, Mexico's Conditional Transfer Program." *Social Policy and Administration* 40(4): 425–49.

Molyneux, Maxine. 2008. "The Neoliberal Turn and New Social Policy in Latin America." *Development and Change* 39(5): 775–97.

Molyneux, Maxine, and Sian Lazar. 2003. *Doing the Rights Thing: Rights-Based Development and Latin American NGOs.* London: Intermediate Technology Publishing Group.

Molyneux, Maxine, and S. Razavi (eds.). 2003. *Gender Justice, Development and Rights.* Oxford: Oxford University Press.

Montenegro, R., and C. Stephen. 2006. "Indigenous Health in Latin America and the Caribbean." *Lancet* 367: 1855–69.

Moore, Donald S. 1997. "Remapping Resistance: 'Ground for Struggle' and the Politics of Place." In S. Pile and M. Keith (eds.), *Geographies of Resistance.* London: Routledge, 87–106.

Moore, Henrietta. 1994. *A Passion for Difference.* Cambridge, UK: Polity.

Moser, Annalise. 2004. "Happy Heterogeneity: Feminism, Development and the Grassroots Movement in Peru." *Feminist Studies* 30(1): 211–37.

Mosse, David. 1994. "Authority, Gender and Knowledge: Theoretical Reflections on the Practice of Participatory Rural Appraisal." *Development and Change* 25: 497–526.

Mukhopadhyay, M., and N. Singh (eds.). 2007. *Gender Justice, Citizenship and Development.* New Delhi, India: Zubaan.

Muratorio, Blanca. 1994. *Imágenes e imagineros: Representaciones de los indígenas ecuatorianos, siglos XIX y XX.* Quito: FLACSO Sede Ecuador.

Nagar, Richa. 2004. "Mapping Feminisms and Difference." In L. Staeheli et al. (eds.), *Mapping Women, Making Politics: Feminist Perspectives on Political Geography.* London: Routledge, 31–48.

Nagar, Richa, Victoria Lawson, and Linda McDowell. 2002. "Locating Globalization: Feminist (Re)readings of the Subjects and Spaces of Globalization." *Economic Geography* 78: 257–84.

Nelson, Diane. 1999. *Finger in the Wound: Body Politics in Quincentennial Guatemala.* Berkeley: University of California Press.

Nelson, Lise. 2006. "Artesanía, Mobility and the Crafting of Indigenous Identities among Purhépechan Women in Mexico." *Journal of Latin American Geography* 5(1): 51–77.

Noxolo, P., P. Raghuram, and C. Madge. 2012. "Unsettling Responsibility: Postcolonial Interventions." *Transactions of the Institute of British Geographers* 37(3): 418–29.

O'Connor, Erin. 2007. *Gender, Indian Nation: The Contradictions of Making Ecuador, 1830–1925.* Tucson: University of Arizona Press.

Okin, Susan. 1999. *Is Multiculturalism Bad for Women?* Princeton, NJ: Princeton University Press.

Oliart, Patricia. 2008. "Indigenous Women's Organizations and the Political Discourses of Indigenous Rights and Gender Equity in Peru." *Latin American and Caribbean Ethnic Studies* 3(3): 291–308.

O'Neill, Onora. 2000. *Bounds of Justice.* Cambridge: Cambridge University Press.

Pacari, Nina. 1998a. "La mujer indígena, medio ambiente y biodiversidad." In R. Torres Galarza (ed.), *Derechos de los pueblos indígenas.* Quito: CONAIE-CEPLAES-Abya Yala, 17–27.

Pacari, Nina. 1998b. "La mujer indígena: Reflexiones sobre su identidad de género." In G. León (ed.), *Ciudadanía y participación política: El abordaje de género en América Latina y su incidencia en los cambios socio-políticos.* Quito: Abya Yala, 59–68.

Pacari, Nina. 2002. "La Participación Política de la Mujer en el Congreso ecuatoriano: Una tarea pendiente." In M. Méndez-Montalvo and J. Ballington (eds.) *Mujeres en el Parlamento: Más allá de los números.* Stockholm: International Institute for Democracy and Electoral Assistance, 45–60.

PAHO. 2003. *La pertinencia de los modelos de atención específicos para mujeres afroecuatorianas e indígenas afectadas por la violencia familiar.* Cuenca, Ecuador: PAHO.

Palacios, Paulina. 2005. "Construyendo la diferencia en la diferencia: Mujeres indígenas y democracia plurinacional." In P. Dávalos (comp.), *Pueblos Indígenas, estado y democracia.* Buenos Aires: CLACSO, 311–39.

Palacios, Paulina, and Vicenta Chuma. 2001. "El sistema de formación de mujeres líderes indígenas Dolores Cacuango." *Boletín ICCI Rimay* 3 (28) (July).

Paredes, Julieta. 2010. *Hilando Fino desde el Femenismo Comunitario.* La Paz, Bolivia: Mujeres Creando.

Parpart, Jane L. 1995. "Deconstructing the Development 'Expert': Gender, Development and the 'Vulnerable Groups.'" In M. Marchand and J. L. Parpart (eds.), *Feminism, Postmodernism, Development.* London: Routledge, 221–43.

Paulson, Susan. 2002. "Placing Gender and Ethnicity on the Bodies of Indigenous Women and in the Work of Bolivian Intellectuals." In R. Montoya et al. (eds.) *Gender's Place: Feminist Anthropologies of Latin America.* Basingtoke, UK: Palgrave Macmillan, 135–154.

Paulson, Susan, and Pamela Calla. 2000. "Gender and Ethnicity in Bolivian Politics: Transformation or Paternalism?" *Journal of Latin American Anthropology* 5: 112–49.

Pazmiño, A. 2008. "Objetivos de desarrollo del milenio: Las opciones para las mujeres indígenas." In L. Donato (ed.), *Mujeres indígenas, territorialidad y biodiversidad en el contexto latinoamericano.* Bogota: Universidad Nacional de Colombia-UNODC, 253–62.

Peake, Linda, and Alissa Trotz. 1999. *Gender, Ethnicity and Place: Women and Identities in Guyana.* London: Routledge.

Peake, Linda, and Alissa Trotz. 2002. "Feminism and Feminist Issues in the South." In V. Desai and R. Potter (eds.), *The Companion to Development Studies.* London: Arnold, 334–38.

Peck, Jamie, and N. Brenner. 2009. "Postneoliberalism and Its Discontents." *Antipode* 41: 94–116.

Pequeño, Andrea (ed.). 2009. *Participación y políticas de mujeres indígenas en América Latina*. Quito: FLACSO-Ministerio de Cultura.

Peredo Beltrán, E. 2004. *Una aproximación a la problemática de género y etnicidad en América Latina*. Serie Mujer y Desarrollo 53. Santiago: CEPAL.

Perreault, Thomas. 2003. "A People with Our Own Identity: Towards a Cultural Politics of Development in the Ecuadorian Amazon." *Society and Space* 21(5): 583–606.

Perry, S., and C. Schenck (eds.) 2001. *Eye to Eye: Women practicing development across cultures*. London: Zed Books.

Pettit, J., and J. Wheeler. 2005. "Developing Rights? Relating Discourse to Context and Practice." *IDS Bulletin* 36(1): 1–8.

Phillips, Anne. 1995. *The Politics of Presence: The Political Representation of Gender, Ethnicity and Race*. Oxford: Clarendon Press.

Phillips, Anne, and S. Saharso. 2008. "The Rights of Women and the Crisis of Multiculturalism." *Ethnicities* 8(3): 291–301.

Phillips, Lynne. 1987. "Women, Development and the State in Rural Ecuador." In C. Deere and M. León (eds.), *Rural Women and State Policy*. Boulder: Westview, 105–23.

Pigg, Stacy Leigh. 1992. "Inventing Social Categories through Place: Social Representations and Development in Nepal." *Comparative Studies in Society and History* 34(3): 491–513.

Pile, Steve. 1994. "Masculinism, the Use of Dualistic Epistemologies and Third Spaces." *Antipode* 26(3): 255–77.

PIO Chimborazo. 2005. *Las Mujeres de Chimborazo construyendo el Plan de Igualdad de Oportunidades*. Riobamba, Ecuador: CONAMU-Municipio de Riobamba-CEDIS.

Poeschel-Rens, U. 2003. "Las marcas de la violencia en la construcción sociohistórica de la identidad femenina indígena." *Debate* 59.

Ponce, J., and A. Acosta. 2010. "La pobreza en la 'revolución ciudadana' o pobreza de revolución?" *Ecuador Debate* 81: 7–20.

Pontón, J., and D. Pontón. 2008. *Situación de las mujeres rurales: Ecuador*. Santiago, Chile: FAO.

Postero, Nancy. 2006. *Now We Are Citizens: Indigenous Politics in Postmulticultural Bolivia*. Stanford, CA: Stanford University Press.

Povinelli, Elizabeth. 2005. "A Flight from Freedom." In A. Loomba (ed.), *Postcolonial Studies and Beyond*. Durham, NC: Duke University Press, 145–65.

Pratt, Gerry. 2005. "Abandoned Women and Spaces of Exception." *Antipode* 37: 1052–78.

Prieto, Mercedes. 2004. *Liberalismo y temor: Imaginando a los sujetos indígenas en Ecuador postcolonial, 1895–1950*. Quito: Abya Yala.

Prieto, Mercedes (ed.). 2005. *Mujeres ecuatorianas: Entre las crisis y las oportunidades, 1990–2004*. Quito: FLACSO-CONAMU-UNFPA-UNIFEM.

Prieto, Mercedes. 2008. "Rosa Lema y la Misión cultural ecuatoriana indígena a Estados Unidos: Turismo, artesanías y desarrollo." In C. De la Torre and M. Salgado (eds.), *Galo Plaza y su época*. Quito: FLACSO-Fundación Galo Plaza Lasso, 157–91.

Prieto, Mercedes. 2015. *Estado y colonialidad: Mujeres kichwas de la sierra del Ecuador, 1925–1975.* Quito: FLACSO.

Prieto, Mercedes, C. Cumiñao, A. Flores, G. Maldonado, and A. Pequeño. 2005. "Las mujeres indígenas y la búsqueda del respeto." In Mercedes Prieto (ed.), *Mujeres ecuatorianas: Entre las crisis y las oportunidades.* Quito: FLACSO-CONAMU-UNFPA-UNIFEM, 155–94.

Quijano, Aníbal. 2000. "El fantasma del desarrollo en América Latina." *Revista Venezolana de Economía y Ciencias Sociales* 6(2): 73–90.

Quijano, Aníbal. 2007. "Colonialidad de poder y clasificación social." In S. Castro-Gómez and R. Grosfoguel (eds.), *El giro decolonial.* Bogota: Universidad Central, 93–126.

Quintero López, R. 2008. *La constitución del 2008: Un análisis político.* Quito: Abya Yala.

Radcliffe, Sarah A. 1996. "Gendered Nations: Nostalgia, Development and Territory in Ecuador." *Gender, Place and Culture* 3(1): 5–21.

Radcliffe, Sarah A. 2002. "Indigenous Women, Rights and the Nation-State in the Andes." In N. Craske and M. Molyneux (eds.), *Gender and the Politics of Rights and Democracy in Latin America.* London: Palgrave, 149–72.

Radcliffe, Sarah A. 2005. "Development and Geography II: Towards a Postcolonial Development Geography?" *Progress in Human Geography* 29(3): 291–98.

Radcliffe, Sarah A. 2007a. "Latin American Indigenous Geographies of Fear: Living in the Shadow of Racism, Lack of Development and Anti-Terror Measures." *Annals of the Association of American Geographers* 97(2): 385–97.

Radcliffe, Sarah A. 2007b. "Tejiendo redes: Organizaciones y capital social en los pueblos indígenas." In S. Marti i Puig (ed.), *Pueblos Indígenas y Política en América Latina.* Barcelona: CIDOB, 31–56.

Radcliffe, Sarah A. 2008. "Las mujeres indígenas ecuatorianas bajo la gobernabilidad multicultural y género." In P. Wade et al. (eds.), *Raza, etnicidad y sexualidades: Ciudadanía y multiculturalismo en América Latina.* Bogota: Universidad del Valle-Universidad del Estado de Rio de Janeiro-Universidad Nacional de Colombia, 105–36.

Radcliffe, Sarah A. 2010. "Epílogo: Historias de vida de mujeres indígenas a través de la educación y el liderazgo: Intersecciones de raza, género y locación." In V. Coronel and M. Prieto (eds.), *Celebraciones centenarias y negociaciones por la nación ecuatoriana.* Quito: FLACSO-Ministry of Culture, 317–48.

Radcliffe, Sarah A. 2012. "Development for a Postneoliberal Era? *Sumak Kawsay,* Living Well and the Limits to Decolonization in Ecuador." *Geoforum* 43(2): 240–49.

Radcliffe, Sarah A. 2014a. "Plural Knowledges and Modernity: Social Difference and Geographical Explanations." In K. Okamoto and Y. Ishikawa (eds.), *Traditional Wisdom and Modern Knowledge for the Earth's Future.* Tokyo: Springer, 79–102.

Radcliffe, Sarah A. 2014b. "Gendered Frontiers of Land Control: Indigenous Territory, Women and Contests over Land in Ecuador." *Gender, Place and Culture* 21(7): 854–71.

Radcliffe, Sarah A. Forthcoming. "The Difference Indigeneity Makes: Socio-Natures, Knowledges and Contested Policy in Post-neoliberal Ecuador." In M. Raftopoulos and M. Coletta (eds.), *Environmental Debates and Policies in Latin America.* London: Institute of Latin American Studies.

Radcliffe, Sarah A., R. Andolina, and N. Laurie. 2002. "Re-territorialised Space and Ethnic Political Participation: Indigenous Municipalities in Ecuador." *Space and Polity* 6(3): 289–305.

Radcliffe, Sarah A., and N. Laurie. 2006. "Culture and Development: Taking Indigenous Culture Seriously in the Andes." *Society and Space* 24(2): 231–48.

Radcliffe, Sarah A., N. Laurie, and R. Andolina. 2004. "The Transnationalization of Gender and Re-imagining Andean Indigenous Development." *Signs* 29(2): 387–416.

Radcliffe, Sarah A., with A. Pequeño. 2010. "Ethnicity, Development and Gender: Tsáchila Indigenous Women in Ecuador." *Development and Change* 41(6): 983–1016.

Rai, Shirin (ed.). 2003. *Mainstreaming Gender, Democratizing the State?* Manchester: Manchester University Press.

Ramalingam, Ben. 2013. *Aid on the Edge of Chaos.* Oxford: Oxford University Press.

Ramírez Gallegos, Franklin. 2001. *La política de desarrollo local en dos cantones indígenas del Ecuador.* Quito: Cuidad.

Ramírez Gallegos, R. 2008. *Igualmente Pobres, Desigualmente Ricos.* Quito: UNDP.

Ramón, G., and V. H. Torres. 2004. *El desarrollo local en el Ecuador: Historias, actores y métodos.* Quito: Abya Yala-COMUNIDEC.

Rankin, Katherine R. 2001. "Governing Development: Neoliberalism, Microcredit and National Economic Woman." *Economy and Society* 30(1): 18–37.

Rankin, Katherine R. 2010. "Reflexivity and Postcolonial Critique: Toward an Ethics of Accountability in Planning Praxis." *Planning Theory* 9(3): 181–99.

Rappaport, Joanne. 2005. *Intercultural Utopias.* Durham, NC: Duke University Press.

Rathgeber, Eva M. 1990. "WID, WAD, GAD: Recent Trends in Research and Policy." *Journal of Developing Areas* 24: 489–502.

Razack, Sherene H. (ed.). 2002. *Race, Space and the Law: Unmapping a White Settler Society.* Toronto: Between the Lines.

Rens, Jef. 1965. "Le programme des indiens des Andes. L'intégration des populations aborigènes dans les plans nationaux de développement économique." *Tiers Monde* 6(21): 41–55.

Rens, Marjan. 2003. *Mitad del Mundo: Mujeres, identidad y simbolismo en Ecuador.* Quito: Abya Yala-Fundación Marjan Rens.

Richards, Patricia. 2004. *Pobladoras, Indígenas and the State: Conflicts over Women's Rights in Chile.* London: Rutgers University Press.

Richards, P. 2007. "Bravas, Permitidas, Obsoletas: Mapuche Women in the Chilean Print Media." *Gender and Society* 21(4): 553–78.

Rivera Cusicanqui, Silvia. 2006. "Chhixinakax utxiwa: Una reflexión sobre prácticas y discursos descolonizadores." In M. Yupi (ed.), *Modernidad y pensamiento descolonizador.* La Paz, Bolivia: PIEB-Instituto Francés de Estudios Andinos, 3–16.

Rivera Cusicanqui, Silvia. 2010. "The Notion of 'Rights' and the Paradoxes of Postcolonial Modernity: Indigenous Peoples and Women in Bolivia." *Qui Parle* 18(2): 29–54.

Rivera Cusicanqui, S. 2012. "Ch'ixinakax Utxiwa: A Reflection on the Practices and Discourses of Decolonization. *South Atlantic Quarterly* 111(1): 95–109.

Roberts, E. F. S. 2012. "Scars of Nation: Surgical Penetration and the Ecuadorian State." *Journal of Latin American Anthropology* 17(2): 215–37.

Rodríguez, G. A. 2007. "Derechos de las mujeres indígenas en Colombia." In L. Donato et al.(eds.), *Mujeres indígenas, territorialidad y biodiversidad en el contexto latinoamericano*. Bogota: Universidad Nacional de Colombia, 113–25.

Rodríguez, Lilia. 2010. "Género y etnia, los cruces de las inequidades en salud." In M. Chiriboga et al. (eds.), *Salud, interculturalidad y derechos*. Quito: Abya Yala, 149–61.

Romo Leroux de Morales, Kitty. 1975. *Situación jurídica y social de la mujer en el Ecuador*. Guayaquil: Universidad de Guayaquil.

Rose, Gillian. 1995. "The Interstitial Perspective: A Review Essay on Homi Bhabha's *The Location of Culture*." *Society and Space* 13(3): 365–73.

Rose, Nikolas. 1996. "Governing 'Advanced' Liberal Democracies." In A. Barry et al. (eds.), *Foucault and Political Reason: Liberalism, Neoliberalism and Rationalities of Government*. Chicago: University of Chicago Press, 37–64.

Rose, Nikolas, and Peter Miller. 2008. *Governing the Present: Administering Economic, Social and Personal Life*. Cambridge, UK: Polity.

Rosero Garcés, R., and A. Reyes Ávila. 1997. *Es como la luna nuestro pensamiento . . . Testimonios e historias de mujeres de Chimborazo*. 2nd ed. Alausí, Ecuador: Proyecto Desarrollo de la Mujer Rural en la Provincia de Chimborazo.

Safa, Helen. 2005. "Challenging Mestizaje: A Gender Perspective on Indigenous and Afrodescendent Movements in Latin America." *Critical Anthropology* 25(3): 307–29.

Said, Edward. 1993. *Culture and Imperialism*. London: Chatto and Windus.

Saldana, P., and T. Paz y Miño. 1999. *Hacia la equidad: Proyectos de mujer y género en el Ecuador*. Quito: CONAMU.

Salman, T., and A. Zoomer (eds.). 2003. *Imaging the Andes: Shifting Margins of a Marginal World*. Amsterdam: CEDLA.

Sanchez-Pérez, H. J., G. Vargas Morales, and J. M. Jansá. 2006. "Vida y salud de la mujer en zonas de alta marginación en México. Es peor ser indígena?" In A. Cimadamore et al. (eds.), *Pueblos indígenas y pobreza: Enfoques multidisciplinarios*. Buenos Aires: CLACSO-CROP.

Sawyer, S. 2004. *Crude Chronicles: Indigenous Politics, Multinational Oil and Neoliberalism in Ecuador*. Durham NC: Duke University Press.

Schech, S. and J. Haggis. (eds.) 2000. *Culture and Development: A Critical Introduction*. London: Wiley-Blackwell.

Schild, Veronica. 1998. "New Subjects of Rights? Women's Movements and the Construction of Citizenship in the New Democracies." In S. Alvarez, E. Dagnino, and A. Escobar (eds.), *Cultures of Politics, Politics of Cultures: Re-visioning Latin American Social Movements*. Boulder: Westview, 93–117.

Schuler, S. R., M. E. Choque, and S. Rance. 1994. "Misinformation, Mistrust and Mistreatment: Family Planning among Bolivian Market Women." *Studies in Family Planning* 25(4): 211–21.

Schurr, Carolin. 2013. *Performing Politics, Making Space: A Visual Ethnography of Political Change in Ecuador*. Stuttgart: Franz Steiner Verlag.

Schurr, C., and D. Segebart. 2012. "Engaging with Feminist Postcolonial Concerns through Participatory Action Research and Intersectionality." *Geographica Helvetica* 67: 147–54.

Scott, Catherine V. 1995. *Gender and Development: Modernization and Dependency Theory Reconsidered*. Boulder: Lynne Rienner.

Secretaría Técnica de Frente Social. 1998. "Retrato de las mujeres: Indicadores sociales sobre la situación de las indígenas y campesinas del Ecuador rural." *Serie: El desarrollo social en el Ecuador #2*. Quito: SIISE-Frente Social.

Selmeczi, Anna. 2009. "'. . . We Are Being Left to Burn because We Do Not Count': Biopolitics, Abandonment and Resistance." *Global Society* 23(4): 519–38.

Seminario Internacional. 1992. *Seminario Internacional de Mujeres Indígenas de las Américas. Memoria: Documentos y Conclusiones*. Santa Cruz, Bolivia: Liga Internacional de Mujeres pro-Paz y Libertad.

Sen, Gita, and Caren Grown. 1987. *Development Crises and Alternative Visions: Third World Women's Perspectives*. New York: Monthly Review Press.

Sharp, Joanne. 2009. *Geographies of Postcolonialism: Spaces of Power and Representation*. London: Sage.

Shaw, Wendy, R. Herman, and R. Dobbs. 2006. "Encountering Indigeneity: Reimagining and Decolonizing Geography." *Geografiska Annaler B* 88(3): 267–76.

Shohat, Ella. 1998. Introduction to E. Shohat (ed.), *Talking Visions: Multicultural Feminism in a Transnational Age*. Cambridge, MA: MIT Press, 1–63.

Shrestha, Nanda. 1995. "Becoming a Development Category." In J. Crush (ed.), *Power of Development*. London: Routledge, 266–77.

Sidaway, James. 2012. "Geographies of Development: New Maps, New Visions?" *Professional Geographer* 64(2): 1–14.

Sieder, Rachel (ed.). 2002. *Multiculturalism in Latin America*. London: Palgrave-Macmillan.

Smith, Neil. 2008 [1984]. *Uneven Development*. 3rd ed. Athens: University of Georgia Press.

Sniadecka-Kotarska, M. 2001. *Antropología de la mujer andina. Biografías de mujeres indígenas de clase media y su identidad*. Quito: Abya Yala.

Speed, Shannon, Aída Hernández, and Lynn Stephen (eds.). 2006. *Dissident Women: Gender and Cultural Politics in Chiapas*. Austin: University of Texas Press.

Spivak, Gayatri C. 1993 [1988]. "Can the Subaltern Speak?" In P. Williams and L. Chrisman (eds.), *Colonial Discourse and Postcolonial Theory: A Reader*. London: Harvester, 66–111.

Staeheli, Lynn. 2011. "Political Geography: Where's Citizenship?" *Progress in Human Geography* 35(3): 393–400.

Staeheli, L., E. Kofman, and L. Peake (eds.). 2004. *Mapping Women, Making Politics: Feminist Perspectives on Political Geography*. London: Routledge.

Stavenhagen, Rodolfo. 1986. "Ethnodevelopment: A Neglected Dimension in Development Thinking." In R. Apthorpe (ed.), *Development Studies: Critique and Renewal*. Leiden: Brill, 71–94.

Stephen, Lynn. 2005. *Zapotec Women: Gender, Class and Ethnicity in Globalized Oaxaca*. 2nd ed. Durham, NC: Duke University Press.

Stoler, Laura A. 1995. *Race and the Education of Desire: Foucault's "History of Sexuality" and the Colonial Order of Things*. Durham, NC: Duke University Press.

Stoler, Laura A. 2002. *Carnal Knowledge and Imperial Power: Race and the Intimate in Colonial Rule*. Berkeley: University of California Press.

Strobele-Gregor, J. 2008. "Ciudadanía y mujeres indígenas: El debate en Ecuador." In S. Kron and K. Noack (eds.), *Qué género tiene el derecho? Ciudadanía, historia y globalización*. Berlin: Tranvía-Verlag Walter Frey, 143–69.

Suárez, Liliana, and Aída Hernández Castillo (eds.). 2008. *Descolonizando el feminismo: Teorías y prácticas desde los márgenes*. Valencia: Cátedra Universidad de Valencia.

Sundberg, Juanita. 2014. "Decolonizing Posthumanist Geographies." *Cultural Geography* 21(1): 33–47.

Swanson, Kate. 2007. " 'Bad Mothers' and 'Delinquent Children': Unravelling Antibegging Rhetoric in the Ecuadorian Andes." *Gender, Place and Culture* 14(6): 703–20.

Swyngedouw, Erik. 1999. "Modernity and Hybridity: Nature, Regeneracionismo, and the Production of the Spanish Waterscape, 1890–1930." *Annals of the Association of American Geographers* 89(3): 443–65.

Sylvester, Christine. 1999. "Development Studies and Postcolonial Studies: Disparate Tales of the 'Third World.' " *Third World Quarterly* 20(4): 703–21.

Sylvester, Christine. 2006. "Bare Life as a Development/Postcolonial Problem." *Geographical Journal* 172(1): 66–77.

Sylvester, Christine. 2011. "Development and Postcolonial Takes on Biopolitics and Economy." In J. Pollard et al. (eds.), *Postcolonial Economies*. London: Zed Books, 185–204.

Telles, E. 2007. "Race and Ethnicity and Latin America's United Nations Millennium Development Goals." *Latin American and Caribbean Ethnic Studies* 2(2): 185–200.

Tene, Carmen. 2000. "Ruptura de la exclusión de mujeres indígenas." In *Seminario "Mujer: Participación y Desarrollo."* Quito: CORDES, 199–224.

Tene, C., et al. 2004. *Programas de microcrédito y capital social entre mujeres indígenas*. Quito: World Bank.

Terán, Pacha. 2004. "Intervención de la delegada del Movimiento Pachakutik-Nuevo Pais." In M. F. Cañete (ed.) *Reflexiones sobre la Mujer y Política*. Quito: Abya-Yala, 83–88.

Terborgh, A., et al. 1995. "Family Planning among Indigenous Populations in Latin America." *International Family Planning Perspectives* 21(4): 143–66.

Thomas, C. 2001. "Global Governance, Development and Human Security: Exploring the Links." *Third World Quarterly* 22(2): 159–75.

Transition Commission. 2011. *Plan de Igualdad, no discriminación y buen vivir para las mujeres ecuatorianas. Marco conceptual, ruta metodológica y estrategia de transversalización 2010–2014*. Cuaderno de Trabajo, January. Quito: Comisión de Transición hacia el Consejo de las Mujeres y la Igualdad de Género.

Transition Commission. 2014. *Agenda Nacional de las Mujeres y la Igualdad de Género 2014–2017*. February. Quito: Comisión de Transición de Género-SENPLADES.

Tsikata, D. 2004. "The Rights-Based Approach to Development: Potential for Change or More of the Same?" *IDS Bulletin* 35(4): 130–33.

Tuhiwai Smith, L. 2012. *Decolonizing Methodologies: Research and Indigenous Peoples.* 2nd ed. London: Zed Books.

Tyner, James A. 2013. "Population Geography I: Surplus Populations." *Progress in Human Geography* 37(5): 701–11.

UN DESA [United Nations Department of Economic and Social Affairs]. 2007. *Indigenous Women and the United Nations System: Good Practices and Lessons Learnt.* New York: United Nations.

UNDP [United Nations Development Program] et al. 2005. *Fortalecimiento del goce de los derechos humanos y los derechos colectivos por parte de los pueblos indígenas en el Ecuador.* Quito: UNDP.

UNIFEM [United Nations Development Fund for Women]. 2008. *Qué está pasando con los derechos de los pueblos indígenas? Estudio sobre buenas prácticas.* Comité para la Eliminación de Discriminación en contra de la Mujer. Bolivia, Ecuador y Perú. Managua: CADPI.

Valdivia, Gabriela. 2009. "Indigenous Bodies, Indigenous Minds? Towards an Understanding of Indigeneity in the Ecuadorian Amazon." *Gender, Place and Culture* 16(5): 535–51.

Van Cott, Donna L. 2000. *The Friendly Liquidation of the Past: The Politics of Diversity in Latin America.* Pittsburgh, PA: University of Pittsburgh Press.

Van der Hoogte, Liesbeth, and Koos Kingma. 2004. "Promoting Cultural Diversity and the Rights of Women: The Dilemmas of Intersectionality for Development Organisations." *Gender and Development* 12(1): 47–55.

Vega Ugalde, S. 2005. "La cuota electoral en Ecuador: Nadando a contracorriente en un horizonte esperanzador." In M. León (ed.), *Nadando contra la corriente: Mujeres y cuotas políticas en los países andinos.* Quito: UNIFEM-UNFPA-FLACSO, 169–206.

Vega Ugalde, S. 2007. "The Role of the Women's Movement in Institutionalizing a Gender Focus in Public Policy: The Ecuadorian Experience." In S. Rai (ed.), *Mainstreaming Gender, Democratizing the State.* Manchester, UK: University of Manchester Press, 117–29.

Velasque, C. 2008. "Testimonio de mi experiencia como mujer, indígena y política con los medios de comunicación." In M. F. Cañete (ed.), *Asamblea, Democracia, Medios de Comunicación.* Quito: Abya-Yala, 81–90.

Velástegui, H. 1984. *Santo Domingo de los Colorados.* Quito: Ediciones Culturales.

Veloz, Alexandra. 1997. "Mujer: Autoestima y éxito." *Yamaipacha Boletín Informativo* (Quito) 2: 9.

Ventura, Monserrat. 1997. "Una visión de la cultura Tsáchila en la actualidad." In J. Juncosa (ed.), *Etnografías mínimas del Ecuador.* Quito: Abya Yala, 1–32.

Ventura, M. 2012. *En el cruce de caminos: Identidad, cosmología y chamanismo tsachila.* Quito: FLACSO-Abya Yala.

Vinding, D. 1998. *Indigenous Women: The Right to a Voice.* Copenhagen: IWGIA.

Volpp, L. 2001. "Feminism versus Multiculturalism." *Columbia Law Review* 101: 1181–218.

Wade, Peter. 2009. *Race and Sex in Latin America.* London: Pluto.

Wainwright, Joel. 2008. *Decolonizing Development: Colonial Power and the Maya.* Oxford: Blackwell.

Walby, S. 2005. "Gender Mainstreaming: Productive Tensions in Theory and Practice." *Social Policy* 12(3): 321–43.

Walsh, Catherine. 2009a. *Interculturalidad, estado, sociedad.* Quito: Universidad Andina-Abya Yala.

Walsh, Catherine. 2009b. "The Plurinational and Intercultural State: Decolonization and State Re-founding in Ecuador." *Kult* 6: 65–84.

Walsh, Catherine. 2010. "Development as *Buen Vivir*: Institutional Arrangements and (De)colonial Entanglements." *Development* 53(1): 15–21.

Walsh, Catherine, F. Schiwy, and S. Castro-Gómez (eds.). 2009. *Indisciplinar las ciencias sociales: Geopolíticas del conocimiento y colonialidad de poder. Perspectivas desde lo andino.* Quito: Universidad Andina-Abya Yala.

Warren, Kay, and Jean Jackson (eds.). 2003. *Indigenous Movements, Self-Representation, and the State in Latin America.* Austin: University of Texas Press.

Watts, Michael J. 2003. "Development and Governmentality." *Singapore Journal of Tropical Geography* 24(1): 6–34.

Weismantel, Mary J. 2001. *Cholas and Pishtacos: Stories of Race and Sex in the Andes.* Chicago: University of Chicago Press.

White, Sarah. 2002. "Thinking Race, Thinking Development." *Third World Quarterly* 23(3): 407–19.

White, Sarah. 2006. "The Gender Lens: A Racial Blinder?" *Progress in Development Studies* 6(1): 455–67.

Wright, Melissa. 2001. "A Manifesto against Femicide." *Antipode* 33(3): 550–66.

Yashar, Deborah. 2005. *Contesting Citizenship in Latin America: The Rise of Indigenous Movements and the Postliberal Challenge.* Cambridge: Cambridge University Press.

Yeh, Emily. 2007. "Tropes of Indolence and the Cultural Politics of Development in Lhasa, Tibet." *Annals of the Association of American Geographers* 97(3): 593–612.

Young, Iris M. 1990. *Justice and the Politics of Difference.* Princeton, NJ: Princeton University Press.

Young, Robert J. C. 1995. *Colonial Desire: Hybridity in Culture, Theory and Race.* London: Routledge.

Yúdice, George. 2004. *The Expediency of Culture: Uses of Culture in the Global Era.* Durham, NC: Duke University Press.

Yuval-Davis, Nira. 2006. Intersectionality and Feminist Politics. *European Journal of Women's Studies* 13(3): 193–209.

Yuval-Davis, Nira, and Floya Anthias. 1989. *Woman-Nation-State.* Basingstoke, UK: Macmillan.

INDEX

Page references in italics indicate illustrations, and t indicates a table.

abandonment, 17–18, 293n23. *See also* ethnic topographies of labor, racism, and abandonment

abjection: definition of, 292n11; economic, 6; of indigenous/racialized women, 155, 160, 171, 176, 178, 213; neoliberal interpretations of, 165; and vulnerability, 149, 178

abortion, 209, 315n19

ACDI-FUNDAMYF (Agricultural Cooperative Development International–Fundación Mujer y Familia Andina), 108, 112, 319n18

addition, metaphors of, 301n66

adoption, 316n22

Africa, development in, 26

Agamben, Giorgio, 295n3

Agrarian Census (2003), 110

agrarian frontier programs, 50

Agrarian Reform (1964), 48

Agrarian Reform (1973), 297n25

Alausí (Chimborazo province, Ecuador): comunas in, 230; EU rural women's project in, 133–38, *135*, 146, 171, 175, *177*; indigenous majority in, 128, 136; poverty in, 133; women's health rights in, 315n6; women's role in government in, 248

Alianza País party, 320n27

Aliméntate Ecuador, 322n10

allegados/arrimados system, 41

Almeida, Milena, 166–67

Alonso, Ana Maria, 194

Amazonia, 48–50, 61, 297–98n29, 305n33, 306n48, 315n6, 318n6

American Indians, 289–90

Ana (case study), 94–95, 228

Ana Maria (case study), 135, 137, 169, 245–46

Andean Mission, 45–46, *46*, 297n19

Andrade, María, 80, 183, 276

Andrea (case study), 229, 240

Anthias, Floya, 194, 310n26

antiviolence statutes, 249

Aurora (case study), 2, 5, 23, 205, 241, 252, 318n9

axis, definitions of, 72–73

Aysabucha, Magdalena, 117, 173, 178, 280, 311n32, 313n17

Ayuda Popular Noruega (APN), 320n33

bananas, 50, 86–87, 303nn17–18

Banivanua, T., 41

bare life, 38–39, 99, 207, 257, 277, 279, 295n3

Bebbington, Anthony, 52–53, 77

Bhabha, Homi: on coloniality, 16–17, 63, 285, 313n20; on the epistemic violence of the postcolonial system, 43; on ethnic performance, 298n35; on female indigeneity, 63, 165; on global postcolonial dynamics, 294n31; on third space, 195, 211 biopolitics, 193–206; and citizenship, 20; cultural decline, 209–10; definition of, 293n29; family size, 201–5, 215; fertility, 206, 314n2, 315n16 (see also family planning methods/programs); Foucault on, 194, 293n29; and health rights/services, 196–206, 200t, 315nn6–8, 315nn10–11, 315n19, 316n25; of indigeneity/indigenous populations, 39–40; infant mortality, 199, 202, 314n2, 316n21, 316n29; intercultural health policy, 211–13, 316–17nn36–38; and the intercultural justice system, 219; and intercultural third space, 211, 214, 222–23; men's role in sexual-reproductive health, 204–6, 215, 316n25; overview of, 193–96

Blaser, Mario, 129, 155

BNF (National Investment Bank), 111

Bolivia, 161, 282–83, 300n54, 324n58

bono payments. See human development bond

border knowledges/thinking, 26, 113, 258–59, 277–78, 307–8n75

Bronstein, Audrey, 38

budgeting, participatory, 138–39

buen vivir/sumak kawsay (living well) development, 257–90; and border thinking, 258–59, 277–78; and citizenship, 21; CONAIE on, 266, 275; definition of, 259–60; emergence and adoption as policy, 35, 258; genealogy of, 260, 322n7; indigenous women's role in/critiques of, 267–73, 281, 323n37, 324n40; meaning of, 321n1; and new developmentalism, 259–61, 322n5, 322nn8–11; overview of, 35, 257–59, 321nn1–3; and Pachamama, 266–67, 272–74, 276–78, 288; and the plurinational state, 266, 274–75, 278–83; and poverty, 269; rights-based development's influence on, 22; and social heterogeneity, 261–67, 283, 285–86, 288, 290, 322nn12–13, 322nn16–17, 323nn21–22, 323n24; women's decolonial interpretation of sumak kawsay,

273–83, 324nn57–58. See also National Development Plans

Cacuango, Dolores, 136, 296n12, 309n15

Caguana, Delia, 23, 179, 181, 189, 275, 291n1, 324n50

cajas (credit clubs): benefits/critiques of, 121, 123, 144; definition of, 112; education funded via, 307n73; gender inequality in, 142, 310n25, 310n27; number of, 141; and participation vs. organization, 143; women's organization/politicization via, 123, 146, 307n74

Calazacón, Abraham, 92, 318n1

Cañar province (Ecuador), 175

Carmen (case study), 75, 233, 252–53, 318n5

Catholic Church, 84, 95, 234, 237, 303n11, 317n44, 319n12

CCT (Conditional Cash Transfer), 228, 265, 270, 323n21. See also human development bond

CEDAW Convention (Convention for the Elimination of Discrimination against Women; 1979), 171–72, 250, 272, 294n39, 299n38, 313n29, 319n23

Cervone, Emma, 60, 308n2

CGLA (association of alternative local governments), 320n33

Chambers, Robert, 134

Chancosa, Blanca, 173

Chatterjee, Partha, 20–21

Chibber, Vivek, 291–92nn7–8, 314n31, 324n59

child care, 90–91

Chimborazo province (Ecuador), 2; comunas in, 230; demographics of, 77, 302n2; development institutions in, 128; farms in, 84, 302n5; grassroots organizations in, 128; HDI for, 77, 128, 302n2, 309n3; health care in, 132; illiteracy rates in, 45; labor/attendance requirements in, 1–2; labor markets in, 47; map of, 31; migration from, 47; population of, 77; poverty in, 99, 295n48; vs. Santo Domingo province,

78–79t (see also ethnic topographies of
labor, racism, and abandonment); social difference/development in, 68–69t;
women's activism in, 216–17. See also
Puruhá pueblo
cholas, 83, 101
Chují, Monica, 268
Chuma, María Vicenta, 59, 71, 180
Chunchi (Chimborazo province, Ecuador), 133–38, 135, 146, 171, 175, 177
Circunscripciones Territoriales Indígenas
(Indigenous Territorial Circumscriptions; CTIS), 323n24
citizenship: vs. bare life, 99, 279; and
buen vivir, 21; insurgent, 236, 254–55;
and participation and indigenous
women's organization, 155–56; and
postcolonial intersectionality/develop-
ment, politics of, 20–25, 294nn30–36;
as practices vs. interventions, 20; substantive, 293n29. See also rights, voice,
and citizenship practices
Ciudad Juarez (Mexico), 219
civil organizations, indigenous, 300n49
Claudia (case study), 114, 134–35, 253
cocoa/cacao, 86, 303nn17–18
CODENPE (Council of Nationalities and
Peoples of Ecuador), 150, 249, 266;
Baños public policy meeting (2010),
179; on collective vs. individual rights,
267; vs. CONAMU, 54; and the Correa
government, 323n23, 323n37; development with identity devised by, 54;
Dolores Cacuango training school co-
funded by, 169; establishment of, 61;
funding for, 323n22; grants to women
vs. men, 153; programs of, 61; staff of,
65; women's participation in, 153–54,
311n49. See also PRODEPINE
Colombia, 161
coloniality: alienation of, 176, 313n20;
colonial difference, definition of,
292n16; and data gathering, 173 (see
also under "indigenous women" policy);
decoloniality, definition of, 294n38;
definition of, 15; of GAD, 13; internal colonies, 15–16, 41, 77, 96, 160,

296n6; and modernity, 6, 10, 16, 25;
and postcolonial intersectionality, 7,
14–20, 292–93nn20–28. See also buen
vivir/sumak kawsay development;
decolonizing social difference, overview of
Colta (Chimborazo province, Ecuador):
comunas in, 230; economy of, 240;
indigenous majority in, 128, 189;
women's groups/leadership in, 217,
237, 245, 320n32
COMICG (Canton Guamote Women's
Organization), 247–48
COMICH (Confederation of the Chimborazo Indigenous Movement), 189, 221,
321n39
complementarity, 59, 144, 154, 299n46
COMPOCIECH (Confederation of evangelical indigenous peoples, organizations
and communities of Chimborazo),
190
comunas (communities): creation of,
43, 230; decapitalization of, 296n6;
decision-making in, 230–36, 318n7,
318n10; and feminist politics, 23; gen-
der/class difference in, 140, 142–44,
152, 310n31; indígenas associated
with/subsumed into, 59, 104, 141;
indigenous mobilization based on,
230, 296n14; membership in, 230–32,
318n7; postcolonial expectations
about, 70; state recognition of, 210;
women's status in, 230–32, 318n10;
work parties in, 235
CONAIE Women's Office, 295n42; on
buen vivir, 266, 275; on gender violence, 222–23; and IBIS, 165; indígenas' participation in public policy encouraged by, 164, 280; on international
rights instruments, 250; landscapes/
livelihoods defended by, 53; on plurinationalism, 266, 279; Political and
Strategic Agenda, 184–85; on the quota
law, 244; on quota/prowomen laws,
244; on sexuality/reproduction issues,
207–9, 208, 223; workshops held by,
152–53, 207–8

CONAMU (National Women's Council), 311n48; abolition of, 263 (*see also* transition commissions); vs. CODENPE, 54; contact with indigenous women, 149; criticisms of, 58; on cultural rights, 313n21; data gathered by, 170–71, 312–13n16; establishment of, 55, 299n39; feminist ties of, 55; gender equity promoted by, 319n25; gender policy oversight by, 55; goals of, 55; on indigenous women as leaders, 163–64; on indigenous women's vulnerability/ lack of agency, 66, 172; PIO (Plan for Equal Opportunities), 132, 150–51, 265–66; and PRODEPINE, 140; on toxic waste spills, 199; user committees registered with, 130–31; on violence against women, 313n28; women's organizations registered with, 309nn12–13; on women's work hours, 308n83

Concepción (case study), 75, 111, 203, 228–29, 234, 237–38, 240

CONMIE (National Council of Indigenous Ecuadorian Women), 177

Consejo Nacional de Desarrollo, 59, 297n19, 308n83

conservation agendas, 276

Constituent Assembly, 156, 258, 263

Constitution (Ecuador, 1998), 301n71

Constitution (Ecuador, 2008), 35, 156, 259–60, 263–64, 268, 271–80, 311n48, 316n19, 323n24

Continental Summit of Indigenous Women of Abya Yala (Colombia, 2013), 272–73

contraception. *See* family planning methods/programs

Convention for the Elimination of Discrimination against Women. *See* CEDAW Convention

cooking, 91, 97

Cornwall, Andrea, 14, 126, 138, 140

Corporación Educativa Macac, 148, 311n35

Correa, Rafael, 320n27

Cotopaxi province (Ecuador), 101, 109, 115–16, 244, 304n23, 312n11

counter-topography. *See* ethnic topographies of labor, racism, and abandonment

CPME (Political Coordinator of Ecuadorian Women), 55, 299n41

crafts, 87, 90

credit, 111–12, 307nn69–70. *See also* cajas; microcredit

Cristina (case study), 167, 172, 199, 228, 232, 241, 253, 318n1

culture: vs. psychology, 291–92nn7–8; social neoliberal politics of, 147–54, 311n38, 311n42, 311nn49–50; strengthening of, 51, 298n32. *See also* ethnodevelopment

Curicama, Mariano, 247, 314n1 (Interlude)

cut-flower industry, 304n25

Cuvi Sanchez, M., 70, 110

Decade for Indigenous Peoples (1995–2004), 160

Decade for Women (1975–1985), 160

Declaration of Barbados (1971), 298n34

decolonizing social difference, overview of, 32, 35, 257–59, 283–90. *See also* buen vivir/sumak kawsay development

De la Cadena, Marisol, 276–78, 297n27, 298n31

development with identity, 54, 63. *See also* ethnodevelopment

Dietz, Mary G., 226, 250, 294n30

"dignified salary" law, 322n8

dignified work, 268, 323n27

discursive colonialism, 15

dispossession, definition of, 292n15

diversity: within diversity, 24, 118, 145, 155, 186–87, 213–14, 258, 272, 286–87, 324n57; racial-ethnic, Ecuadorian, 291n2; UN on, 292n17. *See also* multicultural reforms/multiculturalism

divorce, 231–32, 317n42

DNSPI (National Health Directorate of Indigenous Peoples), 212–13, 317n38, 317n41, 317n44

Dolores Cacuango training school, 168–69, 222, 227, 249, 312nn12–13 domestic servants: and education, 318n4; indigenous men as, 307n64; labor protection for, 318n3; migrants as, 88–89; pay/benefits for, 269

domestic violence, 132, 217–23, 218, 221, 249, 263–64, 318n51

DRI (Desarrollo Rural Integrado) programs, 110

dynamic nominalism, 165

Earth Mother, 296n13. *See also* Pachamama

Ecuador: discrimination in, 62; economy of, 39–40, 48, 297n26; HDI for, 302n2, 309n3; independence of, 39; indigenous population size, 298n32; land ownership in, 47–48, 297n22, 297n25; triple oppression of indigenous women in, 67, 70

Ecuarunari (Andean federation), 149, 168, 274, 320n33. *See also* Dolores Cacuango training school

education: attendance rates by gender and ethnicity, 92, 306n46; average years of, 305n43, 305–6n45; barriers to, 92–96, 94, 305n37, 305n39, 305–6nn41–46; Dolores Cacuango training school, 168–69, 222, 227, 249; expansion of, 305n42; and family planning, 204; night school, 93–94; primary, 92–96, 305n42, 322n9; regional schools, 312n11; rights to, 253; secondary, 92–95, 172, 211, 305n39, 305n44, 307n60, 322n9; training schools, 320n37; training workshops, 113–16, 308n78; university, 93, 305n41; women as educators, 87–88; women's, household decisions about, 307n60

El Búa (Ecuador), 305n39, 310n25

electricity, 91

Elizabeth (case study), 85, 252, 321n46

Elvira (case study), 142, 238, 319n19, 321n46

Engle, Karen, 265

Enlightenment thinking, 313n20

epidermalization of marginalization, 17, 101

epistemic violence: Bhabha on, 43; definition of, 296n8; indigenous women's experience of, 101, 117, 206; of single issue development, 285; against subaltern knowledges, 27, 113, 185–86

Equality Plan (Women of Chimborazo Constructing an Equal Opportunity Plan; 2005), 118, 154

ERPE (Popular Radio Schools of Ecuador), 303n11

Escobar, Arturo, 10, 15, 259, 292n10

essentialism, 118–19, 174–78

ethnic communities. *See* comunas

ethnicity, meanings of, 293n22

ethnic movements, 43, 72–73, 209, 216, 241–42, 317n45. *See also* ethnic rights movements

ethnic politics and gendered contradictions, 193–223; indigenous movements and intercultural agendas, 206–11, 208, 316n31; intercultural health policy, 211–13, 316–17nn36–38; overview of, 32, 35, 193–96, 314n1 (ch. 5); SRH (sexual and reproductive health), 194–98, 200t, 204–5, 207, 211, 213–14, 217, 219, 222–23; women's agenda added to interculturalism, 213–22, 218, 221, 317n42, 317nn44–45, 317n47, 318nn50–51. *See also* biopolitics

ethnic rights forums, 308n80

ethnic rights movements, 138, 145, 223, 250, 257, 272. *See also* ethnic movements

ethnic topographies of labor, racism, and abandonment, 75–119; capabilities/education, 92–96, 94, 305n37, 305n39, 305–6nn41–46; counter-topography, definition of, 75–76; discontent with postcolonial development, 106–18, 307n74, 308n78, 308n80, 308n83; overview of, 75–77, 78–79t, 118–19; and power/essentialism, 118–19; racialization/gendering experiences, 101–6, 118–19, 306n55, 306n57, 307nn60–65; resource control by Kichwa and Tsáchila women, 75–77,

ethnic topographies of labor, racism, and abandonment (*continued*)
96–100, 98, 100, 306nn47–48; topography, definition of, 301–2n1; work/livelihood, 80–92, 81, 302nn3–8, 303n12, 303nn14–18, 303n20, 304–5nn23–33, 305n35

ethnobotanical knowledge, 212, 317n37

ethnodevelopment, 72, 74, 301n66; and colonial thinking, 54, 63; and community, 65, 143, 310n31; emergence of, 60, 139; and GAD, 64; and gender, 54–55, 59, 61, 64–67, 68–69t, 72 (*see also under* participation and indigenous women's organization); as protection of tradition, 34; as racialized, 61–62, 62, 65, 67; and social capital, 141; training in, 301n63; World Bank's support for, 66. *See also* PRODEPINE

"ethnoracial," definition of, 293n22

EU rural women's project, 133–38, 135, 146, 171, 175, 177

family farms, 48, 80, 86, 270

family planning methods/programs, 197, 199–206, 208–9, 214–15, 315n8, 315nn16–17, 316nn23–25

family size, 201–5, 215

Fanon, Frantz, 25–26, 40–42, 101, 176

FEINE (Council of Evangelical Indigenous Peoples and Organizations of Ecuador), 190

feminism: vs. complementarity, 59; in Ecuador, 55; feminist geography, 302n1; global colonial politics of, 149; on household structures, 66; indigenous women's critiques of, 179–80, 222; on mainstreaming, 301n70; vs. multiculturalism, 63–65, 300n57, 300n59, 301n61; on self-esteem, 176–77; on thirdworldwomen, 23

FEPP (Ecuadorian Fund for Popular Progress), 307n68

Ferguson, James, 270, 299n44

fertility, 206, 314n2, 315n16. *See also* family planning methods/programs

feudal peonage relations, 41

firewood, 97

First Nations, 289–90

Florinda (case study), 83–84, 201–2, 205

flower farms, 59, 300n48. *See also* cut-flower industry

FODEPI credit program, 70–71

FODERUMA (Fund for Rural Marginal Development), 58, 110

Fondo Indígena, 312n12

food sovereignty, 263, 322–23n17, 323n26

Foucault, Michel, 194, 291n5, 293n29, 307–8n75

Fraser, Nancy, 241–42

Free Maternity Services Law (Ecuador, 2006), 128

Fuss, Diane, 64

Gabriela (case study), 107–8, 125, 200, 233, 318n4

GAD (gender and development) policy: coloniality of, 13, 177, 313n22; and data gathering, 170; on empowerment/self-esteem, 175–76; and ethnodevelopment, 64; goals of, 37; and hidden histories, 54–55, 58–60, 299nn38–41, 299n43, 299n46; vs. multiculturalism, 54, 147; vs. participatory development, 133; western female-male relations promoted by, 34. *See also* participation and indigenous women's organization

Garcés Dávila, Alicia, 216–17

gender: electoral gender quotas, 242–44, 247, 250, 319nn23–24; and ethnicity, 63–65; and ethnodevelopment, 54–55, 59, 61, 64–67, 68–69t, 72 (*see also under* participation and indigenous women's organization); formalization of rights, 292n18; indigenous women's critiques of concept of, 180–82, 186; inequality based on, 38, 294n36, 299n38; mainstreaming of, 55, 180, 299n40; policies on, 133 (*see also* CONAMU; ethnic politics and gendered contradictions; GAD policy; participation and indigenous women's organization); solidarity based on, 59; violence based on, 132, 217–23, 218, 221, 249, 263–64, 318n51

Gender Mainstreaming Action Plan, 164

genocide, ethnic, 208–9

Gioconda (case study), 200, 203, 215, 222, 235, 237

Gonzalez Casanova, Pablo, 49, 101, 296n42

gossip/social discourses, 99–100

"green economy" initiatives, 276

Gregory, Derek, 38

Grewal, Inderpal, 80, 292n13

group-purity guidelines, 210–11

Guamote (Chimborazo province, Ecuador): comunas in, 230; ecotourism in, 116–17; EU rural women's project in, 133–38, 135, 146, 171, 175, 177; haciendas in, 41, 47, 97; health care in, 132; indigenous majority in, 128, 136, 138, 309n10; poverty in, 133, 138, 309n10; tribute relations in, 42; women's activism in, 217; women's role in government in, 247–48

Guatemala, 300n54

HDI (Human Development Index), 77, 128, 294n35, 302n2, 309n3

healers (yachaqs), 215

health care: and attitudes toward indigenous women, 111, 198, 212; and bare life, 99; caesareans, 200, 315n18; infant/child mortality, 102, 306n57; intercultural health policy, 211–13, 316–17nn36–38; maternal/infant laws/programs, 99, 128–33, 131, 309n6, 309n8; maternal mortality, 197–99, 208, 213, 309n8; during pregnancy and childbirth, 129, 131, 197–99, 306n57, 315n10; racialized access to, 99, 197, 206; sterilization, 315n11, 315–16n19; UN on, 209; women's activism on, 133, 214 (see also under interculturalism); and women's expertise in childbirth, 216. See also family planning methods/programs

heterogeneity, social. See social difference and development

Hodgson, Dorothy L., 26

Holston, James, 236

household structures, 65–66, 301n64

Huacho, Maria, 182–83

huasicama, 42

huasipungo system, 40–42, 47–49, 297n24

human development bond (bono de desarrollo humano), 228, 252, 265, 270, 323n21

Human Development Index. See HDI

hunting, 50, 86–87

IADB (Inter-American Development Bank), 161–65

IBIS (Ibis Education for Development), 165–69

ICCI (Scientific Institute of Indigenous Cultures), 169, 249, 312n12, 320n33

ID cards, 225–30, 318n1

illiteracy, 45, 94, 161, 294n37, 305n37, 305n42, 323n32. See also literacy programs

ILO (International Labor Organization) Convention 169, 250, 300n50, 316–17n36

income/wage inequalities, 323n27; gender-based, 11, 87, 89, 143, 304nn23–24, 304n26, 304n32, 307n61; Gini coefficient in Ecuador, 11, 24–25; race-/ethnicity-based, 11, 24–25, 61–62, 62, 300n55, 307n63; in rural vs. urban areas, 11, 88

indigeneity/indigenous populations: agricultural work by rural, indigenous women, 80–81, 81; biopolitics of, 39–40; and complementarity, 59, 144, 154, 299n46; definition of, 18, 293n21, 293n24; development of indigenous populations (see ethnodevelopment); vs. gender issues, 54, 298nn36–37; indígena, definition of, 19, 32, 293n25; indigenous, definition of, 17; indigenous masculinities, 293n26, 293n28; international law on, 298n35; and male-female difference, 18–19, 22; in postcolonial intersectionality, 17–20; poverty linked with, 80–81, 104, 300n55, 302n3 indigenous movements: health policy's response to, 195; and intercultural agendas, 195, 206–11, 208, 316n31; successes/failures of, 189–91

"indigenous women" policy, 157–87; and at-risk populations, 157–58, 171–73, 185; data on "indigenous women" category, 170–74, 312–13nn15–16, 313n18; Dolores Cacuango training school, 168–69, 222, 227, 249, 312nn12–13; emergence of "indigenous women" category, 157–58, 160, 164, 169–70; and grassroots movements, 162–63, 185; IBIS, 165–68, 312n8; indigenous women as development experts, 178–86, 181, 313nn28–29, 314n31, 314n35, 314n38 (see also UNIFEM); male attitudes toward women's public role, 167–68, 186, 312n10, 314n38; overview of, 32, 34–35, 185–87; political governance, 159–65, 162, 312n4; and self-esteem, 174–78, 182; and social networks, 164

infant/child mortality, 102, 199, 202, 306n57, 314n2, 316n21, 316n29

informal sector, 82–83

informed consent, 53, 181

INGO (international nongovernmental organization), 165

INNFA (National Children and Family Institute), 88

interculturalism: and collective rights, 151–52; CONAMU on, 151, 311n42; definitions of, 151–53, 195; health policy, 211–13, 316–17nn36–38; and indigenous movements, 195, 206–11, 208, 316n31; justice system, 219–20; national cohesion advocated by, 150; as a third space, 195, 207, 211, 214, 222; women's agenda added to, 213–23, 218, 221, 317n42, 317nn44–45, 317n47, 318nn50–51. See also plurinational state

intersectionality. See postcolonial intersectionality

interviews, 295n46

irrigation systems, 97–98

Joaquina (case study), 220, 234

Julia (case study), 166, 231, 233–34

Kaplan, Caren, 80, 292n13

Kapur, Ilan, 126, 146, 148

Katz, Cindi, 75–76, 106, 301–2n11

Kichwa language, 31–32

Kichwa people, 31–32, 295n47. See also under ethnic topographies of labor, racism, and abandonment

labor. See ethnic topographies of labor, racism, and abandonment

land use: in Chimborazo, 84, 87, 302n5; family farms, 48, 80, 86, 270; flower farms, 59, 300n48; Kichwa, 85–86; by rural heads of households, 96–97, 306nn47–48; in Santo Domingo, 86, 303n17; smallholder farms, 47, 97, 297–98n29; Tsáchila, 85–86, 303n18; and Tsáchila-mestizo marriages, 210–11. See also ethnic topographies of labor, racism, and abandonment

Law 103 (against gender violence), 132

Lefebvre, Henri, 295n42

Lemke, T., 70, 174–75, 212

Levantamientos Indígenas (popular uprisings), 62, 190, 238, 239

Ley contra la violencia a la mujer y la familia (Law against violence against women and families), 299n39

LGBTTI (lesbian, gay, bisexual, transgender, travesti, and intersex) individuals, 264

Li, Tania Murray, 29, 158

liberalism, 21. See also neoliberalism

life histories, 295n41

Lind, Amy, 58, 264–65

Lisa (case study), 89, 229–30, 240, 271, 316n24

literacy programs, 95–96. See also illiteracy

Llankari Warmi (Entrepreneurial Woman) scheme, 70

Lucía (case study), 113, 215, 252–53

Lugones, María, 18, 76

machista (patriarchal) society, 306n55

Magdalena (case study), 89, 91, 220, 235, 318n5, 321n43

Mahoney, James, 16, 34, 43

mainstreaming: feminism on, 301n70; of gender, 55, 164, 180, 299n40; institutional, 263, 322n16

Maldonado-Torres, Nelson, 27, 60, 289

malnutrition, 82, 102, 199, 315n15

Mapuche women (Chile), 159–60, 295n2

Margarita (case study), 2, 5, 23

Maria (case study), 202, 319n20

Maria Petrona (case study), 201, 205, 210, 240, 316n23

marriage: and comuna membership, 231–32, 318n7; group-purity guidelines for, 210–11; husbands as primary household decision-makers, 111, 307n69; marital status on ID cards, 229; racialized-gendered-rural subjectivities of, 102–5; women's age at, 196, 199, 201, 210. See also domestic violence

Marta (case study), 215, 220, 229

Marxism, 314n39

maternal mortality, 197–99, 208, 213, 309n8

Maternity Law, 132, 146, 216–17, 309n8

Mayo, Norma, 112–13, 117–18

McEwan, Cheryl, 21, 176–77, 292n10

medicine, traditional, 212

Meentzen, Angela, 127, 170, 308n83

mejoradoras del hogar (female household improvers), 45–46

Memmi, Alberti, 41–42

Menchú, Rigoberta, 164, 246

Mercedes (case study), 88, 114, 218, 240–42, 252

mestizaje (racial ideology), 53, 89, 176, 194–96, 327

mestizo developmentalism, 48, 50–53, 58, 60, 64, 297n27, 298n35

Mexico, 67, 70, 300nn54–55

microcredit, 60, 70–71, 112, 263–64, 301n69

midwives, 45–46, 102, 198, 213, 215, 317n47

Mignolo, Walter, 307–8n75

migrants: Chimborazo's, 304n27; as domestic servants, 88–89; female, 304nn27–29; male, 88, 111

Millennium Developmental Goals, 3, 185, 294n39, 313n29, 324n40

Minh-ha, Trinh, 119

minimum wage, 88, 260

Ministry of Agriculture (Ecuador): EU rural women's project, 133–38, 135, 146, 171, 175, 177; FODERUMA, 58, 110; Household Improvement Department, 46; Rural Development division, 297n19

Ministry of Social Welfare (Ecuador), 49, 51

Mireya (case study), 200–201, 231

mobile cohabitation of differences, 187

Mohanty, Chandra, 15, 27, 183, 311n36

Molyneux, Maxine, 9, 58, 129, 141, 255

more-than-human politics, 98, 267, 275–79, 281–83, 289–90. See also Pachamama

Morona Santiago (Ecuador), 45

Mosse, David, 115–16, 126, 166

mothers-in-law, 220

multicultural reforms/multiculturalism, 21–23, 54, 61–63, 73, 147, 222–23, 300n52. See also under feminism

Nancy (case study), 204, 233, 253, 319n16

Nariz del Diablo tourist site, 90

National Council of Equality for Nationalities and Pueblos, 266

National Development Council (Ecuador), 51

National Development Plans (Ecuador), 55, 58–59, 258–59, 281, 321n2

nationality, definition of, 17

National Planning Secretariat. See SENPLADES

national secretariat of indigenous peoples, 145–46, 311n35

National Social Development Plan (Ecuador, 1996), 70, 148–49, 311n38

National Women's Council. See CONAMU

National Women's Service (Chile), 295n2

Naula, Rosario, 248

neoliberalism: cultural politics of, 9, 174–75, 322n5; and poverty, 53; social, 9–10, 53, 63–67, 68–69t, 70–71 (*see also under* participation and indigenous women's organization); technologies of, 132–33, 174–75

New Poverty Agenda, 128–29

NGOs (nongovernmental organizations), 161, 162, 180. *See also specific* NGOs

Nira (case study), 100, 204

Nizag (Chimborazo province, Ecuador), 90, 116

O'Connor, Erin, 298n36, 304n27

ODM. *See* Millennium Developmental Goals

Office of Indian Affairs (Ecuador), 51

Office of Indigenous Affairs (Ecuador), 298n32

oil revenues/prospecting, 48–49, 52, 93, 298n33

Okin, Susan, 300n59

O'Neill, Onora, 185–86, 314n36

Orellana province (Amazonia, Ecuador), 197

organizing. *See* participation and indigenous women's organization

Orientalist discourses, 173

OSG (Organización de Segundo Grado), 309n4

Otavalo (Ecuador), 45, 176, 318n50

OTG (Organización de Tercer Grado), 309n4

Oxfam América, 308n78

Pacari, Nina, 80, 92, 164, 173, 179–80, 301n71, 312n2

Pachakutik party, 242–46, 312n12, 319n21, 320nn26–27

Pachamama (living earth), 83, 97, 266–67, 272–74, 276–78, 288

PAHO (Pan American Health Organization), 317nn37–38

Palacios, Paulina, 16, 42, 152, 239, 316n31

participation and indigenous women's organization, 125–56; and citizenship rights, 155–56; civic oversight and neoliberal technologies of development, 128–33, 131, 309n6, 309n8; codification of participation, 126; and empowerment, 133–39, 135, 309nn12–13, 310nn17–18; Equality Plan, 118, 154; ethnodevelopment, social capital, and gender, 139–47, 145, 310n23, 310nn25–27, 310n31, 311n35 (*see also* PRODEPINE); male attitudes toward, 137; overview of, 30–32, 34, 125–28, 154–56, 308–9nn2–5; vulnerability/culture, social neoliberal politics of, 147–54, 156, 311n38, 311n42, 311nn49–50

patriarchy, 180, 306n55

Peru, 11, 161, 308n78, 315n5, 315n11

Phillips, Anne, 63

Pilar (case study), 95, 204

PIO (Plan for Equal Opportunities), 132, 150–51, 265–66

Plans for Life, 324n55

Plaza, Galo, 45, 51, 52

plows, women's use of, 82

plurinational state, 184, 195, 266, 274–75, 278–83

postcolonial difference, 27–28, 37, 119, 206, 255

postcolonial intersectionality: and colonial legacies, 7, 14–20, 292–93nn20–28; definition of, 3, 6; and development/citizenship, politics of, 20–25, 294nn30–36; hierarchies of, 4–5, 8; importance in Latin America, 11; limitations of, 292n14; and social difference and development, 6–11, 292nn13–16

postcolonial intersectionality and the colonial present, 37–74; colonial histories of power/dispossession, 38–43, 296nn6–7, 296n12; colonialism in Africa, Asia, and France, 41–42, 296n9; comunas (communities), 43, 47; ethnodevelopment, 54–55, 59, 60–67, 62, 72, 74, 301n63, 301n66;

GAD and hidden histories, 54–55, 58–60, 299nn38–41, 299n43, 299n46; haciendas, 40–43, 47–48, 297n22, 297n24; huasipungo system, 40–42, 47–49, 297n24; "Indian" category, 42; indigenous women as development challenge, 46, 297n20; indigenous women's mobilizations, 47–48, 296n12; internal colonies, 41, 45, 50, 296n6, 296n12; mestizo communities, 40, 42, 44–45, 51, 298n30; mestizo developmentalism, 48, 50–53, 58, 60, 64, 297n27, 298n35; mid-twentieth-century (modernist) development, 43–53, 46, 52, 296–97nn17–21, 297nn24–26, 297–98nn29–31; overview of, 30–34, 37–38, 71–74; protests against, 53, 298n34; single issue thinking, overview of, 53–54, 56–57t, 71–73, 285–87, 298nn36–37; single issue thinking, persistence of, 64, 67, 70; social neoliberalism, 53, 63–67, 68–69t, 70–71; triple oppression of indigenous women, 38, 67, 70, 301n66; and the will to improve, 43–44
Postero, Nancy, 62–63
poverty: in Alausí, 133; and buen vivir, 269; in Chimborazo, 99, 295n48; development's goal of reducing, 20–21; in Guamote, 133, 138, 309n10; indigeneity linked with, 80–81, 104, 300n55, 302n3; neoliberal measures to alleviate, 53; New Poverty Agenda, 128–29; rates by racial-ethnic group, 62; rise in, 294n34; of rural women, 86, 294n37; in Santo Domingo province, 295n48; of women vs. men, 86, 303n21, 307n62
Povinelli, Elizabeth, 288
Pratt, Gerry, 38, 67, 70
prefects, 314n1 (Interlude)
pregnancies, unwanted, 206
Proaño, Leonidas, 303n11
PRODEPINE (Development Project for Indigenous and Afro-Ecuadorian Peoples), 128, 310n19, 310n29; and cajas, 141, 143, 310n25; CODENPE oversight of, 61, 139–40; critiques of, 143–45;

on data gathering, 313n18; goals of, 139–40; male-female difference in, 140–45, 147, 310n23; and social capital, 141; women's leadership/empowerment/participation promoted by, 161
PROLEAD (Program for the Support of Women's Leadership and Representation), 161
PRONADER (National Program of Rural Development), 175
provincial councils, 314n1 (Interlude)
pueblo, definition of, 17
Pumisacho, Dolores, 157
Punín (Chimborazo province, Ecuador), 121–22
Puruhá pueblo (Chimborazo province, Ecuador), 32, 69t, 77, 78t, 302n2

Quijano, Aníbal, 7–8, 39, 53
Quimiag (Chimborazo province, Ecuador), 47, 98, 181, 181
quinoa, 83–84, 237

racialization/racism: definition of, 292n15; discrimination/subordination, 11, 24, 51–52, 177–78, 182–83, 313n24; and family size, 202; importance of, 12; indigenous women on, 182–83, 313n29; race as a system of social difference, 292n15; race as historical, 293n22
railways, 296n7
Ramalingam, Ben, 287
REDD (reducing emissions through deforestation and degradation), 276
Renata (case study), 235, 253
rights, voice, and citizenship practices, 225–56; citizenship, conceptions of, 226–27, 254–55; citizenship via development and welfare, 227–30, 318nn2–5; community decision-making, 230–36, 318n7, 318n10; constitutional rights, 259; cultural rights, defined, 313n21; development projects linked to rights, 251, 254; electoral gender quotas, 242–44, 247, 250, 319nn23–24; ethnic rights movements, 138, 145, 223, 250,

rights, voice, and citizenship practices
(*continued*)
257, 272; gender violence, rights
against, 221–22; ID cards, 225–30,
318n1; indigenous women's definitions
of women's rights, 182; individual vs.
collective rights, 13–14, 151–52, 183,
267, 282–83, 311n42; international
formulations of indigenous rights,
300n50; local government, indigenous
women in, 242–50, 319–20nn21–29,
320nn31–33, 321n39; manuals on
rights and citizenship, 161, 162;
nature's rights, 267, 275–79, 282–83;
overview of, 32, 35, 225–27, 254–56;
rights, defined, 322n6; social security
rights, 229–30; SRR (sexual and
reproductive rights), 214, 222–23,
314n1 (ch. 5), 315n19; uneven access
to rights, 22–23; village leadership by
indigenous women, 236–42, 319n12,
319nn15–16, 319nn18–20; voting
rights, 161; voz y voto (voice and vote),
134, 232; women's conceptions of
rights, 249–54, 321nn41–46
Riobamba (Chimborazo province,
Ecuador), 39, 128
Rivera Cusicanqui, Silvia, 16, 278, 283,
324n57
roads, 98–99, 269, 296n7
Rosa (case study), 75, 251
Rosario (case study), 1–2, 23, 139, 253
Rose, Nikolas, 127, 159
Rosita (case study), 93, 228, 321n45
Rural Women's Support Program, 263

Said, Edward, 173
Santo Domingo city (Ecuador), 86, 100
Santo Domingo province (Ecuador): vs.
Chimborazo, 78–79t (*see also* ethnic
topographies of labor, racism, and
abandonment); demographics of, 77;
farms in, 303n17; map of, 33; poverty
in, 295n48; social difference/develop-
ment in, 68–69t; social programs in,
309n5; urbanization of, 77
savings-and-loan associations. *See* cajas

scattered hegemonies, 80, 292n13
Sebastiana (case study), 95, 225–26, 229,
235
Secretaría Técnica del Frente Social, 148
SEDRI program, 49
self-esteem, 174–78, 182
Sen, Amartya, 280
SENPLADES (National Secretariat for
Planning and Development), 242, 262,
274, 282
sexual and reproductive health. *See* SRH
sexual jealousy, male, 217–18
shigra bags, 90
silence, 219, 312n4
silencing, 182
Simbaña, Teresa, 177
single issue development. *See under*
postcolonial intersectionality and the
colonial present
single motherhood, 102, 202–3
smallholder farms, 47, 97, 297–98n29
Smith, Neil, 8, 296n5
social capital, 9, 61, 65, 141
social consensus, 34, 145, 257
social difference and development, 1–29;
development, definitions of, 5, 291n3;
knowledge production on postcolonial
development, 25–29, 294n37, 294n39,
295n41, 295nn44–46; local vs. global,
5, 291–92n7; overview of, 1–6, 29–30,
292n12; postcolonial difference, 27–28;
racial-ethnic diversity in Ecuador,
291n2; rural vs. urban populations,
4; social difference in development
thinking, 3–4, 11–14, 292nn17–18;
social heterogeneity, defined, 4, 291n4;
standard development categories,
8, 21; and the will to improve, 5–6,
292n10; women vs. men, 3. *See also*
buen vivir/sumak kawsay development;
decolonizing social difference; postcolonial intersectionality
social security rights, 229–30
social spending, 139, 179, 259–61, 265
socionatures, 97–98, 306nn49–50
Soledad (case study), 231, 235, 252
Sonia (case study), 113, 142, 233, 271

Spanish colonial power, 38–39. *See also* postcolonial intersectionality and the colonial present

Spanish language, 51, 96, 101, 103–4, 308n77

spatial strategies, 38

Spivak, Gayatri, 19–20, 27, 40, 74, 76, 106, 313n22

SRH (sexual and reproductive health), 194–98, 200t, 204–5, 207, 211, 213–14, 217, 219, 222–23. *See also* health care

SRR (sexual and reproductive rights), 214, 222–23, 314n1 (ch. 5), 315n19

Staeheli, Lynn, 163, 281, 302n1

Stavenhagen, Rodolfo, 296n42

sterilization, 315n11, 315–16n19

Stoler, Laura A., 61

subaltern category, 106, 292n19, 294–95n41

subaltern counter-publics, 241–42, 250

subaltern knowledges, 27, 113, 185–86, 289–90

subjugated knowledges, 307–8n75

Sucumbíos province (Ecuador), 182, 197, 309n8

Sucumbíos women's movement, 216, 318n50

sumak kawsay. *See* buen vivir/sumak kawsay development

Sylvester, Christine, 25, 196

Taulí Carpuz, Victoria, 71–72

Tene, Carmen, 43–44, 48, 180

Teresa (case study), 14–15, 231–32, 318n2

textiles, 39, 86–87

third space, 195, 207, 211, 214, 222–23

tourism, 87, 90

toxic waste spills, 199

transition commissions, 262–67, 272, 322n16; Transition Commission for Gender Equality (*formerly* CONAMU), 263–64, 311n48, 322nn12–13

transnational justice, 314n36

tribute obligations, 39, 42

Tsáchila people, 32, 33, 51, 52, 165–68, 210–11, 312n8. *See also under* ethnic topographies of labor, racism, and abandonment

Tsafiki language, 32

UN (United Nations): Beijing conference on women (1995), 12, 149, 299n40; Decade for Indigenous Peoples (1995–2004), 160; Decade for Women (1975–1985), 160; on diversity, 292n17; Durban conference on racism (2001), 12, 311n42; on indigenous populations, 18, 293n24; on midwives, 317n47; Permanent Forum on Indigenous Issues, 209; Task Force on Indigenous Women, 164–65

UNDP (United Nations Development Program), 164, 324n53

unemployment, female, 304nn31–32

UNESCO, 324n53

uneven development, 8; costs of, 186; definition of, 296n5; and developmental justice, 260; of education, 92–93; of health services/care, 197, 207–8, 212; rural internal colonies, 41, 77, 160; rural vs. urban living standards/welfare, 11; and sociospatial discourses/practices, 288–89; of women's lives/employment, 89

UNFPA (United Nations Population Fund), 207, 213, 324n53

UNIFEM (United Nations Development Fund for Women; *now* UN Women), 118, 161, 164, 183–84, 221, 249, 324n53

user committees (for health care oversight), 130–32

Vacacela, Rosa María, 179

Venezuela, 161

village leadership by indigenous women, 236–42, 319n12, 319nn15–16, 319nn18–20

Violeta (case study), 139, 203, 219, 232, 241, 251

Virginia (case study), 227, 252

voice. *See* rights, voice, and citizenship practices

Volpp, L., 64, 183, 294n31

vulnerability/culture, social neoliberal politics of, 147–54, 311n38, 311n42, 311nn49–50

WAD (women and development policy), 129, 141–42

wages. *See* income/wage inequalities

Walsh, Catherine, 259, 279

washing, 90–91

Washington Consensus, 9–10, 53

water sources, 91, 97–98

weaving, 90

welfare provisions, 270, 294n35

western skepticism toward subaltern knowledges, 289–90

WID (women in development policy), 160, 185, 314n35

widows, 231–32, 235, 240, 318–19n11

will to improve, 5–6, 43–44, 108, 160, 175, 285, 292n10

women: age at first birth, 196, 201, 309n8; age at first sexual experience, 313–14n3; age at marriage, 196, 199, 201, 210; average number of children, 196, 202, 309n8; as caregivers, 317n44; category of, in development thinking, 10; honesty and financial probity of, 310n26; participation in development (*see* participation and indigenous women's organization); solidarity among, 138; violence against, 132, 217–23, 218, 221, 249, 263–64, 318n51. *See also* gender; health care; village leadership by indigenous women

women and development policy (WAD), 129, 141–42

Women of Chimborazo Constructing an Equal Opportunity Plan (Equality Plan; 2005), 118, 154

Women's, Youth, Child and Family Commission, 299n39

Women's Commission (Tsáchila; Comisión de Mujer y Familia Tsáchila), 166–67, 312n8

women's groups/civic organizations, 213, 236–39, 241, 319n18. *See also* village leadership by indigenous women

women's houses (*casas de la mujer*), 135, 136

women's movement, 24, 55, 72–73, 292n18. *See also* CPME

World Conference on Indigenous Peoples (2014), 324n40

yucca, 86, 303n18

Yuval-Davis, Nira, 7, 194, 293n27, 310n26

We propose Living Well on the basis of the lifeways of our peoples, in which Living Well is living in a community, in brotherhood, and above all in complementarity. Living Well means to share, to complement each other, and not to compete, to live in harmony between people and nature, producing for our needs without ruining the surroundings. It is the basis for the defense of nature, of life itself, and all of humanity. It is the basis for saving humanity and the planet from the dangers of a minority that is individualistic and, above all, hugely selfish.

Face-to-face with the crisis, the Western world is worried. It does not know what to do. It is questioning itself and in search of alternative models and ways of life, since its values are in crisis. They need to get to know the values of the indigenous world, of Living Well. They are anxious to understand our forms of organization. They want to know how we indigenous people have guaranteed balance, how we live in harmony with nature.

Since the indigenous nations are the reserve of ancestral knowledge and of scientific knowledge of life to defend life, as the custodians of Mother Earth for thousands and thousands of years, during which we have lived in harmony with Her, we have the moral force to show the world the way toward the solution of these crises and to recover the health of Mother Earth.

Since the days of our fathers and grandfathers, we have always respected the earth, the water, the air, and the fire. For that reason, we are peoples who have a feeling and respect for our potatoes, our manioc, and our maize, our hills, our days and nights, with all their stars.[1] Since time immemorial, we have been accustomed to talking with our waters and respecting them, to talking with our sun and our moon, with the winds, with the cardinal points, and all the animals and plants of our land that accompany us. In our beginning is the basis of what we are today. We have always considered nature as something as important as we ourselves are. The water we receive from the heavens, the mountains, the forests, and the land still live in the hearts of our people. It is not in vain that we are peoples who still know how to distinguish the sacred taste of living water.

Relating to our Mother Earth, we learned to read the mist, the cold and the heat, the slightest tremor of the earth, and the eclipses. We learned to interpret the sound of our rivers and to converse with the wind that emerges from the natural wells and the underground rivers, to interpret natural phenomena and plan our activities for the year.

The creation of Living Well to counteract the Global Crisis means doing away with consumer society, waste and luxury, consuming more than is necessary, to lower the speed of the global economy to reach levels of production, consumption, and use of energy that remain within the limits that the health and resources of the planet can permit.

In the creation of Living Well, our economic and spiritual wealth is directly linked to respect for Mother Earth and the respectful use of the wealth that She wishes to hand over to us. The only alternatives for the world in this Global Crisis, the only solution for the crisis of nature is for us human beings to recognize that we are part of Mother Nature, that we need to reestablish complementary relations of mutual respect and harmony with her.

Living Well means to return to the planet its fertility, which today is in the hands of sterile enterprises, to reforest the world, to live a simple life close to the earth in communities or small farms, family farms, which are the ones that have conserved the trees and the harmonious variety of species, those that have more water available and survive better. With the eradication of monoculture and of the production of biofuels, we can reincorporate agriculture in the communities, with Mother Nature, and the cultivation of basic food needs.

Instead of exhausting the earth, preying on nature, and within thirty or fifty years finishing off all the gas, the oil, the iron, the tin, the lithium, and all the other nonrenewable natural resources necessary to *living better*, Living Well guarantees life for our children and our children's children, saving the planet on the basis of our stone, our quinoa, potatoes, and manioc, our beans, broad beans, and fresh maize cobs, our mahogany, oca, coconuts, and coca leaves.[2]

Living Well means to increase conservation practices and energy efficiency —that is, slow down, reducing personal consumption in countries where this has been excessive and significantly reducing our use of energy; travel less in motor vehicles, travel less in airplanes; turn off the lights when they are not necessary; put on a sweater instead of turning on the heating; borrow something or buy a used one instead of a new one; recycle; use local foodstuffs, which do not use so much energy in production, storage, packaging, and transport.

It means to set our own rhythm for our joys and sorrows, with the right to learn from our mistakes, all on the basis of our own resources and efforts, as well as trust in ourselves, in our identity and our wisdom.

In this context, Living Well means a communal, sovereign life in harmony with nature, in which we work together for society and for our family, sharing, singing, dancing, producing for the community. It means a simple life that reduces our addiction to consumption and maintains balanced production.

Living Well also means turning off the TV or the Internet and connecting ourselves to the community. It means having four hours a day more with the family, with friends, and in our community, that is, the four hours a day that on average we use to watch a TV full of messages about things they want us to buy. Spending our time in fraternal activities with the community strengthens the community and turns it into a source of social and logistic support, of greater security and happiness. For present-day societies of over-consumption, *less* will be *more*.

Translated by Alison Spedding

Notes

1. These three native American crops—potatoes, manioc, and maize—are the basic carbohydrates that shape people's diet at the three major ecological and altitude levels in Bolivia: potatoes on the altiplano; corn in the valleys; and manioc in the tropics. They also represent metaphorically the traditional productive system as a whole in all the different regions of Bolivia, uniting the Andean people and the lowland indigenous groups, which have been historically and culturally differentiated from one another.

2. Oca is a native Andean tuber somewhat like a parsnip but much less fibrous.

Living Well

David Choquehuanca

"Living well"—vivir bien or buen vivir in Spanish—is a translation of the Aymara term suma qamaña *and the Quechua* sumak kawsay, *which are now officially taken up in the constitutions of Bolivia and Ecuador. The language also circulates in other parts of Latin America and even other continents to refer to a utopian alternative with indigenous roots. It does not refer to an existing institution in Andean communities so much as a set of ideals, values, and pursuits that are under debate and construction. It implies, above all, a dynamic equilibrium in the relations between people and with nature, or Mother Earth, as well as the psychic and spiritual satisfaction that comes with that balance. It contains a critique of predominant development models, which bring highly uneven economic benefits at serious cost to the environment. According to David Choquehuanca's notion, the mainstream approaches mean that only a few live better, while humanity as a whole does not live well. Choquehuanca, from an Aymara community near Lake Titicaca, worked closely with different indigenous groups and helped to train many of the leaders who eventually joined the Movement to Socialism (MAS) party. Named foreign minister in the Evo Morales government in 2006, he was the most prominent cabinet member of indigenous origin and one of the foremost advocates of the utopia of "living well."*

Making believe that we were "the poorest of the poor," absolutely all the development programs implemented by the governments, the NGOs, the Church direct us to seek a better life, insinuating that overcoming indigenous "poverty" signifies access to the "benefits of modernity" and development via "integration with the market."

Instead of talking about development, which is related to *living better*, this Government for Life is working to build the Good Life and not a *better life*, at the cost of someone else. We simply propose Living Well, which is not the same as *living better*, living better than someone else. To *live better* is to accept that some few can be better off than all the rest. But for us to be better off and to see others worse off, that is not Living Well. We don't seek, we don't want anyone to live better. We want all of us to be able to live well. There is an important difference between this Living Well and *living better*.